U.S. BORDER SECURITY

Selected Titles in ABC-CLIO's
CONTEMPORARY
WORLD ISSUES
Series

For a complete list of titles in this series, please visit
www.abc-clio.com.

Books in the Contemporary World Issues series address vital issues in today's society, such as genetic engineering, pollution, and biodiversity. Written by professional writers, scholars, and nonacademic experts, these books are authoritative, clearly written, up-to-date, and objective. They provide a good starting point for research by high school and college students, scholars, and general readers as well as by legislators, businesspeople, activists, and others.

Each book, carefully organized and easy to use, contains an overview of the subject, a detailed chronology, biographical sketches, facts and data and/or documents and other primary-source material, a directory of organizations and agencies, annotated lists of print and nonprint resources, and an index.

Readers of books in the Contemporary World Issues series will find the information they need to have a better understanding of the social, political, environmental, and economic issues facing the world today.

U.S. BORDER SECURITY

A Reference Handbook

Judith A. Warner

CONTEMPORARY WORLD ISSUES

ABC-CLIO

Santa Barbara, California • Denver, Colorado • Oxford, England

Library of Congress Cataloging-in-Publication Data

Warner, Judith.
    U.S. border security : a reference handbook / Judith A. Warner.
      p. cm.—(Contemporary world issues)
    Includes bibliographical references and index.
    ISBN 978-1-59884-407-8 (hard copy : alk. paper)—ISBN 978-1-59884-408-5 (ebook : alk. paper) 1. Border security—United States—Handbooks, manuals, etc. I. Title.
    HV8139.W37   2010
    363.28′50973—dc22   2010009662

ISBN: 978-1-59884-407-8
EISBN: 978-1-59884-408-5

14   13   12   11   10   1   2   3   4   5

This book is also available on the World Wide Web as an eBook. Visit www.abc-clio.com for details.

ABC_CLIO
An Imprint of ABC-CLIO, LLC

ABC-CLIO, LLC
130 Cremona Drive, P.O. Box 1911
Santa Barbara, California 93116-1911

This book is printed on acid-free paper ∞

Manufactured in the United States of America

Contents

Preface and Acknowledgments

The 21st century has brought an unprecedented range of possibilities and threats to the American way of life. In the 20th century, America was by and large secure from external conflict within its borders except for the bombing of Pearl Harbor at the start of World War II and the first World Trade Center attack in 1993. The United States has a history of internal threats marked by such incidents as the 1995 Oklahoma City bombing. It was not until September 11, 2001, and the second terrorist attack on the World Trade Center, that the public learned that a new era of transnational threats had begun.

In 2003, many separate federal law enforcement agencies were reorganized as the Department of Homeland Security (DHS). The failure to prevent the 9/11 tragedy was perceived to be due to the inability of separate federal agencies to coordinate intelligence on terrorist activity; in other words, they failed to "connect the dots" by integrating discrete pieces of evidence. The failed attempt by Umar Farouk Abdulmutallab to explode an incendiary device hidden in underwear during an air flight on December 25, 2009, demonstrated that merging agencies had not solved the problem concerning sharing and interpretation of intelligence.

Historically, security has been viewed in terms of military capabilities for meeting external threats. Since the end of the Cold War, national security has focused on prevention of terrorism, drug trafficking, arms smuggling, and human smuggling or trafficking. Each security threat involves crossing borders, and an efficient border-management system is necessary to protect citizens. Nations police borders and use border guards. Because border control is no longer viewed as a national defense issue, it involves law enforcement, and most states classify border guards as police (Öövel and Varga 2003). U.S. Customs and

Border Patrol is the national policing bureaucracy at the Mexican and Canadian borders.

In the 21st century, globalization of the international economy has made border security a matter of international cooperation and alliances. It has extended the border to sites that perform pre-inspection in other countries connected by air and sea. This complex situation has introduced transnational threats in which organized crime and terrorist groups act globally. The complications produced by new technologies of communication and travel have fostered new types of criminal organizations and necessitate new border-control strategies.

Border security involves the use of border police to protect borders and provide safety for citizens. Security concerns at land, air, and sea borders include:

- unauthorized entry and smuggling of foreign nationals
- human trafficking for purpose of prostitution or work enslavement
- drug trafficking and narcoterrorism
- property offenses (e.g., auto theft)
- terrorism
- smuggling of weapons of mass destruction

Within the United States, policing agencies such as Customs, Border Patrol, ICE, and local or federal law enforcement must work together to address these issues. For example, when cargo is shipped from overseas, it travels in a variety of ways, enters and leaves the custody of various people and organizations, and may necessitate processing up to 40 different documents connected to transit across borders (Lake 2007). The task of law enforcement in preventing smuggling and terrorism is further complicated by the need for cooperation between the DHS and other agencies such as the Drug Enforcement Administration (DEA). The massive consolidation of the DHS did not totally unify the federal law-enforcement bureaucracies.

In the second decade of the 21st century, transnational threats such as drug and arms trafficking will be major border-security issues. Mexico has become the leading transshipment point for cocaine, marijuana, and other illegal drugs. Mexican drug-trafficking organizations have fought over control of the key routes into the interior of the United States, and thousands of Mexicans have been killed in the violence. The freedom to own guns and limitations on gun control in the United States are associated with arms smuggling into Mexico, which increases lethality. The corruption of the Mexican police and government has contributed to a national security crisis for Mexico and brought increased U.S. assistance. While Mexico is considered unlikely to become a failed state, the terroristic use of violence by Mexican narcotics traffickers, known as narcoterrorism, has generated a crisis that can only be solved by binational cooperation. Indeed, border security is a transnational concern.

To this end, understanding the many issues involved in border security and proposed solutions, the book is organized as follows:

Chapter 1 presents a historical outline of U.S. border relations with former North American colonial powers, Canada, and Mexico. The circumstances and settings that give rise to unauthorized immigration, smuggling, and transnational terrorism are investigated.

Chapter 2 looks at border security as a contemporary issue and examines why the borders are critical but porous sites for legitimate and illicit movement of goods and people. It looks at the impact of border control on border and interior communities. Recent attempts to increase security at the land, air, and sea borders are examined. The methods used to try to contain problems are evaluated from different points of view. In particular, the control of transnational threats involves multiple national, binational, and international agencies and processes, necessitating the development of coordination and cooperation.

Chapter 3 examines the international impact of U.S. border security, particularly on the neighboring countries of Mexico and Canada. Security is represented as a bidirectional process in which the policies of one nation have a feedback relationship, often producing unintended consequences for another nation. Border control is a difficult issue because criminal violations cross borders, which precludes a unilateral solution and necessitates bilateral and multilateral effort.

Chapter 4 presents a chronology of key events in the colonial and postcolonial history of demarcation of the borders. It lists successive laws passed to regulate immigration, drugs, and, since 1993, terrorism. The issues examined concern how the regulatory apparatus and border-control methods deployed have intensified and impacted society in the 21st century.

Chapter 5 presents the biographies of key government officials and social analysts who offer viewpoints and structure border-security policies. In addition it examines major criminals who have engaged in narcoterrorism, which has challenged the security of Mexico and its people and poses the possibility of spillover violence in the United States.

Chapter 6 presents statistics, research information, and key legislative documents relating to border control of unauthorized immigration, terrorism, and drug trafficking. Through the use of URL addresses provided, the reader can access the vast resources on this issue for download on the internet.

Chapter 7 provides information on governmental agencies, intergovernmental organizations (IGOs), and nongovernmental organizations (NGOs) that shape policy and advocate for various border-control strategies and or humanitarian concerns. These agencies and organizations provide the data for analysis of the effectiveness of border security. Governmental organizations are impacted by the reports of NGOs such as human rights organizations and IGOs connected to the United Nations and supra-regional government structures such as the Organization of American States.

Chapter 8 provides information on books, articles, and films concerning border security. It lists key reports from government, intergovernmental, and nongovernmental organizations. The bibliographic review and Internet sites allow the reader access to mechanisms that will generate very easy-to-use statistical data.

My special thanks go to Mildred Vasan for bringing attention to this topic and to Robin Tutt and Jane Messah of ABC-CLIO for the determination and enthusiasm they brought to this project. I would like to thank the administration of Texas A&M International for supporting the research that led to this book with faculty leave. Finally, I would like to thank Brother Bob Warren; you are no longer residing on the border, but your interest in the issues is not forgotten.

References

Lake, Jennifer E. 2007. "CRS Report for Congress: Border Security: The Complexity of the Challenge." Washington, DC: Congressional Research Service. http://fpc.state.gov/documents/organization/80215.pdf.

Öövel, Andrus, and Beata Varga. 2003. "Recommendations on the Topic of Border Security Reform." Paper presented at the SSR-Track Panel at the 6th Annual Conference of the PfP Consortium for Defense Academies and Security Studies Institutes, Berlin. http://www.dcaf.ch/pfpc/ev_berlin_papers_oovel.pdf.

1

Background and History

Introduction

The United States' borders coincide with land, water, and the air. A border is a geographic boundary of a nation and defines its legal jurisdiction. Its borders define national sovereignty and the right to citizenship. National sovereignty is defined as "the possession of the sole decisionmaking authority in defining one's policies" (Bagwell and Staiger 2003, 6). Every country exercises sovereignty, the right to make policy decisions, over the people, goods, animals, and plants allowed to enter and exit its borders. Nation-states like the United States protect their citizens by providing for security within their borders (Biersteker 2003). Yet the goal of security is not always compatible with the free movement of people and goods across borders—a source of economic security and improved living standards.

U.S. national security increasingly is based on good border relations throughout the more than 7,500 miles covering the U.S. borders with Canada and Mexico. Because these nations are the two largest trading partners of the United States, there are benefits from allowing the free flow of goods and services between the borders. However, there are concerns about allowing an unregulated flow of what are increasingly considered "dangerous goods and people"; therefore, border security is essential.

All citizens desire an optimal sense of security from foreign threats. National security involves legislating to secure borders against military attack and controlling the traffic in goods and people. Since 9/11 the prevention of international terrorism has become the major border-security issue. The United States has ongoing concerns regarding unauthorized immigration, drugs, weapons, and contraband trafficking. Attempts to control national borders in an age of increased international connections create issues such as how to maintain important diplomatic and economic ties with other nations while countering threats to security. After 9/11 trade and immigration across borders became critical counterterrorism issues and triggered policy and legislative changes.

Geography of the Borders

The United States shares a land and river border with Mexico and a land and lake border with Canada. The land and water borders of the United States, including Alaska and Hawaii, cover 19,841 miles (Beaver 2006, 1–5). There are 95,000 miles of shoreline and defined air space. The United States maintains 327 official ports of entry at its land, sea, and air borders. The ports enforce immigration and import/export law. Customs inspectors also examine any agricultural and wildlife products brought into the country.

The U.S.-Mexican border is 1,933 miles long and partly defined by the Rio Grande River (Beaver 2006, 1–5). Traditionally, the southern border has been the site of extensive drug smuggling and unauthorized entry but no known terrorist efforts. There are 24 official ports of entry in California, Arizona, New Mexico, and Texas. Laredo, Texas, is the busiest port on the Mexican border and has the fastest growth rate because it handles trucks carrying manufactured goods and agricultural products from Mexico. Mexico's border is very controversial because of unauthorized immigration, drug trafficking, arms trafficking from the United States, drug-related violence, and the possibility of terrorist entry.

The United States' geographically complex northern border with Canada stretches for approximately 5,000 miles of both land and water (Beaver 2006, 1–5). This area is sparsely inhabited and includes a border with Alaska that extends into the Arctic. It has been a security zone considered the longest unguarded border in the world and often referred to as "undefended." There are 133 ports of entry, most of which are in unpopulated or wilderness areas. U.S.-Canadian border security is problematic because of size, wilderness, and water boundaries. Unlike Mexico, Canada has a history of terrorist activity, has been used as an entrance corridor, and is thought to harbor some terror cells. While unauthorized immigration is a lesser issue, the smuggling of high-potency marijuana to the United States and untaxed cigarettes to Canada are recurrent issues.

Canada is uniquely a border nation because 75 percent of its population resides within 100 miles of the boundary and 90 percent within 200 miles (Thompson 2001, 14). In certain sectors the border is unmarked; in others it is only a ditch. Yet Canadians stand in an asymmetric relationship to the more powerful United States, referred to as "subservience" despite a prosperity partly based on trade (Winterdyk and Sundberg 2010b, 29). For them, the border may protect their political, economic, and cultural rights against the power of the United States.

Like Canada, the developing nation of Mexico stands in an asymmetric relationship with the United States, only it is even more lopsided. Mexico's seat of government is Mexico City. Since the 1960s and the development of export processing zones with factories called *maquiladoras*, border development and urbanization have proceeded at a rapid pace but at a distance from its national government (Martinez 2006). The Mexican border is an area of cultural contact and hybridization that has led to concerns about de-Mexicanization, a concept that refers to the Americanization of Mexicans living in the border zone (Martinez 2006, 113, 114, 115).

Challenges of Border Security

Despite asymmetries of power, both Canada and Mexico have extensively cooperated with the United States in strengthening border security. The evolving border relationship is one in which the three countries have worked together on mutual protection from external threats. Yet border security is controversial because of the size of the task. The need to have porous borders for the passage of people and trade is counterbalanced by the need to stop the smuggling of people and drugs and to prevent terrorism. Some consider it possible to successfully manage this tradeoff and attain border security. Others believe that the extent of resources needed is self-defeating and that border control is primarily image management (Andreas 2000, 7–9).

Public attention has concentrated on the land borders, particularly Mexico, but the terrorist threat is more widely dispersed.

On September 11, 2001, 19 jihadist air hijackers flew three commercial jets into the World Trade Center skyscrapers in New York City and the Pentagon in Washington, DC. One additional jet crashed due to passenger resistance and was unable to reach a second Washington, DC, target. The action horrified the world and pointed to weak aviation security. Afterward, the 9/11 Commission (Eldridge et al. 2004) found that prior to the attacks border security had not been considered a national security issue. In the face of the unknown after the tragedy, it was impossible to overreact, yet many of the immediate steps taken lacked planning.

When the terrorists' actions to overcome the system were identified, plans for greater security for Americans were put into action. The 9/11 Commission and the newly created Department of Homeland Security completely reorganized border security while employing and reinforcing much past practice and adding some policy innovations. The depth of the response was due to the Bush administration's zero tolerance for risk. The 9/11 hijackings and subsequent mass fatalities marked a new era in border-security management.

Historically, borders have been sites of conflict over territory. The emergence of contemporary nations led to the association of sovereignty with the right to regulate cross-border movement. Many major boundary disputes between Mexico or British America (now Canada) and the United States have occurred, including Britain's (Canada's) objections over the boundaries of Oregon and Alaska, and Mexico's over Texas. Often these conflicts did not occur until politics or economic or strategic change made a border region desirable to both governments. Boundary disputes still occur, but the massive extent of the border and the low intensity of these disputes compare favorably to the rest of the world.

U.S.-Canada Border

Early History of European Expansion

Canada is the world's second largest country, stretching from the Pacific to the Atlantic and into the Arctic (Bothwell 2006, 4).

In 1534 Jacques Cartier staked a claim for New France in the area of the Saint Lawrence Valley. In the 1570s and 1580s, English exploration led to colonies in Newfoundland and Virginia. In the 16th century, Samuel de Champlain established a colony in Quebec. Sixty years of Iroquois wars repressed the growth of French colonial enterprise as the English and Dutch developed colonies along the North Atlantic seaboard. This set the stage for conflict among the European nations over control of territory (Bothwell 2006, 17, 21, 31–35).

In the 17th century, the English forced the Dutch to sign over their New Amsterdam colony and entered into competition with France over Hudson Bay and New York. In 1686, France entered into a war with England that lasted until 1697. Queen Anne's War involved the Iroquois, traditional enemies of the French and allied Algonquin tribes. This conflict resulted in French colonial seizure of Hudson Bay forts but took place mostly in Europe. France was bankrupt, and the Treaty of Utrecht ceded all of Acadia (now Nova Scotia) and Newfoundland to the British, who emerged as the major colonial power (Bothwell 2006, 57, 64–65).

From 1689 to 1815 North America was the seat of warfare between the European nations and the Indian nations. The Seven Years' War (1755–1761) resulted in Great Britain's takeover of the French territories and land east of the Mississippi that became British America (Bothwell 2006, 63, 87–88). Subsequently, the American Revolution resulted in the recognition of the United States.

Origins: Territorial Conflict

The U.S.-Canadian border was first established by the 1783 Treaty of Paris that ended the war between the thirteen U.S. colonies and Great Britain. Afterwards, a series of border disputes between the United States and Great Britain, involving British America, occurred because of desire for territorial expansion. The western boundary was especially a source of territorial conflict. An 1818 U.S.-British agreement placed the British America border at the 49th parallel from the Lake of the Woods to the Rockies (Bothwell 2006, 158). Lake of the Woods is a body of water in the Canadian provinces of Ontario and Manitoba that borders on the U.S. state of Minnesota. Britain and the United States agreed to jointly occupy Oregon territory, west of the Lake of the Woods, for 10 years. This was extended to a further 10 years in 1827 (Bothwell 2006, 109–110, 158).

After 1838 disputes arose over which nation had the right to Oregon. In the 1840s, the American settlers drove their wagon trains across the Oregon Trail, so the United States sought to claim territory up to the 54th parallel. To avoid war, a compromise between the U.S. and Great Britain placed the border at the 49th parallel. The dispute was settled by the 1846 Oregon Treaty (Bothwell 2006, 159). It established the boundary from the 49th parallel at the Lake of the Woods to the Strait of Georgia. This treaty granted the United States control of the territories that became the states of Oregon, Washington, Idaho, and Montana. The British retained Vancouver Island and the right to navigation on a portion of the Columbia River.

In 1837 a rebellion of Canadian settlers in Eastern British America led Americans to consider annexation. U.S. citizens living proximate to the border assisted the rebels. At one point, several hundred western? New Yorkers crossed into Canada and entered into armed conflict with British soldiers. This provoked British Canadians into crossing into the United States. They killed a Canadian rebel and burned the rebel's supply ship, the American-owned *Caroline*. The United States asked for an apology and reparations, but was refused. Later, the boundary with Maine became a source of dispute as lumberjacks sought control of northern Maine and eastern Brunswick. In 1842 the Webster-Ashburton Treaty allocated 7/12ths of the disputed territory in Maine and New Brunswick to the United States (Bothwell 2006, 159, 175–183).

Cross-Border Interactions

In the 19th century, the Canadian border was relatively unmonitored, and no barriers or fees faced Canadians or Americans who chose to visit or immigrate (Ramirez 2001). The unguarded northern border had few checkpoints to monitor crossing, and both Canadians and Americans crossed and even changed citizenship. Canadian immigrants were viewed positively as "thrifty, industrious and belonging to all trades and occupations, both skilled and unskilled" (U.S. Bureau of Immigration 1897, 6 Cited in Ramirez, 2001). As Western Hemisphere immigrants, like Mexicans, Canadians were not subject to a head tax.

At the end of the 19th century, concern about the U.S.-Canada boundary developed because overseas immigrants were using it to avoid inspection and paying the head tax. In 1890, for example, about 20% of all European immigrants had come through the Canadian border to enter (Ramirez 2001). In the 1890s, U.S. checkpoints with immigration inspectors were established and Canadians underwent scrutiny regarding their criminal, health, and labor contract backgrounds.

Borders involve different rules of law and invite smuggling. Border dwellers who smuggle do not consider it a crime. The 20th century brought a clash of governmental policies over issues such as U.S. Prohibition and smuggling across both Canadian and Mexican borders. From 1920 to 1933, the Eighteenth Amendment, from its passing in 1920 to its repeal in 1933, prohibited the making, importing, sale, or transport of liquor in the United States. Canada was a source for bootleg alcohol as well as a tourist destination for those seeking to drink.

Through both world wars, Canada and Mexico supported the United States despite the legacy of conflict over expansion. Nevertheless, the power differential in income and resources between these nations has often meant that the United States has been seen as trying to impose its will on these nations and even engaging in territorial conquest. Mexico has experienced asymmetry of power to a greater degree than more prosperous Canada and lost considerable territory to 19th century U.S. expansionism.

U.S.-Mexico Border

Origins: Territorial Acquisition

In the 19th century, borders and boundaries were mostly clearly interpreted lines on maps which often coincided with physical barriers such as mountains or freshwater rivers and oceans. North America was subdivided among the United States and colonies ruled by fading colonial powers such as Spain and Great Britain. Originally a Spanish territory, Mexico became an independent nation in 1821. Mexico faced many issues in trying to integrate its northern "borderlands" territories (Martinez 2006, 11–12), whose administration collapsed after independence. Approximately 15,000 people lived in the frontier territories, and they did not identify with Mexico's central region, where the process of nation-building had concentrated. While the 1924 Mexican Constitution gave the states extensive autonomy in decision-making, the frontier territories were under the control of the Mexican Congress. In addition, the territory of Texas was merged with Coahuila. The frontier periphery began to have strained relations with the center.

The possession of physical territory became a major source of dispute. Conquest was perceived as a source of economic expansion. The United States was involved in a rush to acquire territory and promoted the ideology of manifest destiny to control land on the continent, including all of Mexico. Mexico encouraged U.S. citizens to immigrate to its territories, but the colonization policy proved a mistake. Americans came to outnumber Mexicans in Texas and California. Asserting control, the Mexican government outlawed slavery, which was practiced in Texas, and levied high taxes. Texans rebelled and became independent in 1836. The Texas Rebellion resulted in Mexico's first loss of territory (ibid., 12, 13).

The United States annexed Texas in 1845 and war broke out in 1846. The U.S.-Mexico War ended with the signing of the Treaty of Guadalupe Hidalgo in 1848. This treaty included the forced sale of one-third of Mexico to the United States. After the Gadsden Purchase, Mexico lost one-half of its territory altogether. The consolidation of the United States was based on a partial conquest of Mexican territory and set the stage for the power asymmetry in relations that exists today (ibid., 16–18).

After the U.S.-Mexico War, U.S. citizens continued to try to expand into Mexico, and border conflict was intense. "Filibusters" were incidents of armed aggression directed against Mexican citizens on Mexican territory. Through the first quarter of the 20th century U.S. citizens who were independent adventurers ignored national sovereignty and acted as revolutionary agents and colonizers seeking to "liberate" northern Mexican territory both for personal enrichment and so that the territory could become part of the United States. These unlawful invasions occurred because of the Mexican government's weakness and instability. Mexico held on to its northern territory for a variety of reasons. Filibustering failed because of "inadequate planning by the aggressors, insufficient resources, poor judgment, lack of official support and Mexican resistance" (ibid., 31–32, 46–47).

As colonial expansion ended in the 20th century, the ideal of sovereign nonintervention was proclaimed and geographic borders gained in importance (Biersteker 2003, 157–158). After

World War I, the 1919 Covenant of the League of Nations specified that its members should not intervene in independent
nations. After World War II ended in Europe in 1945, the Char-
ter of the United Nations reaffirmed this idea. National boundaries began to be used as means of regulating the movement
of people and goods. Nation-states began to authorizel the entry
of immigrants across boundaries and to exercise control of capital through international monetary agreements meant to stabilize their economies. Treaties were created to form alliances to
protect national security and territories.

Early in the 20th century, border concerns centered on the
U.S.-Mexico border and military or migration issues caused by
the Mexican Revolution, which had caused Mexican citizens to
flee over the border line (Martinez 2006, 82). From 1910 to 1920,
the United States protected its territorial sovereignty and the
security of citizens while enforcing neutrality law regarding the
outcome of the Mexican conflict. The United States engaged in
surveillance of Mexican revolutionary activities, stopping raids
into its territory, preventing gun smuggling to Mexico, and protecting U.S. border citizens by using local, state and federal
law enforcement (83). For example, federal troops, the Texas
Rangers, and state National Guards were mobilized along with
border sheriff–led civilian posses and police. A military incident occurred in March, 1916 when Pancho Villa crossed the
border at Columbus, New Mexico, and killed 17 U.S. citizens
while burning and looting. The United States responded with a
military invasion led by General John "Black Jack" Pershing.

Cross-Border Incursions and Illicit Activities in Mexico and Canada

After the end of the U.S.-Mexico War of 1848, banditry was a concern for both the United States and Mexico at the borders. The U.S.
military was often involved in tracking down the bandits, which
included American Indians on raids (Martinez 2006, 54–55). In
1878 the Posse Comitatus Act restricted but did not preclude military involvement in domestic law enforcement. U.S.-Mexico border law enforcement raids involved vigilantes and unofficial
posses as well as military crossing the border to pursue bandits.
This activity continued into the early 20th century.

During Prohibition, when production and consumption of
alcohol were outlawed in the United States, smuggling of alcohol

from Mexico and Canada was a major concern (Moore 2004, 3–4). Americans flocked to both Mexican and Canadian border towns to drink. In the case of Mexico, American investors provided capital to start entertainment establishments featuring drinking and prostitution because both were legal in Mexico (Martinez 2006, 108–109). During this period, the Mexican border towns became stereotyped as "sin cities" and centers for vice. The Great Depression brought a decline in border tourism, and the repeal of Prohibition ended a period in which many American citizens left the country to drink.

Today legal prostitution in Mexico brings sex tourists to border towns, and women and some men work this trade while subject to mandatory medical exams (Martinez 2006). Teenagers may cross to Mexico to drink legally if the age limit is lower than the corresponding American state; they also may go if they perceive the trip as an "exotic" experience. To their parents, of course, it is a source of consternation, especially regarding the potential for binge drinking. In the late 20th century, the availability of liquor, drugs, and sex work businesses in the United States decreased the demand for such experiences in the Mexican border cities.

Ongoing Issues

While major U.S.-Canada and U.S.-Mexico boundary disputes have been settled for years, governmental policies still clash. An important difference between the two borders is the status of the two countries: Canada is a developed nation while Mexico is a developing nation. As a result, the degree of law enforcement at the two borders is very disparate. The United States has created an increasingly fortified border with Mexico to prevent economic migration and, more recently, drug trafficking. The Canadian border has a history of being relatively unguarded and of less concern (Ackleson and Heyman 2010, 39). For all three nations, too careful regulation of people and commodities crossing the borders is viewed as causing costly delay in the flow of legitimate goods under the North American Free Trade Agreement (NAFTA). It is a contradiction in terms that billions in investment in security gravitates to the U.S.-Mexico border, posing constraints to this increasingly economically important trade. Security policies and related post-9/11 laws have often negatively influenced the goodwill of trans border relationships and are shadowed by the legacy of conflicted border relations.

Border Security

Three concerns have dominated U.S. border enforcement: immigration, drugs, and international terrorism (Payan 2006, 1–21). Mass unauthorized migration has resulted in the growth of a U.S. Border Patrol–led interdiction regime (Heyman 1999, 619–622). Persons and vehicles crossing at a port of entry are inspected. This is usually done without prior intelligence gathering and is an example of mass enforcement. During the 20th century, the United States' efforts to control contraband have focused on drugs, for example, marijuana, opiates such as heroin and cocaine, and methamphetamines. International terrorism developed as a concern in the 1990s, after the 1993 World Trade Center bombing, and emerged as the primary border concern after the 9/11 attacks.

The focus of counterterrorism is the apprehension of terrorists crossing borders, developing intelligence about transnational networks, and stopping supplies for violent activities. Interdiction relies on mass screening, including radiation monitors used on cargos to detect weapons of mass destruction. Pinpoint actions are used against a limited number of people and conveyances identified by intelligence (Ackleson and Heyman 2010, 38–39).

Border Trade

The 1980s United States–Canada Free Trade Agreement and the 1990s North American Free Trade Agreement (United States, Canada, and Mexico) were signed to reduce or eliminate export tariffs in several industries including agriculture, automobiles, and textiles. These agreements resulted in a need for infrastructure growth to manage trade. The 1995 United States–Canada Accord on Our Shared Border and the 1999 United States–Canada Partnership Forum addressed these issues but were found inadequate after the 9/11 attacks.

After 9/11, many considered that further transnational integration of the NAFTA economies was precluded by national security needs and demonstrated a negative consequence of globalization. Although the Mexican border has been long considered problematic, for the first time, the porosity of the Canadian border came into question. In 2002, the United States and Canada signed the Smart Border Declaration. In 2005, the Trilateral Security and Prosperity Partnership (SSP) a North American initiative involving the United States, Canada, and Mexico, took another step towards addressing border security needs (Villareal and Lake 2005). At the 2005 North American Leaders Summit, "smart and secure borders" was established as a priority for SSP. Leaders seek to coordinate security procedures in order to avoid duplication such as repeat inspection of baggage and cargo, but this initiative may not be enough to address new security challenges.

Representative Silvestre Reyes (Democrat–Texas) has stressed,

> Inadequate staffing and outdated infrastructure at our land ports of entry are making America less safe. We need to provide our federal law enforcement agencies with the tools and resources they need to effectively combat the flow of drugs, money, and weapons that are illegally transported between the United States and Mexico. (Reyes 2009)

Customs Fees and Border Smuggling

Borders, by their nature, create opportunities for smugglers because of the desire to evade taxes on imports called customs duties. The U.S. Customs Service has the job of collecting duties on legal imports and keeping out illegal or untaxed goods, known as contraband. After passage of the Tariff Act of 1789 on July 4, 1789, U.S. Customs began operation on July 31, 1789 (CBP.gov 2009). The fledgling United States was close to bankruptcy and a tax on imported goods, known as a tariff, was imposed to raise money. In the first year of operation $2 million in duties was collected. In 1886, Customs inspectors on horseback patrolled the Mexico border. Revenue cutters sought to prevent coastal smuggling. Customs was the chief source of federal revenue until 1913, when an amendment authorizing an income tax was passed.

Canada Customs was established by the Customs Consolidation Act of 1841 (McIntosh, 1984). In 1906, the Canadian Immigration Department was created by the Immigration Act of

1906 (Kelly and Treblecock 1998). The Royal Canadian Mounted Police (RCMP) was established February 1, 1920. At this point, Canada initiated a tripartite border strategy in which customs inspectors, immigration officers, and police work to maintain border security (Winterdyck and Sundberg 2010b, 23). Customs is based at all prominent land crossings, airports, and harbors. Immigration officers work alongside Customs inspectors at major ports of entry. The Royal Canadian Mounted Police patrol remote areas and between ports of entry.

U.S. Customs is expected to ensure that all imported and exported goods comply with federal law. It collects and protects tariff duty revenue, excise taxes, and any fees or penalties due on imports (CBP.gov 2009). It seeks to interdict and seize contraband, particularly narcotics, and it apprehends individuals suspected of trying to circumvent U.S. Customs and related law. Even intellectual property rights law is enforced. A new mission of U.S. Customs has been to protect national security by enforcing prohibition on the export or import of critical technology used to develop weapons of mass destruction and to provide defense against money laundering.

Unfortunately, U.S. Customs inspectors are subject to the temptation of corruption. The profit from contraband has meant that U.S. Customs has to wage a perpetual battle against bribery of inspectors. In 1998 Congress asked the Treasury Office's Department of Professional Responsibility to study corruption and U.S. Customs programs to detect it (CBP.gov 2009). The study did not detect organized corruption networks but found that individual Customs inspectors were at great risk of bribery and that there were problems in detecting it. The international drug trade and related arms smuggling present a serious challenge to the ethics of U.S. Customs inspectors, and some give in and accept bribes to wave drugs through.

Immigration

Immigrants cross by land, sea, and, since the mid-20th century, air to enter the United States. After U.S. independence from Great Britain, a period of open entry to the United States occurred and Europeans were recruited to come. As immigrant origins became diversified, racial and ethnic disputes led to passage of a series of laws restricting entry. In 1882 the Chinese Exclusion Act began what was often a racist process of immigrant exclusion. In 1882

U.S. Customs inspectors were asked to prevent smuggling of Chinese. In 1904 the Immigration Service undertook this activity. Beginning in 1917, it became necessary for individuals crossing from Mexico into the United States to demonstrate literacy and pay a crossing fee. Because of the porous nature of the land boundary, the era of unauthorized Mexican migration began. Following the passage of restrictive immigration laws in 1920 and 1924, the U.S. Border Patrol was established. Initially it had a budget of $1 million and 450 officers (Lee 2006, 10, 12–13).

Immigration control is a domain of international law enforcement. The United States' borders are the primary focus of its enforcement efforts. International policing is often synonymous with local policing at the border. The border is a zone of liaisons with foreign officials, boundary crossing, and a concentration of federal law enforcement agencies. Because of the United States focus on immigration control, the United States has focused on interdiction of those who would enter without authorization. Periodic intensification and escalation of immigration enforcement, however, has never ended unauthorized immigration, and associated policies have become increasingly like crime control.

Crossing a border without document inspection or using fraudulent documentation violates the national sovereignty of the United States. The presence of an estimated 11.3 million unauthorized immigrants in the United States indicates that legislation regulating immigration and border enforcement has not succeeded. A majority of unauthorized immigrants originate in North America. Mexicans are most represented, followed by other Latin Americans (Passel and Cohn 2008, iii). Europeans, Asians, and Africans are relatively few in comparison. Mexicans comprise 61% of all unauthorized immigrants, and they have been in the majority since 1990 (Hoefer Rytina and Campbell 2006, 4). The Central American countries of El Salvador, Guatemala, and Honduras are the origin of about 12% of unauthorized immigrants. Other countries represented among the unauthorized include India, Korea, China, and Vietnam.

Legal and unauthorized immigration is a response to the "pull" factor of economic motivation, employer demand, and the "push" factor of lack of economic opportunity in "sending countries," the countries of origin of immmigrants. The United States has one of the world's most active economies, while Mexico and Central America are developing economies in which many must struggle to survive. Mexican workers are pulled by the wage differential with the United States. In Mexico the minimum wage is set at $4.86 an hour (Freebairn 2007). The U.S. federal minimum wage is $6.55 an hour and 24 states have set their minimum wage rate higher than federal law requires (CNN 2008). State minimum wages range from a high of $8.07 in Washington to $6.65 in Missouri.

Opponents of immigration argue that unauthorized immigrants drive down the wages of native-born workers. Economists George J. Borjas and Lawrence F. Katz (2005) indicate that Mexican immigrants have less education than native-born workers. Their 1980–2000 econometric statistics indicate that lack of education is associated with low wages for Mexican immigrants. Borjas and Katz state: "The large Mexican influx in recent decades widened the U.S. wage structure by adversely impacting the earnings of less-educated native workers and improving the earnings of college graduates" (42–43). Their calculations indicate that native-born high school dropouts experience a wage reduction of "about 4.8 percent" (39). In contrast, the wages of native-born college graduates were improved because they benefit from the greater availability and reduced prices of goods and services provided by unskilled immigrants.

Immigration critics consider that unskilled unauthorized workers do not receive the minimum wage and that employers refuse to pay overtime. In semi- and low-skilled day labor and the manufacturing and food processing industries, the wages are relatively low. In 2008, as a severe economic recession developed, wage theft became a major complaint at workers' rights centers (Associated Press 2009). The National Day Laborer Organizing Network reported that an estimated 50% of day laborers, of whom 120,000 work on any given day in the United States, fail to receive some portion of their wages.

Wage theft is pervasive in low-skill jobs. A study of 4,378 workers in low-waged industries in Chicago, Los Angeles, and New York City indicated numerous violations of payment of the minimum wage or overtime, the right to take meal breaks, and access to worker's compensation when injured (Bernhart et al. 2009, 43). Wage theft rates were lowest among U.S.-born workers: 14.9% of men and 16.1% of women. Among foreign-born authorized workers, 13.5% of men and 24.2% of women experienced wage violations. Unauthorized foreign-born workers experienced the highest rate of violations: 29.5% of men and 47.4% of women. The research indicates that minimum-wage violations range from 3% to 43% across industries and that certain industries so commonly violate the law that it appears to be standard business practice (Bernhart et al. 2009, 39). Among sewing and garment workers, 40% experienced a minimum-wage violation and 70% experienced an overtime violation. Private household employment also had a high rate of violations. Among child-care workers, 66.3% experienced a wage violation while 49.6 % of beauty, dry cleaning, and general repair workers received illegally reduced pay.

Those in favor of restricting immigration believe that unauthorized workers are subject to poor working conditions. For example, the U.S. General Accountability Office (GAO 2005) and the Bureau of Labor Statistics (2007) indicate that food processing has one of the highest rates of injury and illness. Musculoskeletal injuries and respiratory and dermatological problems occur at significant rates. Poultry processing has a very high industry rate of injury (Bureau of Labor Statistics 2007). Poultry part cutting mechanization and assembly line production require lengthy periods of standing and repetitive motion. Speed on the assembly line, close proximity, and use of hand tools generate stress, contributing to injury. The use of immigrant labor complicates the likelihood of reporting injury because unauthorized individuals fear deportation.

In an America's Voice 2009 poll, 87% of Americans supported a path to legalization for unauthorized immigrants and 89% favored "cracking down" on employers of unauthorized labor (Brodnitz 2010). Of voters, 67% favored making immigrants without legal documentation into registered taxpayers. One question is whether unauthorized workers make it possible for employers to cut corners. Employers are economically motivated to increase profits by failing to pay living wages and violating workplace safety laws. Many of these jobs are cash only and the lack of paperwork disguises wage violations. Non-hourly payment and lack of paper wage-reporting statements facilitate this crime and make it difficult for workers to report it (Bernhart et al. 2009, 39). Workers may want jobs that are off the books because taxes are not deducted from the wage. Regardless, cash-payment work deprives states and the federal government of taxes on income. Critics also believe that the lack of legal status of unauthorized immigrants leaves them unable to challenge hazardous working conditions.

Will citizens avoid taking unskilled and semiskilled jobs because of the low pay and poor working conditions? A PEW

Hispanic Center national survey (2006) found that 65% of respondents believe that immigrants take jobs that Americans "mostly don't want" while 24% believe they deprive the native-born of employment opportunity. The most impacted native-born group is minority high school dropouts. There is mixed evidence concerning whether unauthorized workers substitute for less-educated native-born workers. Borjas (2003) estimated that unauthorized immigrants displaced about 10% of native-born workers with low education. Meanwhile, the number of native-born high school dropouts has decreased by 1.2 million, creating the possibility that more unskilled labor was needed than could be provided by native-born workers. Kochar's (2006) examination of the impact of foreign workers on the native-born did not show a consistent pattern of favorable or unfavorable job outcomes. Instead, from 1990–2005, eight states (North Carolina, Arizona, Arkansas, South Carolina, Tennessee, Oklahoma, Kentucky, and Alabama) had above-average growth for the foreign-born population and below-average employment rates for native-born workers. In contrast, 14 states (Minnesota, Nebraska, Colorado, Iowa, Utah, Kansas, Georgia, Delaware, Nevada, Idaho, Indiana, Oregon, Texas, and Washington) with above-average growth in the foreign-born population had above-average employment rates for the native-born.

The post-2007 economic downturn in the United States has led to increased scrutiny of the impact of immigrants on employment. Initially, the recession resulted in a 17% unemployment rate among immigrants working in construction who were impacted by the decline in housing prices and reduced new construction (Orrenous and Zavodny 2009). In particular, unauthorized Latin American immigrants are often less educated and work at unskilled jobs, making them especially vulnerable to fluctuations in the business cycle. Overall, recessions impact on native-born workers to a greater degree than immigrants with the exception of the severely impacted housing sector.

Lamar Smith (Austin American Statesmen PolitiFact Texas 2009) cited March 2008 data when stating, "allowing millions of illegal immigrants to stay and take jobs away from citizens and legal immigrants is like giving a burglar a key to the house. Illegal immigrants currently occupy 8 million jobs. Those stolen jobs rightfully belong to citizens and legal immigrants." The Center for Immigration Studies (CIS 2009) argues that the recession, combined with unauthorized immigration, has hurt U.S.-born blacks and Hispanics without a high school diploma. In December 2008, the unemployment rate for native-born blacks without a high school education was 24.7%. Unemployment among Hispanics with less than a high school education was 16.2%. At this time, rising unemployment dropped jobs estimated to be held by unauthorized immigrants to 6 to 7 million. CIS considers that unemployed native-born high school dropouts could potentially fill some of these jobs. About 12.8 million native-born who held a high school diploma or less were unemployed. Among less-educated immigrants without a high school education, unemployment was 10.6% and those with a high school education faced 11% unemployment.

Gordon H. Hanson, an economist, thinks that "Policy inaction [on immigration] is a result not only of a partisan divide in Washington, but also of the underlying economic reality that despite its faults, illegal immigration has been hugely beneficial to many U.S. employers, often providing benefits that the current legal immigration system does not." The availability of less-educated unauthorized workers does put a downward pressure on wages for unskilled employment. Hanson points out that unauthorized immigrants take unskilled employment because they most often lack a high school education. Their job opportunities are further limited by their lack of legal status. In 2008 unauthorized immigrants worked at labor-intensive agriculture (25%), building and maintenance staff (19%), construction (17%), food preparation and serving (12%), and production labor (10%). They are 5% of the civilian labor force. Losing these workers would cause economic disruption. According to Hanson, the demand from labor-intensive employers is such that only an increase in visas for unskilled workers, making legal immigration policy responsive to market conditions, would legalize this immigration flow (Hanson 2009).

Conservative Patrick Buchanan believes that "As immigrants work for less than Americans, they drive down the wages of our working people. And they represent a wealth transfer from the poorest Americans to the richest" (2006, 264). As a result, he advocates for enforcement of employer sanctions but would not legalize the unauthorized population. An opposing view is given by Robert Scheer, who has worked as a journalist for the *Los Angeles Times* and is a contributing editor for *The Nation*:

Some 2 million immigrant workers now earn less than the minimum wage and millions more work without

the occupational safety, workers' compensation, overtime pay and other protections legal status offers. Con-
sequently, when the president says that immigrants
perform work that legal residents are unwilling to do,
he may be right—but we don't know. The only way to
test that hypothesis is to bring this black market labor
pool above ground. (Scheer 2006)

The incompleteness of border control has created a dilemma of
an unauthorized population whose economic impact is incompletely understood and whose solution it is difficult to agree
upon. The political sensitivity of the issue has led to repeated
delays in addressing it.

The proximity of Mexico and Central American countries
to the southern land border facilitates migration. This border is
the only one in the world between a developed and a developing country. Nevertheless, 2,410,000 immigrants are estimated
to have come from non–North American countries using other
means (Hoefer, Rytina, and Campbell 2006). Problems with the
U.S. visa entrance and exit system and the openness of coasts
permit people of many ethnicities to enter legally and fail to
depart or to come without inspection along the coasts and over
the Canadian border. Globalization has also broadened patterns
of unauthorized entry to encompass all types of borders, land,
sea, or air, although Americans are not as aware of this issue.

Attempted Solutions

U.S. Border Patrol

Since the 1970s, the expansion of U.S. Border Patrol personnel
has been a consistent policy response to concern about unauthorized immigration and, later, drug trafficking across the U.S.-
Mexico border (see Andreas 2000, 34, 55–56, 87–93, 98; Ackleson
and Heyman 2010, 43). Before 9/11, border entry was more monitored than border exit, when inspection was often not carried out
or any data entered. Border inspectors either allowed or turned
back entrants. They charged unauthorized entrants trying to cross
without inspection and documents with fraudulent entry. The
first attempt is a civil offense and the second is a felony.

The U.S. Border Patrol, originally part of the Immigration and Naturalization Service (INS), now in the Department of Homeland Security, manages land interdiction and has the largest budget and political constituency. In 1980, there were 2,268 agents of which 87.2% were at the southern border and 9.3% at the northern border (TRAC 2006a). In 2001 there were 9,651 Border Patrol officers, of whom 93.9% were stationed at the U.S.-Mexico border and 3.4% at the Canadian border (TRAC 2006b).

Public concern about unauthorized immigration has led to a political response that continually increases the size of the Border Patrol and adds new surveillance equipment (Ackleson and Heyman 2010, 42–44). For example, helicopters, fixed-wing aircraft, and motion sensors are increasingly used. By 2000, there were 13,000 sensors, although some were not functionally operational (Kosolowski 2006).

In the 1990s the Border Patrol implemented a new tactic: line watching (Ackleson and Heyman 2010, 43–44) in operations like San Diego's Operation Gatekeeper (Nevin 2002), El Paso's Hold the Line (Dunn 2009, 51–96), Operation Rio Grande in McAllen, Texas (Maril 2004), and Operation Safeguard in Tucson, Arizona. Vehicles were placed close together, a few hundred feet apart and almost on the border line. This was done in urban zones to deter individuals from crossing before they even tried.

Criminalization of Immigration

Criminalization refers to the process of designating particular human behavior, such as crossing a country's border without its authority, as criminally illegal. In the United States, an individual's first crossing is a civil offense. Repeated attempts are a criminal felony. The language of immigration is complicated by the media's use of the term "illegal aliens" and, more recently, the unqualified "criminal aliens" for all apprehended migrants, because the first entry is a a misdemeanor (Warner 2006). A more neutral term used by the federal government is "unauthorized immigrants," while a term preferred by immigrant advocates is "undocumented immigrants."

The first attempt at expanding criminalization, of mixed success so far, was directed at citizen and permanent resident employers of unauthorized workers. In 1986 the Immigration

Reform and Control Act (IRCA) passed. Its "amnesty" legalized unauthorized immigrants who could prove they were in the country prior to January 1, 1982, and made employers who hired unauthorized workers subject to civil and criminal penalties referred to as "employer sanctions" (Green and Ciobanu 2006). Regardless of the law's intent, spending on interior enforcement never matched the amount expended on expanding U.S.-Mexico border enforcement to control unauthorized immigration. The target has always been apprehending unauthorized migrants, a task to which securing the nation from possible terrorists was later added in what is now referred to as the securitization of immigration.

Further criminalization of immigration began in the late 1980s after the passage of IRCA, when the United States began to develop a two-tier system of rights for citizens and noncitizens. It has gradually deprived noncitizens, including permanent resident aliens who had committed certain crimes, of their due process rights under the Constitution. Traditionally foreign-born individuals entering without inspection (EWI) have been deported from the country unless they successfully asked for asylum, which the government does not award to economically motivated migrants. In 1988 deportation was relabeled as "removal" and the Immigration and Naturalization Service (INS, now ICE) began the Institutional Removal Program (IRP) to review the immigration status of federal prisoners (Office of the Inspector General 2002, 1). This program was created to identify and then remove noncitizen prisoners immediately after their prison time was concluded (1999). The IRP later evolved into the Criminal Alien Program (CAP) (ICE 2008). Criminal aliens are defined by the Government Accountability Office as: "noncitizens who are residing in the United States legally or illegally and convicted of a crime" (GAO 2005, 3). The first permanent residents to be designated criminal aliens committed aggravated felonies, a legal concept that has evolved to encompass an expanded set of offenses.

In the late 1980s both immigration and crime control were major public issues. Permanent resident aliens who had committed crimes were subject to additional penalties. Congress began to pass laws that expanded the basis for removal (deportation) of permanent resident aliens who had committed crimes. The War on Drugs began with the 1988 Omnibus Anti-Drug Abuse Act, which specified that if a permanent resident alien was convicted of homicide, rape, drug trafficking, and/or arms trafficking, that person would be given expedited removal upon finishing his or her sentence without further access to a lawyer and with expanded exclusion from reentry (Podgorny 2009). These were among the first "criminal aliens" to be expelled. Because the law was retroactive, the numbers deported exceeded those actually finishing criminal sentences in any given year.

In 1993, the first attack on the World Trade Center was carried out; it had been planned by Ramzi Yousef, who had claimed political asylum, and other conspirators (Reeve 2002), creating a linkage between who is allowed to enter and the possibility of terrorism. In 1996 the Anti-Terrorism and Effective Death Penalty Act (AEDPA) and the Illegal Immigration Reform and Immigrant Responsibility Act (IIRIRA) linked immigration to the terrorism concern, which is the hallmark of later securitization (Chacon 2008; Podgorny 2009). These laws added 50 offenses to those designated as "aggravated felonies" (Garcia 2006). Further, any crime resulting in a sentence of more than a year, including misdemeanor crime like drug possession and shoplifting, was to be a basis for expulsion. Even a suspended sentence was to be a criterion for mandatory detention and removal. As a result, another wave of deportation of criminal aliens occurred. After removal, many convicted of aggravated felonies were banned for a lifetime while others might have to wait 5, 10, or 20 years before returning.

Denying noncitizens the constitutional right to due process of law is another aspect of criminalization. The attempt to control the high volume of unauthorized immigration led to taking away the right to obtain a lawyer and appear at a hearing before an immigration judge, denying the possibility of being pardoned for meritorious behavior and the need to support a family (Siskin and Wasem 2006). Often immigration officials at the nation's borders make a life-changing decision for an individual seeking asylum with only limited information. Similarly, in the interior, permanent-resident aliens subject to removal for aggravated felonies have no access to a legal appeal before they are summarily removed.

Expedited removal is applied to unauthorized entrants arriving at the land, sea, or air borders and permanent-resident or unauthorized-resident aliens serving time in detention or prison. For convicted noncitizens, any time in the United States after a prison sentence is completed is to be spent in mandatory detention without release on bond, which further isolates individuals from legal help. The denial of access to legal representation and immigration court means that there is little transparency in treatment of noncitizens.

The reason for expedited removal is to avoid the costly, time-consuming legal procedures. The combination of detention and expedited removal is supposed to deter individuals from attempting to enter without authorization. Opposition to expedited removal has come from immigration advocates who argue that the process denies asylum applicants of the legal opportunity to state their case (Human Rights First 2000). At present, asylum seekers who attempt to enter and have their initial claim denied are placed in mandatory detention, often in jails with criminals due to lack of space.

A penultimate step in the criminalization of immigration, irrespective of the legal entrance status of noncitizens, was the 2001 USA PATRIOT Act. It specified that immigration enforcement could detain or deport any noncitizen considered a possible threat to national security without due process of law. This legislation has been criticized for promoting racial profiling of Arabs and Muslims who were then expelled, often based on immigration violations such as overstaying a legal entrance visa, regardless of criminal or terrorist involvement (Cole 2003).

Terrorism

Terrorists have sought to enter the United States in the guise of visitors coming for tourism or business and as asylum applicants or legal immigrants. Although terrorists are thought, at present, to constitute only a handful of the millions of people entering and exiting the United States, their potential for harm has led the country to take extraordinary steps to exercise control over the flow of people.

Before 9/11 the pattern of disallowing constitutional rights to noncitizens was established. Subsequent securitization initiatives have taken this path by applying immigration law rather than developing new criminal laws to control terrorist suspects (Stumpf 2006, 12–24). After government officials understood the threat of international terrorism, immigration and interdiction of unauthorized immigrants became more important as a national security issue.

Although airlines screened passengers to avert hijackings, nothing stood in the way of the largest terrorist action in U.S.

history on 9/11. This failure of preparation occurred despite prior known terrorist crossings of the Canadian border. The 9/11 hijackers entered legally by air on various types of legitimate and fraudulent visas and passports (Eldridge et al. 2004). As a consequence, the United States undertook the drastic actions of the War on Terror. Ports of entry acquired new significance as increased scrutiny of visitors for business or pleasure, asylum applicants, and new immigrants occurred.

Counterterrorism before and after 9/11

Prior to 9/11, the United States had warning that it could be an international terrorist target and that the direction of the threat came from the northern border. In 1988 U.S. Customs arrested three Syrian terrorist group members linked to al-Qaeda for attempting to bring explosives across the Canadian border (Winterdyk and Sundberg 2010b, 19–20). The 1993 World Trade Center bombing was connected to Islamic terrorism, and certain plotters entered the United States from Canada (Hataley 2007; Winterdyk and Sundberg 2010b, 22).

In 1999 Ahmed Ressam, a member of al-Qaeda, was stopped at the U.S.-Canadian border after being tracked by Canadian intelligence for linkage to a bomb plot (Winterdyk and Sundberg 2010b, 22–23). The "millennium bomber" had planned to bomb Los Angeles International Airport during the 2000 Millennium celebration and was later convicted of terrorism and given a sentence of 22 years. The Royal Canadian Mounted Police (RCMP) first collected intelligence on Ressam, and then he was arrested when he attempted to cross the border to the United States in a joint operation with the United States (Ackleson and Heyman 2010, 48).

Before 9/11, security priorities were the interdiction of unauthorized migrants and contraband, especially drugs, on land at the U.S.-Mexico border, by air travel, or at sea, off Florida (Ackleson and Heyman 2010, 42–43). Less attention was given to port of entry security, the visa and admission process, and the U.S.-Canadian land and maritime borders, which include the Great Lakes. The 9/11 attack initially resulted in inspecting all entrants and vehicles at the borders, including the trucks that are a major element of international trade (Ackleson and Heyman 2010, 50). This created massive backups (Andreas 2003, 10), including a 36-mile traffic line at the Windsor, Ontario, and

Detroit port of entry bridges. Counterterrorism surveillance procedures increased border-crossing time, and migrant apprehensions for unauthorized entry dropped. The intensive enforcement created transaction costs for international business and slowed or diverted trade to other countries.

After 9/11, the Bush administration sought to maintain borders that were open to entry but the major emphasis was on lengthy background checks, aggressive immigration enforcement, and new border controls. Border security has been enhanced in many ways but many of the policies undertaken are a continuation of past trends. Initial response to the attack was marked by confusion and the need to reassess all aspects of border-security policy. The attack provoked both innovation and greater investment in prior programs (Ackleson and Heyman 2010, 49–50). In the post–World Trade Center attack world, planners began to consider a wide variety of terrorist attacks that could be carried out on U.S. soil. Border-control strategies that were emphasized after 9/11 included nonintrusive scanning equipment for cargo and differentiating trusted (low risk) shippers from those unknown or suspected of smuggling contraband.

The 9/11 Commission (see Eldridge et al. 2004) found that the United States was slow to react to the development of international terrorism. Al-Qaeda terrorism against U.S. embassies and military abroad did not result in improved U.S. border security. Terrorism, rather than immigration or drug smuggling, became the major border-security issue after 9/11, although terrorists have been few and seldom encountered in the United States (Ackleson and Heyman 2010, 58–59). As a result, most border-security efforts concentrate on unauthorized entry and drug control. The initiatives undertaken are mostly a reprioritization of established programs for improving surveillance technology, fencing, and certain enforcement procedures. Federal terrorism prosecutions, never more than marginal in number, rose in the 12 months after 9/11 and then declined (TRAC 2006c). To illustrate, there were 355 international terrorist prosecutions in 2002 and 19 in 2006.

Monitoring Ports of Entry

Originally, ports of entry had dual governance (Ackleson and Heyman 2010, 40–41). The Immigration and Naturalization Service (INS) in the Department of Justice inspected noncitizen visitors, immigrants, and citizens in transit. Customs, in the Treasury

Department, regulated legitimate goods and sought to prevent smuggling through inspection of land vehicles and airplane inspections, a task shared with the Federal Aviation Agency (FAA). Customs shared oceanic vessel inspection with the Coast Guard, in the Department of Transportation. Further inspection was carried out by the Animal and Health Inspection Service in the Department of Agriculture and the Nuclear Regulatory Commission in the Department of Energy.

Every nation exercises border control and seeks to confine transit to special zones known as ports of entry. Ports of entry, places where movement occurs across borders, are deterritorialized from physical borders when individuals enter at international airports or seaports. Since 1976, the legal case of *U.S. v. Martinez-Fuente* has allowed the establishment of permanent or fixed checkpoints on highways within 100 miles of the border. These have been situated above the Mexican border. Vehicles traveling through these checkpoints are checked for individual documentation and contraband such as drugs. The inspections must be brief and a warrant is not required.

Ports of entry regulation is central to border security, and Customs inspectors make many arrests. The port traffic of legal entrants is 1,000 times that of unauthorized entries; 500,000 enter via the ports, and it is loosely estimated that at least 500 million attempt clandestine entrance each year. Major publicity is given to land borders outside of the ports, especially abutting Mexico. Entrance between ports, by air, land, or sea, is unauthorized. The Border Patrol is in charge of preventing unauthorized entry over the land borders. The Department of Defense is responsible for air interdiction, and the Coast Guard patrols the coast (Ackleson and Heyman 2010, 41, 42).

Before 9/11 residents of the two countries bordering the United States had two different procedures which reflected the relative social inequality between the nations. Canadian citizens, from a prosperous country, did not need a visa (Ackleson and Heyman 2010, 48). Mexican citizens, from a developing nation, were required to have a border-crossing card or visa. The card for Mexico was biometric and allowed 72-hour visits within 25 miles of the border. These visits could be extended if approved at a port of entry or consulate. An additional 27 prosperous countries had visa waivers and could enter with a passport. This was a key vulnerability, as these countries, with low rates of unauthorized immigration to the United States, were known to harbor terrorists or were a part of terrorist travel patterns.

Both pre- and post-9/11, the Department of State has regulated visas for nonimmigrant travel. Pre-9/11 immigrant visas involved the Immigration and Naturalization Service (INS) and the Department of State. The 9/11 terrorists used visas, some fraudulent, and their entry was linked to lack of consular and port inspector training in examining terrorist travel patterns or identifying fraudulent documents. The 9/11 Commission found that U.S. Consulates prioritized prevention of unauthorized immigration over screening for potentially dangerous terrorists (Eldridge et al. 2004, 7, 73–74, 82; Ackleson and Heyman 2010, 42, 47).

Land port inspectors were and are under pressure to clear traffic (Andreas 2000, 46, 47; Heyman 1999, 626–627) but are also mandated to interdict drugs, and checking people was deemphasized (Ackleson and Heyman 2010, 46). Staffing and port-of-entry expansion had not kept up with demand. Individuals crossing at land borders were waved through after very brief questioning. Trucking connected the manufacturing of commodities in the U.S.-Mexico economic partnership. The volume of such traffic meant that port inspectors had heavy work schedules and substantial overtime. Previously, land-port workers were pressured to clear goods quickly while searching for contraband and inspection of visitors was not emphasized. Seaports prioritized clearance of cargo over security while the Coast Guard concentrated on interdiction of Haitian and Cuban migrants and drugs (Ackleson and Heyman 2010, 46). Terrorism had not been a priority and the United States was caught by surprise.

Screening at airports was cursory because of pressure to clear passenger entries. Air travelers and luggage/goods were screened by the INS and Customs. International airports gave priority to clearing passengers instead of inspection of travelers for immigration violations. Before 9/11 the United States was one of the most open countries in the world to visit. After 9/11, it was found that the United States had been underprepared in addressing international terrorism with border-security measures (Eldridge et al. 2004, 3).

Before 9/11 biometric electronic databases containing biographical, criminal, and security information were being developed (Eldridge et al. 2004, 87–96; Ackleson and Heyman 2010, 46). These included IDENT, IBIS, NAILS, TECS, and TIPOFF.

Despite their availability, use of these databases was discretionary. Identity documents were not machine readable for comparison. Oral declarations of citizenship were accepted at the discretion of the land-port officers. The biometric database was to be used for immigration enforcement and port security officials were distracted from searching for terrorists. After 9/11, new systems and procedures heavily regulated visa applicants and increased the difficulty for visitors, foreign students, and temporary workers trying to enter the United States.

Department of Homeland Security

Prior to their reorganization into the U.S. Department of Homeland Security, border-control and law-enforcement agencies were fragmented and did not share intelligence (Eldridge et al. 2004). The Bush administration adopted a zero-tolerance risk-management approach to improving border security. They sought to balance concerns about identifying and preventing terrorist entry, stopping unauthorized immigration, and preventing criminals' entry with economic concerns.

The most significant development after 9/11 was the reorganization of federal agencies under the umbrella of the U.S. Department of Homeland Security (Ackleson and Heyman 2010, 51–52). The 9/11 Commission had substantially faulted the lack of cooperation among government intelligence agencies (Eldridge et al. 2004). They indicated that the United States had not been prepared to counter a major terrorist attack because of lack of coordination of intelligence agencies and law enforcement. The Homeland Security Act of 2002 joined 22 federal agencies and 180,000 employees. The U.S. Immigration and Naturalization Service (INS) ceased to exist on March 1, 2003. Its functions were reallocated to the Bureau of Citizenship and Immigration services (CIS), U.S. Immigration and Customs Enforcement (ICE), and U.S. Customs and Border Protection. The DHS director became a Cabinet-level member of the government. Whether the huge bureaucratic organization, which was again reorganized in 2004, has been successfully integrated has been questioned (Carafano and Heyman 2004). The DHS budget has consistently had massive and constant increases.

The U.S.-Canadian border was proudly referred to as the "longest undefended border" in the world, but that changed dramatically after 9/11 (Winterdyk and Sundberg 2010a, 27).

Armed police and paramilitary organizations patrol this bilateral border. In a move parallel to the United States' creation of the Department of Homeland Security, Canada created the umbrella Canadian Border Services Agency (CBSA) to house the former customs, immigration, and food inspections services, and it became the first armed service to patrol. In 2006, the Canadian government allocated $101 million to arm 4,800 Border Services officers. They wear ballistic vests and carry handguns to operate as a paramilitary organization.

Layered Traveler Screening

The 1996 Illegal Immigration Reform and Immigrant Responsibility Act (IIRIRA) had mandated the development of a data system to track foreign visitor arrival and departure as did the Immigration and Naturalization Service Data Management Improvement Act of 2000 (Ackleson and Heyman 2010, 57). The system was to integrate the Department of Justice and Department of State databases. The goal was to identify unauthorized entrants, not terrorists. The original databases were faulty as immigration and consular watch lists lacked comprehensive information. This was partly due to lack of cooperation among intelligence agencies, the State Department, and the FBI, which the 9/11 Commission later noted. Although consular terrorist watch lists were electronic, they were incomplete.

The 9/11 Commission determined that better information from a layered approach would identify high-risk travelers to maintain security and be less disruptive to regular travel (Eldridge et al. 2004). They determined that the border of the United States should be electronically "moved abroad" to begin the process of security checks for a layered defense (Ackleson and Heyman 2010, 56). This necessitated working with foreign governments to begin checks. The physical border and its inspectors would be the last—not the first—step in security screening.

The Uniting and Strengthening America by Providing Appropriate Tools Required to Intercept and Obstruct Terrorism Act (USA PATRIOT Act) of 2001 sought to strengthen surveillance and intelligence sharing (Ackleson and Heyman 2010, 53). It focused on review of immigrants and noncitizen visitors. A new deadline was set for requiring machine-readable passports for nations that were not required to request a visa to travel. The Enhanced Border Security and Visa Entry Reform

Act of 2002 changed security reviews for visa applicants, established data sharing, and sought to integrate the entry and exit systems at U.S. ports of entry (Ackleson and Heyman 2010, 54).

Changes in the visa-application process were a needed counterterrorist response. The United States is seeking to unify consular and international travel system watch lists for visa screening. Before 9/11, the CIA, FBI, and Defense Department watch lists were integrated but they did not share data, permitting duplication and waste of intelligence (Ackleson and Heyman 2010, 55–56). A new Terrorist Screening Center is unifying watch lists and has information on individuals and their records. The security of the original sources is protected while the information is shared.

Layered inspection is occurring (Ackleson and Heyman 2010, 56). The first step is to apply for a visa at consulates (although many European countries and Canada have this process waived). At step two, pre-inspection of documents against watch lists is done and individuals may be questioned prior to boarding airplanes or ships. Certain individuals may be denied transit if they are on a "no-fly list." The Secure Flight program uses a computerized risk assessment algorithm (Automated Targeting System) which searches by computer to indicate "no fly" or further inquiry of "selectees." Step three involves three procedures: document inspection, a watch-list check, and questioning at entry. A preflight manifest is sent to international airports under Secure Flight and inspectors have backgrounds and risk scores. This approach is also used at sea and air freight entry points. All individuals entering and cargo paperwork are inspected. Most actual air or marine cargo is not inspected.

A necessity for control of terrorism is screening of aircraft flight lists. In the 1995 Bojinka plot, Ramzi Yousef and Khalid Shaikh Mohammed planned to bring down 11 Trans-Pacific commercial jets (Hamm 2007). Although the United States recognized its vulnerability, before 9/11 foreign air carriers only cooperated voluntarily, and countries like Saudi Arabia refused to do so. The United States now operates the Advanced Passenger Information System (APIS) and receives information on foreign passengers from all international airlines.

Border Inspections

The Intelligence Reform and Terrorism Prevention Act (IRTP) of 2004 ended the passport exemption for travel among the

United States, Canada, and Mexico (Ackleson and Heyman 2010, 58). Under the Western Hemisphere Travel Initiative (WHTI) everyone must have a passport or another approved identity document to cross over the borders. Communities located on the borders were concerned about impact on cross-border traffic and increased crossing times. Previously, U.S. citizens could verbally declare their status and cross without verification. WHTI has caused consternation in border communities concerned about crossing times (Abelson and Wood 2007).

A trusted traveler program was created to pre-clear certain noncitizens. Preferred flows of travelers have been established to structure inspection programs. Identity card standards were raised and standards for "breeder documents," birth certificates, and other documents used to establish personage were set. SENTRI is the Secure Electronic Network for Traveler's Rapid Inspection and is meant to expedite entry of cleared individuals (Ackleson and Heyman 2010, 55). This program is called NEXUS in Canada.

In 2002 the Container Security Initiative (CSI) was begun, as was the Customs-Trade Partnership Against Terrorism (C-TPAT) (Ackleson and Heyman 2010, 55; DHS 2007a). These public and private initiatives created a risk-based automated targeting system and signed up businesses for a trusted shipper program in which they would agree to guarantee security of goods from their supply chain. It is a layered form of security because goods are inspected prior to coming to the border and may be inspected at the port of entry. Radiation screening and advanced inspection technology are used to detect weapons of mass destruction such as nuclear materials for a dirty bomb.

Pressure exists for speedy border transit because inspection can create bottlenecks in the international transport grid. Both business owners and politicians push for fast transit of people and goods. Yet the completeness of the inspection process is inversely related to speed. Despite the emphasis on paying fees for passage of legal goods and apprehending smugglers and taking contraband, most shipping is not inspected. The 9/11 Commission Act of 2007 requires that 100% of air cargos be physically inspected by August, 2010 (GAO 2009). Similarly, 100% of maritime shipping containers are to be inspected by July, 2010. The Government Accountability Office (2009) reports that 100% scanning of inbound foreign maritime cargo is not feasible and the deadline has been extended to 2014. In 2009, about 50% of nonexempt air cargo was being screened due to labor and resource issues. A formal declaration is made for all shipped goods, and tariff fees and regulations are applied.

The 2004 Border Strategic Plan made terrorism the most important issue but has focused on the U.S.-Mexico border corridor. Border Patrol officers have been given access to terrorist and criminal watch databases and are apprehending criminal non-citizens attempting reentry. Border communities are receiving increased street patrolling.

Overall, the massive efforts to arrest terrorists after 9/11 have produced few solid leads resulting in prosecution. Immigration law was used to detain noncitizens on the basis of nationality and religion without charge and for lengthy periods of time without bond. A major problem is that immigrant communities were alienated from cooperating to find potential terrorists. Counter-terrorism and immigration enforcement have begin to overlap.

Although the basic thrust of legislation has been countering terrorism, most funded initiatives impact visitors, cargo, and citizens crossing the borders. These changes primarily address the past issues of immigration and smuggling while incorporating concerns about terrorism. The DHS has continued its integration of formerly separate agencies and the ID system at U.S. consulates and airports has been strengthened.

Canada has resisted fortification of its border, and Smart Border screening and entry will be the major strategy. In North America, policy was based on Smart Border Accords and the Security and Prosperity Agreement of the United States, Mexico, and Canada. Trilateral cooperation in intelligence, inspection, and prescreening was arranged. After establishing that the al-Qaeda hijackers did not cross as unauthorized entrants, screening was the priority. Although no system is infallible, new strategies seek to assess and manage indirect and unintended risks (Naim 2005). Screening involves filtering for threats using a layered approach (Ackleson and Heyman 2010). Developed countries have a Smart Border preference and the resources to implement it.

The original Canada-U.S. Smart Border Declaration initiated a biometric identification system in Canada and sharing of intelligence data. The Security and Prosperity Agreement of the United States, Canada, and Mexico extended intelligence sharing to Mexico and established a trusted traveler program for all three countries. The three security priorities are (1) traveler and cargo inspection and bioprotection; (2) shared critical infrastructure protection, port security, and intelligence against transnational threats; and (3) trusted travel (Ackleson and Justin 2006; Villareal and Lake, 2009).

Conclusion

The 9/11 incident demonstrated that border security involves more than the land borders. The air and sea ports of entry need careful monitoring and application of intelligence data to prevent terrorism. Consulates issuing visas and passports are carrying out layered screening. The DHS and the Terrorist Screening Center have integrated electronic watch lists. Homeland Security now has officers at some consulates. Implementation of intelligence-led law enforcement is under way. Despite or because of this upgrading, the land and sea ports have operational problems. Inspectors turned away 200,000 inadmissible entrants in 2006, but it is estimated that they missed 20,000 (GAO 2007). It is thought that the inspection process is inconsistent. This may be due to ports being understaffed by 7–25%. There is an extreme workload with poor training, outdated facilities, and a lack of full documentation standardization. It is not surprising that there are delays, inadequacies in security, low morale, and high turnover among inspectors. In 2007 the exit check at land ports was abandoned, making calculation of visa overstayers problematic. The DHS lacks the capacity to arrest all visa violators.

The United States is attempting to safeguard its physical length and numerous borders against "terrorism." Terrorism is hard to combat because, relative to an issue like unauthorized immigration, looking for terrorists is like searching for a needle in a haystack (Winterdyck and Sundberg 2009). It is suggested that border-security personnel should search for criminals rather than terrorists (Hamm 2007). Meanwhile, the U.S. Government Accountability Office (GAO 2008) has determined that the huge and complex Department of Homeland Security is expending billions of dollars without appropriate oversight, including 15 major investments deemed to be underperforming.

References

Abelson, D., and D. Wood. 2007. "People, Security, and Borders: The Impact of the Western Hemisphere Travel Initiative in North

America." White paper. Foundation for Educational Exchange between Canada and the United States of America. http://www. wilsoncenter.org/index.cfm?fuseaction=events.print&event_ id=237749&stoplayout=true.

Ackleson, J., and Josiah McHeyman. 2010. "United States Border Security after 9/11." In *Border Security in the Al-Qaeda Era*, ed. John A. Winterdyk and Kelly W. Sundberg, 37–76. New York: CRC Press.

Ackleson, J., and K. Justin. 2006. "The Security and Prosperity Partnership of North America." *American Review of Canadian Studies* 36: 207–232.

Andreas, Peter. 2000. *Border Games: Policing the U.S.-Mexico Divide.* Ithaca: Cornell University Press.

Andreas, Peter. 2003. "A Tale of Two Borders: The U.S.-Canada and U.S.-Mexico Lines after 9–11." In The Rebordering of North America, ed. Peter Andreas and Thomas J. Biersteker New York: Routledge.

Associated Press. 2009. "As Wage Theft Rises, States and Cities Crack Down." December 16. http://abcnews.go.com/Business/wireStory? id=9359168.

Austin American Statesmen PolitiFact Texas. 2009. "Rep. Lamar Smith Says Immigrants Hold 8 Million Jobs." http://www.politifact.com/ texas/statements/2010/jan/12/lamar-smith/rep-lamar-smith-says- immigrants-hold-8-million-job/.

Bagwell, K., and R. W. Staiger. 2003. "National Sovereignty in an Interdependent World." http://www.intertic.org/Unions%20Papers/ bagwell-staiger.pdf.

Beaver, Janice Cheryl. 2006. "CRS Report for Congress: U.S. International Borders: Brief Facts." http://fpc.state.gov/documents/ organization/76897.pdf.

Bernhart, Annette, Ruth Milkman, Nik Theodore, Douglas Heckathorn, Miribai Auer, James DeFillipis, Ana Luz Gonzalez, Victor Narro, Jason Perelshteyn, Diana Polson, and Michael Spiller. 2009. *Broken Laws, Unprotected Workers: Violations of Employment and Labor Laws in American Cities.* Joint Report of the Center for Urban Economic Development, University of Illinois–Chicago, National Employment Law Project of New York, NY, and the UCLA Institute for Research on Labor and Employment, Los Angeles, California. http://www.nelp. org/page/-/brokenlaws/BrokenLawsReport2009.pdf?nocdn=1.

Biersteker, Thomas J. 2003. "The Rebordering of North America? Implications for Conceptualizing Borders after September 11th." In *The Rebordering of North America: Integration and Exclusion in a New Security Context,* ed. Peter Andreas and Thomas J. Biersteker, 153–166. New York: Routledge.

Borjas, George J. 2003. "The Labor Demand Curve Is Downward Sloping: Reexamining the Impact of Immigration on the Labor Market." *Quarterly Journal of Economics* 118: 1335–1374.

Borjas, George J., and Lawrence F. Katz. 2005. "The Evolution of the Mexican-Born Workforce in the United States." National Bureau of Economic Research Working Paper 11281. Cambridge, MA: National Bureau of Economic Research. http://www.hks.harvard.edu/fs/ gborjas/Papers/w11281.pdf.

Bothwell, Robert. 2006. *The Penguin History of Canada*. Toronto: Penguin Group (Canada).

Brodnitz, Pete. 2010. "Immigration Reform: National Polling." Benensen Strategy Group for America's Voice. December. http:// amvoice.3cdn.net/e8038e6eb31fa1bd2e_gfm6vati2.pdf.

Buchanan, Patrick. 2006. *State of Emergency: The Third World Invasion and Conquest of North America*. New York: Thomas Dunne Books.

Bureau of Labor Statistics, U.S. Department of Labor. 2007. "Survey of Occupational Injuries and Illnesses in Cooperation with Participating State Agencies." Washington, DC: U.S. Department of Labor. http:// www.bls.gov/iif/oshwc/osh/case/ostb1951.txt.

Carafano, James J., and David Heyman. 2004. "DHS 2.0: Rethinking the Department of Homeland Security." Washington, DC: The Heritage Foundation. http://www.heritage.org/Research/ HomelandDefense/upload/72759_1.pdf.

Center for Immigration Studies (CIS). 2009. *Unemployment for Immigrants and the U.S.-Born: Picture Bleak for Less-Educated Black and Hispanic Americans*. Washington, DC: Center for Immigration Studies. http://www.cis.org/December2008Unemployment.

Chacon, Jennifer. 2008. "The Security Myth: Punishing Immigrants in the Name of National Security." In *Immigration, Integration and Security: America and Europe in Comparative Perspective*, ed. Ariane Chebel d'Appollonia and Simon Reich. Pittsburgh: University of Pittsburgh Press.

Cole, David. 2003. *Enemy Aliens: Double Standards and Constitutional Freedoms in the War on Terrorism*. New York: Free Press.

CNN. 2008. "Minimum Wage Laws, State by State." July 24. http:// money.cnn.com/2008/07/24/smallbusiness/state_minimum_wages. fsb/index.htm?postversion=2008072411.

Department of Homeland Security (DHS). 2007a. "Container Security Initiative Strategic Plan." http://www.dhs.gov/files/programs/gc_ 1165872287564.shtm.

Department of Homeland Security (DHS). 2007b. "DHS Announces Predeparture Screening of International Passengers and First Step

Towards Secure Flight." http://www.dhs.gov/xnews/releases/pr_1186668114504.shtm.

Dunn, Timothy J. 2009. *Blockading the Border and Human Rights: The El Paso Operation That Remade Immigration Enforcement.* Austin: University of Texas Press.

Eldridge, Thomas R., Susan Ginsberg, Walter T. Hempel II, Janice L. Kephart, and Kelly Moore. 2004. "9/11 and Terrorist Travel. Staff Report of the National Commission on Terrorist Attacks Upon the United States." http://govinfo.library.unt.edu/911/staff_statements/911_TerrTrav_Monograph.pdf.

Freebairn, William. 2007. "Mexico Raises Daily Minimum Wage to $4.86 in 2008." *Bloomberg News, December 21.* http://www.bloomberg.com/apps/news?pid=20601086&sid=a0nqGGuVgzzo&refer=latin_america.

GAO. 2005. "Information on Criminal Aliens Incarcerated in Federal and State Prisons and Local Jails." http://www.gao.gov/new.items/d05337r.pdf.

GAO. 2007. "Border Security: Despite Progress, Weaknesses in Travelor Inspections Exist at Our Nation's Ports of Entry." http://www.gao.gov/highlights/d08219high.pdf.

GAO. 2008. "Department of Homeland Security: Billions Invested in Major Programs Lack Appropriate Oversight." http://www.gao.gov/new.items/d0929.pdf.

GAO. 2009. DHS's "Progress and Challenges in Key Areas of Maritime, Aviation and Cybersecurity." http://www.gao.gov/new.items/d10106.pdf.

Garcia, Michael John. 2006. "CRS Report for Congress: Immigration Consequences of Criminal Activity." http://fpc.state.gov/documents/organization/78335.pdf.

Green, Thomas C., and Illiana M. Ciobanu. 2006. "Deputizing—and Then Prosecuting—America's Businesses in the Fight Against Illegal Immigration." *American Criminal Law Review* 43 (3): 1203–1224.

Hamm, Mark S. 2007. *Terrorism as Crime: From Oklahoma City to Al-Qaeda and Beyond.* New York: New York University Press.

Hanson, Gordon H. 2009. "The Economics and Policy of Illegal Immigration to the United States. Migration Information Source." Washington, DC: Migration Policy Institute. http://www.migrationpolicy.org/pubs/Hanson-Dec09.pdf.

Hataley, T. S. 2007. "Catastrophic Terrorism at the Border: The Case of the Canada–United States Border. Homeland Security Affairs." Supplement no. 1. http://www.jsaj.org/?special:article=supplement.1.2.

Heyman, Josiah Mc. 1999. "Why Interdiction? Immigration and Law Enforcement at the United States–Mexico Border." *Regional Studies* 33: 619–630.

Hoefer, Michael, Nancy Rytina, and Christopher Campbell. 2006. "Estimates of the Unauthorized Immigrant Population Residing in the United States: January, 2006." http://www.dhs.gov/xlibrary/assets/statistics/publications/ill_pe_2006.pdf.

Human Rights First. 2000. "Is This America? The Denial of Due Process to Asylum Seekers in the United States." http://www.humanrightsfirst.org/refugees/reports/due_process/due_process.aspx.

Kelly, N., and M. Treblecock. 1998. *The Making of the Mosaic: A History of Canadian Immigration Policy.* Toronto: University of Toronto Press.

Kochhar, Rakesh. 2006. "Growth in the Foreign-Born Workforce and Employment of the Native-Born." Washington, DC: PEW Hispanic Center. http://pewhispanic.org/files/reports/69.pdf.

Kosolowski, R. 2006. "Immigration Reforms and Border Security Technologies. Border Battles: The U.S. Immigration Debates." Social Science Research Council. http://borderbattles.ssrc.org/Koslowski.

Lee, Erika. 2006. "A Nation of Immigrants and a Gatekeeping Nation: American Immigration Law and Policy." In *A Companion to American Immigration,* ed. Reed Ueda. New York: Routledge.

Maril, Robert. 2004. *Patrolling Chaos: The U.S. Border Patrol in Deep South Texas.* Lubbock: Texas Tech University Press.

Martinez, Oscar. 2006. *Troublesome Border.* Rev. ed. Tucson: University of Arizona Press.

McIntosh, D. 1984. *The Collectors: A History of Canada Customs and Excise.* Toronto: NC Press (in association with Revenue Canada, Customs and Excise and Supplies and Services Canada).

Moore, Stephen T. 2004. "Defining the 'Undefended': Canadians, Americans, and the Multiple Meanings of Border during Prohibition." *American Review of Canadian Studies* 34(1): 3–32.

Naim, Moises. 2005. *Illicit: How Smugglers, Traffickers, and Copycats Are Hijacking the Global Economy.* New York: Doubleday.

Nevins, Joseph. 2002. *Operation Gatekeeper: The Rise of the "Illegal Alien" and the Making of the U.S.-Mexico Boundary.* New York: Routledge.

Office of the Inspector General. 2002. "Audit Report: Immigration and Naturalization Service Institutional Removal Program." http://www.usdoj.gov/oig/reports/INS/a0241/final.pdf.

Orrenius, Pia M., and Madeline Zavodny. 2009. *Tied to the Business Cycle: How Immigrants Fare in Good and Bad Times.* Washington, DC: Migration

Policy Institute. http://www.migrationpolicy.org/pubs/orrenius-Nov09.pdf.

Passel, Jeffrey and D'Vera Cohn. 2008. "Trends in Unauthorized Immigration: Undocumented Inflow Now Trails Legal Inflow." Washington, DC: PEW Hispanic Center. http://pewhispanic.org/files/reports/94.pdf.

Payan, Tony. 2006. *The Three U.S.-Mexico Border Wars: Drugs, Immigration, and Homeland Security.* Westport, CT: Praeger Security International.

PEW Research Center for the People and the Press and PEW Hispanic Center. 2006. *America's Immigration Quandary.* Washington, DC: PEW Research Center for the People and the Press and PEW Hispanic Center. http://pewhispanic.org/files/reports/63.pdf.

Podgorny, Diana R. 2009. "Rethinking the Increased Focus on Penal Measures in Immigration Law as Reflected in the Expansion of the 'Aggravated Felony Concept.'" *Journal of Criminal Law and Criminology* 99 (1): 287–315.

Ramirez, Bruno. 2001. "Canada in the United States: Perspectives on Migration and Continental History." *Journal of American Ethnic History* 20(3): 50–71.

Reeve, Simon. 2002. *The New Jackals: Ramzi Yousef, Osama Bin Laden, and the Future of Terrorism.* Boston: Northeastern University.

Reyes, Silvestre. 2009. "Border Security." http://reyes.house.gov/Issues/Issue/?IssueID=4437.

Scheer, Robert. 2006. "There Is No Immigration Crisis." *Huffington Post. March 29.* http://www.huffingtonpost.com/robert-scheer/there-is-no-immigration-c_b_18080.html.

Schuck, P.H. and J. Williams 1999. "Removing Criminal Aliens: The Pitfalls and Promises of Federalism." *Harvard Journal of Law and Public Policy* 22(2): 367–464.

Siskin, Alison, and Ruth Ellen Wasem. 2006. "Congressional Research Service Report for Congress: Immigration Policy on Expedited Removal of Aliens." Washington, DC: Government Printing Office. http://fpc.state.gov/documents/organization/54512.pdf.

Stumpf, Juliet. 2006. "The Crimmigration Crisis: Immigrants, Crime, and Sovereign Power." *American University Law Review* 56: 368–419.

Thompson, Wayne C. 2001. *Canada 2001.* Harper's Ferry, WV: Stryker-Post Publications.

Transactional Action Clearinghouse (TRAC). 2006a. "Border Patrol Agents: Southern Versus Northern Border." http://trac.syr.edu/immigration/reports/143/include/rep143table2.html.

Transactional Action Clearinghouse (TRAC). 2006b. "Border Patrol Expands: But Growth Rate After 9/11 Much Less Than Before; Division Between North/South Border Little Changed. http://trac.syr.edu/immigration/reports/143/Transactional Action Clearinghouse.

Transactional Records Clearinghouse (TRAC) 2006c. "Criminal Terrorism Enforcement in the United States During the Five Years Since the 9/11/01 Attacks." http://trac.syr.edu/tracreports/terrorism/169/.

U.S. Customs and Border Patrol (CBP.gov). 2009. "U.S. Customs Service—Over 200 Years of History." http://www.cbp.gov/xp/cgov/about/history/legacy/history2.xml.

U.S. Immigration and Customs Enforcement. 2008. "Fact Sheet: Criminal Alien Program." http://www.ice.gov/doclib/pi/news/factsheets/criminal_alien_program.pdf.

Villareal, M. Angeles, and Jennifer E. Lake. 2009. *CRS Report for Congress: Security and Prosperity Partnership of North America: An Overview and Selected Issues*. Washington, DC: Congressional Research Service. http://www.fas.org/sgp/crs/row/RS22701.pdf.

Warner, Judith A. 2006. "The Social Construction of the Criminal Alien in Immigration Law, Enforcement Practice and Statistical Enumeration: Consequences for Immigrant Streotyping." *Journal of Social and Ecological Boundaries* 1(2): 56–80.

Winterdyk, John A. and Kelly W. Sundberg, 2010a. "Introduction." In *Border Security in the Al-Qaeda Era*, ed. John A. Winterdyk and Kelly W. Sundberg, xvii–xliv. New York: CRC Press.

Winterdyck, John A., and Kelly W. Sundberg. 2010b. "Shifts in Canadian Border Security." In *Border Security in the Al-Qaeda Era*, ed. John A. Winterdyk and Kelly W. Sundberg, 3–36. New York: CRC Press.

2

Problems, Controversies, and Solutions

Introduction

Our world is being transformed by a high rate of internationally interconnected social changes that are beyond individual nations' capacity to control. Economic globalization involves a process of integration of the world economy and travel circuits. Globalization was widely viewed as a social force leading to a new era of economic integration and peace. Instead nonstate criminal actors such as terrorists and organized criminals are using new technology to exploit opportunities within the growing web of global linkages. Transnational threats are not confined to one nation; they cross borders and are not subject to sovereign control (Thachuk 2007, 3, 8). They include terrorism, drug, arms, and human trafficking, money laundering, and corruption. Three major trends are increasing transnational threats: (1) the globalization of trade and communications has generated unequal opportunities while increasing awareness of new technology; (2) the number of politically unstable states is increasing; and (3) the ethnic and religious hatred that produces terrorism, civil conflict, and war has increased. Nonstate actors are as important to maintaining national and border security as nation-states.

Increasingly nation-states are presented with the serious issue of how to deal with transnational threats and maintain economic ties while cooperating to stop transnational terrorism and crime. Nonstate actors smuggle and traffic goods, services,

41

and people. Kimberly Thachuk of the Center for Technology and National Security Policy at the National Defense University notes; "While much of this illicit trade brings great misery and sorrow to many, so too does it provide jobs and buoys up sagging economies, often blending seamlessly into busy commerce." Newly democratic nations that are struggling to develop economically during globalization face survival issues (Thachuk 2007, 3–5). These countries may choose to look the other way or participate in corruption as they seek income. Criminal enterprise may be deeply embedded within legitimate activities, which complicates the task of keeping the social order. For example, illicit goods like drugs are often smuggled in regular cargos. Criminals may commit terroristic acts like the multiple murders committed by Mexican drug-trafficking organizations in conflict over territory and the police. Nations must learn to integrate law enforcement with military defense activities. Further, the types of threats that are faced are not discrete but interconnected, as when terrorists commit crimes to raise money such as al-Qaeda trafficking heroin.

Thachuk suggests that power is no longer solely located in societal institutions. Individuals and loosely organized collectives have taken advantage of the fluidity of global networks. According to Thachuk,

> Errant individuals of indeterminate origins, loosely knit gangs of determined killers, small bands of criminal clans with excessive international connections and numerous other combinations of nonstate actors, many of whom possess statelike capabilities, are proving to be elusive, sophisticated, and deadly enemies, not only in the war on terror but also for the stability of many sovereign states in a number of regions. (2007, 5)

Governments are subject to corruption and extortion, and citizens are threatened by violence and experience economic distortion caused by criminal investment. As a result, domestic security is no longer distinct from national security and international military conflict. The key event precipitating this change is 9/11. The "War on Terror" is a domestic and international policy involving border security and international armed conflict in Afghanistan and Iraq.

Al-Qaeda is a loosely networked terrorist organization. It cannot be addressed without international cooperation, although nations are often unwilling to cooperate if their sovereignty is threatened. Terrorism is merged with criminal activity as al-Qaeda has smuggled both drugs and diamonds. The U.S. Department of State indicates that many major international terrorist groups have ties to drug traffickers (Thachuk 2007, 16). The money raised is used for the cause. In 2002, the FBI caught an American and two Pakistanis trading 5 metric tons of hashish and 600 kilograms of heroin for four Stinger antiaircraft missiles ("Feds Break Up" 2002). Other criminal activity linked to terrorists includes extortion, kidnapping, document forgery, identity theft, and credit card fraud. The international scope of this activity makes them a threat to global security and stability rather than just a law enforcement problem (Thachuk 2007, 17–18). Violence and corruption can destabilize governments, making individuals and their organizations as powerful as some nation-states.

The development of transnational terrorism occurred before a comprehensive security strategy could be developed. Controlling jihadist terrorists is difficult for four reasons: (1) jihadists are deliberately distributed in multiple countries to make detection more difficult; (2) the United States has a large flow of visitors and asylum applicants arriving each year; (3) intolerance is a problem if jihadist terrorist profiling is solely based on race/ethnicity and religion; and (4) the problem of jihadist terrorism can be "homegrown" by social alienation if the second and third generations after immigration are not socially integrated into American society.

After 9/11, the prevention of terrorism became a major element of border policy. In the struggle to monitor access to the United States for business and travel while preventing entry of terrorists, two positions came to predominate among the nation's leaders (Alden 2008). In Washington, DC, technocrats proposed a risk-management strategy for border security that adhered to the Constitutional Bill of Rights and utilized information and surveillance technology to better monitor border access. Advocates of this strategy included former Secretary of Homeland Security Tom Ridge and, to a moderate extent, Robert Bonner, former Commissioner of Customs and Border Security.

A competing perspective on border control is that taken by law-enforcement advocates who used existing immigration law to screen immigrants and prevent terrorist entry. The key advocate of this position was former Attorney General John Ashcroft, who stated, "If a terrorism suspect committed any legal infraction at all, regardless how minor, we would apprehend and charge him" (Alden 2008, 81).

An intelligence-based approach to terrorism is developing but, once again, the priority is immigration and law enforcement at the U.S.-Mexico border. Politicians have focused on immigration and promote special operations and building a wall at the U.S.-Mexico border. The U.S. Border Patrol is the primary agency targeted for increased funding. In September 2006, it was comprised of 12,300 agents, and it grew to 18,875 in April, 2009: a 53% increase in under three years (Kouri 2009). Adding a large number of new hires has a potential for problems. The standards for hiring may be lowered, training attenuated, and less experienced agents are likely to be less worthy in the field. In contrast, the Canadian border had 980 officers in September 2005 and 1,128 in May 2008 (Heyman and Ackleson 2010: 59). The Canadian- border agents are 8.8% of U.S. Border Patrol staffing as compared to 7.1% in prior years.

Free Trade and Security

The North American Free Trade Agreement (NAFTA) was followed by an expansion of trade among the United States, Canada, and Mexico. Experts disagree about the extent to which NAFTA itself widened economic ties (Teslik 2009). According to the Office of the U.S. Trade Representative (2008), "From 1993 to 2007, trade among the NAFTA nations more than tripled, from $297 billion to $930 billion." Tellingly, trade between the NAFTA nations constitutes 80% of Canadian and Mexican trade and is over one-third of U.S. trade (Teslik 2009).

In Canada, the extent of trade makes the degree to which cross-border traffic is scrutinized a major business-cost issue. Of Canadian exports, 82% are to the United States, its major international trade partner; in contrast, 22% of U.S. exports are sent to Canada. Canada inspects an estimated 4.5% of shipments. At the Canadian border, Free and Secure Trade (FAST), NEXUS, and C-TPAT are risk-management programs that seek to preclear low-risk shipments based on shipper compliance. The degree of importance that should be attached to protecting key U.S.-Canada ports of entry relative to less trafficked locations is open to debate. One-third of all truck traffic goes through Windsor,

Canada, and Detroit. Two-thirds of traffic utilizes four crossings in Southern Ontario. Eight of the top 10 crossings in use are bridges or tunnels. The key ports of entry are more vulnerable to terrorist disruption because of the volume of traffic.

Mexico's border-security apparatus has developed parallel to the United States' War on Terror (Heyman and Ackleson 2010). The Mexican International Migration Institute (El Instituto Nacional de Migración, INM) is developing a biometric immigration document system. The Secure Electronic Network for Traveler's Rapid Inspection (SENTRI) promotes the free and rapid flow of people. In Mexico, the Container Security Initiative and the Customs-Trade Partnership Against Terrorism (C-TPAT) for shipment certification are being deployed.

Terrorism

The terrorist threat faced by the United States and other Western nations has changed dramatically since 9/11. Historically, terrorism involved state-sponsored military activity directed toward changing the foreign policy of other nations. Today's terrorism is a privatized non–nation state activity using criminal financing. Three trends distinguish transnational terrorism (Armitage 2008). First, international agreements promoting economic liberalization such as NAFTA and the European Common Market promoted the free movement of people, goods, and capital across borders. As a result, regional borders were opened. Second, advances in global communication and transportation made it easier for international organization and travel. Al-Qaeda is a global network using commercial travel routes and the Internet. Third, major political events such as the collapse of the Soviet Union, wars in the Balkans, and the Gulf War destabilized societies and increased the opportunity for organized crime.

Pre-globalization terrorist organizations were involved in perpetrating fraud, extortion, theft, bank robbery, and counterfeiting. The contemporary organized criminal activities of terrorist organizations include drug trafficking, smuggling of arms and weapons of mass destruction (WMD), kidnapping, money laundering and other financial crimes, and human trafficking. Terrorist financial crimes include theft of identity, cell phones, and credit cards. Transnational organized crime and terrorist organizations have much in common. For al-Qaeda, the need to commit crime to raise money is an "Achilles heel" because it attracts law enforcement. Islamic jihadist groups have banked in the Middle East and Africa, making it difficult to control money laundering. As might be expected, Middle Eastern countries are not receptive to Western oversight of banking.

The collapse of the Soviet Union has exposed its substantial nuclear armament to diversion for sale to terrorists. Soviet activity in Afghanistan, Azerbaijan, and Tajikistan left behind potentially catastrophic weaponry. For example, in 2002, al-Qaeda used a Russian antiaircraft missile in an attempt to shoot down an Israeli jet in Kenya. National security investigators know that terrorist organizations have repeatedly tried to purchase WMDs on the black market.

Weapons of Mass Destruction and Security

After hijackers used airplanes to destroy skyscrapers, the world entered a new era of global threats from weapons of mass destruction (WMD). Dick Cheney (Vanderbilt, Harris, and Allen 2009) considers that: "the ultimate threat to the country" is "a 9/11-type event where the terrorists are armed with something much more dangerous than an airline ticket and a box cutter—a nuclear weapon or a biological agent of some kind." Texas Governor Rick Perry (Texas Border Sherrif's Coalition 2007) points out: "A vulnerable border also gives terrorists opportunities to smuggle weapons of mass destruction into the U.S. undetected."

During the Cold War, the United States was very concerned about the possibility of a Soviet nuclear strike. After the breakup of the Soviet Union, concern turned to the lack of security for nuclear materials in its stockpiles (Smigielski 2007, 53). The Russian military dispersed, and tens of thousands of atomic scientists went without pay for months. Policy planners became concerned that rogue regimes and terrorists would gain access to nuclear materials and the means to construct a device. In the United States, the Cooperative Threat Reduction (CTR) Program is active in preventing nuclear smuggling, particularly from the Russian stockpile.

The transnational threat of nuclear smuggling is constrained by the availability of materials and the intention of the end user.

Thachuk (2007, 14) has stated: "While great fear is generated by the chance that a nuclear weapon will be smuggled into the wrong hands, the probability is low." More probable scenarios are the smuggling of nuclear materials or components used to make weapons. Four types of nuclear search by terrorists occur in illicit markets. They seek weapons, raw materials, technological components, and expertise. Rogue regimes and terrorists are known to have tried to acquire a nuclear bomb (Smigielski 2007, 54–55). Muammar Qadhafi of Libya is believed to have offered the Chinese government almost $1 billion for nuclear weapons and was declined (Federation of Nuclear Scientists, n.d.). Another terrorist option is acquiring fissionable materials, the industrial means to enrich them to bomb quality, and the help of experts. Because terrorists lack the national territory (a state-based homeland) for bomb development, if they wanted to build a bomb they would try to produce a "dirty bomb," which is a low-tech radiological weapon. Al-Qaeda is known to have tried to acquire a nuclear weapon or materials. It is considered unlikely that nuclear bombs will be smuggled because they are guarded. Nevertheless, a rogue technician could attempt insider theft.

Weapons-grade fissile uranium and plutonium require refinement and separation technology. Nuclear-weapon construction requires detonators and timers (Smigielski 2007, 57). Computer design programs and specialized machinery are necessary. Technicians with knowledge of nuclear physics, fissionable material, and weapons manufacture are needed. Furthermore, nuclear materials that have been intercepted have never amounted to enough for bomb construction (Smigielski 2007, 56). Plutonium is toxic when handled outside special facilities. A smuggler attempting to transit sufficient nuclear materials for a bomb would likely be killed by radiation. Nevertheless, highly enriched uranium is easier to use and handle and can be shielded to a degree that would make it difficult to detect with conventional U.S. Customs technology. Dogs are unable to detect uranium and plutonium because they have no odor. The availability of uranium on the black market is the major factor impacting terrorists' ability to construct a dirty bomb.

The manufacture of a dirty bomb requires only low-grade radioactive material and a casing. Most people are unaware that dirty bombs are not considered a WMD because they do not cause casualties outside of the area of the explosion. Dr. Henry

Kelly, in March 2002 testimony before the Senate Committee on Foreign Relations, stated:

> While radiological attacks would result in some deaths, they would not result in the hundreds of thousands of fatalities that could be caused by a crude nuclear device. Attacks could contaminate large urban areas with radiation levels that exceed . . . health and toxic materials guidelines [and] would require prompt evacuation and create terror in large communities even if radiation casualties were low. (Federation of American Scientists 2002)

Dirty bombs have been labeled "weapons of mass disruption" because they cause panic among the public (Smigielski 2007, 56). In November 1995, Chechen rebels placed a cesium-137 radioactive bomb in a Moscow park to cause terror, but it was disabled.

In 1991, concerns about the security of Russia's nuclear stockpile resulted in the Nunn-Lugar Cooperative Threat Reduction Program. The U.S. Department of Defense cooperated in an international program to prevent nuclear smuggling at the source (Smigielski 2007, 58–59). Dismantled Russian warheads were secured and fencing and surveillance for deterrence were provided. Russian weapons-grade reactors were converted to nuclear power plants and enriched uranium was blended with lower-grade uranium to stabilize it.

David Smigielski (2007, 60–61), an analyst at the Central Intelligence Agency (CIA), suggests that the U.S. effort to prevent smuggling by helping Russia must be broadened to other countries. In 2001, al-Qaeda was reported to have contacted Pakistani nuclear scientists (Kelly 2001). The Pakistani scientists indicated they would only go to Afghanistan if their government approved and, fortunately, it did not. Later, al-Qaeda contacted A. Q. Khan, a nuclear scientist in Pakistan who was found to have sold nuclear components to Libya.

Although attention is focused on fissile nuclear material, nonfissile material including medical and scientific radioactive waste can be used to make a dirty bomb with devastating consequences (Smigielski 2007, 61). A cesium-137 or strontium-90 bomb exploded in New York City would contaminate tens of square miles and necessitate building demolition costing trillions of dollars. Smigielski considers that preventing nonfissile dirty bomb attacks requires greater attention than nuclear materials.

Border Documents and Visas

Acts of terrorism by noncitizens have been very limited in the United States. Most individuals entering on visas are travelers on business or pleasure. The United States needs to maintain security at the ports of entry and overcome vulnerabilities in the legal visitation and immigration system. Major violations include extending a stay without authorization after entering on a visa, known as visa overstay, and using fraudulent documents to enter. Nevertheless, Americans associate unauthorized immigration with U.S.-Mexico border migrants who enter without inspection. The reality is that about 45–50% of the unauthorized population is estimated to be comprised of visa overstayers who enter legally using nonimmigrant visas or border crossing cards (PEW Hispanic Center 2006). The tracking of international visitors is an important aspect of the securitization of immigration.

Keeping track of immigration is a major task at the air borders because of business and tourist visitation. It is estimated that 250,000–350,000 of the unauthorized population entered with permission and overstayed (PEW Hispanic Center 2006). This is about 1–1.5% of visitors and they comprise 35–45% of the annual increase in unauthorized residents. This number is augmented by individuals who cross at the Canadian or Mexican borders with border-crossing cards and overstay. Immigration monitoring is far more complex than just policing the Mexican border as it involves any land, sea, or air port of entry and searching within the interior of the United States for unauthorized entrants.

Air borders have been a site for U.S. vulnerability to terrorism. Two of the 9/11 hijackers were on a terrorist watch list on the day they passed through air security (Eldridge et al. 2004). The training camps developed by terrorist groups like al-Qaeda teach military and criminal skills for unauthorized entry. Altering visas, passports, and other documentation is a part of the lesson. The 9/11 terrorists entered on temporary visas, and some used fraudulent documents while coming by air. The 9/11

Commission recommendations (Eldridge et al. 2004) resulted in many changes to immigration policy for both business and visitation to the United States.

The knowledge that the 9/11 terrorists had traveled from foreign nations using visas obtained by legal or fraudulent means has generated new security and detention regimes. New biometric identification requirements for visitors, security checks prior to issuing visas, and mandatory detention of asylum applicants and unauthorized entrants are major initiatives to contain the threat of terrorism. Stringent visa screening policies have resulted in processing delays. Applicants often have a long waiting period before they can be interviewed by a consular official. Visitors applying for a visa need to prove that they are coming for a limited period of time and a specified objective, such as business or tourism. The portion of visitors for whom the interview is not waived increased as a result of 9/11 Commission identification of laxness in carrying out visa policy.

On December 25, 2009, the continued vulnerability of the air borders became evident as Umar Farouk Abdulmutallab, a Nigerian citizen, was observed attempting to light a powder and liquid explosive on a Northwest Airlines flight from Holland (O'Conner and Schmidt 2009). The passengers and crew subdued the terrorism suspect while the plane was landing at Detroit's airport. Although he was allowed to fly, Abdulmutallab was in a law-enforcement intelligence database because his father had reported his radicalization. He later stated that al-Qaeda in Yemen had sponsored him (Baker 2010). The intelligence community has been criticized for not integrating intelligence information that Abdulmutallab could be connected to terrorism with reports that al-Qaeda was training a Nigerian suicide bomber.

President Obama ordered immediate changes in the use of the terrorism database to increase the number of individuals from Nigeria and Yemen who are on a terrorism watch list. Millimeter full body scanning technology, not available in most airports, might have detected the explosive device. Intelligence can identify potential terrorists and targets for additional security precautions and multilayered, unpredictable screening to deter attempts. Anytime security is heightened at airports, it increases delays.

After the 9/11 World Trade Center attacks one might expect that a viable entry *and exit* tracking system would be in operation but, as the December 25, 2009, Northwest Airlines incident has demonstrated, that is not the reality. The visa process entails checking both terrorist watch lists and no-fly lists. Abdulmutallab is another case in which the United States had access to information indicating he was a terrorism suspect, but he was not subjected to a pat-down search or placed on a no-fly list.

The U.S. VISIT (U.S. Visitor and Immigrant Status Indicator) Program uses biometric identification (digital photographs and fingerprints) to scan travelers before flying and at arrival but it is not used at exit. This new identification system supplements the arrival and departure forms referred to as "I-95s" that air travelers are supposed to fill out by hand when they enter through U.S. Customs at ports of entry. This pre-computer age form is typed into a computer network at entrance, when identification documents are also inspected to verify personal identity and checked against watch lists. A problem is that the departure form is not always received. At departure, forms are collected and not always entered into a national or global database to verify that a visa holder exited. Further complications occur when the two I-95 departure and exit forms do not match (GAO 2004). In 2001 20% of I-95 departure forms were estimated to be uncollected. In the process, some people leave without being registered and some unauthorized entrants stay and become unauthorized immigrants.

Despite the connection between visa overstay and unauthorized immigration, the United States is still unable to track departures (McKinley and Preston 2009). Although Congress passed legislation mandating the creation of such a universal exit electronic monitoring system, inspection only occurs at arrival, not at departure. In 2009, Hosam Maher Husein Smadi, a 19-year-old Jordanian national who overstayed a tourist visa, was arraigned on charges of plotting to bomb a Dallas skyscraper. This directed attention to the gap in the visa-monitoring system. In 2008, 2.9 million people came to the United States on temporary visas and some were never officially recorded as checking out. The current exit system relies on turning in a paper stub with personal information. Approximately 93% turn in this paperwork. Some of the remainder exit without knowing how to process their departure forms. About 200,000 may have overstayed their visas and joined the unauthorized population. It is estimated that 40% of the population of unauthorized immigrants overstayed their visas.

DHS has indicated that, with over one million visitors a day, monitoring exits is a formidable task (McKinley and Preston 2009). Pilot exit programs have not functioned in a speedy manner to facilitate visits and commerce through borders. Airlines have refused to take photographs and fingerprints of departing passengers. This inability to track departure has led DHS to emphasize the role of law enforcement in apprehending terrorists. In addition, the penalty for visa overstay has been greatly increased. Failure to renew a visa for additional time of stay could result in deportation and being banned from returning to the U.S. for 10 years.

Border-crossing cards are issued to Canadian and Mexican citizens for facilitating border transit. In 1998 the federal government began a process of issuing biometric border-crossing cards to Mexican citizens. A U.S.-Mexico border-crossing card authorizes a visit of no longer than 30 days within a 25-mile radius of the border in California, Texas, and New Mexico, and 75 miles in Arizona. In order to obtain a visa for a longer stay, an individual must fill out an additional application. Many requests are denied when individuals cannot show financial means in an effort to prevent undocumented economic migration.

Border-crossing cardholders are not checked when they exit the border, which creates vulnerability in the tracking system. In addition, crossing at U.S.-Mexico ports of entry does not mean that biometric data is verified. It is estimated that 1.7% of legal border crossers overstay (PEW Hispanic Center 2006). At the inland border mileage limit checkpoints, all vehicles stop and the occupants are asked about citizenship, but many vehicles are waved on after a verbal validation without the documents being checked for everyone in the car. Interior checkpoints do not have the necessary computers or staffing to validate all vehicle occupants.

At borders, an economic premium is placed on getting people across in a speedy manner. The U.S. Government Accountability Office (GAO 2008) found that individuals in a test program sent across the Canadian border without documentation or with counterfeit driver's licenses or passports were almost uniformly allowed to enter without detection of their unauthorized status. The U.S. Customs and Border Patrol (CBP) responded that they lacked the resources to inspect all documents at land crossings and the situation was acute at the northern border. The implementation of the Western Hemisphere Travel Initiative (WHTI) ended the ability to enter the U.S. with only a verbal declaration and no document inspection.

U.S.-Canada Border Issues

The American media constantly focus on the Mexican border although no terrorists have ever been apprehended at that border (Chavez 2009). In contrast, the Canadian border has been the site of major arrests of terrorist plotters. Hataley (2007, 1) states: "A catastrophic event at the U.S.-Canadian border would be an event having the potential to seriously disrupt . . . economic linkages vital to the well-being of Canadians and the Canadian state." Besides the vulnerability of border economic infrastructure, tunnels and bridges are major targets. These transit points across the border function as "chokepoints" (Ackleson 2009, 345) for disrupting trade. According to Hataley (2007, 2), 80% of Canadian trade uses a very limited number of checkpoints which would make terrorist attacks more damaging at these crossings.

In congressional testimony prior to 9/11, Congressman Lamar Smith of Texas said that police investigator Claude Pacquette criticized Canada as a "Club Med for terrorists" (Committee of the Judiciary 2000, 12). The Canadian immigration and refugee system is viewed as creating a U.S. security risk. Approximately 30,000 refugees are allowed to enter Canada each year, and claims are made that efforts to determine terrorist connections are not sufficient. It is easier to enter Canada than the United States, and there is facility of movement within Canada and potentially to the United States. The Canadian Security and Intelligence Service (CSIS) found that Canada's entrance rules had attracted terrorists. Ward Elock, director of the CSIS, states,

> the following terrorist groups or front groups acting on their behalf have been and are active in Canada: Hezbollah and other Shiite Islamic terrorist organizations, several Sunni extremist terrorist groups, including Hamas, with ties to Egypt, Libya, Algeria, Lebanon and Iran; . . . the Tamil Tigers [Sri Lankan]; the Kurdistan Worker's Party (PKK); and all of the world's major Sikh terrorist groups. (Emerson 2000, 7, citing Elock)

Prior terrorist attempts to cross the Canadian border into the United States have resulted in arrests on two occasions and successful entry by certain 1993 World Trade Center bombers (Hataley 2007). U.S. intelligence believes there are terrorist sleeper cells in Canada and that its border represents a security risk. Prior to 9/11, Canada began tightening its policies by passing the Immigration and Refugee Act of 2000 (Adelman 2002, 22–23). In response to the terrorist security risk, the Post 9/11 Public Safety Act has provisions for denying asylum to individuals connected to terrorism and detaining such individuals at the border or in the interior of Canada.

Canada's passing of securitization legislation is not considered sufficient. Stewart Bell (2004) and Clark Kent Erwin (2006) have suggested that the United States faces a major risk of terrorists crossing from Canada. Former U.S. ambassador to Canada Paul Cellucci stated: "It is inevitable that terrorists would look to Canada as a potential launching pad to get into the U.S." (Dawson and Fife 2005).

Ackleson (2009, 341) believes the unease created in the United States by 9/11 has caused the United States to think of Canada and its border as a major security threat. Canada is criticized by DHS Secretary Janet Napolitano as lax in immigration and refugee policy. The United States wants the same level of scrutiny given to Canadian applicants for asylum and immigration that foriegn applicants receive when they come to the United States.

The U.S. Northern Command considers Canada a "favorable" environment for terrorism because of its immigration policies toward Pakistani, Afghan, and Egyptian applicants. The Great Lakes region and areas of upstate New York, Vermont, and New Hampshire were cited for concern about terrorist network formation. Suggestions for increasing security include intelligence sharing through both cross-border criminal and terrorist databases and law-enforcement programs, such as the extant Integrated Border Enforcement Team, which targets dangerous people. More complicated would be coordinating Canadian and United States visa policies for foreign entrants to have matching entrance criteria (McNeill and Nguyen 2009).

Bolstering Canadian Security

Global terrorists have developed the communications and logistical capacity to form international networks and to cross borders. Both "homegrown" and foreign-born terrorists figure in these networks. The bombing of London mass transit in 2005 was the first example of a self-organized terrorist group not composed of foreign nationals. A 2006 Canadian plot to bomb buildings was disrupted by the Royal Canadian Police (CBC News 2010). Seventeen young Muslim males were arrested on charges of participating in a terrorist group. Three were charged with importing weapons and ammunition while 12 were charged with planning a bombing. As with earlier plots, a Muslim imam had preached violence. Their arrest led to an investigation of their possible ties to jihadist groups in the United States, Great Britain, and other countries.

Serious concerns exist about Canadian border-security infrastructure. The U.S. Government Accountability Office (GAO 2007) found areas of the border designated as "unmanned and unmonitored" and simulated movement of radioactive materials that went undetected in tests. They concluded: "Our work shows that a determined cross border violator would likely be able to bring radioactive materials or other contraband undetected into the United States by crossing the U.S.-Canada border at any of the locations we investigated" (GAO 2007, 1). CBP responded that a lack of visible Border Patrol agents did not mean that the border was not monitored. The ground surveillance camera, radar, and mobile infrared detection sensor systems are being upgraded and increased.

On June 1, 2009, the Western Hemisphere Travel Initiative (WHTI) was implemented. Individuals from countries other than Canada, Western Europe, Japan, and select other countries need to attend an interview with a U.S. embassy official regardless of the reason for entry: visits, business, study, or work. Prior to 9/11, it was thought that international visitors posed little risk. Concerns have been raised that long delays required for interviews will block the flow of people and trade over the borders. Since 2004, most visa applicants must come for an interview, photograph, and fingerprinting, which results in delays of up to months. Young men from Muslim nations, regardless of religious orientation, must undergo an additional questionnaire interview including information on U.S. family, contacts, and income. Upon departure, they need to notify U.S. border inspectors that they are leaving or face a ban of five years or more. Individuals previously cleared for U.S. entry who travel back to the country of origin undergo "secondary screening" for return. One result of tightened security is that the number of visitors, workers, and foreign students applying for visas has dropped. Foreign investors have also been discouraged. The United States has to pay a price in loss of talent as well as money to maintain exceptional security standards (Alden 2008).

A process of militarization largely began after 9/11 at the previously "unguarded" Canadian border. The northern strategy has relied on high-tech detection equipment including sensors and radar because only a little over a thousand U.S. Border Patrol agents are stationed there. Ongoing efforts include identifying high-threat areas and intelligence sharing across databases. Canada and the United States are high-income countries and the funding and development of cross-border initiatives involves more bilateral decision-making than at the Mexican border but is still unequal. Due to U.S. pressure, Canada has undertaken a series of securitization measures that parallel those of the United States. Patrick Lennox (2007, 1021) states: "Given the vast asymmetry in power capabilities between the two countries, the United States has and continues to have the prerogative to define and determine the means to deal with threats to the continent." The size and relatively lower degree of enforcement of the Canadian border are ongoing issues.

Immigration

Although the passage of tough immigration laws in the 1990s was meant to resolve public concern, throughout the first decade of the 21st century, immigration has been a divisive issue. Notably, a series of Presidents, Democrat Bill Clinton, Republican George W. Bush, and Democrat Barack Obama, have all successfully backed legislation to support policing of the borders and failed to gain Congressional authorization for legalization of unauthorized entrants residing sub rosa in the country. The only remaining form of leniency has been for the first attempt at unauthorized entry to remain a misdemeanor civil offense instead of passing legislation making it a felony crime.

Key Players

The Clinton administration and Congress passed tougher laws to deter unauthorized immigration and remove "criminal aliens." This legislation included the 1996 Anti-Terrorism and

Effective Death Penalty Act (AEDPA) and Illegal Immigration Reform and Immigrant Responsibility Act (IARIRA. President Clinton (1993) stated:

> The simple fact is that we must not—and we will not—surrender our borders to those who wish to exploit our history of compassion and justice. . . . But the solution to the problem of illegal immigration is not simply to close our borders. The solution is to welcome legal immigrants and legal, legitimate refugees and to turn away those who do not obey the laws. We must say no to illegal immigration so we can continue to say yes to legal immigration.

In 2001, President George W. Bush indicated that immigration would be a signature issue but attempts to achieve a bipartisan compromise on immigration reform were unsuccessful. President Bush (2006) supported the legalization of undocumented immigrants and a new guest-worker program. Bush introduced an approach to legalization with penalties that was promoted by Senators Ted Kennedy and John McCain and shapes current proposals on legalization. Bush (2006) stated:

> Illegal immigration puts pressure on public schools and hospitals, it strains state and local budgets, and brings crime to our communities. These are real problems. Yet we must remember that the vast majority of illegal immigrants are decent people who work hard, support their families, practice their faith, and lead responsible lives. They are a part of American life, but they are beyond the reach and protection of American law.

The election of Barack Obama as president was accompanied by the creation of a two year Democratic majority in the Senate and House of Representatives. In 2009, the issue of immigration was placed on the back burner, but slated for future action. President Obama (2009) has stated:

> Here's what I believe: We are a nation of immigrants, number one. Number two, we do have to have control of our borders. Number three, that people who have

been here a long time and have put down roots here have to come out of the shadows, because if they stay in the shadows, in the underground economy, then they are oftentimes pitted against American workers. Since they can't join a union, they can't complain about minimum wages, et cetera, they end up being abused, and that depresses the wages of everybody, all Americans.

So I don't think we can do this [immigration reform] piecemeal. I think what we have to do is come together and say, we're going to strengthen our borders. We have to combine that with cracking down on employers who are exploiting undocumented workers. (Obama 2009)

Obama's views on immigration reform involve supporting legalization of unauthorized residents who pay a fine, return to Mexico, and then enter the legal immigration system. As a part of legalization, they would be expected to learn English. To control unauthorized economic migrants, an effective employment-verification system would be set up. In this regard, many aspects of the renewed immigration reform initiative are not new.

Opposing Viewpoints on Immigration Reform

It has been hard to achieve immigration reform because some favor all out-border control and immigration restriction while others suggest that a combination of border and interior enforcement, legal immigration reform, and legalization is needed. The two positions have stalled congressional debate as border enforcement advocates have refused to consider changes to the legal immigration system until the problem of unauthorized immigration is solved. Five key issues of this debate are as follows: (1) Can a level of border enforcement be reached that prevents unauthorized immigration? (2) What is the role of employer sanctions and/or interior enforcement to locate unauthorized immigrants in the solution? (3) Should the unauthorized population be legalized and under what specific conditions—or should they be deported? (4) Should legal immigration be primarily based on admitting skilled workers or family reunification? and (5) How many unskilled permanent or guest workers should be allowed into the United States?

Republican and Democratic conservatives had a major role in preventing passage of the Senate Comprehensive Immigration Reform (CIR) bills of 2006 and 2007 (Orchowski 2008, 169). Conservatives in the House emphasized securing the border and visa restriction rather than legalization, which they negatively call "amnesty," which was an aspect of the Senate bill. Conservative Republican grassroots organizations sent over a million faxes or phone calls to defeat CIR. These bills failed because there was a deadlock over whether the "broken immigration system" can be fixed through just border control and immigration restriction or if a redesign of the criteria for legal residence is needed. Neoconservative Charles Krauthammer (2007) summed up the prior failure to pass a bill as follows:

> Comprehensive immigration reform is in jeopardy because it is a complex compromise with too many moving parts and too many competing interests. Employers want a guest-worker program; unions want to kill it. Reformers want to introduce a point system that preferentially admits skilled and educated immigrants; immigrant groups naturally want to keep the existing family-preference system. Liberals want legalization now; conservatives insist on enforcement "triggers" first.

Current attempts to pass immigration legislation will involve a degree of compromise that only wholehearted intraparty and bipartisan support can provide. Neither the Republican nor the Democratic Party speak with one unified voice. There are three Republican groups: corporate libertarians, neoconservatives, and traditional conservatives (Orchowski 2008, 169). The Democratic Party is divided into centrist progressives, populist progressives, moderates, and conservatives. Conservative and moderate Democrats meet in the "Blue Dog Caucus" which has a maximum membership of 47 (Orchowski 2008, 175).

The late Senator Ted Kennedy, former chair of the Senate immigration subcommittee, was the most vocal supporter of immigrants in Washington, DC. Kennedy was a supporter of the 1965 Immigration and Nationality Act and an architect of the Immigration Reform and Control Act of 1986, which had a one-time amnesty for individuals resident in the United States prior to 1986. Orchowski (2008, 171) considers that both Kennedy and former President George W. Bush represent libertarians in favor of more permissive immigration. Nevertheless, Bush wanted immigration for economic reasons while Kennedy promoted humanitarianism and social justice.

"Corporate libertarians" include corporate lobbyists, many of whom are representatives of industries involved in mass hiring of unauthorized workers and legal immigrants (Orchowski 2008). Daniel Griswold (2009), the director of the Center for Trade Policy Studies at the Cato Institute, has urged the adoption of a guest-worker program which corporate libertarians connect to positive economic expansion. This reform of the legal immigration system would occur in addition to legalization. Centrist Democrats favor expanding work visas and legalization. To illustrate how complex the issue is, some centrist Democrats want to simultaneously increase border control and interior enforcement of immigration laws to contain the immigrant population. This implies that they do not believe opening more legal ways to enter, such as a guest-worker program, will stop the problem of unauthorized border crossing for immigration.

Democratic Senator Charles Schumer (2007) of New York presents a pro-legalization view in his book, *Positively American: Winning Back the Middle Class Majority One Family at a Time.* Schumer advocates a balanced approach through his "50% solution": reducing unauthorized immigration by 50% and increasing legal immigration by 50%. Interior enforcement of labor law through employer sanctions and legalization is emphasized in this strategy. Both centrist and populist progressive Democrats favor social justice for the poor and minorities. As a result, they are concerned about public opinion on interior immigration enforcement such as raids impacting immigrant communities. Progressive think tanks representing this position include the Center for American Progress and People for the American Way. Media proponents include Jon Stewart at Comedy Central and Keith Olbermann of MSNBC. Other advocates of liberal immigration policy include *The Progressive, The Nation, In These Times,* and the American Catholic Church.

Many centrist progressive Democrats are allied with conservative Republicans in wanting increased border enforcement. The conservative position on immigration is tied to individual politicians rather than political parties. Patrick Buchanan (2006, 250), editor of the *American Conservative,* is a strong advocate of immigration restriction and believes in an "immediate moratorium on all immigration" and removal of the unauthorized population.

He emphasizes border control as the major strategy by supporting a "permanent fence along the entire 2,000 mile border with Mexico, defining, sealing and securing it forever" (P. Buchanan 2006, 254). Many Democrats who are Blue Dog Caucus members favor enforcement without legalization, known as the SAVE proposal, which was cosponsored by congressmen Heath Shuler (D-NC) and Brian Bilbray (R-CA). Opinion is further divided as some would increase enforcement and expand immigration permits as well.

Conservatives are said to have a media pipeline through supportitive news anchors: Bill O'Reilly of FOX News and Lou Dobbs, a former CNN anchor who works in talk radio. Bill O'Reilly supported the border fence and legalization of the unauthorized population via an initial U.S. Post Office administered Department of Homeland Security registration program tied to later passing a criminal background check. With this initiative, employers hiring workers without legitimate documents would be penalized. Since leaving CNN, Dobbs has continued to promote border control. He considers: "We need to be able to influence the direction of the conversation toward securing the border because until we can control immigration, we cannot meaningfully, substantively alter immigration law because it would have no point if we cannot establish the basis for the control of the flow of people across that border" (Rhee 2009). Dobbs's views changed after he left CNN as he had not previously emphasized "humane immigration policy" or the "ability to legalize illegal immigrants under certain conditions."

Given the public's acceptance of border control as the main strategy for ending unauthorized immigration, support for legalization, often referred to as a new "amnesty," is a divided issue. Kris Koback (2009), a law professor and advisor to the Attorney General on immigration law and national security (2001–2003), indicated that the size of the undocumented population makes legalization ill-advised because of "(1) the inability of U.S. Citizenship and Immigration Services (USCIS) to implement the amnesty and (2) the national security risks that would result. He considers that undertaking legalization in one year would present a monumental task and that there would be insufficient time for background checks.

The negative public attitude towards "illegal immigration" has been viewed as a moral panic. "Moral panics" refer to a situation in which the public is falsely manipulated to believe in the existence of a threatening social problem. According to this view, since the 1970s, undocumented immigrants have been repeatedly made scapegoats for employment problems related to fundamental changes in the global economy. Due to the 21st-century emphasis on counterterrorism, U.S.-Mexico border enforcement has been strengthened, but critics say it does more to give the appearance of protection than actually achieving a concrete goal of stopping undocumented immigration or terrorism (Andreas, 2000; Rothe and Muzzatti 2004; Sharma 2006).

Progressive U.S.-Mexico border scholars view negative media and political attention toward unauthorized entrants as a form of cultural violence. "Cultural violence" refers to symbols and ideas that rationalize, appear to make legitimate, or mystify the impact of structural violence. According to proponents of this idea (Spener 2009), cultural violence occurs when "illegal immigrants" are stigmatized while their human dilemma as citizens of developing nations who have a difficult time economically supporting their families is overlooked.

In light of the representation of "illegals" as scapegoats, it is surprising that the American public favors remedial action. An America's Voice opinion poll conducted by the Berenson Strategy Group of 1,000 likely voters in May 2009 (Immigration Forum 2009) indicated that 75% wanted congressional action on immigration reform; and 68% supported a path to legalization, including 62% of Republicans. Respondents reported that 71% wanted unauthorized workers to become legal taxpayers and also considered that they do not deprive American citizens of jobs. These results were somewhat higher than a PEW Research Center poll of a sample of 1,000 taken in May 2009 indicating 63% of voters and 50% of Republicans supported a path to citizenship (Immigration Forum 2009).

Immigration reform has always been difficult to pass, but public opinion is definitely in favor of ending "illegal immigration." A November 2008 America's Voice national poll of 1,000 respondents found that 78% of voters considered it a "serious problem" (Immigration Forum 2009). In a November, 2009 speech at the Center for American Progress, DHS Secretary Janet Napolitano (DHS 2009) stated:

> a larger segment of the American public has embraced the need to engage this debate and arrive at a sensible

solution to this problem. . . . There are leaders of the law enforcement community speaking out, saying that immigration reform is vital to their ability to do their jobs keeping Americans safe. Faith leaders, including the National Association of Evangelicals, have announced their support for immigration reform as a moral and practical issue. We are seeing more business leaders and more labor leaders engaged in this debate in a constructive way than we have ever seen before.

In 2009 Rep. Luis Gutierrez (D-IL) introduced an immigration bill: The Comprehensive Immigration Reform for America's Security and Prosperity Act (CIR ASAP). It is supported by 90 House members, including the Congressional Hispanic Caucus, the Congressional Black Caucus, the Congressional Asian Pacific Caucus, and the Progressive Caucus. CIR ASAP provides a path to legalization, updates the family and employment-based legal immigration system, provides more resources for border ports of entry to deter unauthorized immigration and drug and arms smuggling, sets standards for detention and provides for community alternatives, repeals the Section 287 program linking federal immigration enforcement with local and state police, restores due process through judicial review of immigration proceedings, and provides for an electronic employment verification system. The progressive group Reform Immigration FOR America has organized more than 600 business, community, faith, labor, and civil rights organizations to support immigration reform and is organizing media events to support it.

Federal Government

The securitization of immigration is connected to the move of immigration visa and citizenship processing and enforcement from the Department of Justice (DOJ) to the Department of Homeland Security (DHS). The July 2002 "National Strategy for Homeland Security" of the Bush administration focused on mobilization to protect the homeland from terrorism. The 2002 "National Security Strategy of the United States of America" included immigration policy. The DHS is a counterterrorism bureaucracy and more militarized than the policing-oriented

DOJ. Immigration and Customs Enforcement (ICE) is now located in the DHS national security bureaucracy. This led to increased militarization of ICE and the U.S. Border Patrol (Lovato 2008).

Begun in the late 1980s, policies to criminalize immigration are increasingly deployed in an effort to arrest, detain, and deport unauthorized entrants. As a result, an unprecedented policing bureaucracy has been developed. The fear that terrorists might use the same forms of unauthorized entry as other migrants over the land borders has created a domestic security industry (Lovato 2008). Billions of dollars have been awarded in military contracts for Boeing, General Electric, and Haliburton to build virtual walls, ground sensor systems, radar systems, drones, and surveillance technology for a geographically complex border.

Law Enforcement

The apprehension of undocumented residents in the interior is an important aspect of border security because it is thought to deter further attempts at unauthorized entrance. Historically, the United States has primarily relied on interdiction at the U.S.-Mexico border instead of in the interior. Conservatives such as Carafano and colleagues (2006) have suggested that worksite enforcement and *not* legislating legalization of undocumented residents would send a stronger message to individuals considering migration. Janet Napolitano, DHS Secretary, notes: "border security by itself will not stop illegal entrants into our country. Our border strategy must be combined with better enforcement of the immigration laws within the United States" (McKinley 2009).

The Immigration Reform and Control Act of 1986 is ineffective because it instituted worker document checks but did not require employers to verify if they were valid. INA Section 274A authorized employer sanctions for hiring unauthorized workers (Smith 2005). It prohibits *knowing* hiring of undocumented immigrants and provides for civil fines of $250 to $10,000 per worker and a criminal sanction of up to six months imprisonment. To comply, employers submit I-9 forms showing that a Social Security card, driver's license, voter registration card, passport, or other identification indicates an individual is a citizen or a U.S. resident alien.

In the mid-1980s, the failure to make an employer responsible for document verification resulted in the development of a cottage fraudulent-document industry followed by organized criminal document rings (Simcox 2000). Traditionally, interior enforcement has been understaffed and unable to track the level of fraudulent document use. This is shown by the undetected cases of Zoe Baird, Kimba Wood, Linda Chavez, and others unable to gain high-ranking federal positions because they had hired unauthorized labor. After 9/11, diversion of resources to counterterrorism reduced enforcement through employer audits. They declined from 1,300 in 1990 to less than 500 in FY2003 (Brownell 2005). As a result, many unauthorized workers submit work-related documents that are false (such as a made-up Social Security number unconnected to an individual) or fraudulent (a Social Security number connected to an individual, i.e., illegal use of an authenticated identity).

ICE workplace raids were stepped up during the second half of the Bush administration. Yet only 863 out of 4,077 "administrative arrests" in FY2007 involved owners, managers, or human resource supervisors (ICE 2007). Those who suffer the penalty for this white-collar crime are the unauthorized workers. In 2008, out of 7.4 million employers, 42 companies were raided and 16 had administrative employees who were arrested and convicted (some cases pending appeal) (ICE 2009). At the end of the decade, ICE shifted its priorities and sought to target employers rather than conduct numerous workplace raids. Nevertheless, ICE audits are still connected to mass firings of unauthorized workers.

Immigration enforcement has especially targeted criminal aliens. The 287(g) program authorized by the 1996 Illegal Immigration Reform and Immigrant Responsibility Act (IIRIRA) provides for cooperation in immigration enforcement between the fed and state and local law enforcement (ICE 2010). Participating municipalities enter the program by signing a Memorandum of Agreement (MOA). At the prompting of the Obama administration, the DHS has expanded the 287(g) immigration enforcement program and has issued a revised MOA. Participating 287(g) police are supervised by Immigration and Customs Enforcement.

Criticism of 287(g) has come from both immigrant advocates concerned about racial profiling and those who support tougher enforcement, who claim that prioritizing criminal aliens would lead to neglect of unauthorized immigrants. The U.S. Government Accountability Office (GAO 2009a, 4) audit of police departments participating in 287(g) found that:

> while ICE officials have stated that the main objective of the 287(g) program is to enhance the safety and security of communities by addressing serious criminal activity committed by removable aliens, they have not documented this objective in program-related materials consistent with internal control standards. As a result, some participating agencies are using their 287(g) authority to process for removal aliens who have committed minor crimes, such as carrying an open container of alcohol. While participating agencies are not prohibited from seeking the assistance of ICE for aliens arrested for minor offenses, if all the participating agencies sought assistance to remove aliens for such minor offenses, ICE would not have detention space to detain all of the aliens referred to them. ICE's Office of Detention and Removal strategic plan calls for using the limited detention bed space available for those aliens who pose the greatest threat to the public, until more alternative detention methods are available.

Evidence exists indicating that 287(g) had not met its targets but resulted in arrest of nonviolent unauthorized migrants. In El Paso, Texas, the Sheriff's Office's Operation Linebacker, connected to 287(g), resulted in the arrest of 1,076 unauthorized entrants and four noncitizens on drug-related charges (Staudt 2008a, 303). Kathleen Staudt, a political scientist, considers that did not reflect the emphasis placed on stopping drug- and violence-related crime. Due to concerns expressed by the GAO (2009a) and immigration advocates, ICE has changed its 287(g) agreements to stress that its priority is to remove dangerous criminal aliens. 287(g) is designed to increase apprehension of noncitizens that commit violent crimes, human smuggling, gang/organized crime activity, sexual-related offenses, narcotics smuggling, and money laundering.

Reliance on ICE and the U.S. Border Patrol occurs because immigration enforcement is a federal responsibility. When local and state police are allowed to use immigration status as a factor in questioning and arrest, they are considered a "multiple force amplifier" One argument for this involvement is that four of the 9/11 hijackers were subject to routine traffic stops and could have been detained for visa violations (Eldridge et al. 2004). An argument against giving local and state police this power is it could foster alienation of immigrant communities, which often contain many unauthorized residents. Immigrants may hesitate to report crime and victimization or otherwise cooperate with the police if they fear family or community members will be deported (Romero 2006; Martinez 2007).

Community policing strategies rely on steady contact between police and neighborhood residents, which is difficult if there is a fear of the police (Martinez 2007). Many immigrants originate from nations where the police are corrupt and not trusted. They bring this attitude to the United States and are aware of negative public attitudes toward immigrants. Another problem associated with nonfederal police involvement is the possibility of screening based on racial and ethnic profiling rather than suspicious behavior (Kretsedemas 2008, 346–351).

The federal government has taken many steps to offer immigration enforcement authority to state and local police but municipalities have not uniformly responded (Kretsedemas 2008, 341–342). Regardless, information on noncitizens with immigration violations and, after 9/11, noncitizens under suspicion of terrorist activity, has been incorporated into a National Crime Information Center (NCIC) database. The database includes noncitizens with both criminal and civil violations.

Arizona bypassed the 287(g) federal and state law enforcement linkage program when Governor Jan Brewer signed Senate Bill 1070 into law on March 23, 2010 (Archibold 2010b). The bill makes unauthorized entrance and presence of a migrant in the United States a state misdemeanor crime. It stipulates that state and local police should check an individual's immigration status if there is reasonable suspicion that a person is an unauthorized alien. If an individual cannot prove legal residency, law enforcement officers can make a warrantless arrest if there is probable cause that an individual is an unauthorized alien. Upon arrest, individuals cannot be released unless they establish legal immigration status under § 1373(c) of Title 8 of the United States Code. The first offense carries a $500 fine and up to a six-month jail term. In order to avoid arrest, permanent resident aliens and visitors holding visas must carry identification. The documentation necessary to prove legal status includes Arizona driver's licenses, Arizona nonoperating identification licenses, or any form of valid federal, state, or local identification which can certify immigration status. Arizona's law is the first to require state and local police to check immigration status. It is considered that the law makes a failure to carry immigration documents a crime.

Because immigration is a matter of federal law, Arizona's bill may be unconstitutional. Multiple law suits at the federal and state level have been filed by the American Civil Liberties Union, the Mexican American Legal Defense and Educational Fund, and Phoenix, AZ mayor Phil Gordon. The ACLU lawsuit makes the argument that the bill violates the Supremacy Clause of the U.S. Constitution, which provides for federal authority over the states, including on immigration matters. Erwin Chemerinsky, Dean of the School of Law at the University of California Irvine, is quoted: as follows: "The law is clearly pre-empted by federal law under Supreme Court precedents." Defenders of the bill, including Kris W. Kobach, a co-drafter of the AZ bill and law professor at the University of Missouri-Kansas City School of Law, present the principle of "concurrent enforcement": that the state law parallels the federal law which makes first entry without authorization a misdemeanor (Schwartz and Archibold 2010).

President Barack Obama criticized passage of the law, stating that it would "undermine basic notions of fairness that we cherish as Americans, as well as the trust between police and our communities that is so crucial to keeping us safe" (Archibold 2010b). Arizona governor Brewer defended the law as: "another tool for our state to use as we work to solve a crisis we did not create and the federal government has refused to fix" (Archibold 2010b). The mandated use of state and local police in immigration enforcement and the requirement for possession of immigration documents generated national protests. Major social criticism includes that the bill justifies racial profiling and will lead to discrimination against both legal immigrants and minority citizens. Former Arizona Attorney General Grant Woods said that: "People will be profiled because of the color of their skin" (Schwartz and Archibold 2010).

Public reaction to the Arizona immigration law included a protest gathering of over one thousand during the signing of the law in Phoenix, Arizona. U.S. Congressman Raul Grijalva, representative for Arizona's 7th Congressional District, called for an economic boycott of Arizona state products and tourism (Archibold 2010a). The nation's major Spanish language newspaper, *La Opinión*, and the Reverand Al Sharpton were among those supporting a boycott. It is likely that the new Arizona immigration law will galvanize both continued legal reaction and public protest until constitutional issues and probable individual anti-discrimination lawsuits are resolved.

Militarization of the U.S.-Mexico Border

The U.S.-Mexico border has been subject to repeat military buildups. From 1978 to 1992, when the War on Drugs was initiated, the military was directly deployed to stop drug trafficking (Dunn 1996). In theory, if the supply of drugs was reduced or eliminated, it was thought that drug usage would decline and this social problem would be controlled. Initially, the antidrug campaign was conducted in foreign nations such as Colombia (Payan 2006, 28; Andreas and Nadelman 2006, 130–131). Troops fought growers and associated smuggling operations in the Caribbean with military technology and succeeded in disrupting the Colombian-Caribbean connection. This diverted cocaine trafficking to the Mexico border in the late 1980s. At the same time an increase in Mexican economic migration and Central American war refugees became a military concern.

Attempts to control undocumented entry and drug smuggling resulted in the militarization of the U.S.-Mexico border with armed services troops, the National Guard, and military technologies used to secure the border (Dunn 1996, 147–156). Since the 1980s, given substantial reliance on military surveillance technology, the military has backed up the Border Patrol and Customs at all types of borders: land, sea, and air. The 1878 Posse Comitatus Act proscribes the military from enforcing civilian law, but the National Guard, which is controlled by the states, can and has been repeatedly ordered to the U.S.-Mexico border (Banks 2002; Dunn 1996, 106–108). The National Guard was involved in the first border wall construction at the San Diego, California, urbanized border (Nevins 2002). The Armed Forces and the National Guard have worked on construction, given logistical support, engaged in intelligence gathering and interpretation, and conducted ground reconnaissance and surveillance.

For example, Joint Task Force-Six (JTF-6, later renamed JTF North) has been stationed at Fort Bliss in El Paso, Texas. It provides military personnel for assistance to the Border Patrol via observations, reconnaissance, analysis of data, and training (Heyman and Ackleson 2010, 61). During the first eight years of JTF-6, it conducted numerous covert troop operations, mostly at the request of the Border Patrol. Military units patrolled until 1997 when a reconnaissance unit killed a U.S. citizen near Redford, Texas (Dunn 2001, 9). In May 1997, Esequiel Hernandez, a U.S. citizen of Mexican American descent, was shot and killed by four marines during a covert operation. This stopped military patrols but not support and technological assistance by military personnel. In addition, the family of Esequiel Hernandez was awarded $1.9 million in a settlement for wrongful death (Lubbockonline 1998).

The Immigration Reform and Control Act of 1986 initiated a two-decade expansion of policing of the U.S.-Mexico border. In 1993, border deterrence began to involve walls and line-watch duties for U.S. Border Patrol officers. It was augmented by militarization through the use of troops or military technology. The classic line-watch operations, Operation Gatekeeper in San Diego, Operation Hold the Line in El Paso, and Operation Rio Grande in the McAllen/Laredo, Texas sector, have greatly reduced the possibility of a successful unauthorized migrant urban border crossing (Nevins 2002; Dunn 2009; Maril 2004). Due to line-watching, from 1980 to 2000, U.S. Border Patrol agent staffing increased 3.7 times; line-watch hours were upped by 6.5 times and the cost increased by a factor of 12 (Massey 2009).

Although unauthorized immigration apprehensions began to decrease, the War on Terror brought renewed focus to fortifying the U.S.-Mexico border. Jeb Bush, Thomas F. McLarty, and Edward Alden (2009) state, "In a post 9/11 world in which the U.S. must be able to thwart terrorist plots by extremists coming from abroad, illegal immigration . . . creates an unacceptable security risk." The addition of preventing terrorist entry to the mix of duties that the U.S. Border Patrol handles must be evaluated. Alden (2008, 291) believes that "immigration enforcement and counter-terrorism are two different things, and for either to be effective, they must be separated." Since 9/11, massive federal expenditure has occurred to support border enforcement. Douglas Massey, a sociologist (2009), states,

> Border enforcement nonetheless rose exponentially after September 11, with the Border Patrol Budget increasing 95 times its 1980 level and the number of line-watch hours rising 111 times. After 9/11 deportations also began a marked increase, rising from just 11,000 in 1980 to some 350,000 in 2008.

In 2006, the governors of New Mexico and Arizona requested that the National Guard support border law enforcement. By June 2006, 6,000 National Guardsmen ordered by President George W. Bush were at the California, Arizona, New Mexico, and Texas borders (CNN 2006). They have not been assigned to direct law enforcement. They assist with road and wall or fence construction and operate ground-level radar, visual and other surveillance devices that communicate immediate intelligence about crossing attempts. National Guardsmen are deployed to perform surveillance using high-tech devices that allow USBP officers to be in the field. Currently, many Border Patrol officers are assigned to line-watch duty at the geographical boundary to deter migrants from attempting to cross, but many areas of the border are not watched or do not have ready response units.

In 2009, Governor Rick Perry of Texas requested 1,000 National Guard troops, but a conflict occurred over whether the federal or state government would pay it. This forestalled deployment (Office of the Governor, Rick Perry 2009a). Instead, the Texas Rangers were called in (Office of the Governor, Rick Perry 2009b). Perry has sent Ranger Recon teams combining Texas Rangers and Texas National Guard Counter Drug Forces to conduct surveillance, identify high-intensity smuggling routes, and assist in operations to reduce border-related crime connected to drug trafficking and migrant smuggling. In Texas there has been an increase in burglaries of rural ranches, homes, and hunting camps. Land owners along the Texas boundary also face extortion demands or threats from organized criminal groups connected to drug smuggling.

Although Congress has sought to give the military search, arrest, and seizure assignments along the border, which would be a major escalation, such bills have never passed. Critics argue that immigration enforcement is a civil—not military—matter and that troops should not be assigned to the border.

Physical and Technological Barriers

Whether or not walls work to deter unauthorized immigration has been a major concern. Migrants have responded by crossing in different locations, which is a displacement effect (Dunn 2009; Haddal, Kim, and Garcia 2009). There have been temporarily successful efforts to tunnel under walls as well. Although walls have been represented to the public as a deterrent to unauthorized entry, the reality is that they displace migrants to more rural and remote, even hazardous, areas to cross (Garcia-Goldsmith 2007).

The Secure Fence Act of 2006 directed the DHS to build two layers of secured fencing and to place additional physical barriers, roads, and surveillance technology in five areas of Arizona, California, New Mexico, and Texas (Haddal, Kim, and Garcia 2009). Walls and fencing were to be placed along 850 miles. Border communities selected for the wall and fencing project have objected to the impact on the local environment and their properties. Former Department of Homeland Security Secretary Michael Chertoff won the right to waive seven environmental and historic preservation laws including the Endangered Species Act, the Federal Water Pollution Control Act (Clean Water Act), and the Safe Drinking Water Act. DHS has used the waivers on four locations.

Alternately represented as both successful and controversial in cost and consequences, border walls are extremely expensive to build and maintain (GAO 2009b). By 2009, 613 miles of border wall and fence authorized by the Secure Fence Act of 2006 had been built. J. D. Hayworth (2009, 3), former congressional representative from Arizona, indicates that the bills call for double-layer fencing; however, only 200 miles are double. The single-layer fence and vehicle barriers are being overcome by smugglers who use portable ramps.

Early in his term, President Obama deemphasized the need for fencing and advocated stepping up border patrols and deploying surveillance technology. Yet the likelihood that fencing and walls will be scaled back was reduced by Mexican drug-cartel violence. The problem of border violence is exacerbated by arms smuggling from the United States to Mexico. Although DHS Secretary Janet Napolitano was initially opposed to border fencing as governor of Arizona, she came to believe that walls and fences improve operational control. She has authorized completion of the final 60 miles of fencing projected to cost $4 million a mile (Reese 2009). Napolitano also initiated southbound inspection of entry into Mexico to curtail traffic in weapons.

Passed in 2008, the Department of Homeland Security (DHS) appropriations bill requires consultation with federal agencies, state and local officials, and local property owners before building fencing. DHS allocated $50 million in 2009 to compensate for damage to animal and plant habitat or issues with Native American religious sites. The fence could be modified to curb flooding or restore habitats of endangered or threatened species. Previously about $40 million had been spent on restorative activities. Jaguars, ocelots, deer, javelinas (wild pig species), and owls are among the species affected by the wall, which blocks their migratory routes and reduces habitat.

Those favoring border-fence construction use data from the San Diego Sector, where border fencing originated during Operation Gatekeeper. This sector is almost completely fenced pending a small section (Haddal, Kim, and Garcia 2009). Significantly fewer migrants are being apprehended because of the barrier. The U.S. Border Patrol believes that border fencing is a force multiplier because it allows the patrol to concentrate enforcement resources on other activities. The Border Patrol views the diversion of unauthorized migration to more remote rural regions as giving its agents a tactical advantage in apprehending unauthorized entrants (Dunn 2009). Those in opposition to extensive border-fencing expenditures view the existing fencing as funneling migrants away and not stopping undocumented entry (Garcia-Goldsmith et al. 2007). They view greatly increased U.S. Border Patrol staffing and resources as the cause of increased apprehensions, not the fencing.

The overall number of undocumented border-crossing arrests in 2004 was very close to the figure for 1992 (Haddal, Kim, and Garcia 2009). The major difference is that most arrests in 1992 occurred in San Diego while in 2004 arrests were highest in the Tucson and Yuma, Arizona, sectors. Fencing appears to funnel migrants to less densely populated and hazardous areas. In fenced areas, individuals have cut holes, used ladders, dug tunnels, and employed various other means to get across.

This suggests that fencing only modifies the efforts of migrants who want to enter without papers. Options for dealing with these problems include more tamper-resistant and expensive fencing and investing in tunnel-detection technology.

There are a number of arguments against border walls and fences. Both Mexican and Canadian diplomats have protested any extension of border fencing. The Canadian government is concerned that it has not been consulted enough by the United States. Overall, opponents of border barriers consider them to be akin to the "Great Wall of China" or the "Berlin Wall." The U.S. government needs to consider if the need for national security is more important than alienating its border neighbors and if border nationa should be bilaterally consulted about fencing (Haddal, Kim, and Garcia 2009). The securitization of the border necessitates international cooperation in intelligence sharing and policing, and border fences create problems for working together.

Cross-border tunnels and subterranean passages have been used for smuggling drugs, people, and contraband. From May 1990 through 2008, 101 tunnels were discovered (Haddal, Kim, and Garcia 2009). The largest had lighting, ventilation, and drainage systems and contained two tons of marijuana when discovered. Intensive Border Patrol enforcement has thought to have increased the number and sophistication of tunnels and encouraged drug traffickers to expend the time and investment. Intelligence gathering for suspicious patterns of behavior and sophisticated tunnel-detection technology are being improved. For deterrence, the 2006 Border Tunnel Prevention Act increased criminal penalties for cross-border tunneling. There is a 20-year maximum sentence for constructing or financing tunnels.

One alternative to walls is a $6.7 billion "virtual fence" of cameras, sensors, and other communications equipment (Heyman 2008). The Border Patrol has used airplanes and helicopters for decades, and electronic motion detectors were installed in some areas in the 1970s. In the 1980s airplanes and balloons with instrumentation were deployed to monitor unauthorized border-crossing traffic. A virtual wall increases the density of high-tech devices and upgrades them. Drones, which are unmanned flying vehicles, carry surveillance cameras. Upgraded detection equipment will use wider electromagnetic bands, near ground radar, and high-resolution cameras on towers. Even National Security Administration satellites may be used for monitoring.

Surveillance technology such as the Integrated Surveillance Intelligence System (ISIS) and the America's Shield Initiative (ASI) had operational issues in deployment, readiness, and system integration (GAO 2006, 29–44) and was later replaced by the high-tech SBInet, part of the Secure Border Initiative (SBI). The SBI was a multibillion-dollar program initiated in 2005 to sustain border security and reduce unauthorized immigration. It focused on the Mexican border at locations deemed vulnerable and had programs at the Canadian border to increase Border Patrol personnel and install radiation portal monitors to scan for radioactive material. SBI surveillance technology involved cameras, unattended ground sensors, radar systems, communication systems, mounted laptops for U.S. Border Patrol vehicles, helicopters, and drones as well as walls and fencing (GAO 2009b, 10). Command, control, and communications technologies (C3I) were to include hardware and software to produce a "common operating picture (COP)," uniform activity data presentation for command centers and agent vehicles (GAO 2009b, 13). In March, 2010, $50 million in SBI funding was taken for use with more "tested" surveillance technologies (DHS 2010). DHS Secretary Napolitano was responding to SBI technology problems.

Theoretically, tracking of people and vehicles can be confused by irrelevant information such as animal migration, rancher activity, and even dust in the air. SBI has faced problems in system integration and a $400 million cost overrun by the contractor, Boeing. The U.S. Government Accountability Office (GAO 2008, 2) conducted a study that concluded, "It is imperative that [DHS] immediately re-evaluate its plans and approach in relation to the status of the system and related development acquisition and testing activities." In 2007 and 2008 tests showed that the surveillance technology often failed in application due to software, communication, and user failures. The GAO (2009b, 15) determined that SBI had problems including the failure to involve U.S. Border Patrol agents in developing its requirements, limited oversight of program contractors, and underestimation of the scope and complexity of what was needed.

Impact on Migrant Smuggling

The repeated intensification of border control has led migrants to increasingly hire coyotes (Spener 2009, 231; Andreas 2000, 21–26; Spagot 2006). Like other forms of smuggling, adaptation occurs when old routes are blocked. Intensive enforcement in the San Diego sector, the site of Operation Gatekeeper (Nevins 2002), is associated with attempts to smuggle people in motor boats. More unauthorized crossings are occurring through ports of entry as individuals are concealed in vehicles or purchase fraudulent documents. U.S. Customs and Border Patrol is unable to thoroughly inspect all individuals and vehicles because of the time demand on personnel and the need to quickly move people and trade over the border. Human smugglers have responded to the continual process of tightening enforcement with innovative strategies. The rising cost of assisted unauthorized entry and the reduced penalties for human smuggling, as opposed to drug smuggling, were thought attractive for organized crime. David Spener's (2009) field research on the use of *coyotes* (human smugglers) in South Texas demonstrates that the hierarchical, top-down structure of organized crime has not developed. Instead, horizontal organization and loose connections permits coyotes to flexibly adapt to heightened enforcement. In this respect, their degree of organization is characteristic of lower level transnational crime groups across the globe (Thachuk 2007).

In the negotiation between migrants and coyotes, a fee is agreed upon which is paid on delivery by their relatives in communities in the interior. Indeed, these operations are dependent on linkages between families and friends in the sending communities in Mexico and the receiving communities in the United States. According to Spener (2009, 166), migrants utilize the social capital of these network ties to try to accomplish at least a portion of the following:

- give them information they needed to cross the border successfully, including recommending them to affordable and reliable coyotes;
- being guided/advised while making the journey across the border;
- send them money at no interest to finance the crossing, including money to pay the coyotes' fee;
- drive them to their final destination in the United States after the migrants get past the last immigration checkpoint; and
- provide them with food, housing, and assistance with finding a job after arrival in the U.S. destination.

Spener (2009, 152–153) identifies the basic operational structure of human smuggling in the South Texas border region as follows:

- someone to recruit migrants in Mexico;
- someone at the border who could receive migrants, form a crossing party, and verify via telephone that migrants had respondents in the destination city who would pay for their passage;
- someone who could guide migrants through brush around the *segunda garita* [the ring of traffic checkpoints away from the border];
- someone with a car, van or truck who could pick migrants up as they emerged from the brush and drive them on to San Antonio, Austin, Dallas or Houston or other destinations; and
- someone living in the destination city who could house migrants in an apartment, mobile home or private residence and collect the remaining fees from their respondents.

Migrant deaths have been publicized in Mexico, but individuals feel financial pressure to migrate, hire smugglers and take the risk. After the expansion of border enforcement, migrants are increasingly choosing to remain in the United States and become immigrants (Massey 2009). After a successful unauthorized entry, migrants are bottled up and do not return. An unexpected consequence of the deterrent strategy is shaping circular migrants into long-term immigrants, and they are bringing family members and forming households in the United States (Casteneda 2007). This is changing a pattern of circular migration back and forth from Mexico to permanent immigration as the cost of smuggling has risen and risk has increased. This means that there are fewer times that individuals are exposed to apprehension after a successful crossing and that reduced apprehensions do not necessarily represent deterrence.

Deportation versus Detainment

Unauthorized entrance has been handled through deportation or, as an additional sanction, mandatory detention followed by deportation. The Illegal Immigration Reform and Immigrant Responsibility Act of 1996 (IIRIRA) mandated that the Immigration and Naturalization Service (now ICE) detain increasing numbers of unauthorized entrants and asylum applicants who petitioned to stay. In 1996, 20,000 were detained. Annually, the figure is now over 300,000. The federal government was never prepared for this extent of detention. In 2004, Congress authorized building detention centers with 40,000 beds by 2010. This is a major expansion of what has been described as a "prison-industrial complex" (Dow 2004).

Annually, ICE detains hundreds of thousands of immigrants at its facilities or in jails and prisons where the government can purchase bed space. In 2008, 378,582 were placed in detention facilities. There were 32,000 detention beds available in FY2008 at a cost of $90–118 per day (ICE 2008b). There are over 350 detention centers with at least one in almost every state, but most detention sites are actual jails and prisons rather than centers operated by ICE. Local governments and states subcontract their facilities through intergovernmental service agreements (IGSA). Sixty-seven percent of detainees are held in ICE IGSA facilities (Human Rights Watch 2009, 1).

ICE is estimated to detain 31,000 prisoners daily (ICE 2008b). Because many detainees are sent to jails or prisons, they are placed with prisoners and exposed to the same conditions. Regardless of whether a detainee has committed a civil or a criminal offense, he or she has experienced a combination of handcuffs, belly chains, and leg shackles. Journalist Mark Dow (2004) went to various ICE and IGSA detention facilities and discovered problems whether a detainee was in ICE custody or under contract to a jail or prison. Detention conditions included verbal and physical abuse, poor diet and health facilities, and use of solitary confinement—for individuals who had attempted unauthorized entry or asylum applicants who had committed no crime. It has been difficult for detainees to challenge these conditions due to lack of legal consultation, which led some to hunger strikes or attempted suicide.

The Office of the Inspector General (OIG 2006) audited six ICE and subcontracted IGSA facilities. Health violations included not giving required physical examinations, failure to respond to nonemergency health issues in a reasonable amount of time, and problems monitoring detainees on hunger strikes or suicide watch lists. In terms of environment, issues occurred with rodents, insects, vermin and adequate temperatures when cooking meat. From 2003 to 2008, under these conditions, 74 people died in ICE detention (ICE 2008c).

The rate at which detainees are transferred, which complicates contact with relatives and receiving legal advice, has greatly increased. Because IGSA facilities are for local, state, and federal prisoners and ICE detention space is limited, detainees are being transported long distances to be placed in a facility. Detainees are first held in a location near their residence but often transferred to remote regions such as Arizona, Texas, and Louisiana (Human Rights Watch 2009, 1–2). Transfers are made between immigration gateway cities like Los Angeles to distant states like Texas. ICE data released to Human Rights First indicates that from 1999 to 2008, 1.4 million detainee transfers occurred. There were 122,783 transfers in 2003 and 261,941 in 2007. These transfers make it difficult for detainees to have access to their families and retain legal counsel.

Human Rights Watch (2009, 2–4) has compared the rights of citizens, as prisoners, to those given to noncitizen detainees. The Sixth Amendment of the Constitution provides the right to be tried in the jurisdiction in which a crime occurred. Detainees are often moved from the district in which they violated immigration law and are distant from witnesses and evidence relevant to their case. Commonly citizen prisoners are not transferred until they have received access to counsel and been convicted. Noncitizen detainees can be transferred away from their attorneys. Citizen prisoners can also be located in a state or federal locator system, often updated every 24 hours, while detainees are "lost" with no access. Noncitizen detainees, nonetheless, have a right to access an attorney under international human rights law.

The detainee-transfer system disrupts attorney-client relations because lawyers are not informed. ICE expects detainees to contact attorneys but does not typically provide the means. Attorneys are then forced to spend days or weeks determining where their clients are. A distant location can terminate attorney representation. If an attorney agrees to represent a client over the phone or by video, a particular immigration judge can deny it. Unfortunately, some detainees are transferred, often to remote locations, before they have legal representation and are unable to obtain it. In 2008 60% of noncitizens appeared in immigration court without representation (Human Rights Watch

2009, 4). The legal process is further complicated because detainees are often denied a bond hearing because the transfer prevents family and character witnesses to speak in their defense.

Human Rights Watch (2009) criticizes the transfer system for preventing detainees from gaining access to an attorney and receiving their legal rights. ICE cares for hundreds of thousands of people and argues that it needs to make transfers. It claims that limitations on its ability to transfer detainees would prevent it from making cost-effective use of access to detention beds. Requests for change of venue to return to attorneys and witnesses are most often denied (Human Rights Watch 2009, 5). Although detainees have the right to a hearing to contest removal, the transfer process often works against it.

An alternative to detention, the former "catch-and-release" policy, involved releasing unauthorized Mexican entrants at a border crossing into their home country, which led to multiple crossing attempts. Andreas (2000) referred to this as "border games." Since 2005, Operation Streamline has required first-time undocumented entrants to be detained. This effort began in the high-traffic border zone of Del Rio, Texas (U.S. Customs and Border Protection 2005), and was extended to Tucson, Arizona, and other sectors (U.S. Customs and Border Protection 2007). Previously, the first entry without inspection (EWI) was a misdemeanor that did not require detention. Currently, a zero-tolerance policy, when available detention space allows for it, has led to detention of these migrants for up to 180 days rather than deportation over the border into Mexico or otherwise returning the migrants.

Critics of this mass-detention policy point out that it generates massive need for U.S. attorneys, public or pro bono defense lawyers, federal courthouse space, U.S. marshalls (for prisoner transport), prison beds, and other resources (Ackleson and Heyman 2010, 60). Operation Streamline has strained judicial and detention capacity. A chief judge for the U.S. District Court for New Mexico reacted to the new operation's volume of detainees: "We were obviously alarmed because where would we put our bank robbers? Our rapists? Those who violate probation?" (Associated Press 2007). Congressional testimony by Heather E. Williams, First Assistant Federal Public Defender, District of Arizona, concluded that "Operation Streamline may well be one of the least successful, but most costly and time consuming ways of discouraging [unauthorized] entries and re-entries" (Hsu 2008).

It is difficult for Operation Streamline courtrooms to pro-vide procedural due process and access to legal counsel. Defendants are arraigned in groups: up to 80 in Del Rio, Texas, 70 in Tucson, and 20 in El Paso (Lydgate 2010, 12). In 2009, the Ninth Circuit Court of Appeals ruled that mass proceedings in Tucson violate Federal Court Rule 11 procedures of due process before a guilty plea can be accepted. These rules include a per-sonal address for the defendant and making sure that he or she understands constitutional rights are being waived and the plea is voluntary. Alternate procedures are being implemented in Tucson, and other districts are not yet impacted.

The end of the catch-and-release policy in 2006 raised detention costs. The states are supposed to be paid by the fed-eral State Criminal Assistance (SCAP) program for detention costs, but they are not fully reimbursed. Unauthorized immi-gration has serious financial impacts on 24 counties located on the U.S.-Mexico border. From 1999 through 2006, the 24 U.S.-Mexico border counties reported $1.23 billion in law enforce-ment expenditures for processing unauthorized migrants with criminal charges (U.S.-Mexico Border Counties Coalition 2008). In FY 2006, $192 million was expended. In 2006, the SCAP pro-gram federal appropriation was $400 million and the 24 border counties received $4.7 million. This raises serious cost implica-tions for U.S.-Mexico border counties receiving an increased detention population.

One reason that the United States often released Mexican migrants to Mexico after apprehension was the monumental size of the task of detention. Because the border-deterrence strategy funnels migrants rather than discouraging them for attempting entry, the end of the catch-and-release policy has meant that the federal government does not have enough detention space and is having a hard time paying for the expense. The old policy of voluntary departure was cheaper, although more individuals made multiple attempts until they succeeded without forfeiting time and earnings to detention.

Human rights organizations have argued that there are cost-effective alternatives to detention. These include a system of conditional release and bond or a financial deposit (Amnesty International 2009). Reporting and electronic monitoring can cost $12 a day (Detention Watch Network 2009). When alterna-tives are used, 93% of those apprehended still appear for a hearing at an immigration court. Congress approved a funding increase to explore alternatives but ICE used it to monitor those eligible for release rather than persons to be detained. At present, ICE operates two supervised release programs using electronic bracelets, telephone check-in, home visits, and restricted-movement guidelines. Electronic monitoring is available throughout the nation, but it is in limited use. Amnesty International (2009) believes that individuals should only be detained if it is established that it is necessary and proportional after considering alternative measures. Further, it argues that electronic monitors should not be placed on people who are not security or flight risks.

At the end of the Bush presidency, ICE released new detention standards for staff-detainee communication. The Obama administration has responded to criticism of immigrant detention by creating an Office of Detention Policy and Planning in ICE and increasing federal oversight. DHS will move away from a decentralized, jail-oriented approach. This would reestablish a right eroded by the process of criminalization and securitization of immigration and require further change in law. DHS detention reforms include new oversight of contracted detention facilities, using detention in relation to risk, expanding alternatives to detention, and improving medical care in detention.

The prosecution and detention of individuals in the United States without authorization are projected to deter new migrants. Conservatives such as Rep. James Sensenbrenner (R-WI) have argued for stronger sanctions against unauthorized migrants, but human rights activists are concerned that the detention system denies detainee rights and is not operated humanely. While the most recent increase in detention involves migrants apprehended in the U.S.-Mexico border region, asylum applicants and unauthorized immigrants apprehended in the interior are also being held. The pressure to prevent terrorism and problems in having border arrivals who are not authorized to stay present themselves before an immigration court with "absconding" have generated mass detention.

Border Conditions

The U.S.-Mexico border region is marked by poverty and lower levels of education than in the interior (Anderson and Gerber 2007). Overall, the region has higher levels of unemployment than in the rest of the United States. The degree of poverty increases from west to east as one travels from the affluent city of San Diego, California, east across to Texas, ending at the city of Brownsville, Texas. Economic differences between the American and Mexican sister cities are less than between comparable American and Mexican cities of the interior of these two nations. The Mexican border cities tend to be relatively better off than the Mexican interior.

There are five major U.S.-Mexico sister cities: (1) San Diego and Tijuana, Baja California; (2) El Paso and Ciudad Juarez, Chihuahua; (3) Brownsville and Matamoros, Tamaulipas; (4) Laredo, Texas, and Nuevo Laredo, Tamaulipas; and (5) McAllen, Texas, and Reynosa, Tamaulipas. U.S.-Mexico border cities function as trade routes and ports of entry with trade bridges. The railways were important in the development of trade to the interior, and NAFTA greatly increased the economic significance of these cities for both countries (Anderson and Gerber 2007). The desire to avoid customs levies means that smuggling for the black market is important. For example, Mexico has a tariff on used clothing, but much *"ropa"* is taken into Mexico with the cooperation of corrupt Mexican border guards. Regarding economic fluctuations, the border cities are typically more impacted than the interior. U.S. Border cities experience declines in Mexican consumer purchases when there are peso devaluations or Mexican layoffs in American-owned factories when the United States is experiencing a recession.

Crime and Human Rights Violations

On the U.S.-Mexico border and in the interior, "criminal aliens" have been represented in the media as a security threat involved in the drug trade and violent crime (Dell'Agnese 2005; Mains 2004). In contrast, national crime trends indicate that immigrant destination cities have lower violent crime rates (Martinez 2006, 12). Sociologist Ruben Rumbaut and his colleagues (2006b, 70) analyzed 2000 U.S. Census data to determine that foreign-born immigrant men between age 18 and 39 were half as likely as similarly situated non-Hispanic native-born men and thirteen times less likely than African American native-born men to be incarcerated in federal or state prisons and local jails. Nevertheless, incarceration rates for the native-born second generation were four times that of the foreign men regardless of level of education.

Rumbaut and colleagues (2006, 73) state:

> The finding that incarceration rates are much lower among immigrant men than the national norm, despite their lower levels of education and minority status, but increase significantly among their co-ethnics by the second generation, suggest that the process of "Americanization" leads to downward mobility and increased rates of involvement with the criminal justice system among a significant segment of this population.

The policy implication is that the nation needs to oversee and invest in the development of the second-generation offspring of immigrants. Progressives view investment in immigrant education and services, rather than the criminal justice system, as more cost-effective.

Research results on immigrant crime trends in U.S. border cities are contrary to public belief about the connection between unauthorized immigration and crime. Matthew Lee (2003) found that Latino immigrant neighborhoods in El Paso and San Diego had lower homicide rates. Factors associated with homicide included poverty, joblessness, and residential instability—all factors associated with social disorganization. Jacob Stowell's (2007) statistical research found that immigrants of varied national origin were less likely to commit violent crime but that immigrant groups living in high-crime impoverished neighborhoods had an increased violent crime rate.

The U.S. border cities have been ranked among the 50 safest in the United States (Albuquerque 2007, 77). Looking at crime rates from 1996 to 2001, Pedro H. Albuquerque states,

> Cities on the American side of the border have experienced impressive reductions of homicide rates from peak levels, which were significantly larger than the reductions observed in most American cities outside the border region; for example, four border cities saw reductions of homicide rates varying from 72.3 to 73.1%, comparable therefore with the famed New York City reduction of 73.6%.

Overall, both violent crime and property crime rates in the five American border cities have fallen since the 1990s and were lower than median city rates, although larceny theft increased in Brownsville, Laredo, and McAllen (Albuquerque 2007). In the border region itself, the rate of property crime among minors is impacted by special conditions (Richardson and Resendez 2006). The demand for vehicles in Mexico promotes auto theft and shoplifting is an attractive source of criminal income.

Mexican twin-city homicide rates are higher than on the U.S. side. From 1985 to 2001, prior to development of drug-cartel violence, Mexican twin cities' homicide rate declined relative to the countrywide Mexican rate. Albuquerque's (2007) analysis of crime data indicates that U.S. Border Patrol line-watch hours reduce homicide rates in Mexican border cities. From 1985 to 2004, line-watch hours increased 370%. Rodriguez makes a conservative statistical estimate that 991 lives may have been saved in Mexican border cities and an optimistic estimate that 2, 371 lives were saved (Albuquerque 2007, 76, 86). Nevertheless, escalating drug related violence has greatly increased homicide in Mexican border cities.

The higher population density in Mexican cities is a structural factor contributing to the homicide rate. Mexican cities may have higher homicide rates, due to severe problems with organized crime and institutional inefficiencies such as lack of training and law enforcement corruption. The Comisión para Asuntos de la Frontera Norte (2002, as cited in Albuquerque 2007) indicates that drug trafficking, arms smuggling, chaotic urban growth, low civic participation, and a "culture of impunity" increase crime. Mexican twin-city homicide rates have a moderate spillover effect on American border cities. Albuquerque found that a 10% increase in Mexican homicide rate correlated with a 2% increase in twin-city homicide rate (Albuquerque 2007, 83). Through the first decade of the 21st century, relatively little spillover violence has occurred (Lake et. al., 2010).

The concept of impunity is important in understanding violent Mexican crime. To act with impunity means to have no concern for the consequences. The weakness of the Mexican police fosters lawless, violent behavior. In the border city of Ciudad Juarez, Mexico, the repeat rape, mutilation, and killing of young Mexican women, many of whom work in factories (maquiladoras), is of great concern. Since 1993 over 400 women have been murdered in what has been described as femicide. The institutional ineffectiveness of Mexican law enforcement is illustrated by the loss of murder reports and evidence, mysterious case closings or "solutions," and the fact that the number killed changes with the Mexican political party in power (Staudt 2008b, 33).

Various theories attempt to explain the murder and abandonment of young women's bodies in the desert. These include multiple serial killers or gangs, drug traffickers having sport, "sons of the rich," sex trafficking, snuff films produced for U.S. citizens, and even the black market in organs. International and Mexican human rights organizations have tracked a situation in which justice is elusive. Kathleen Staudt points to activism against violence against women as a partial answer for reducing femicide (2008b, 1–2, 13). She views the homicides as related to a gendered culture of violence against women on both sides of the border.

Sensational media stories represent U.S. and Mexican border communities as war zones heavily impacted by unauthorized migrant crossings. Realistically, migrants attempting to enter must use stealth and do not visibly enter into the daily life of most border citizens. Border violence is associated with the peril of crossing without documents from Mexico. Migrants who cross the Rio Grande in Texas face robbery and rape by bandits (Richardson and Resendez 2006). For example, Richardson interviewed Rodolfo about his experiences in crossing the Rio Grande with his pregnant wife, Rosario:

> "It was around seven in the evening," he says, "and we had just crossed the river. We had not even finished getting dressed, when out of nowhere came three guys. Two of them had knives and the other said he had a gun. They threatened us and demanded money. When we explained to them that we had almost no money, they got mad and began verbally harassing my wife. Since she was five months pregnant, I started defending her. This made matters worse because they started to beat me up. My wife was screaming hysterically and I was afraid to fight back because they were armed. The only thing that mattered to me was the baby's well-being. When they were finally satisfied that we had given them all we had, they left, taking all of our belongings, including some of the clothing we were wearing. I was badly beaten and Rosario was shaking and crying. To top it all, we were half naked. We finally had the strength to

make it up the nearest street, where, because of our appearance, we were picked up by immigration. Since we did not have any documents, they returned us to Reynosa [Mexico]. Fortunately, they provided us with food, clothing and medical attention. I was grateful for that."

The Mexican bandits know that unauthorized crossers are unlikely to risk contacting law enforcement to report their victimization. These crimes may only be detected if migrants are apprehended by the Border Patrol. The smugglers are not trustworthy and may set up the migrants, robbing them and taking their possessions.

Petty property crime such as stealing food for survival from homes and trespassing is common in remote rural areas where unauthorized migrants are trekking overland (Hagan and Pallioni 1999). These crimes are acts of desperation as the migrants may be thirsty and starving. Arizona ranchers and rural residents have repeatedly experienced this as a result of the diversion of migrants from urban crossing areas by fences and line watching. Unfortunately, refuse such as plastic water jugs and bags litters the desert, and grazing land is damaged by the foot traffic and refuse. Residences have been burglarized for basic staples, and trespassing on private land is frequent. Some ranchers become vigilantes and migrant shootings have occurred.

As border enforcement has intensified, the number of incidents of violence against U.S. Border Patrol officers has escalated. In FY2005, there were 773 attacks on USBP agents and in FY2008 1,097 occured (Nunez-Nieto 2008, 28–29). These incidents included being fired at, rocking, and being doused with a flammable liquid and set ablaze. "Rocking" refers to when individuals on the Mexican side of the border throw rocks and other items at U.S. Border Patrol agents and their vehicles (Haddal, Kim, and Garcia 2009). As a result, the fenced area of the Yuma sector uses armored vehicles for patrol. U.S. Border Patrol agents prefer open view fencing, such as more easily compromised chain link to less costly concrete, because they can limit rockings and have a tactical advantage for apprehensions.

Migrant apprehensions often number over 1 million per year; and, historically, immigration enforcement is primarily non-violent. The concentration of drug trafficking at the U.S.-Mexico border in zones where migrants may be attempting to cross exposes the USBP to violent incidents, although migrants and especially smugglers have been occasionally reported to engage in violent acts.

Policing organizations are often accused of using undue force on suspects or violating their rights, and the U.S. Border Patrol is no exception. Immigrant advocacy and social justice groups have documented what would be termed human rights abuses under international law and violations of the U.S. Constitution. There are documented incidents of illegal search of people and property (Seltzer and Korous 1998). Abuse includes verbal, psychological, and physical violence. Migrants have been deliberately deprived of food and water, refused medical attention, and tortured. There have been incidents of assault, battery, and murder. Human rights and immigrant advocates state that migrant interrogation routinely involves verbal abuse and threats. Mexicans and Central Americans are humiliated and intimidated. Much of this abuse is never reported by the vulnerable migrant population.

An immigrant advocate research (Huspeck, Martinez, and Jiminez 1998) found that 24% of encounters with USBP agents involved psychological abuse. Of migrants, 13% were physically abused and 13% were sexually assaulted. As migrants may be carrying personal property, at the minimum—food, water, and clothing—theft or destruction of their goods has occurred. This was documented for 9% of cases. Racial and ethnic profiling is discriminatory but this immigrant advocacy research found that 24% of the migrant arrests investigated were based on ethnic physical appearance, and the number may be underestimated.

The USBP, like other policing organizations, enters into life-threatening situations due to the intrusion of drug traffickers into the migrant routes. U.S. Border Patrol officers' lives may be on the line, and they can make poorly thought out decisions in the heat of the moment. U.S.-Mexico border-crossing zones are becoming dangerous and violent places. Sometimes officers quickly decide to use force when suspects are not trying to flee. Harm can be prevented through training and safety programs.

The militarization of the U.S. border and media representations have hardened public views of "illegal immigrants." American citizens and many border residents stereotype unauthorized crossers as invaders and criminals (Chavez 2009, 89–94). Since

2000, civilian watch groups have formed because of a concern that border-control efforts are insufficient. Using weapons and surveillance technology, the Minutemen, Ranch Rescue, and the American Border Patrol have monitored undocumented migrants trying to cross in rural areas. Watch-group members view these migrants as criminals, enemies, and a national security threat (Kil and Menjivar 2006). In reaction, immigrants have called them "migrant hunters." Jim Gilchrist (2006) of the Minuteman Project stresses that the "Minuteman volunteers only observe and report; they do not chase or confront. . . . There has never been a violent incident initiated by volunteers."

President George W. Bush (2005) labeled the citizen volunteers as vigilantes, stating, "I am against vigilantes in the United States. I am for enforcing the law in a rational way. That's why you got a Border Patrol, and they ought to be in charge of enforcing the border." Many civilian watch-group members have active or past memberships in nationally organized racist groups. The Department of Justice has categorized the American Patrol as a "hate group," and their alleged hate crimes are being documented by the Southern Poverty Law Center (Buchanan and Kim 2006). The Minutemen have been viewed firing shots, loosing biting dogs, assaulting with a flashlight, and kicking and verbally harassing migrants while taking them prisoner, which is illegal but tolerated. As a result of the presence of racists in citizen watch groups, many progressives have labeled them as vigilantes.

Ranchers in the U.S.-Mexico border region have endorsed the activities of civilian watch groups and engage in their own offensive and defensive actions against migrants who may trespass and even damage their property. Arizonan Roger Barnett has a 22,000-acre cattle ranch located one mile from the Mexican border. Undocumented migrants frequently come onto the land with smugglers in large groups or in small parties on their own. He alleges that men patrolling his ranch have reported over 14,000 undocumented migrants to the U.S. Border Patrol and intercepted drug shipments. Barnett has stated, "It's time we take our country back" (Barnetts Arizona.com 2009).

Barnett and his brother Donald are alleged to have held migrants at gunpoint, chased after them in all-terrain vehicles, and used dogs to attack them (Buchanan and Kim 2006). In the Morales incident, a Mexican American father and three girls were fired upon. Frustrated at Cochise County's lack of action, the Southern Poverty Law Center, a human rights group, took Barnett to civil court on charges of assault, intentionally inflicting emotional distress, and false imprisonment (Buchanan 2007). Attorneys for the Morales family alleged that the incident caused the Morales' three girls to suffer post-traumatic stress disorder. After deliberation, the jury found for the plaintiff and awarded $99,000 in damages.

Concern exists about whether citizen watch-group members will harm unauthorized entrants. Shawna Forde, the leader of American Minuteman Defense, a Washington State citizen group that patrols the border, and two other individuals are suspected of attempting a home invasion in Aravaca, Arizona (McKinley and Wollan 2009). A man and a child were killed in what has been called an attempt to gain money and drugs to finance vigilantism. Suspects were charged with first-degree murder, assault, and burglary. There has been disagreement among citizen watch-groups, and while some merely monitor the border, others advocate more confrontational tactics. Forde has been linked to both the Minuteman Project and the Federation for American Immigration Reform because of appearances in Washington State at which she appeared listed as a speaker for these groups.

The Minuteman Project and other border watch groups have been successful in gaining media attention for issues of border security. Whether they have any major impact on unauthorized border crossing is disputed. California governor Arnold Schwarzenegger (Associated Press 2005) considered that the groups "cut down the crossing of illegal immigrants by a huge percentage." Nevertheless, it is difficult to locate accurate statistics that can untangle their impact from that of the U.S. Border Patrol. Like the U.S. Border Patrol, citizen watch-groups may deter migrants from crossing where they are located but divert them to other, less patrolled areas.

U.S.-Mexico Border Migrant Deaths

A disturbing consequence of the southern border deterrent strategy has been unprecedented increases in border migrant crossing deaths. Wayne Cornelius found that, from 1994 to 2004, 2,978 border migrants died. Cornelius (2006, 784) indicates: "To put this death toll in perspective, the fortified U.S. border with

Mexico has been more than ten times deadlier to migrants from Mexico during the last nine years than the Berlin Wall was to East Germans throughout its twenty-eight year existence."

A funnel effect (Garcia-Goldsmith et al. 2007) due to intensified border enforcement in California and Texas essentially diverted migrant crossing attempts to Arizona. One thousand deaths are estimated to have occurred in Arizona, and this is only a count of bodies that were found. Deaths cannot be fully counted because of the remoteness of this desert and mountainous region. The GAO (2006) indicated that Arizona was the site of 78% of increased migrant deaths. Sadly, over 80% of those killed were under the age of 40 and there has been an increase in deaths of individuals under 18.

Three primary causes of migrant death are exposure-heat (35%), drowning (21%), and motor-vehicle accidents (11%) (Guerette 2007a). Deterring migrants from crossing in urban areas sent them toward the hot southwestern deserts where water sources are scarce and it is easy to get lost. Drowning occurs in Texas along the Rio Grande River or in California's Colorado River. Both riverine systems are connected to irrigation works, and migrants may drown when an area is suddenly flooded.

Migrant deaths were first recognized as a major issue in 1998 (Eschbach, Hagan, and Rodriguez 1999) when the United States and Mexico agreed on the Border Safety Initiative (BSI). This is a joint effort to alert migrants about crossing risks, to organize rescue in remote, high-risk regions, and to seek to arrest smugglers and human traffickers. BSI is a harm-reduction method for border policing (Guerette 2007b). The plan has four elements: (1) public media campaigns in Mexico about the risks of border crossing and the posting of signage about risks in remote border-crossing areas; (2) Border Search, Trauma, and Rescue (BORSTAR) teams; (3) U.S. Border Patrol training in search-and-rescue methods; and (4) data analysis to determine areas of highest risk to migrants. One example of a BSI initiative is the placing of high towers with strobes that have a button for stranded migrants to call for rescue (Sapotka et al. 2006). Unmanned drones also search for migrants in need of rescue.

Immigration reform has not resulted in any alleviation of pressures to migrate in Mexico. As a result, situational crime prevention has been proposed as a way to reduce mortality

(Clarke 1997; Guerette 2007a). Warning migrants with a hazardous condition alert system and placing Spanish and English warning signs are two measures to deter crossing at specific sites. For example, a weather warning system could prevent death events.

U.S. citizens have been dismayed at the increasing migrant death rate. Volunteer groups have maintained water stations and watched from airplanes for distressed migrants. The U.S. government has allowed these groups to operate and taken notice of the increased deaths. Humane Borders founder Reverend Robin Hoover believes that the Border Patrol "cannot encourage death. [The Border Patrol is] losing the P.R. war. . . . Their only other option is to say: 'We like death, let's have some more'" (quoted in Scharf 2006, 167).

Rights of Immigrants and Suspected Terrorists

After the World Trade Center was destroyed, many nations faced difficult decisions about how to balance the rights of individuals with the need for security. Both U.S. citizens and permanent resident aliens were subject to a loss of constitutional rights in the name of security. The events of 9/11 introduced issues of electronic eavesdropping and warrantless surveillance that gave the law enforcement system and government unprecedented power.

Ultimately, a borderless world is turned on itself when security does not stop at the border but encompasses everyone. The U.S. Constitution gives citizens the right to privacy. After 9/11 the USA PATRIOT Act and the Presidential Directives of George W. Bush (2001–2009) cut back on these rights to fight the War on Terror. This program was later extended by the Protect America Act of 2007. The Bill of Rights affords individuals the right to privacy and necessitates warrants for search and seizure. The crime control orientation of counterterrorist initiatives resulted in the suspension of privacy rights to ostensibly track terrorist organizations' financing and money laundering and produced warrantless searches for information that would ordinarily violate the Fourth Amendment to the Constitution. Warrantless surveillance included electronic eavesdropping.

The United States spends billions per year on surveillance. Electronic eavesdropping and wiretapping allow the government potential access to terrorist conversations when attacks are being plotted. Nevertheless, the government has been able to listen to any phone call made in the United States, which means that citizens are under surveillance without their consent. In 2005 the *New York Times* released a story to the effect that the National Security Administration was listening to billions of phone calls, emails, cellular and other communication (Risen and Licthblau 2005). This news led to the warrantless surveillance controversy, congressional investigation, and major lawsuits. The Protect America Act of 2007 extended the provisions for unrestricted communications access for the government. President Barack Obama has supported the continued operation of these information sweeps.

Because of the volume of communication, the government indicates that it is focused on monitoring terrorism suspects, which may protect citizens to a degree. Regardless, the Office of the Inspector General (OIG 2009) issued an unclassified report indicating that the monumental wiretapping project, while expensive, has uncovered little of value. Presumably much of this information is classified and difficult to evaluate for efficacy. One of the known cases of its use is that of former governor of New York Elliot Spitzer, who was found to have patronized prostitutes in a wiretapping operation, and that certainly was not terrorist activity. The program continues, as in August 2008, the U.S. Foreign Intelligence Surveillance Court of Review found the 2007 Protect America Act to be constitutional. The constitutionality of this program is likely to be further debated and decided in the courts.

After 9/11 the NSEERS program was used to round up Arab Muslim men. Those who had overstayed their visas or where otherwise unauthorized were summarily deported. This was done in the name of fighting terrorism, but only one conviction occurred: Felix Padilla, a U.S. citizen. Despite this lack of productive findings, the suspension of rights resulted in a practice that had previously been declared unconstitutional by the Supreme Court: indefinite detention. Arabic and/or Muslim foreign-born men were held indefinitely—often prior to deportation—after a series of sweeps. At present, all immigrants entering the United States who request political asylum are detained. For those whose application is turned down, but refuse a return to their homeland, the possibility of indefinite detention looms. Foreign nationals from 25 countries designated as terrorist-harboring nations now face additional scrutiny if trying to enter. Foreign students are monitored and U.S. consulates are free to turn down visitation or immigration applications if they find an individual's background suspicious.

The War on Terror was a response to immense deficits in intelligence that left the federal government unaware of exactly who had exited the country (Eldridge et al. 2004). The unauthorized population, estimated to have peaked at 12 million, represented an unknown in terms of terrorist threat. The initial response in registering noncitizens from nations labeled as sponsoring terrorists was a reaction to a massive failure in intelligence and recordkeeping. The stringent measures undertaken have potentially harmful consequences for the U.S. economy.

Politicians and academicians have predicted that the "Global War on Terror" may last indefinitely. This war is based on intelligence, law enforcement, and improvement in homeland security defenses. As an enemy, terrorists are difficult to strategize, and progress cannot be easily measured. The task of preventing terrorism involves air, sea, and the Mexican and Canadian land borders. The focus on the southern border and arrest and detention of Mexican and Central American unauthorized migrants moves the focus from terrorists to mass enforcement of immigration law (Heyman and Ackleson 2010).

U.S. border security has been enhanced, but there have been tradeoffs from the War on Terror impacting the vitality of the economy and foreign relations. International immigration of the most educated and talented suffered setbacks (Alden 2008) and only slowly recovered over time. Critics of how homeland security has been managed maintain that it is wrong to conflate counterterrorism with immigration enforcement. Zero tolerance of risk can have harsh consequences for the functioning of international trade and managing the process of legal immigration.

The United States was unprepared for the 9/11 terrorist attacks, but it implemented a securitization regime that many view as draconian. The overall policy of deterrence of unauthorized immigration, now characterized by mass arrests and detention at the southern border, has never been evaluated as a failure. The public views the Mexican border, rather than the interior, as the place to deal with both unauthorized entry and drug trafficking (Heyman and Ackleson 2010). Internal steps to reduce the employment of the undocumented and reduce demand for drugs are minor compared to the outlay to the south. Josiah Heyman (2008) thinks that a combination of virtual or physical walls and the current mass enforcement policy is likely to be ineffective.

The Future of Border Control

The achievement of border security by air, land, and sea is a complicated task (Lake, 2007, 3–4). It involves five different missions which are difficult to coordinate. First, it involves discovery and interdiction of terrorists attempting entry or smuggling weapons of mass destruction from abroad. Second, border law enforcement seeks to interdict unauthorized migrants, smuggled goods, and terrorists. Third, interior law enforcement is used to control unauthorized immigration, confiscate contraband, and interdict terrorists. Fourth, the protection of people and critical infrastructure all over the United States is monitored. Fifth, it includes an element of emergency preparation and response to terrorist attack or natural disaster.

It is difficult to balance the need for rapid flow of legitimate people and goods with guarding against transnational threats. Smugglers and terrorists seek to embed themselves in this traffic or to cross themselves or illicit goods in remote, less secure ways away from ports of entry. Examining all of the different processes for authorized border entry by air, land, and sea is a major step towards understanding current efforts to securitize the borders and what is needed in the future. Providing security at the borders involves governmental agencies, foreign governments, and private individuals. Each situation at a land, air, or sea border necessitates a fine-tuned strategy. One emergent effort has been to "move the border" to the countries in which individual travel and shipment of goods originate (Lake 2007). This is done by initiating clearance procedures at United States consulates and international ports of departure. Another strategy has been to harden the border through hiring more agents, using high technology, and getting assistance from the military. This is referred to as the militarization of the border and has been critiqued. One unanticipated consequence is increased attacks on U.S. Border Patrol officers.

Globalization changes the tactics and organization of groups which are transnational threats. The response to transnational threats is increasingly complicated by the interchangeability of criminal networks. Trafficking networks may form ties with terrorists and can switch from smuggling drugs to weapons. Those who provide fraudulent documents to migrants who seek to enter to work could potentially sell them to terrorists. Transnational criminal organizations are becoming sophisticated and flexible. The loose horizontal linkage between specialist groups in criminal organizations facilitates shifting activities and makes it more difficult for international and border law enforcement to apprehend criminals. One of the crucial needs will be to develop bilateral and multilateral policing cooperation because deterring transnational threats will involve actions in more than one country. If the joint involvement of federal agents and state or local police can be viewed as a "force multiplier," then efforts to engage foreign governments, their internal police forces, and international policing agencies are key to dealing with transnational threats. Interpol, Europol, and intelligence sharing with many countries will facilitate prevention of terrorist plots.

After the 9/11 attacks, the cancellation of air flights and the closure of the Canadian and Mexican borders placed legitimate travel and commerce on hold. U.S. Customs was placed on high alert and every vehicle or truck was searched, causing delays of up to twelve hours in crossing the border at crossings in New York and Michigan (Andreas 2003). This situation generated major economic losses and negatively impacted the auto industry and other cross-border industries using just-in-time shipping for production. On September 13, Daimler-Chrysler closed a plant, and Ford followed by closing five plants the following week. As a result, border-security policies which reinforce national security while permitting legitimate traffic across borders are a goal. These policies are simultaneously evaluated in terms of how they facilitate legal activities and impede illicit ones.

Since the 9/11 terrorist attack, many border-security policy decisions have been made in a climate of uncertainty. These decisions will have consequences, intended and unintended, that will take the measure of the United States as a world power. In an era of globalization, American discussions of border control externalize the problem as originating from outside. In short, other nations and groups are represented as causing the problems. Examination of the many issues of border security reveals that the issues are inevitably linked: crossing borders. The policy decisions which have been made or avoided by the United States have contributed to current border-security problems. Similarly, the policies of neighboring Canada and Mexico impact on border control, and through the sea and air borders, world policy comes to impact the United States.

The media and public focus extensively on the U.S.-Mexico border and undocumented immigration. Fears about terrorists have led to concerns that terrorists might use the Mexican border for covert entry. Realistically, known terrorists have primarily used the air borders to transit to the United States (9/11 attacks) or the Canadian border (first World Trade Center attack, 1993). After the 12-25-2009 failed attempt to explode an incendiary device on a Northwest Airlines flight into Detroit, the National Counterterrorism Center has been given authority to respond to the threat of al-Qaeda attacks by hiring hundreds of intelligence specialists to join teams to monitor emergent terrorist plots (Schmidt 2010). White House review found that no one in the new intelligence bureaucracy had sole authority to interpret disparate intelligence information. This action occurred in conjunction with tightened airport screening, new watch-list rules, and increased revocation of permission to fly. The human right of freedom of movement is increasing challenged by procedures which make crossing borders a heavily regulated privilege.

World history is marked by conflict and border disputes as groups have sought to become more powerful. Although current boundaries have been politically designated and geospatially mapped, the desire of individuals for freedom of movement is in conflict with ideals of sovereign control of territory. The Department of Homeland Security, and particularly the U.S. Border Patrol, have been viewed as the key to border security despite the range of land, sea, and air borders. Control of unauthorized immigration, particularly at the southern border, is a major federal expense, and current border-control strategies are subject to criticism. David Carafano and Heyman (2004) consider, "U.S. border operations are likely to fail regardless of what security (e.g., manpower and fences) is added because in the months and years required to implement new means of security, the hundreds of thousands seeking to enter the United States will find ways to circumvent these measures."

The classic criminological theory of deterrence makes the case that increased level of punishment and risk of being caught will reduce traditional criminal behavior. The southern border strategy has emphasized "prevention through deterrence." Deterrence has involved continual expansion of the U.S. Border Patrol, increasing walls and fencing in traditional urban crossing zones, building new fortified checkpoints above the border, placing expensive high-technology sensing devices, and mounting special operations. The U.S. Congress is committed to both the building of an expensive border fence and the further development of electronic surveillance systems.

Lou Dobbs (2007), former CNN journalist and news anchor, has stated: "We cannot reform immigration law until we control immigration, and we cannot control immigration until we control our borders and our ports." In this regard, his views are in line with those in the House of Representatives who supported 2007 border-security bills and resisted legalization. Proposed comprehensive immigration reform legislation contains provisions for increased border enforcement and a legalization program to deal with unauthorized immigrants in the interior. Another issue is increasing visas for unskilled workers as a way of reducing demand for unauthorized workers.

One way of measuring the success of border interdiction is to look at control of unauthorized entry. Mexico is the primary source of undocumented immigrants in the United States. Douglas Massey (2009) has testified to the Senate Subcommittee on Border Security, Immigration, and Citizenship that Mexican Migration Institute data indicates that the probability of making initial unauthorized entry into the United States has decreased since 1990 and the probability of making subsequent trips after return to Mexico has declined since 2000. These decreases occurred regardless of the current border buildup.

Intensified enforcement did increase the costs of unauthorized crossing involving smugglers from $600 to $2,200 in constant dollars. Mexicans responded to the increased cost and risk of death of border crossing by staying in the United States. Massey (2009) indicates that between 1980 and 2005, the probability of returning to Mexico within 12 months of unauthorized entry decreased by more than half. The odds of apprehension did not rise and successful border migrants stayed longer and chose settlement. Massey states, "It was because of a decline in return migration and not an increase in entry from Mexico that the undocumented population ballooned during the 1990s" (Massey 2009).

Intensified border enforcement and increased interior deportations have coincided with a small decline in the size of the undocumented population (Passel and Cohn 2008). Nevertheless, Massey believes that it also reflects a decline in labor demand. The 2007–2009 recession in the United States increased unemployment, but settled Mexican migrants have not returned. Simultaneously, the federal government quietly provided a legal means for unskilled Mexican workers to come. Massey indicates, "According to official data, the number of temporary legal workers entering from Mexico rose from 3,300 in 1980 to 361,000 in 2008, rivaling numbers last seen during the Bracero Program [a Mexican guest-worker program] of the late 1960s" (Massey 2009).

He continues, "Mexican migration is not and has never been out of control. It rises and falls with labor demand and if legitimate avenues for entry are available, migrants enter legally." This sentiment was shared by former Secretary of Homeland Security Michael Chertoff (2008), who commented, "If the economy suddenly changes in the next year or two and particularly if a differential between the economy in other countries and the U.S. becomes more marked, yes, that is going to probably encourage some more people to try to come across."

The process of criminalization of immigration has added the threat of detention and deportation to the risk faced by unauthorized entrants. The securitization of immigration policy involves adding new controls to the legal process of entry into the United States. Media have fostered fear of terrorism and xenophobic fear of new immigrants. Because of political and public emphasis on border control as a means to prevent unauthorized immigration and terrorist entry, it is unlikely that research on the unintended consequences of the southern border strategy, such as increased migrant deaths, will end the staffing and high-technology buildup of enforcement. There is humanitarian concern about the increase in deaths of unauthorized migrants who attempt to cross in harsh and remote regions of the U.S.-Mexico border connected to urban line-watch U.S. Border Patrol Operations such as Operation Gatekeeper.

Jeb Bush, Thomas S. McLarty III, and Edward Alden (2009) consider "Getting immigration policy right is fundamental to

[U.S.] national interests—our economic vitality, our diplomacy and our national security." The deep divisions within both the Republican and Democratic parties indicate that immigration reform will not be easily achieved. Proponents of legalization are criticized as attempting "amnesty," giving something for nothing to "lawbreakers." Although this solution would bring the cooperation of undocumented immigrants, the scale of the effort is considered more than U.S. Citizenship and Immigration Services (USCIS) could handle without a massive increase in staffing and reorganization.

Few stop to think about the consequences of attempting to remove the unauthorized population, estimated at almost 11.3 million. ICE deports approximately 300,000 per year. Human and civil rights issues could back up the courts as many "mixed status" (legal and unauthorized) families have U.S.-born children whose lives would be disrupted. Beyond these concerns are the citizens who "aided" these undocumented immigrants: their employers, service providers such as landlords, and their friends. The U.S. citizens involved in this situation have never been implicated in any solution except for businesses, if they are asked to undertake more fool-proof employment verification such as e-verify.

The question of whether it is possible to fully control the borders is seldom raised. Particular problems, such as unauthorized immigration, first led to attempts to control land and sea borders followed by the challenge of protecting the passengers of the air. Terrorism connected the immigration issue to one encompassing security at all land, sea, and air routes of entrance. Perhaps the size of the problem automatically leads to focusing on one issue at a time such as Mexican migration. Yet a broader view of how nation-states interconnect is developing in the 21st century. Regarding the massive investment in multiple methods of border control, Edward Alden (2008, 291) believes: "managing the risk of terrorism means exactly what it says, which is accepting that there are risks and that the consequences of trying to eliminate all those risks are worse than learning how to live with them."

The way forward in dealing with a climate of risk involves a new style of international negotiation and ties. Ackleson (2009, 344) states that: "most scholars agree that security in both Canada and the United States can be increased, not only through new domestic policies but also through increased multilateral cooperation." He emphasizes rediscovering common ground and rebuilding trust and mutual confidence. The infrastructure of the northern border is outdated, and there is a need to invest in more bridges, lanes, and crossings to foster trade. Regarding the Department of Homeland Security, firm leadership is needed. Although Ackleson believes that development of a North American security perimeter is too controversial, he does advocate for shared border management. It would include intelligence cooperation, joint law enforcement, and expansion of pre-clearance programs for the movement of people and goods.

Border control involves preventing unauthorized immigration, drug smuggling, and terrorist entry. Public focus is on immigration and terrorism. Yet former representative Jim Kolbe (R-AZ) has commented: "Our intelligence agents will tell you that there has been no evidence of any serious attempt of terrorists to come into the United States through the southern border" (LoMonaco 2005). Regarding the Canadian border, Sen. Charles Schumer (D-NY) indicates: "Northern New York has hundreds of miles of remote land and lakes that straddle the border with Canada that could easily be crossed by terrorists. Those wishing to do our nation harm tend to follow the path of least resistance" (LoTemplio 2007). Schumer emphasized the disparity in staffing and resources between the northern and the southern borders and blamed the Bush administration for neglect.

If unauthorized entrance could be controlled by previously unheard of massification of border enforcement, an employer verification system immune from fraudulent document use, and the legalization of the current unauthorized population, would drug trafficking, arms smuggling, and terrorism become the focus of U.S.-Mexico border control? The *Arizona Republic*, Arizona's largest newspaper, wrote a front page editorial after the controversial Arizona immigration law requiring state and local police to check immigration was passed. It stated: "Comprehensive [immigration] reform will make the border safer. When migrant labor is channeled through the legal ports of entry, the Border Patrol can focus on catching drug smugglers and other criminals instead of chasing busboys across the desert" (Arizona Republi 2009). Many voices speak in favor of fixing a broken immigration system, and resolving transnational threats such as drug and arms smuggling and terrorism is connected to political cooperation and reform in Washington, DC.

References

Ackleson, Jason. 2009. "From 'Thin' to 'Thick' (and Back Again?): The Politics and Policies of the Contemporary U.S.-Canada Border." *American Review of Canadian Studies* 39(4): 336–351.

Adelman, Howard. 2002. "Canadian Borders and Immigration Post 9/11." *International Migration Review* 36: 15–28.

Albuquerque, Pedro S. 2007. "Shared Legacies, Disparate Outcomes: Why American South Border Cities Turned the Tables on Crime and Their Mexican Sisters Did Not." *Crime, Law and Social Change* 47: 69–88.

Alden, Edward. 2008. *The Closing of the American Border: Terrorism, Immigration, and Security since 9/11*. New York: HarperCollins and the Counsel on Foreign Relations.

Amnesty International. 2009. "Jailed Without Justice: Immigrant Detention in the USA." http://www.amnestyusa.org/uploads/JailedWithoutJustice.pdf.

Anderson, Joan, and James Gerber. 2007. "Introduction." In *Fifty Years of Change on the U.S.-Mexico Border*, ed. Joan Anderson and James Gerber, 1–12. Austin: University of Texas Press.

Andreas, Peter. 2000. *Border Games: Policing the U.S.-Mexico Divide*. Ithaca, NY: Cornell University Press.

Andreas, Peter. 2003. "A Tale of Two Borders: The U.S.-Canada and U.S.-Mexico Lines After 9–11." In The Rebordering of North America, ed. Peter Andreas and thomas J. Biersteker. New York: Routledge.

Andreas, Peter and Ethan Nadelman. 2008. *Policing the Globe: Criminalization and Crime Control in International Relations*. New York: Oxford University Press.

Archibold, Randal C. 2009. "Border Plan Will Address Harm Done at Fence Site." *New York Times*, January 16. http://www.nytimes.com/2009/01/17/us/.

Archibold, Randal C. 2010a. "In Wake of Immigration Law: Calls for an Economic Boycott of Arizona." *New York Times*, April 26. http://www.nytimes.com/2010/04/27/us/27arizona.html.

Archibold, Randal C. 2010b. "U.S.'s Toughest Immigration Law Is Signed in Arizona." *New York Times*, April 23. http://www.nytimes.com/2010/04/24/us/politics/24immig.html.

Arizona Republic. 2010. "Editorial: Stop Failing Arizona; Start Fixing Immigration." *Arizona Republic*. May 1. http://www.azcentral.com/news/articles/2010/05/01/20100501arizona-immigration-problem.html.

Armitage Jr., David T. 2007. "U.S. and EU Efforts to Fight Terrorism: Same Ends, Different Means, or Same Means, Different Ends."

Presented at European Union Studies Association Bienniel Conference, May 17–19, Montreal, Canada.

Associated Press "Canadian Terror Probe Expands to Seven Nations." 2006. *USA Today*, June 6. http://www.usatoday.com/news/world/2006-06-05-canada_x.htm.

Associated Press. 2005. "Schwarzenegger Praises Minuteman Volunteers for Watching Arizona Border." *USA Today*, May 1. http://www.usatoday.com/news/nation/2005-05-01-minutemen_x.htm.

Associated Press. 2007. "Southwest Border Courts Swamped with Immigration-Related Felony Cases." April 27. http://www.foxnews.com/story/0,2933,268961,00.html.

Baker, Peter. 2010. "Obama Says Al Qaeda in Yemen Planned Bombing Plot, and He Vows Retribution." *New York Times*, January 2. http://www.nytimes.com/2010/01/03/us/politics/.

Banks, William C. 2002. "Troops Defending the Homeland: The Posse Comitatus Act and the Legal Environment for a Military Role in Domestic Counterterrorism." *Terrorism and Political Violence* 14: 41.

Barnett's Arizona.com. 2009. http://barnettsaz.com/towingABOUTowners.htm.

Beleda, Alex. 2002. "Nuclear Fuel Rod Reported Missing from DRC." Voice of America, June 24.

Bell, Stewart. 2004. *Cold Terror: How Canada Nurtures and Exports Terrorism to the World*. Ottawa: John Wiley.

Bernstein, Nina. 2009. "Immigration Detention System Lapses Detailed." *New York Times*, December 2. http://www.nytimes.com/2009/12/03/us/03immig.html?partner=rss&emc=rss.

Brownell, Peter. 2005. "The Declining Enforcement of Employer Sanctions." Washington, DC: Migration Policy Institute. http://www.migrationinformation.org/Feature/display.cfm?ID=332.

Buchanan, Patrick. 2006. *State of Emergency: The Third World Invasion and Conquest of America*. New York: Saint Martin's Griffin.

Buchanan, Suzy. 2007. "Vigilante Justice: Rancher Roger Barnett Faces a Comeuppance." Southern Poverty Law Center. Spring. http://www.splcenter.org/intel/intelreport/article.jsp?aid=758.

Buchanan, Suzy, and Tom Kim. 2006. "The Nativists." Southern Poverty Law Center Intelligence Report. http://www.splcenter.org/intel/intelreport/article.jsp?pid=1251.

Bush, George W. 2005. "President Meets with President Fox and Prime Minister Martin." March 23. http://georgewbush-whitehouse.archives.gov/news/releases/2005/03/20050323-5.html.

Bush, George W. 2006. "President Bush Addresses the Nation on Immigration Reform." May. http://georgewbush-whitehouse.archives.gov/news/releases/2006/05/20060515-8.html.

Bush, Jeb, Thomas F. McLarty III, and Edward Alden. 2009. "Op-Ed: A Bipartisan Blueprint for Immigration Reform." *Los Angeles Times*, July 13. http://www.cfr.org/publication/19860/bipartisan_blueprint_for_immigration_reform.html.

Carafano, James J., and David Heyman. 2004. "DHS 2.0: Rethinking the Department of Homeland Security." Heritage Foundation Special Report #2, December 13. http://www.heritage.org/Research/HomelandSecurity/sr02.cfm.

Carafano, James J., Brian W. Walsh, David B. Mulhausen, Laura P. Keith, and David D. Gentili. 2006. "Better, Faster and Cheaper Border Security." Heritage Foundation Backgrounder #1967. http://www.heritage.org/Research/HomelandSecurity/bg1967.cfm.

Casteneda, Jorge. 2007. *Ex-Mex: From Migrants to Immigrants*. New York: The Free Press.

CBC News. 2009. "Van Loan Signs Border Security Pact with Homeland Security Head." http://www.cbc.ca/canada/story/2009/05/26/border-security-van-loan-napolitano.html?ref=rss.

CBC News. 2010. "'Toronto 18' Case: Key Events in the Case." http://www.cbc.ca/canada/story/2008/06/02/f-toronto-timeline.html.

Chavez, Leo R. 2009. "Mexicans of Mass Destruction: National Security and Mexican Immigration in a Pre- and Post- 9/11 World." In *International Migration and Human Rights: The Global Repercussions of U.S. Policy*, ed. Samuel Martinez, 82–97. Berkeley: University of California Press.

Chertoff, Michael. 2008. "Remarks by Homeland Security Secretary Michael Chertoff on the State of Immigration and the No Match Rule." October 23. http://www.dhs.gov/xnews/speeches/sp_1224803933474.shtm.

Chisti, Muzzafer, and Claire Bergeron. 2009. "New and Revised ICE Agreements with State and Local Law Enforcement Met with Criticism." Washington, DC: Migration Policy Institute. http://www.migrationinformation.org/USfocus/display.cfm?ID=738.

Clarke, Ronald V., ed. 1997. *Situational Crime Prevention: Successful Case Studies*. 2nd ed. New York: Harrow and Heston.

Clinton, William Jefferson. 1993. "Protecting Borders Against Illegal Immigration: Remarks Made at Announcement of Immigration Policy." U.S. Department of State dispatch. August 9. http://findarticles.com/p/articles/mi_m1584/is_n32_v4/ai_13263265/.

CNN. 2006. "Gen. Blum: "Not Every Guardsmen on Border Will Be Armed." May 17. http://www.cnn.com/2006/POLITICS/05/17/cnna. blum/index.html.

Committee of the Judiciary, House of Representatives Subcommittee on Immigration and Claims. 2000. Hearing on Terrorism and Threats. http://commdocs.house.gov/committees/judiciary/hju64355.000/ hju64355_0.HTM.

Comisión para Asuntos de la Frontera Norte. 2002. Seguridad Pública y Procuración de Justicia. In *Programa de Desarrollo Regional Frontera Norte 2001–2006*, 563–597. Tijuana: CAFN.

Cornelius, Wayne A. 2006. "Controlling 'Unwanted Immigration': Lessons from the United States, 1993–2004." *Journal of Ethnic and Migration Studies* 31 (4): 775–794.

Dawson, Anne, and Robert Fife. 2005. "Don't Lose Fear of Terrorists, U.S. Envoy Cellucci Warns." *Ottawa Citizen*, February 7, A5.

Dell'Agnese, E. 2005. "The US–Mexico Border in American Movies: A Political Geography Perspective." *Geopolitics* 10: 204–221.

Detention Watch Network. 2009. "About the U.S. Detention and Deportation System." http://www.detentionwatchnetwork.org/ aboutdetention.

DHS (Department of Homeland Security). 2009. "Prepared Remarks by Secretary Napolitano on Immigration Reform at the Center for American Progress." http://www.dhs.gov/ynews/speeches/sp_ 1258123461050.shtm.

Discover America Partnership. 2006. "Discover America Partnership/ RT Strategies Survey of International Travelers." November 20. http:// www.tia-dap.org/pdf/International_Travek_Survey_Summary.pdf.

Dobbs, Lou. 2007. "New Immigration Plan Ignores History's Lessons." CNN.com, May 23. http://www.cnn.com/2007/US/05/22/Dobbs. May23/index.html.

Dow, Mark. 2004. *American Gulag: Inside U.S. Immigration Prisons*. Berkeley: University of California Press.

Dunn, Timothy. 1996. *The Militarization of the Border, 1978–1992: Low-Intensity Conflict Doctrine Comes Home*. Austin: Center for Mexican American Studies, University of Texas.

Dunn, Timothy. 2001. "Border Militarization Through Drug and Immigration Enforcement: Human Rights Implications." *Social Justice* 28 (2): 7–30.

Dunn, Timothy. 2009. *Blockading the Border and Human Rights: The El Paso Operation That Remade Immigration Enforcement*. Austin, TX: University of Texas Press.

Eschbach, Karl, Jacqueline Hagan, and Nestor Rodriguez. 1999. "Death at the Border." *International Migration Review* 33 (2): 430–454.

Eldridge, Thomas R., Susan Ginsberg, Walter T. Hempel II, Janice L. Kephart, and Kelly Moore. 2004. *9/11 and Terrorist Travel. Staff Report of the National Commission on Terrorist Attacks upon the United States.* http://govinfo.library.unt.edu/911/staff_statements/911_TerrTrav_ Monograph.pdf.

Erwin, Clark Kent. 2006. *Open Target: Where America Is Vulnerable to Attack.* New York: Palgrave Macmillan.

Federation of Nuclear Scientists. 2002. "Testimony of Dr. Henry Kelly before the Senate Committee on Foreign Relations." www.fas.org/ ssp/docs/030602-kellytestimony.htm.

Federation of Nuclear Scientists. N.d. "Libya Special Weapons." www. fas.org/nuke/guide/lbya/index.html.

"Feds Break Up Drug Smuggling Linked to Terrorist Groups." 2002. *New York Times,* November 6.

GAO. 2004. *Over-Stay Tracking: A Key Component of Homeland Security and a Layered Defense: A Report to the Chairman, Committee on the Judiciary, House of Representatives.* Washington, DC: U.S. Government Printing Office. http://www.gao.gov/new.items/d04170t.pdf.

GAO. 2006. *Border Crossing Deaths Have Doubled since 1995; Border Patrol's Efforts to Prevent Deaths Have Not Been Fully Evaluated.* Washington, DC: U.S. Government Printing Office. http://www.gao. gov/new.items/d06770.pdf.

GAO. 2007. *Border Security: Security Vulnerabilities at Unmanned and Unmonitored U.S. Border Locations.* Washington, DC: U.S. Government Printing Office. http://www.gao.gov/new.items/d07884t.pdf.

GAO. 2008a. "Border Security: Summary of Covert Tests and Security Assessments for the Senate Committee on Finance, 2003–2007." http://www.gao.gov/new.items/d08757.pdf.

GAO. 2008b. "Secure Border Initiative: DHS Needs to Address Significant Risks in Delivering Key Technology Investment." http:// www.gao.gov/new.items/d081148t.pdf.

GAO. 2009a. "Immigration Enforcement: Better Controls Needed over Program Authorizing State and Local Enforcement of Federal Immigration Laws." http://www.gao.gov/new.items/d09109.pdf.

GAO. 2009b. "Secure Border Initiative Fence Construction Costs." http://www.gao.gov/new.items/d09244r.pdf.

Garcia-Goldsmith, Raquel, M. Melissa MucCormick, Daniel Martinez, and Inez Magadalena Duarte. 2007. *The "Funnel Effect" & Recovered Bodies of Unauthorized Immigrants Processed by the Pima County Office of the Medical Examiner, 1990–2005.* Binational Immigration Institute. http://www.borderhealth.org/files/res_763.pdf.

Gilchrist, Jim. 2006. "Don't Fall for Media's Spin about the Minutemen." CNN.com. October 26. http://www.cnn.com/2006/US/10/25/gilchrist.commentary/index.html.

Griswold, David. 2009. "As Immigrants Move In, Americans Move Up." *Free Trade Bulletin* #38: 1–4. http://www.cato.org/pubs/ftb/FTB-038.pdf.

Guerette, Rob T. 2007a. "Immigration Policy, Border Security, and Migrant Deaths: An Impact Evaluation of Life-Saving Efforts under the Border Safety Initiative." *Criminology and Public Policy* 6 (2): 245–266.

Guerette, Rob T. 2007b. *Migrant Death: Border Safety and Situational Crime Prevention on the U.S.-Mexico Divide.* New York: LFB Scholarly Publishing.

Haddal, Chad C., Yule Kim, and Michael John Garcia. 2009. "Congressional Research Service: Border Security: Barriers Along the U.S. International Border." March 16. http://www.fas.org/sgp/crs/homesec/RL33659.pdf.

Hagan, John, and Alberto Pallioni. 1999. "Sociological Criminology and the Mythology of Hispanic Immigration and Crime." *Social Problems* 46(4): 617–632.

Harris, John F., Mile Allen, and Jim Vandehei. 2009. "Cheney Warns of New Attacks." *Politico, February 4.* http://www.politico.com/news/stories/0209/18390.html.

Hataley, Todd S. 2007. *Catastrophic Terrorism at the Border: The Case of the Canada–United States Border.* Homeland Security Affairs, Supplement No. 1. http://www.hsaj.org/pages/supplement/issue1/pdfs/supplement.1.2.pdf.

Hayworth, J. D. 2009. Testimony before the United States Senate Committee on the Judiciary, Subcommittee on Immigration, Border Security and Citizenship, Hearing on Securing the Borders and America's Ports of Entry, What Remains to Be Done. May 20. http://judiciary.senate.gov/pdf/5-20-09HayworthTestimony.pdf.

Heyman, Josiah Mc. 2008. "Constructing a Virtual Wall: Race and Citizenship in U.S.-Mexico Border Policing." *Journal of the Southwest* 50 (3): 305–334.

Heyman, Josiah Mc. 2009. "Ports of Entry in the 'Homeland Security' Era: Inequality of Mobility and the Securitization of Transnational Flows." In *International Migration and Human Rights: The Global Repercussions of U.S. Policy,* ed. Samuel Martinez, 44–62. Berkeley: University of California Press.

Heyman, Josiah Mc, and Jason Ackleson. 2010. "United States Border Security after 9/11." In *Border Security in the Al-Qaeda Era*, ed. John A. Winterdyk and Kelly W. Sundberg, 37–76. New York: CRC Press.

Human Rights Watch. 2009. "Locked Up Far Away: The Transfer of Immigrants to Remote Detention Centers in the United States." December. http://www.courthousenews.com/2009/12/03/HumanRtsRep.pdf.

Huspek, Michael, Roberto Martinez, and Leticia Jimenez. 1998. "Violations of Human and Civil Rights on the U.S.-Mexico Border, 1995–1997: A Report." *Social Justice* 25 (2): 110–130.

Hsu, Spencer S. 2008. "Immigration Prosecutions Hit New High." *Washington Post*, June 2. http://www.washingtonpost.com/wp-dyn/content/article/2008/06/01/AR2008060102192_pf.html.

ICE. 2007. Workplace Enforcement Fact Sheet. http://www.ice.gov/pi/news/factsheets/worksite.htm.

ICE. 2008a. ICE/DRO Detention Standard: Staff-Detainee Communication. http://www.ice.gov/doclib/PBNDS/pdf/staff_detainee_communication.pdf.

ICE. 2008b. Immigration and Customs Enforcement, Detention Management Program. http://www.ice.gov/partners/dro/dmp.htm.

ICE. 2008c. "Mortality Rates at ICE Facilities." http://www.ice.gov/pi/news/factsheets/detention_facilities_mortality_rates.htm.

ICE. 2010. Immigration and Customs Enforcement, Delegation of Immigration Authority Section 287(g) Immigration and Nationality Act. http://www.ice.gov/pi/news/factsheets/section287_g.htm.

Immigration Forum. 2009. "Polls Show Most Americans Support Comprehensive Immigration Reform." http://amvoice.3cdn.net/ad908a806f9a2997e8_6om6b9tju.pdf.

Johnson, David, and Scott Shane. 2009. "Terror Case Is Called One of the Most Serious in Years." *New York Times*, September 24. http://www.nytimes.com/2009/09/25/us/25zazi.html.

Kelly, Jack. 2001. "Terrorists Courted Nuclear Scientists." *USA Today*, November 12.

Kil, Sang Hea, and Cecilia Menjivar. 2006. "The 'War on the Border': Criminalizing Immigrants and Militarizing the U.S.-Mexico Border." In *Immigration and Crime: Race, Ethnicity and Violence*, ed. Ramiro Martinez Jr. and Abel Valenzuela Jr., 164–188. New York: New York University Press.

Koback, Kris. 2009. Testimony before the United States Senate Committee on the Judiciary, Subcommittee on Immigration, Border Security, and Citizenship, Hearing on Comprehensive Immigration Reform in 2009, Can We Do It Now and How? April 30. http://judiciary.senate.gov/pdf/09-04-30KobachTestimony.pdf.

Kouri, Jim. 2009. "GAO: Funding Needed for New Border Patrol Agents." *Law Enforcement Examiner*, June 19.

Krauthammer, Charles. 2007. "The Jeopardy of Reform." *Washington Post*, June 15. http://townhall.com/columnists/CharlesKrauthammer/2007/06/15/the_jeopardy_of_reform?page=full&comments=true.

Kretsedemas, Philip. 2008. "What Does an Undocumented Immigrant Look Like? Local Enforcement and New Immigrant Profiling." In *Keeping Out the Other: A Critical Introduction to Immigration Enforcement Today*, ed. David Brotherton and Philip Kretsedemas, 334–364. New York: Columbia University Press.

Lake, Jennifer E. 2007. "CRS Report for Congress: Border Security: The Complexity of the Challenge." Washington, DC: Congressional Research Service. http://fpc.state.gov/documents/organization/80215.pdf.

Lake, Jennifer E., Kristin M. Finklea, Mark Eddy, Celinda Franco, Chad C. Haddal, William J. Krouse and Mark A. Randol. 2010. CRS Report for Congress: Spillover Border Violence: Issues in Identifying and Measuring Spillover Violence. Washington DC: CRS Research Service. http://www.opencrs.com/document/R40135/2009-06-01/

Lee, Matthew T. 2003. *Crime on the Border: Immigration and Homicide in Urban Communities*. New York: LFB Scholarly Publishing.

Lennox, Patrick. 2007. "From Golden Straitjacket to Kevlar Vest: Canada's Transformation to a Security State." *Canadian Journal of Political Science* 40 (4): 1017–1038.

LoMonaco, Claudine. 2005. "Border Security: Line Blurs on Terrorism." *Tucson Citizen*, September 11. http://www.tucsoncitizen.com/daily/local/25753.php.

LoTemplio, Joe. 2007. "Schumer Blasts Administration over Northern Border." PressRepublican.com. September 28. http://www.pressrepublican.com/.

Lovato, Roberto. 2008. "Building the Homeland Security State." *NACLA Report on the Americas* 41 (6): 15–22.

Lubbockonline. 1998. "Family of Teen Shot by Marine Patrol gets Settlement." August 12. http://www.lubbockonline.com/stories/081298/LD0703.shtml.

Lydgate, Joana. 2010. "Assembly-Line Justice: A Review of Operation Streamline." Berkeley: The Chief Justice Earl Warren Institute on Race, Ethnicity and Diversity, University of California, Berkeley Law School. http://www.law.berkeley.edu/files/Operation_Streamline_Policy_Brief.pdf.

Mains, S. P. 2004. "Imagining the Border and Southern Spaces: Cinematic Explorations of Race and Gender." *GeoJournal* 59: 253–264.

Maril, Robert. 2004. *Patrolling Chaos: The U.S. Border Patrol in Deep South Texas*. Lubbock: Texas Tech University Press.

Mann, Jack. 2010. "DHS Pulls SBInet Funding." *GovCon Executive*. March 17. http://www.govconexecutive.com/2010/03/dhs-pulls-sbinet-funding/.

Martinez, Ramiro. 2006. "Coming to America: The Impact of the New Immigration on Crime." In Immigration and Crime: Race, Ethnicity and Violence, ed. Ramiro Martinez and Abel Valenzuela, 1–35. Berkeley: University of California Press.

Martinez, Ramiro. 2007. "Incorporating Latinos and Immigrants into Policing Research." *Criminology and Public Policy* 6 (1): 57–64.

Massey, Douglas. 2009. Testimony before the U.S. Senate Committee on the Judiciary, Subcommittee on Immigration, Border Security, and Citizenship, Hearing on Securing the Borders and America's Ports of Entry, What Remains to Be Done. May 20. http://judiciary.senate.gov/hearings/testimony.cfm?id=3859&wit_id=7939.

Martinez, Ramiro, Jr. 2006. "Coming to America: The Impact of the New Immigration on Crime." In *Immigration and Crime: Race, Ethnicity, and Violence,* ed. Ramiro Martinez Jr. and Abel Valenzuela Jr., 20–35. New York: New York University Press.

McKinley, James C., Jr. 2009. "Napolitano Focuses on Immigration Enforcement." *New York Times*, August 11. http://www.nytimes.com/2009/08/12/us/12border.html?_r=1.

McKinley, James C., Jr., and Julia Preston. 2009. "U.S. Can't Trace Foreign Visitors on Expired Visas." *New York Times*, October 11. http://www.nytimes.com/2009/10/12/us/12visa.html?pagewanted=1&_r=1&partner=rss&emc=rss.

McKinley, Jesse, and Malia Wollan. 2009. "New Border Fear: Violence by a Rogue Militia." *New York Times,* June 26. http://www.nytimes.com/2009/06/27/us/27arizona.html?_r=2.

McNeill, Jena Baker, and Diem Nguyen. 2009. "U.S., Canada Working Together on Border Security." Heritage Organization. http://www.heritage.org/Research/HomelandSecurity/wm2329.cfm.

Nevins, Joseph. 2002. *Operation Gatekeeper: The Rise of the "Illegal Alien" and the Making of the U.S.-Mexico Boundary*. New York: Routledge.

Nunez-Nieto, Blas. 2008. *Border Security: The Role of the U.S. Border Patrol*. Congressional Research Service. http://www.fas.org/sgp/crs/homesec/RL32562.pdf.

Moreno, S. 2006. "Along Part of the Border; A Zero Tolerance Zone: Tough Program Is Discouraging Illegal Crossings." *Washington Post*, June 18, A03.

O'Conner, Anahad, and Eric Schmidt. 2009. "Terror Attempt Seen as Man Tries to Ignite Device on Jet." *New York Times*, December 25. http://www.nytimes.com/2009/12/26/us/26plane.html?scp=1&sq=December%2025%20terror%20attack&st=cse.

Obama, Barack. 2009. "The President of the United States Supports Comprehensive Immigration Reform." Costa Mesa Town Hall Meeting, March 18. http://latimesblogs.latimes.com/washington/2009/03/obama-text.html.

Office of Border Patrol. 2004. *National Border Patrol Strategy.* Washington, DC. http://www.au.af.mil/au/awc/awcgate/dhs/national_bp_strategy.pdf.

Office of the Governor, Rick Perry. 2009a. "Statement by Governor Rick Perry on the Obama Administration's Plan to Combat Mexican Drug Cartels." March 24. http://governor.state.tx.us/news/press-release/12119/.

Office of the Governor, Rick Perry. 2009b. "Gov. Perry Announces Highly Skilled Ranger Recon Teams as Texas' Latest Efforts to Enhance Border Security." September 10. http://www.governor.state.tx.us/news/press-release/13577/.

Office of the U.S. Trade Representative. 2008. "NAFTA—Myth vs. Facts." http://www.ustr.gov/sites/default/files/uploads/factsheets/2008/asset_upload_file71_14540.pdf.

OIG (Office of the Inspector General), Department of Homeland Security. 2006. "Treatment of Immigration Detainees Housed at Immigration and Customs Enforcement Facilities." http://www.dhs.gov/xoig/assets/mgmtrpts/OIG_07-01_Dec06.pdf.

"On the Trail of the Traffickers." 2009. *The Economist*, March 7.

Orchowski, Margaret Sands. 2008. *Immigration and the American Dream: Battling the Political Hype and Hysteria.* New York: Rowan and Littlefield.

Papademetriou, Demetri, and Aaron Terrazas. 2009. *Immigrants and the Current Economic Crisis: Research Evidence, Policy Challenges, and Implications.* Washington, DC: Migration Policy Institute. http://www.migrationpolicy.org/pubs/lmi_recessionJan09.pdf.

Passel, Jeffrey S., and D'Vera Cohn. 2008. *Trends in Unauthorized Immigration: Undocumented Inflow Now Trails Legal Inflow.* Washington, DC: PEW Hispanic Center. http://pewhispanic.org/files/reports/94.pdf.

Payan, Tony. 2006. *The Three U.S.-Mexico Border Wars: Drugs, Immigration, and Homeland Security.* Westport, CT: Praeger Security International.

PEW Hispanic Center. 2006. *Modes of Entry for the Unauthorized Migrant Population Fact Sheet*. Washington, DC: PEW Hispanic Center.

Preston, Julia. 2009. "Obama to Push Immigration Bill as One Priority." *New York Times*, April 8. http://www.nytimes.com/2009/04/09/us/politics/09immig.html?hp.

Ramos, Jorge. 2005. *Dying to Cross: The Worst Immigrant Tragedy in History*. New York: HarperCollins.

Reese, April. 2009. "U.S.-Mexico Fence Building Continues Despite Obama's Promise to Review Its Effects." *New York Times*, April 16. http://www.nytimes.com/gwire/2009/04/16/.

Rhee, Foon. 2009. "Hard Line Immigration Group Pulls Backing from Dobbs." *Political Intelligence*, December 3. http://www.boston.com/news/politics/politicalintelligence/2009/12/hardline_immigr.html.

Richardson, Chad, and Rosalva Resendez. 2006. *On the Edge: Culture, Labor and Deviance on the South Texas Border*. Austin: University of Texas Press.

Risen, James, and Eri Licthblau. 2005. "Spying Program Snared U.S. Calls." *New York Times*, December 21. http://www.nytimes.com/2005/12/21/politics/21nsa.html.

Roebuck, J. 2008. "Some Fear 'Streamline' Could Overburden Federal Courts." *The Monitor* (McAllen, TX), June 10. http://www.themonitor.com/articles/illegal_13020_article.html/border_immigration.htm.

Romero, Mary. 2006. "Racial Profiling and Immigration Law Enforcement: Rounding Up of Usual Suspects in the Latino Community." *Critical Sociology* 32 (2–3): 447–473.

Rothe, Dawn, and Stephen L. Muzzatti. 2004. "Enemies Everywhere: Terrorism, Moral Panic, and U.S. Civil Society." *Critical Criminology* 12: 327–350.

Rubio-Goldsmith, Raquel, M. Melissa McCormick, Daniel Martinez, and Inez Magdelena Duarte. 2006. *The "Funnel Effect" and Recovered Bodies of Unauthorized Immigrants Processed by the Pima County Office of the Medical Examiner, 1990–2005*. Report Submitted to the Pima County Board of Supervisors. Tucson: Binational Immigration Institute, Mexican American Research and Studies Center, University of Arizona.

Rumbaut, Ruben, Roberto G. Gonzales, Golnaz Komaie, and Charlie V. Morgan. 2006a. "Debunking the Myth of Migrant Criminality: Imprisonment among First and Second Generation Young Men." Washington, DC: Migration Policy Institute. http://www.migrationinformation.org/Feature/display.cfm?ID=403.

Rumbaut, Ruben, Roberto G. Gonzales, Golnaz Komaie, and Charlie V. Morgan. 2006b. "Immigration and Incarceration: Patterns and Predictors of Imprisonment among First- and Second-Generation Young Adults." In *Immigration and Crime: Race, Ethnicity, and Violence,* ed. Ramiro Martinez Jr. and Abel Valenzuela Jr., 64–89. New York: New York University Press.

Scharf, David A. 2006. "For Humane Borders: Two Decades of Death and Illegal Activity in the Sonoran Desert." *Case Western Reserve Journal of International Law* 141: 141–172.

Schmidt, Eric. 2010. "New Teams Created to Connect Dots of Terror Plots." *New York Times*, January 29. http://www.nytimes.com/2010/01/30/us/30intel.html.

Schwartz, John, and Randall C. Archibold. 2010. "A Law Facing A Tough Road Through the Courts." *New York Times*, April 27. http://www.nytimes.com/2010/04/28/us/28legal.html.

Schumer, Charles. 2007. *Positively American: Winning Back the Middle Class Majority One Family at a Time.* Emmaus, Penn: Rodale Books.

Schumer, Charles. 2009. Remarks at the 6th Annual Immigration and Law and Policy Conference, Migration Policy Institute, June 24. http://www.migrationpolicy.org/pubs/Schumer-remarks-Law-Policy-Conference-06-24-09.pdf.

Sele, Andrew. 2009. "'Money, Guns, and Drugs': Are U.S. Inputs Fueling Violence on the U.S.-Mexico Border?" Testimony by Andrew Sele to the House Subcommittee on National Security and Foreign Affairs, March 9. http://nationalsecurity.oversight.house.gov/documents/20090313115456.pdf.

Seltzer, Nate, and George Kourous. 1998. "Persistent Impunity, Growing Problems: Immigration Law Enforcement and Human Rights Abuses." *Borderlines* 6 (9): 1–4.

Sharma, Nandita. 2006. "White Nationalism, Illegality, and Imperialism: Border Control as Ideology." In *(En)gendering the War on Terror: War Stories and Camoflauged Politics*, ed. Krista Hunt and Kim Rygiel, 121–144. Aldershot, UK.

Simcox, David. 2000. *Inalienable Identification: Key to Halting Illegal Employment*. Washington, DC: Center for Immigration Studies. http://www.cis.org/articles/2000/back100.html.

Smigielski, David. 2007. "Addressing the Nuclear Smuggling Threat." In *Transnational Threats: Smuggling and Trafficking in Arms, Drugs, and Human Life,* ed. Kimberly L. Thachuk, 53–63. Westport, CT: Praeger Security International.

Smith, Alison. 2005. "CRS Report for Congress: Unauthorized Employment of Aliens: Basics of Employer Sanctions." Washington, DC: Congressional Research Service. http://fpc.state.gov/documents/organization/49088.pdf.

Spagot, Elliot. 2006. "Border Crackdown Fuels Smuggler's Boom." *Washington Post,* December 30. http://www.washingtonpost.com/wp-dyn/content/article/2006/12/30/AR2006123000471.html.

Spakota, Sanjeeb, Harold W. Kohl III, Julie Gilchrist, Jay McAuliffe, Bruce Parks, Bob England, Tim Flood, Mark Sewell, Dennis Perrota, Miguel Escobedo, Corrine E. Stern, David Zane, and Kurt B. Nolte. 2006. "Unauthorized Border Crossings and Migrant Deaths: Arizona, New Mexico, and El Paso, Texas, 2002–2003." *American Journal of Public Health* 96 (7): 1282–1287.

Spener, David. 2009. *Clandestine Crossings: Migrants and Coyotes on the Texas-Mexico Border.* Ithaca, NY: Cornell University Press.

Staudt, Kathleen. 2008a. "Bordering the Other in the Texas Southwest: El Pasoans Confront the Local Sheriff." In *Keeping Out the Other: A Critical Introduction to Immigration Enforcement Today,* ed. David Brotherton and Philip Kretsedemas, 291–313. New York: Columbia University Press.

Staudt, Kathleen, 2008b. *Violence and Activism at the Border: Gender, Fear, and Everyday Life in Ciudad Juarez.* Austin: University of Texas Press.

Stowell, Jacob. 2007. *Immigration and Crime: The Effects of Immigration on Criminal Behavior.* New York: LFB Scholarly Publishing.

"Surge in Immigration Prosecutions Continues." 2008. Transactional Record Clearinghouse. http://trac.syr.edu/immigration/reports/188/.

Teslik, Lee Hudson. 2009. *Council on Foreign Relations Backgrounder: NAFTA's Economic Impact.* New York: Council on Foreign Relations. http://www.cfr.org/publication/15790/naftas_economic_impact.html.

Texas Border Sheriff's Coalition. 2007. "The Governor's View on Border Security." http://www.tlc2.uh.edu/TBSC/News/news_item.2007-05-30.6007901817/newsitem_view?month:int=1&year:int=2010.

Thachuk, Kimberly L. 2007. "An Introduction to Transnational Threats." In *Transnational Threats: Smuggling and Trafficking in Arms, Drugs, and Human Life,* ed. Thachuk, 3–20. Westport, CT: Praeger Security International.

Thompson, Ginger. 2009a. "A Shift to Make the Border Safe, from Inside Out." *New York Times,* April 5. http://www.nytimes.com/2009/04/06.

Thompson, Ginger. 2009b. "Work Under Way on Virtual Fence." *New York Times*, May 8. http://www.nytimes.com/2009/05/09.

Waugh, W. L. 2003. "Terrorism, Homeland Security, and the National Emergency Management Network." *Public Organization Review: A Global Journal* 3: 373–385.

Wassem, Ruth Ellen. 2008. "Visa Issuances: Policy, Issues, and Legislation." Congressional Research Service. http://italy.usembassy.gov/pdf/other/RL31512.pdf/.

U.S. Customs and Border Protection. 2005. "DHS Launches Operation Streamline II." http://www.cbp.gov/xp/cgov/newsroom/news_releases/archives/2005_press_releases/122005/12162005.xml.

U.S. Customs and Border Protection. 2007. "Operation Streamline Nets 1200-Plus Prosecutions in Arizona." http://www.cbp.gov/xp/cgov/newsroom/news_releases/archives/2007_news_releases/072007/07242007_3.xml.

U.S.-Mexico Border Counties Coalition. 2008. "Undocumented Immigrants in U.S.-Mexico Border Counties: The Costs of Law Enforcement and Criminal Justice Services." The University of Arizona Eller College of Management. http://www.bordercounties.org/vertical/Sites/%7BB4A0F1FF-7823-4C95-8D7A-F5E400063C73%7D/uploads/%7B690801CA-CEE6-413C-AC8B-A00DA765D96E%7D.pdf.

U.S.-Mexico Border and Immigration Task Force. 2009. "Accountability, Community Security, and Infrastructure on the U.S.-Mexico Border: Policy Priorities for 2009–2010." http://borderaction.org/bordertaskforce/2009.Border.Policy.Report.Final.pdf.

Vanderbilt, Jim, John F. Harris, and Mile Allen. 2009. "Cheney Warns of New Attacks." *Politico*, February 4. http://www.nbcdfw.com/news/archive/Cheney_warns_of_new_attacks.html?f=y&orderpar=regular&com=4.

Villareal, M. Angeles, and Jennifer E. Lake. 2009. "CRS Report for Congress: Security and Prosperity Partnership of North America: An Overview and Selected Issues." Washington, DC: Congressional Research Service. http://www.fas.org/sgp/crs/row/RS22701.pdf.

3

Border Security in an International Context

Introduction

Securing the U.S. borders has become a major expense for the nation. Enforcement for interdiction of unauthorized migrants has been continually stepped up at the U.S.-Mexico border without ever more than partially succeeding by temporary declines or diversion to more remote regions. It has had the unanticipated consequence of increasing the size of the undocumented population in the United States and decreasing the more temporary pattern of circular migration (Massey 2009). In the meantime, new transnational threats in the form of terrorist acts, various forms of trafficking, and money laundering are developing from international criminal and terrorist networks. This threat is driven by the desire for prosperity in an imbalanced world of "haves" and "have-nots."

Global Inequalities: Economic and Security

Global inequality has a major negative impact on human lives and health within and between nations. Unfortunately, income inequalities are increasing in almost all world countries (International Labor Organization 2008). International agreements like the North American Free Trade Agreement (NAFTA), which includes the United States, Mexico, and Canada, are meant to increase incomes and decrease inequality through economic integration

117

after a difficult transition phase. NAFTA represents a form of financial liberalization that has not yet improved global productivity or employment growth. Financial globalization has not equally benefited everyone as inequalities between social classes have deepened inside impacted nations. From 1990 to 2000 income inequality between and within world nations has increased, and, through 2008, executive pay was a major cause of increasing income inequality within the economies of high-income nations.

Since 2000 U.S. income inequality has rapidly increased, following a trend that began in the 1970s (OECD 2008). The average income of the richest 10% is $93,000 in purchasing power. The poorest try to make do on $5,800. The top 1% of earners control 25–33% of the wealth and the top 10% control 71%. The United States has become a nation of earners living on wages and salaries that are decreasing relative to elite earners. In the mid-1980s, income inequality began to increase in Canada (OECD 2008). The elite earners receive $71,000 in purchasing power per year. Poverty has increased among all age groups. Of children, 15% live in poverty. Fearful American workers advocate for keeping the rest of the world out without realizing how U.S. prosperity is increasingly dependent on international economic ties.

Mexico has a higher degree of inequality than the United States or Canada, but the United States has the third-highest level of inequality of the 30 OECD nations, challenging ideas about the affluence of the American population (OECD 2008). Inequality has been increasing among the world's high-income countries due to a widening gap between high earners and the poor. In both the United States and Canada, middle-income earners are falling behind. The situation of widening inequality in these high-income nations raises important questions about the benefits of financial globalization (International Labor Organization 2008; OECD 2008). Nevertheless, once the process has been initiated, it is unlikely that nations can withdraw from this new world economic system.

Mexico is classified as an upper-middle-income country by the World Bank (World Bank 2001). Its economy, although developing, is the twelfth largest in the world (High 2009). NAFTA was meant to end the exclusion of Mexico from the United States and Canadian economies, but disproportionate resources have meant that Mexico has not benefited to the degree one might expect. Mexico's economy is driven by NAFTA-related international trade, oil, tourism, and remittances, money sent from abroad by migrants and immigrants working in the United States. Since

NAFTA was implemented in 1994, trade has tripled from $297 to $930 billion (High 2009). About 80% of Mexico's exports are sent to the United States (High 2009). Yet NAFTA is not sufficient to drive the economy of Mexico. Remittances peaked at $27 billion in 2007 and dropped after the world economic crisis of 2008–2009 (Banco de Mexico 2009).

Since NAFTA was enacted, social inequality has been slightly reduced in Mexico as income poverty (people who live on less than half of the median income) decreased from 21% to 18% (OECD 2008). (OECD 2008). Despite this positive change, 42.6% of the Mexican population is estimated to live in poverty and 13.8% in extreme poverty (CONEVAL 2009). The young and the elderly are particularly affected; 22% of children and about 30% of those over 65 live in households with a below–poverty-level income.

The United States has asymmetric power relations with both Canada and Mexico. The gap in resources between the high-income countries of the United States and Canada and the high-middle-income of Mexico limits Mexican multilateral political influence. Similarly, Canada faces limitations on its ability to influence American policy. Powerful countries like the United States have less initiative to cooperate with the less powerful on binational issues. Many security issues devolve from the inequality of access to global resources in Mexico and the desire of Canadians to maintain independent policies rather than follow the lead of the United States, a country with world objectives that do not always overlap with Canadian views.

Globalization is connected to processes of economic liberalization that have implied that the significance of borders will decline. Security concerns have meant that the U.S.-Mexico border is more tightly controlled while other borders, such as the internal borders in the multination European Union, are more relaxed (Andreas and Snyder 2000). Economic and political inequality results in disproportionate control over which people and goods will cross the border. Ports of entry and associated borders are subject to diverging levels of control. The sizable security investment in the Mexican border as opposed to the Canadian border demonstrates this. The political economy of the world system of nations results in the unequal movement of capital and social value and persons across borders.

U.S. citizens, who are at a higher income level, are allowed to cross the Mexico border with greater ease than Mexican citizens, although some members of the middle and working classes or peasants from Mexico are allowed (Heyman 2004). U.S. tourists seek better prices when crossing the border. The mobility of financial capital has increased as a result of NAFTA, allowing a certain potential for Mexican development. Similarly, raw materials are assembled in Mexico, where value is added by low-priced labor, an unequal value transfer perceived as vital to American prosperity. Manufacturers gained access to labor and investors to markets at favorable rates. The mobility of goods and people over the border does not contribute to extensive change in the relation of inequality in resources between the three countries. Canada is a "medium-power" country in relation to the United States (Ackleson and Krasner 2006, 219) and NAFTA basically extended the United States' economic norms to both Canada and Mexico, impacting the two border states to a greater extent. The Security and Prosperity Partnership extends the same pattern of interstate power relations.

The World Bank (2001) has taken the position that "economic and social stability *and human security* are preconditions for sustainable development" (emphasis added). Because of power asymmetries, the United States is viewed as imposing its own rules on Canada (Weinburg 2009) and Mexico. This tendency for one country to dominate another is referred to as unilateralism. A more coordinated approach is multilateralism. The economic situation of its bordering countries and all world nations is increasingly tied into the major problems the United States faces: unauthorized immigration, drug trafficking, and transnational terrorism. Borders lend themselves to reciprocal influence for better or worse. The U.S. consumer demand for drugs and relative freedom of access to guns means that internal measures are needed to combat drug and arms trafficking and reduce violence on the border and in Mexico. Similarly, many Mexicans and Central Americans want to cross the border for better opportunities. The economic development of Mexico and Central America is a strategy for dealing with unauthorized immigration. To a greater degree, attempts to coordinate and stabilize world development may ease transnational threats.

Human Trafficking: Causes and Consequences

Mexicans migrate to the United States for better wages, the availability of jobs, and family reunification. Mexico is very dependent on remittances from migrants and immigrants in the United States. The need for remittances is heightened by the dependency of many families on unmechanized subsistence-level agriculture. Because there is little irrigation, unpredictable rainfall is needed for crops to thrive. The impoverishment in the countryside pushes Mexicans, along with Central Americans and an array of potential immigrants from all over the globe, to look for work in the United States.

Intensified border enforcement has led to an increase in the hiring of smugglers by U.S.-Mexico border migrants. For individuals attempting to gain entry from other continents, smugglers may be their only choice. Smugglers range from one person to group operations and charge a fee, now substantial, to get a person across the border without inspection. In recent years, the fee for assistance in unauthorized crossing of the southern border has risen to $2,000 or more. Certain individuals working the cross-border passage of immigrants mean to make more than just money from helping them to cross. Traffickers take advantage of restrictions on global movement to practice debt bondage and slavery.

Human smuggling involves abetting unauthorized entry, which is a violation of immigration law. It occurs by mutual consent of the smuggler and the undocumented migrant (Kleeman 2009, 409). In contrast, *human trafficking* is defined by the use of force, fraud, coercion, or deceit to exploit the unauthorized entrant. Human traffickers who bring unauthorized entrants are distinct from smugglers because of their transnational and organized criminal connections and motivation. Recent attempts to illuminate the dark figures of human trafficking have resulted in the estimate that from 600,000 to more than 4 million persons are annually trafficked worldwide (Lehti and Aromaa 2006, 183–215).

The U.S. Congress enacted the Victims of Trafficking and Violence Protection Act (VTVPA) to bolster the Thirteenth Amendment to the Constitution, which outlawed slavery. The VTVPA defines the two "severe forms of trafficking" as "sex trafficking in which a commercial sex act is induced by force, fraud, or coercion, or in which the person induced to perform such an act has not attained 18 years of age"; and "the recruitment, harboring, transportation, provision or obtaining of a person for labor or services, through the use of force, fraud or coercion for the purpose of subjection to involuntary servitude, peonage, debt bondage or slavery" (U.S. Department of State 2008, 6).

Forms of exploitation of trafficking victims include forced prostitution or labor, slavery, and/or removal of body organs. In 2001 the Protocol to Prevent, Suppress and Punish Trafficking in Persons, Especially Women and Children, an international law, was passed, making antitrafficking a principle of international law (United Nations 2001). Both immigration and organized crime laws are broken when human traffickers bring a victim to the United States illegally.

The United States is thought to be the destination for thousands of men, women, and children primarily from Mexico and East Asia (U.S. Department of State 2009, 57). Other source regions include South Asia, Central America, Africa, and Europe. It is estimated that 600,000 to 800,000 people per year are trafficked worldwide. Profit drives this illegal practice and only drugs and arms trafficking are more profitable. Seven to ten billion dollars a year may be realized by human trafficking. Traffickers believe that they have a lower probability of being arrested and convicted of this crime as compared to arms and drugs trafficking because they believe they are not likely to be caught and that the law will not be enforced.

Human trafficking is a crime that occurs in stages. The first stage does not necessarily involve criminal activity but it concerns the social characteristics of the victims, which create vulnerability. Poverty and hopelessness combined with the desire for a better life make individuals in developing countries turn to traffickers in a search for economic opportunity (Kleeman 2009, 416; Lehti and Aromaa 2006). They believe that traffickers can find them employment in an overseas host country and are not aware of any danger or that they may lose their freedom and be forced to engage in criminal activities or enslaved. Often these individuals want to go overseas to earn money to support their relatives and/or families in the homeland and are not aware that they may disappear into a criminal underground. The ultimate cause of this situation is economic instability and lack of economic opportunity in their home countries, which are developing nations and lack the perceived opportunities of developed economies

Recruitment is the second stage of trafficking. A local person often recruits an acquaintance or friend of the victim who knows the culture and understands vulnerability (Kleeman 2009, 417). Often these recruiters are women. Recruiters speak of ways to earn undreamed of amounts of money and may even use help-wanted ads to attract victims. The trust of the victims and their false sense of security lead to willing consent to travel and to accept illegal aspects of the situation, such as obtaining a fraudulent passport, and they will even provide a down payment for travel. The countries of origin lack resources to stop trafficking and corrupt officials may abet it. The United States, a frequent destination, is known to receive victims from Thailand, China, Russia, Ukraine, and the Czech Republic (U.S. Department of State 2008). A major origin region for trafficking victims is the former Soviet Union, where Belarus, Moldavia, the Russian Federation, and Ukraine are the source of many sex trafficking victims (United Nations Office on Drugs and Crime 2006).

Recruitment can occur by force but this practice is not common (Kleeman 2009, 417). Trafficker organizations kidnap or use drugs to pacify victims. Refugee relocation camps holding those who flee war or disasters are a target for abduction. Another type of abduction occurs when individuals are taken from streets, schoolyards, or everyday locations in which police or capable guardians are not available to intercede. After recruitment, individuals are transported abroad. At this stage, many are consenting victims who expect normal employment, but some are coerced into traveling along routes traffickers typically use.

The uncovering of the deception and exploitation of trafficking victims often occurs upon arrival at the destination. Traffickers withhold passports and other identification documents, and victims are told that they have a huge debt to pay through their labor. In sex trafficking, this coerced labor is facilitated by the development of perverted social relationships, intimidation, extremely close monitoring, and violence (Kleeman 2009, 417). Victims are enslaved to a purchaser or the trafficker. Sex traffickers coerce women and children to work in prostitution, exotic dancing, or other "entertainment." Less commonly, victims may work in factories, on farms, in mines, or as domestic servants. Although forced labor is given, with the hope of eventual freedom, "interest" on the smuggling debt makes release unlikely unless severe illness occurs such as a prostitute contracting HIV/AIDS and being no longer able to work.

Exploitation of trafficking victims occurs simultaneously with psychological and verbal abuse that extends to torture. Physical abuse, such as beatings and rape, is not uncommon. This abuse ensures that the trafficking victim will be compliant with customers and will be worn down and therefore not try to escape. Another form of abuse is confined living quarters that may be shared by up to 20 people in the presence of guards. Victims are always under supervision to prevent attempts to get help or escape.

For some victims, the only resolution to trafficking is death. They could be tortured to death or die trying to pay off the smuggling debt. For those who escape, it is often not possible to return to the home country because they would be socially ostracized. In many cultures, prostitution is not acceptable and trafficking victims forced to do such work are considered unclean. Trafficking victims who do return often find themselves without economic opportunity again and may even let themselves be recruited by a new smuggler or trafficker.

The Protocol to Prevent, Suppress and Punish Trafficking in Persons, Especially Women and Children is an international legal agreement that requires its signatory countries to take action to prevent trafficking, prosecute traffickers, and provide victim protection. In the United States, the Victims of Trafficking and Violence Protection Act (VTVPA) requires international cooperation with sending countries to identify human traffickers. Law-enforcement task forces include the FBI (Federal Bureau of Investigation) and Immigration and Customs Enforcement (ICE) agents, which work with international police to acquire intelligence on human-trafficking rings. The U.S. government seeks to educate women abroad about trafficking and provides funding to create economic opportunities in developing countries. The VTVPA of 2000 began a sanctions-based system in which countries are ranked into three tiers based on the degree to which they have introduced antitrafficking initiatives and are attempting prevention and prosecution. The U.S. Department of State has recognized 26 countries as Tier 1, considered acceptable. Tier 2 countries are considered to need more preventative efforts but are not subject to sanctions. Tier 3 countries are subject to sanctions.

Sending countries in the developing world which are successful in assisting prosecution of human trafficking receive economic aid. Countries involved in human trafficking which have not made steps toward dealing with the problem are ineligible for funding. Since it is economic problems which encourage human trafficking, this economic sanction is likely to have the reverse impact of increasing human trafficking if a country does not have the resources to combat it and the VTVPA sanctions are enforced because more individuals will seek to migrate.

In the United States, VTVPA, in conjunction with the Peonage Abolition Act of 1867, which made it a crime to force labor of any man, woman, or child as a slave, provides for prosecution and sentencing of human traffickers. The new law makes it a crime to deceive or threaten harm to coerce work irregardless of whether it is sex work or any other kind of labor. Traffickers and knowing customers can receive up to 20 years' imprisonment for forcing adult labor. In the case of child labor, or if an adult victim dies, is kidnapped, or endures severe sexual abuse, the sentence expands to life imprisonment. This act also specifies that any U.S. citizen traveling to another country for sex tourism can be imprisoned for up to 30 years.

Pursuing and Prosecuting Human Trafficking

The VTVPA authorizes two types of immigration relief for trafficking victims: Continued Presence (CP) and T visas. "Continued presence" is a temporary status issued by law enforcement which allows a victim of severe trafficking to stay in the United States during an investigation. A "T visa" gives nonimmigrant status to victims of severe forms of trafficking who are at or near a port of entry because of trafficking, have helped with investigation or prosecution of trafficking, or are under 18 years of age and who would suffer extreme hardship if deported. They may stay in the United States up to four years and the stay may be extended of it is needed for an antitrafficking investigation. After three years, holders of T visas can apply for an adjustment to permanent resident status.

In FY2007, 122 people received CP status. Their origins were Mexico, El Salvador, and China. Immigration gateway cities such as Los Angeles, New York, Newark, and Houston were sites of the most requests. In FY2007, 279 people received T visas. Since 2001, 1,974 victims and immediate family members have received T visas (Office of the Attorney General 2008, 19–20).

Police corruption in sending countries extends to accepting bribes or even participating in human-trafficking organizations. Police who are involved are called "corrupt guardians" (Farr 2005). Bribery can ensure that false identification and travel documents are accepted, and even some American inspectors are not above taking money to allow fraudulent entry. Alarmingly, corrupt guardians may help to enforce enslavement if they recapture and turn over victims or take bribes to protect businesses using forced labor. They may also warn traffickers of investigations and raids (Farr 2005).

Border-security efforts are considered a method to fight human trafficking. The difficulty with this approach concerns the recruitment of individuals who travel voluntarily and make unauthorized entrance before the situation turns against them (Kleeman 2009, 419). Because most individuals who are forced into labor have entered the United States and other countries without authorization and giving consent, police become complacent about offering assistance and may view these individuals as immigration law violators. Police treat trafficking victims as criminal aliens and put them into deportation proceedings, which occur without due process rights accorded to citizens such as access to a lawyer. The use of fraudulent documents and payment to traffickers makes these victims appear to be willing accomplices. Because the victims consented to illegal entry, police are reluctant to assign a victim status. Victims engaging in prostitution and other sex trade labor also are less likely to be helped by police because they have committed yet another type of crime even though it was against their will. Police complacency and resultant inaction produces a forgotten population of forced labor and further victimizes this group. Lack of police action then encourages human traffickers to operate with impunity. Another factor in police complacency that encourages traffickers is lack of knowledge of how to conduct trafficking investigations.

The U.S. VTVPA provides for protection of victims of human trafficking found in the United States. Victims are to be placed in shelters with security and given psychological, medical, legal, and job assistance. They are to be provided with temporary visas for their testimony against traffickers and will ultimately qualify for permanent resident visas. The United States has faced issues in carrying out this law because of problems in prosecuting cases where the individual gave consent. They may have consented to use of fraudulent documents and unauthorized entry. The VTVPA requires proof of harm and that work was forced or coerced. It is hard to prosecute cases of travel across international borders or instances where individuals agreed to work in the sex industry. The victim has to prove their victimization. Individuals are evaluated in a process called certification by the Department of Health and Human Services to determine if severe treatment due to trafficking occurred before receiving a temporary visa. This means that individuals who have difficulty proving their case may be deported and subject to retaliation in the home country.

Drug Trafficking

In the 1960s, the United States began a law-enforcement campaign against domestic and international drug trafficking (Andreas and Nadelman 2006, 128–131). The U.S. official policy narratives have emphasized the importance of prohibition of drug use rather than alternative harm-reduction approaches including drug treatment. This approach has resulted in organized crime involvement in both Canada and Mexico as there is consumer demand for narcotics and smuggled cigarettes at lower cost.

The U.S.-Canada Border (1960–present)

The Canadian border is a two-way drug-trafficking transshipment point. All methods of border crossing are used. Commercial and private vehicles take drugs overland, and some are brought on foot. Marine borders used for smuggling include the Great Lakes, the Saint Lawrence River, the Washington–British Columbia Strait, and open ocean. Aircraft are used as well in this very profitable illicit venture. Canada has become a source of high-grade marijuana brought to the United States. Heroin and precursor chemicals are trafficked to a lesser extent. The Canadian border is a world source of methamphetamines and ecstasy (National Drug Intelligence Center 2001, 2–18).

The U.S. border is used to smuggle cheaper, tax-exempt cigarettes into Canada. By 1994 it was estimated that one-third of all Canadian cigarettes were smuggled to avoid tariff taxation (Beare 2003). Of greater concern for the Canadians is that the United States has been the major transshipment point for cocaine to be smuggled into Canada and is the main source of smuggled weapons because of its gun-control policy.

In contrast to the increasingly fortified Mexican border, the Canadian border received far fewer resources over time, and was viewed as much less of a priority (Ackleson and Heyman 2010, 66).

In the 1980s the United States passed major antidrug-trafficking legislation, and Canada follows international conventions and its own Controlled Drugs and Substances Act (National Drug Intelligence Center 2001, 21). The United States and Canada have mutual drug demand reduction goals and, with greater resources available than Mexico, have bilateral law-enforcement cooperation. Cross-border cooperative efforts prior to 9/11 include Integrated Border Enforcement Teams, Intelligence Collection Analysis Teams, and the Canada-U.S. Cross-Border Crime Forum.

In Canada, organized Asian criminal groups and outlaw motorcycle gangs such as the Hells Angels control marijuana production and distribution (National Drug Intelligence Center 2001, 4–5). British Columbia is the primary growing area for marijuana, producing "BC Bud," although Quebec also produced "Quebec Gold." BC Bud is used in exchange for cocaine from the United States, and drug smugglers are caught along the border on a regular basis. As the drug trade becomes entrenched, Vancouver, British Columbia, is experiencing drug-related violence.

Mexican Drug Trafficking (1960–present)

The militarization of the U.S.-Mexico border is a social project that began with drug control and has been expanded to immigration (Dunn 1996). Both the United States and Mexico have increasingly involved the armed forces, including the U.S. National Guard, to perform surveillance on the Mexican border.

Since the 1980s the U.S.-Mexico border has emerged as the major site of drug trafficking into the United States, a national security threat (Payan 2006, 28). It threatens the Mexican government due to high levels of violence and associated corruption. Mexican drug-trafficking organizations grow and transport marijuana and heroin and manufacture methamphetamines. Of the cocaine entering the United States from South America, 90% is trafficked by the Mexican cartels over the southwest border (U.S. Department of Justice National Drug Intelligence Center 2006). The smuggling of drug money and arms south is equally significant.

The successful enforcement effort against the Colombian Cali and Medellin cartels led to the emergence of Mexican drug-trafficking organizations (DTOs) which took over the trade (Payan 2006, 28). Previously, Colombians trafficked cocaine through Florida. Mexican smugglers made ties with Colombian traffickers and relocated the problem to the southern border. The Mexican government has a history of tolerating drug-trafficking organizations (Beittel 2009, 7–8). In the 1980s and 1990s, it pursued a policy of accommodation in which government officials and police accepted bribes while appeasing the United States by making some arrests and running a crop-eradication program. Cooperative efforts between the United States and Mexico were viewed with mistrust by U.S. officials because of known corruption in Mexico.

From 1986 through 1992, the U.S. president was required to certify the degree of foreign government cooperation in combating DTOs and Mexico was criticized, which led to a negative Mexican government reaction (Beittel 2009, 2–3). In 2002 the United States changed to a policy of designating countries considered to be deficient in combating narcotics trafficking and withholding assistance. After the election of Mexican President Vincente Fox (2000–2006) of the National Action Party (PAN) ended 71 years of PRI (Institutional Revolutionary Party) rule, binational cooperation against DTOs increased as Mexico strengthened its commitment to democracy rather than one-party rule.

Narcoterrorism

Narcoterrorism is defined as the use of terrorism to increase profits from drug trafficking or taking the profits from drug trafficking to fund terrorism (Casteel 2003). In the case of Mexico, drug organizations have used executioners, gangs, and paramilitary groups to terrorize and intimidate the public and government officials (Cook 2007, 6–9; Beittel 2009, 5–6). Police chiefs, prosecutors, elected government representatives, journalists, and civilians of all ages have been killed (Beittel 2009, 10–12). The violence is considered terroristic because of the torture which marks some of the threats used to intimidate, killings, and their extent. DTOs are torturing and maiming victims and decapitating the corpses (Bunker, Campbell, and Bunker 2010, 146–148). Torture is practiced for intimidation and extortion and can include beatings, breaking bones, knife lacerations, starvation, and sexual abuse. More extreme torture methods include acid, fire, water, electricity, and suffocation. Maiming in connection with murders can involve decapitation, placing bodies in car trunks, drums, or acid baths, taping the eyes and mouth shut, and quartering of the body.

Since 2007, the Mexican government estimates that 22,700 people have been killed in drug-related violence (Castillo 2010). In 2009, 9,635 people were murdered, more than triple the total of 2,837 in 2007. Since, 2006, 4,324 of these deaths occurred in Ciudad Juarez, a Mexican border city. In the first four months of 2010, 3,365 died. This 2010 total includes the deaths of a pregnant U.S. Consulate employee and her husband and another husband of a U.S. Consulate employee (Lacey and Thompson 2010). DTOs made threats against U.S. diplomats stationed on the U.S.-Mexico border prior to the incidents. A short time previously, the State Department decided that consulate workers could evacuate their families across the border for protection in the United States. Mexican president Felipe Calderón considers Mexico's drug-related violence a threat to the nation (Beittel 2009, 3). As of yet, Mexican drug traffickers have not been linked to international terrorism, but the groups that launder money often work with both drug and terrorist organizations.

Despite many attempts and reputed success in corrupting some government officials, Mexico has taken the initiative and cooperated with the Drug Enforcement Administration (DEA) to combat the cartels. From 2000 through 2006, 79,000 people were arrested on drug trafficking–related charges (Cook 2007, 3–4). Although 78,831 were low-level drug dealers, 428 hitmen, 74 lieutenants, 53 financial officers, and 15 cartel leaders were arrested, including Tijuana leader Francisco Javier Arellano Felix and Osiel Cárdenas Guillén, the head of the Gulf organization. Mexico has experienced conflict between major drug organizations, and the arrest of DTO leaders has led to a turf war between the Gulf/Tijuana and Sinaloa organizations (Cook 2007, 11–12).

Mexico drug organizations transit narcotics to 230 U.S. cities and directly operate in 195 cities. In Mexico narcoterrorism is increasing in response to intensified enforcement. Since Calderón became president of Mexico, 70 tons of cocaine, 4,000 tons of marijuana, and 43,000 tons of methamphetamine drug processing precursors have been confiscated (Berrong 2009). This is due to the militarization of Mexico's antidrug effort, which involves federal law enforcement and 45,000 members of the Mexican military (Beittel 2009, 3, 13–14). Mexican law enforcement has arrested 90,000 traffickers, 400 hitmen, and several cartel leaders (Moore 2009). The United States extradited 95 Mexican nationals in 2008 and increased drug-seizure rates. Ironically, top-level arrests increase inter-drug organization violence and narcoterrorism as they fight over control of the most profitable drug routes. Six thousand Mexicans, including 530 police officers, were killed in drug-related violence during 2008.

Mexican traffickers' most profitable crop is marijuana—as cocaine and heroin smuggling has somewhat declined with increased enforcement (Moore 2009). They use tunnels and ramps over border barriers to move it. As drug-trafficking efforts have become concentrated at the Mexico border, violence against Border Patrol officers has increased, including use of automatic weapons like machine guns. Increasingly, Mexican drug organizations are growing indoor marijuana in the United States and competing with Asian networks and individual growers while making contacts with street and prison gangs.

Major drug-trafficking organizations are the Tijuana Cartel Federation, the Sinaloa Cartel Federation, the Gulf Cartel Federation, and the Federation (Sinaloa, Juarez, and Valencia) (Cook 2007, 1–2). The arrests of Tijuana cartel leaders Francisco Javier Arellano Felix and Guild cartel leader Osiel Cárdenas Guillén led to an inter-cartel alliance. Project Reckoning, a DEA initiative, further disrupted the Gulf Cartel's U.S. and European distribution networks (U.S. Attorney, Southern District of New York 2008). Six hundred were arrested and 12,000 pounds of cocaine and $72 million in U.S. currency were confiscated. In the U.S. interior, the DEA moved against the Gulf organization and arrested 750 while targeting 70 distribution networks. Twelve thousand kilograms of cocaine and $60 million in U.S. currency were confiscated.

Narcoterrorism in Mexico has become a leading threat to Mexican national security (Casteel 2003; Grayson 2010). The DTOs attempt to bribe or intimidate Mexican law enforcement, the military, and the government. Police in Nuevo Laredo, Mexico, have reportedly kidnapped members of rival cartels to turn over to the Gulf organization. The Mexican government has conducted numerous operations to purge police of drug organization enforcers. Nuevo Laredo was originally the site of highly publicized drug-organization conflict because of its proximity to Laredo, Texas, its sister border city and the profitable I-35 trafficking route. Hundreds of Mexicans and 60 American citizens have been kidnapped (Blumenthal 2005). Violence has included the murder of government officials, and threats against American journalists have led their newspapers to take protective action. Drug organizations seek to intimidate both the media and police as a way of reducing coverage and reaction to their activities. The U.S. State Department has urged American citizens to take precautions when traveling in Mexico. In April, 2010, a grenade was hurled at the U.S.

Consulate in Nuevo Laredo, which was closed indefinitely (Lacey 2010). It is considered that threats against U.S. interests in Mexico are due to U.S. backing of President Calderón's anti-drug offensive.

The U.S. Joint Forces Command (2008, 36) characterized Mexico as a possible "failing state." Mexican officials have contested this position, and Secretary of State Hillary Clinton (Clinton 2009) has stated that she does not believe that Mexico has any "ungovernable territories." Alternately, Mexican President Calderón claims that the DTOs have been weakened and are turning against each other due to shrinking market share (Malkin 2009). A third view is that drug traffickers need to subvert the state by corrupting government and law enforcement rather than defeat it (Jane's Information Group 2009).

Controversy exists over the cause of rapidly accelerating drug-related violence during the Calderón presidency (Lacey and Thompson 2010). Michele Leonhart, acting Enforcement Administration administrator, considers that: ". . . the violence we have been seeing is a signpost of the success our very courageous Mexican counterparts are having" (Peters 2009). The Mexican government has maintained that the deaths are primarily of individuals involved in drug trafficking and involve conflict between the military or law enforcement and gangs and DTOs or inter-cartel turf wars generated by arrests of high-ranking DTO leaders. Former Foreign Minister Jorge Castañeda has stated that: "The argument is absurd that the killings are a sign of his [Calderón's} success." The January, 2010 deaths of 16 Mexican teenage students at a birthday party were characterized by Felipe Calderón as "a settling of accounts" between drug gang members. In fact, the youth were from a rough neighborhood and had avoided involvement with the drug trade. This incident and the killing of a U.S. Consulate worker has led to increased criticism of President Calderón's military offensive. A new effort will be made to involve Mexican citizens and deal with the rupture in the social fabric of Mexican society.

Janet Napolitano (2009), director of Homeland Security, indicates that cartel violence in Mexican border cities has a spill-over effect in the United States. Spillover violence is defined as planned attacks on U.S. citizens, officials, or physical infrastructure in the United States (Peters 2009). There have been inter-cartel murders in the United States, kidnappings, and attacks on

U.S. Border Patrol officers attempting interdiction of drug smugglers. Law-enforcement monitoring indicates Mexican DTOs maintain drug distribution networks or supply drugs to distributers in 230 U.S. cities (GAO 2009). The *National Drug Assessment, 2010* states that: "Direct violence similar to the conflicts occurring among major DTOs in Mexico is rare." (Department of Justice National Drug Intelligence Center 2009, 16). Nevertheless, "indirect violence" including kidnapping and other forms of DTO "discipline," are occurring. Kidnappings of drug customers occur when payment has not been made. Inside DTOs, the discipline of members can include beatings, kidnappings, torture, and/or death of members who do not deliver drugs or money. Drug-related violence includes assaults against members or the families of DTOs that are establishing homes in the United States for safety. Phoenix, Arizona has experienced an increase in drug and human smuggling related kidnappings in 2007 (260), 2008 (299), and 2009 (267) (Department of Justice National Drug Intelligence Center 2009, 16).

The expansion of Mexican DTOs into the United States led to raids in 19 states by Project Coronado against La Familia Michoacana (LFM), a methamphetamine distributing cartel (McKinley 2009). Three hundred and three people were arrested. Simultaneously, Mexican law enforcement arrested two midlevel commanders and four other LFM members. In Mexico, LFM tortures and beheads its victims, including police officers. Attorney General Eric H. Holder Jr. indicates: "The sheer depravity and level of violence that this cartel has exhibited far exceeds what we, unfortunately, have become accustomed to from other cartels. While this cartel may operate from Mexico, the toxic reach of its operations extends to nearly every state within our country." Arrests occurred in 38 cities including the major distribution centers of Dallas, Atlanta, and Seattle. Since 2006, over 900 members of La Familia Michoacana have been arrested in the United States.

The degree of violence impacting the United States, particularly border communities, is not as severe as in Mexico. For example, El Paso, Texas, reported 17 murders in 2008 and 13 murders through 12-25-2009 in comparison to over 1,600 drug-related murders in Ciudad Juarez, Mexico (Johnson 2009). In 2009, murder rates actually declined during the first six months of 2009. According to Texas governor Rick Perry, this is due to increased patrols. Nevertheless, DHS has added ICE officers to deal with criminal aliens in the border region and is funding increased assistance to state and local law enforcement and Mexico (Department of Homeland Security Office of the Press Secretary 2009). In addition, the United States is enacting plans to increase security by installing x-ray devices to check certain southbound cars for drugs, arms, and cash. Both the DHS and the state of Texas have developed border-security initiatives for any surge of border spillover violence. The most drastic scenario concerns the possibility that drug violence may cause Mexico to become a failed state. When the Pentagon raised this possibility, Mexican President Calderón denied it.

Drug Addiction in Mexico

Mexico has been developing an internal drug-addiction problem as drugs become cheaper and more available. In 2009, Mexico passed a statute said to decriminalize drug possession (Lacey 2009a). Individuals found in possession of small amounts of drugs will not be prosecuted. Instead, they will receive referrals to treatment programs. Individuals found with drugs a third time would be forced to enter a treatment center. The measure is intended to free prison space for more dangerous criminals. Critics of the new law argue that it will promote border drug tourism and increase addiction. It can be viewed, however, as a step toward mandatory sentencing because previously only sale or purchase was criminalized. The amount in possession is very small, making possession of larger amounts a criminal offense. Border drug tourism is less likely because of the higher risk of arrest and imprisonment in Mexico. While drug-related violence in Mexico remains a serious problem, individuals may forego exposing themselves to danger while obtaining drugs in Mexico.

The United States has been the world leader in enacting a drug-prohibition agenda (Andreas and Nadelman 2006). Critics of the War on Drugs consider it a disastrous policy damaging U.S. security interests in Mexico and other drug-exporting nations (Lacey 2009a). They advocate harm reduction through legalization of drugs and associated taxation to pay for the costs. The United States and Mexico have a policy of interdiction and eradication of drug crops. Advocates of this policy believe that the drug supply has been reduced while critics consider that the government has held back data which shows that cocaine prices have dropped due to an increase in supply. The Mexican government and drug-policy critics believe that the

United States needs to reduce citizens' demand for drugs, which allows cartels to earn billions. Strategies for demand reduction include drug-prevention programs and treatment. Five billion dollars has been committed to the integration of substance-abuse services into the U.S. health care system for early screening and care with an emphasis on prevention. Advocates of this approach argue that drug treatment is more cost effective than interdiction.

The United States' power asymmetry with Mexico, a developing country, can be viewed as contributing to the problem. Mexico regards U.S. assistance as sensitive because it sees U.S. intervention as a violation of its sovereignty. Many Latin American countries dislike the United States' unilateral drug-enforcement strategy and would prefer multilateral cooperation. The relative inequality between developed and developing nations, weak institutions, and poverty create a social environment in which organized drug crime can flourish. Confronting the systemic problems of Mexico could benefit counternarcotics efforts.

The Merida Initiative and Mexican Law Enforcement

Drug trafficking and organized crime are problems in Mexico, Central America, and the Caribbean. It has been difficult for the developing nations of the North American region to address drug transit and crime. Organized crime develops in weak nations, and strong and credible national governments are needed to address it (Olson and Donnelly 2009). Although democratic institutions are not absolutely essential, it is thought that they further crime control. Corruption of government officials and law enforcement has allowed drug organizations to exercise control in trafficking nations. Corruption becomes endemic due to a lower standard of living and salaries. As a result, law enforcement and the judiciary are weak in these neighbor nations.

The Merida Initiative involves the United States, Mexico, Central America, the Dominican Republic, and Haiti. It addresses drug trafficking, arms smuggling, money laundering, and organized criminal activity. The United States will input $1.5 billion over three years. Technological assistance and training will be provided, with much investment in helicopters, speedboats, and computerized intelligence systems to share databases.

Organized crime thrives in ungoverned spaces: nations where the government is weak and undemocratic. The drug-trafficking crisis of violence in Mexico has led to citizen protests and major reform of law enforcement. The federal police have been restructured into a national police force. Major problems exist at all levels of law enforcement because low salaries and poor working conditions attract less-educated personnel to what is a low social prestige occupation. Police are very vulnerable to corruption to augment their pay, and there is a history of corruption in both law enforcement and government, especially at the state and municipal levels (Grayson 2010).

The Mexican criminal justice system needs greater equity and transparency to reduce corruption and increase its credibility (Grayson 2010). It lacks resources for the investigation and prosecution of organized crime. Criminal justice personnel lack scientific, technical, and legal training. Organized criminals have infiltrated law enforcement, the courts, and prisons. Compounding this problem is a lack of institutional oversight.

Mexico is moving from an inquisitorial to an adversarial system of justice such as is practiced in the United States (Olson 2008). In inquisitorial systems prosecutors compile evidence and issue recommendations resulting in verdicts given behind closed doors. Individuals are not presumed innocent until evidence is provided and there is an absence of oral prosecution and defense, witness cross-examination, or defendant examination of evidence. This has led to inefficiency and human rights violations. Defendants are held until proven innocent. It is predicted that it will take into 2015 to switch completely over to an adversarial system.

Mexico has endemic corruption due to drug-organization payouts to officials and law-enforcement officers. Mexican federal, state, and local police, as well as the military, have been penetrated by organized crime and subject to bribery (Grayson 2010). For many Mexican government officials, corruption has been considered the norm rather than deviant. As a result, the professionalization of law enforcement has been a priority. Mexico has involved 24,000 of the military in counter-trafficking and preliminary evidence indicated that although violence is reduced where they are deployed, it is displaced, or a stalemate occurs. Nevetheless, the increase in drug-related violence since involvement of the Mexican military has led to a refocusing of the Merida Initiative on strengthening civilian law enforcement and providing support, screening of goods and people prior to border crossing, and strengthening Mexican communities with high poverty and crime rates, particularly Ciudad Juarez and Tijuana (Thompson and Lacey 2010).

The Calderón administration has sought to strengthen control over the military whose officers are involved in civilian law enforcement against drug trafficking. Amnesty International (2009) has issued a report documenting five cases in which the Mexican army is alleged to have committed extrajudicial killings, torture, arbitrary detention, and enforced disappearance—all human rights violations. This NGO believes that these cases establish a pattern of violation of international human rights law. In Mexico crimes committed by the military have been tried in a separate judicial system, which may not be constitutional. Amnesty International (2009, 20) believes that: "military courts lack the independence and impartiality to be able to try the cases of human rights violations implicating members of the military in line with international law." Both the United Nations and the Inter-American Court on Human Rights have issued policies or rulings that such cases should be tried in civilian courts. If Mexico's army is found to be in violation of human rights law, it would cause a withholding of 15% of Merida Initiative funding.

Recommendations for changing policy to deal with the Mexican drug crisis include reducing the demand for drugs among developed nations while increasing the costs of doing business for organized crime. Mexico has a crisis of public security. This is due to homicide, kidnappings, robbery, and piracy. The United States recognizes that public demand for drugs creates this social problem. Another issue is gun control as firearms trafficking is linked to drug-related violence.

Weapons Smuggling

Drug-related violence is connected to traffic in weapons smuggled from the U.S. border states to Mexico. During the first two years of Calderón's presidency, 31,000 weapons and 4 million rounds of ammunition have been seized. Over 3,000 grenades have been confiscated and 56,000 criminals arrested (Berrong 2009). The U.S. civilian gun market in Texas, Arizona, and California provides access to military weaponry for drug traffickers (GAO 2009). The absence of gun control in what is a lightly regulated form of commerce has resulted in constant piecemeal smuggling of arms to

Mexico. Gun shows, where individuals sell weapons without a background check, and other private sales are major sources. Dealers have seldom been investigated. Addressing this issue will be difficult because of powerful civilian pro-gun organizations in the United States. Among measures suggested are stopping import of assault weapons, extending gun checks to the secondary market of individual sales, and targeting border region gun dealers for yearly inspections and revoking the licenses of those found to be a prime source of trafficked weapons.

The smuggling of guns has negatively impacted U.S.-Mexico border security and caused increased weapons-related violence in both Mexico and Canada (Cook, Cukier, and Krause 2009). Although American citizens are not used to being connected to a trinational problem, both Mexico and Canada must deal with a side effect of relatively less-strict U.S. gun-control laws that allow purchase of weapons that are then smuggled across the border (Cook, Cukier, and Krause 2009, 275). Drug-related violence on the Mexico border and in the Mexican interior has intensified due to the illicit trade in U.S. weapons. Canadian gangs have an increased rate of homicide due to use of smuggled weapons in intergang conflict and against police or bystanders (Li 2008). Canadian police documented 117 gang-related homicides in 2007 and 69% were committed with a gun (Li 2008). British Columbia has experienced increased gun violence due to Mexican drug traffickers' conflicts with Canadian drug dealers. From January to March 2009 there were 40 shootings and 17 deaths. As a result, British Columbia's attorney general signed a joint agreement to combat weapons trafficking with Baja California, Mexico, state officials (CTV News 2009).

The United States has readily accessible guns. They can be purchased in small lots and smuggled at low cost using routes already established for other contraband trade. Guns can be legally bought from federal firearms licensees (FFLs) as long as the purchaser does not have a felony record and is a permanent resident alien or citizen (Cook, Cukier, and Krause 2009, 268, 272). Handguns may be purchased in multiples in the state of residence, but this type of sale needs to be reported by FFLs to the Bureau of Alcohol, Tobacco, Firearms, and Explosives (ATF). A criminal background check is meant to curb illegal purchases although false documentation can be used. In addition, firearms dealers may have knowledge that guns will be smuggled. Another way of purchasing illicit weapons in most states is at gun shows where private parties can sell without a background check (Wintermute 2007, 151). It is possible to buy a substantial number of guns this way although mass purchases of hundreds would likely come to the attention of authorities. Theft from FFLs and diversion from manufacturers and distributors are another source of guns (Cook, Cukier, and Krause 2009, 272).

False documentation, concealing guns, and false declaration are used to cross weapons over the Mexican and Canadian borders (Cook, Cukier, and Krause 2009, 275). Border inspectors are under time pressure and may inadvertently pass smuggled arms. Some inspectors may be bribed to let guns pass. The Mexican pattern is to purchase guns in the United States and send a few across the border at a time (Lumpe 1998, 2000). Although few guns are risked at once, a source such as a dealer can provide major quantities (Cook, Cukier, and Krause 2009, 276). ATF data analysis indicates that from 1996 to 2003, more than 30,000 firearms were involved in 127 cases with a 124-gun average (Cook, Cukier, and Krause 2009, 276).

Limited data from firearms tracing indicates that the United States is the main source of handguns used in Canadian crime and of crime weapons used in Mexico (GAO 2009). The illicit arms trade in Mexico is organized around point sources, dealers, and trafficking organizations rather than multiple diffused sources as the same dealers are used repeatedly (Cook, Cukier, and Krause 2009, 277). In recent years, high-caliber and power weapons such as the AK and AR-15 semiautomatic rifles are being trafficked into Mexico, especially from southwestern border states (GAO 2009, 4).

The United States is mobilizing border intelligence and security to apprehend arms traffickers (Cook, Cukier, and Krause 2009, 280). AFT processes online gun trace requests from Mexican officials through Project Gun Runner. One hundred special agents and 25 industry operations investigators are combating smuggling and weapons-related violence in border communities on both sides. Armas Cruzadas, a joint law-enforcement project with Mexico, facilitates intelligence sharing and coordination of operations (Seelke 2008, 18). Drug-related violence in Mexico is peaking and to curb arms smuggling, Mexico will inspect 1 in every 10 cars going south (Asbury 2008).

ATF trace data indicates that the major source states providing arms to Mexico are Texas (39%), California (20%), and

Arizona (10%) (GAO 2009, 4). Most firearms traced come from gun shops and pawn shops. About 6,700 gun and pawn shops are located in southwestern border states. Gun dealers can operate at gun shows or out of their own homes. "Straw purchasers," individuals without a criminal record, are paid by middlemen or drug-trafficking organizations to buy from shops and at gun shows (Cook, Cukier, and Krause 2009, 272). The bulk of guns smuggled to Mexico are used by drug-trafficking organizations who maintain support staff to procure weapons (Cook, Cukier, and Krause 2009, 281). Bringing weapons across the border in personal or commercial vehicles has been very successful.

Attempts to prevent arms trafficking are held back by loose inspection regulations and problems in organizing ICE and ATF to coordinate their efforts (Cook, Cukier, and Krause 2009, 280). Problem areas include no requirement for background checks on private firearm sales and limits to reporting of multiple sales. ATF has no history of cooperation with ICE and the two agencies lack a clear agreement on how to coordinate activities and what their cooperative roles should be. Gun-ownership tracking is problematic because data is not systematically collected on arms-trafficking confiscation and the investigation and prosecution of cases.

Cook, Cukier, and Krause (2009, 280), academicians, consider that the best policy option for reducing international gun trafficking out of the United States is legislating gun-control laws. This would be opposed by the gun lobby, including the National Rifle Association. Expansion of state regulations would better control buyers, such as legislating gun show laws for Arizona, New Mexico, and Texas, like those in place in California. Improved enforcement of existing laws that prohibit illicit sales at gun shows and more investigations of gun running would make it more difficult to traffic in arms.

If the United States is successful in reducing gun smuggling to Mexico, the price of arms will increase and other international sources will be sought (Cook, Cukier, and Krause 2009, 280). The military and Central America are alternate weapons sources. In Central America, millions of weapons used in various armed conflicts are still in use. Corruption in Mexico could lead to sale of police and military arms to organized crime groups.

If weapons became very costly and access to other sources could be checked, then weapons-related violence could be controlled but it is unlikely to eliminate gun smuggling. Canada has strong gun-control laws, a lower likelihood that guns would be diverted from the military or police, and vigorous enforcement, yet gun smuggling persists (Cook, Cukier, and Krause 2009). Curtailing gun smuggling would be likely to reduce gun availability, particularly for handguns, but the impact on the rate of violence is less predictable. The billions in profit from drug trafficking would permit cartels to seek alternate international sources.

Comparing and Contrasting: European Union v. North America

The United States maintains conventionally guarded land borders with Canada and Mexico. In contrast, the European Union (EU) has eliminated many of the internal land borders demarcating its members for its citizens, although noncitizen travel is documented. The Schengen agreement created a "borderless Europe" through which its citizens can freely travel without being stopped for inspection (Europa 2009). The EU countries include Austria, Belgium, Bulgaria, Cyprus, the Czech Republic, Denmark, Estonia, Finland, France, Germany, Greece, Hungary, Iceland, Italy, Latvia, Lithuania, Luxembourg, Malta, the Netherlands, Poland, Portugal, Romania, Slovakia, Slovenia, Spain, Sweden, Switzerland, and the United Kingdom. In 2009, Turkey was negotiating to join.

The Schengen agreement is named after a town in Luxembourg near where it was signed. In 1985, signing occurred in a boat on the Moselle River that demarcates the border between Luxembourg and Germany. The Convention applying the Schengen agreement took five more years for negotiation. The central idea of Schengen was to allow "free movement of persons."

Border-security arrangements for the European Union are substantially different than those of the United States. The external borders of the Schengen countries are the focus of entry and exit management. The Schengen agreement eliminated internal borders between the member states. Official ports of entry allow noncitizens in. Noncitizens are separated from EU citizens at these ports. If a U.S. citizen enters a Schengen country, he or she may continuously travel within the European Union. American citizens coming as visitors do not have to apply for a visa to travel if staying less than 90 days but must carry a passport valid for three months beyond expected departure (U.S. Department of State, n.d.). A visa is needed if the purpose is for employment, study, or like activities. Borderless travel has resulted in many unstaffed internal borders. Noncitizens entering the European Union need to have their passport stamped at an official port of entry for each country entered. Failure to document the visit can result in questioning, fines, and other consequences.

The Schengen agreement created a shared external border and EU member state rules for policing and surveillance of the common border. Shared policy includes hot pursuit: police can cross borders to chase criminals. The Schengen Information System (SIS) allows consulates and police agencies to pool and share information on criminals and stolen property (The Schengen acquis No date). Joint efforts are made to stop drug-related criminal activity. The policy for entry and visa issuance is coordinated between Schengen countries. A common policy on asylum is held in the region.

Article 2.2 of the Schengen treaty allows member countries to reinstate border control for security reasons over a short period of time. France reinstated border control for the 60th anniversary of D-Day in June 2004 and after the London bombings of 2005. Portugal, Finland, and Germany temporarily maintain border control for major sporting events such as the 2006 FIFA World Cup.

The European Union has a common external border and coordinates border surveillance. In light of the international terrorist threat, the open borders within the European Union have decreased control over travel within at a time when increased scrutiny of noncitizen entrants has increased importance. The contradiction between the free movement of people and goods and the need to regulate passage of people is difficult to resolve.

The European Union's cooperation in the visa issuance process has made it easier to attract educated and talented international migrants while allowing a unified process of sharing intelligence on terrorism. In the European Union, one visa is accepted by 24 member nations. The visa process often does not require an interview, and the wait time for processing is about three weeks. Externally, the European Union admits citizens of more countries without a visa than the United States. Although the United States has been the world's leading nation for immigration, the European Union is now friendlier.

In this context, it is helpful to examine the response of the European Union to boundary maintenance pre- and post-9/11.

Prior to the World Trade Center attacks, the European Union signed the Schengen agreement, dissolving its borders and permitting travel without passports for citizens of the European Union. After 9/11, the European Union departed from the United States' practice of limiting citizens' rights by emphasizing intelligence-led policing.

If terrorists are viewed as criminals who engage in routine activities, then police surveillance and citizen engagement can help to interdict them. The United States has invested billions in border security in the hope of intercepting terrorism suspects. The European Union has relied on policing and intelligence to prevent terrorism. Its tradition of dealing with nationalistic terrorism has led it to police terrorism as a crime rather than to become involved in major overseas wars like the United States. The European Union tries to rely on diplomacy, and the difference in international strategy has led to reduced support for the United States. Although the European Union is emphasizing external borders to allow freedom of movement internally, this concept does not seem likely to be adopted for North America. Canadians have rejected the idea of a "security perimeter" because of their need to retain a sense of Canada as a separate nation. Canada will cooperate in creating a Smart Border but will not relinquish national sovereignty. The asymmetry in power relations between the United States and Canada causes them to favor national border regulation rather than international policing cooperation, perhaps permanently postponing a "Fortress North America."

North American Continental Security Perimeter

Good border relations with Canada and Mexico are important to U.S. prosperity. Because these nations are the two largest trading partners of the United States, there are benefits from allowing the free flow of goods and services, as well as migrant labor, between the borders. However, there are concerns about having an unregulated free flow; therefore, security is essential. Thus far, high technology for open surveillance and direct inspection has been used to deal with gridlock in the movement of goods. After 9/11, the idea of a common external border for

North America was explored. Canadians rejected development of a continental security perimeter (see Diez 2007) because it was thought to compromise Canadian sovereignty. The greater economic and military strength of the United States creates an asymmetry in power relations between both the United States and Canada. The desire of Canada and Mexico to remain autonomous may preclude the formation of a continental security perimeter or an even more integrative regional economy such as that of the European Union. Terrorism increased the perceived importance of borders as sites of risk.

Defining Borders: Counterterrorism

European Union

The European Union must deal with terrorist threats from Islamist, ethnonationalist, and separatist terrorist groups. In comparison to the United States and Canada, the level of terrorist activity is much higher in Europe. The most notable European terrorist events have included March 2004 train bombings, July 2005 London mass-transit bombings, August 2006 plots in the United Kingdom and Germany, and the July 2007 London and Glasgow attacks that were prevented.

In 2008, terrorist activity in EU member states except for the United Kingdom decreased by 24 percent as compared to 2007 (Europol 2009). In 2008, 515 terrorist attacks were prevented before mission accomplishment. Over 1,000 terrorist suspects were arrested in 13 EU states. Most arrests were on suspicion of membership in a terrorist organization. Other arrests occurred for attack-related offenses, media propaganda, and the financing of terrorism. Most arrests are to prevent or disrupt terrorist actions.

After 9/11, Islamicist terrorism is perceived as the world's greatest threat. Nevertheless, the European Union experienced only one Islamicist attack in 2008 which occurred in the United Kingdom (Europol 2009). Separatist terrorism is highly prevalent, including Basque terrorist acts in Spain and France and Corsican terrorism in France. Four persons died in separatist attacks in 2008. As in Canada and the United States, the number of "homegrown" (i.e., within country) terrorist groups is increasing. The Islamicist terrorist threat is linked to the situation in warring and/or politically unstable countries: Iraq, Afghanistan, Pakistan, Somalia, Yemen, and India. Terrorist volunteers increasingly travel to Afghanistan, Pakistan, or Yemen rather than Iraq to fight.

Despite the relatively lower rate of Islamicist terrorist activity in the European Union, such attack plans aim at perpetrating indiscriminate mass casualties (Europol 2009). The wars in Afghanistan and Iraq and ethnic antagonism associated with anti-Muslim attitudes in Europe are thought to increase the threat of terrorism. Prisons and the Internet (Stenersen 2008), rather than mosques and public locations, are thought to be the focus for radicalization and recruitment because of anonymity. It is thought that second- and third-generation recruits are attracted to global jihad because they do not identify with the culture of their immigrant forebears but do not feel accepted in the West, which continues to view them as foreigners. Muslims in certain European nations continue to feel excluded after living there for years. Research on 242 European jihadist terrorists found that 40% were born in Europe and 55% were raised in Europe or were long-term residents (Baker 2007). As in the United States, adopting a strategy for fostering assimilation and identification of Muslim immigrants within European host societies would be proactive. Assimilated immigrants make a long-term commitment and can be socially included, not excluded. Unfortunately, al-Qaeda encourages Muslims who feel excluded in Europe to associate their social condition with regional conflicts such as those between Palestine and Israel and in Afghanistan, Iraq, and Pakistan. A failure to act to integrate new Muslim immigrants may create youth alienation and interest in Islamic jihad.

Law-enforcement activities for prevention of terrorism involve substantial investigations of funding, including criminal activities, and Internet recruitment (Europol 2009). Criminal investigation has established that Islamic terrorist organizations have perpetrated fraud while separatist organizations have been accused of extortion. These organizations actively use high-speed Internet and low-cost communication devices because of anonymity and lack of regulation (Stenersen 2008). They are used to spread propaganda and recruit.

European experts believe that terrorism will be a constant threat to national security (Europol 2009). Western nations' policies such as the wars in Afghanistan and Iraq and support of Israel are used to justify global jihad. Along with the United

States, European countries having a military presence in Muslim countries has precipitated jihadist video threats. "Homegrown" terrorism is likely to increase as radical imans are augmented by Internet recruitment. Homemade explosives are most likely to be used in attacks and present a constant risk in a chemical-using society.

The European Union has had a great deal more experience in combating terrorism than the United States and Canada. Prior to 2001, the European Union did not have a common definition of terrorism or penalties. A common policy was rapidly developed, but EU counterterrorism efforts substantially diverge from the U.S. War on Terror, which has external (wars in Afghanistan and Iraq) and internal dimensions. The interior and justice ministries, rather than defense, and intelligence services seek to disrupt terrorist networks. The European Security and Defense Policy (ESDP) has little input into counterterrorism within EU nations. It is not acceptable for the European military to be involved in homeland defense in the way that the U.S. armed forces and National Guard have been active at the U.S.-Mexico border. For example, instead of using a composite agency like the Department of Homeland Security (DHS), in the European Union, the transport ministries have increased airport security. The Agency for the Management of External Borders (FRONTEX) manages overseas external border management and risk analysis. Handling of counterterrorism is divided between many EU ministries.

The Europeans have utilized criminal law to deal with the terrorist threat. This is unlike the United States, where the criminalization of immigration law has greatly reduced rights of noncitizens. The internal problems of separatist and other nonjihadist terrorists and 1970s and 1980s experience with jihadist terrorism have led to intelligence-based counterterrorism programs. Great Britain is an example of a country with prior experience in terrorist prevention. Terrorist incidents initiated by the Irish Republican Army (IRA) led to the development of sophisticated intelligence-gathering operations in Great Britain. Although the European Union took security precautions after 9/11, its approach has emphasized international policing cooperation rather than the development of a surveillance net depriving citizens of constitutional protection of privacy as in the United States. To the degree that the European Union has been involved in the war in Afghanistan through the North

Atlantic Treaty Organization (NATO), and that Great Britain and Spain were involved in Iraq, they have increased their jihadist terrorist threat.

North America

Unlike the United States, Canada has used criminal law, not immigration law, as a method of controlling terrorists (Winderdyck and Sundberg 2010). Canada has allocated resources to interdiction of "irregular migrants" to prevent or intercept the entrance of terrorism suspects (Aiken 2006). On November 20, 2001, Canada passed its Anti-Terrorism Act. Although surveillance was increased, it included measures to safeguard the rights of Canadians under the Canadian Constitution (Royal Assent 2001). This act was criticized on the grounds that it would lead to racial profiling and a discriminatory arrest pattern.

Mexico's foreign policy is one of nonintervention, and cooperation with the United States only occurs if it is reciprocal. Mexico has a historic concern with how its undocumented citizens fare in the United States, and the lack of softening of U.S. response has created constraints on such cooperation (Hussain 2008). Mexico has a National Security Council, the Consejo Nacional de Seguridad Privada de Mexico (CNSP). The CNSP is over Centro de Información de Seguridad Nacional (CISEN), the directorate that gathers and interprets civil intelligence, and it develops and implements national security policy based on a prioritized Institutional Risks Agenda. Due to a history of asymmetry in relations between the United States and Mexico, there is no direct binational cooperative linkage between national security organizations.

Mexico has established the Sistema Nacional de Seguridad Publica (SNSP) (Presidency of the Republic 2009). It controls, among other public security tasks, the Policia Federal de Preventiva (PFP). The Mexican Federal Police have jurisdiction over many activities connected to border security, including customs, immigration, and efforts to counter drug trafficking. The PFP controls the Inter-Institutional Coordination Unit Gruppa Antiterrorista (UCIDGAT). UCIDGAT deals with insurgencies in Mexico and, with the PFP and the Mexican military, has been active at the border.

A major issue in Mexico has been low pay for police and corruption. The PFP and UCIDGAT pay better than other Mexican police agencies and are seeking to end or control corruption over the long term, although drug traffickers appear to have succeeded in corrupting some special police as investigations are under way.

Islamic terrorist groups that may have established a presence include the Lebanese Shi'ite group Hezbollah, which is thought to be in Monterrey, Mexico, where there are Palestinian and Lebanese communities. The Mexican government does not believe that al-Qaeda operatives are established there.

Conclusion

The land, air, and maritime borders of the United States involve a degree of international linkage unprecedented in human history. As a result, transnational threats have developed which require bilateral and international cooperation in law enforcement. It is likely that Interpol and other international policing organizations will become more prominent in efforts to control transnational crimes such as sex, drug, and arms trafficking. A major question is whether U.S. politicians will come to recognize the degree to which unilateral solutions can impede transnational crime control efforts.

The War on Terror provides an example of how international cooperation can dissolve in the face of unilateral actions. The United States faces unprecedented challenges to its economy due to globalization and had the sympathy of the world after the 9/11 attacks. This developed in cooperation in the war in Afghanistan, which was primarily begun in an effort to dismantle al-Qaeda and capture Osama bin Laden. Almost a decade later, bin Laden was still at large and the Taliban was attempting to retake the country. The war in Iraq, with its failure to locate weapons of mass destruction, the use of torture and extraterritorial detention, and other unilateral actions, alienated many countries. To combat transnational crime, there must be international policing cooperation on a global scale rather than just with Canada and Mexico and political ties must be renewed.

The United States has dimmed its democratic luster in the eyes of the international community despite its record in the promotion of international crime initiatives in the area of trafficking. Tremendous amounts of taxpayer income are spent on border control, particularly at the U.S.-Mexico border, with less attention paid to the international linkages involved. For example, the Merida Initiative involves the United States, Mexico, and Central America but the cocaine trafficked through Mexico originates in Colombia. In the manner in which armed conflict united countries through such venues as NATO, the fight against transnational threats will involve giving up antiquated unilateral initiatives for binational and especially, multilateral ventures.

References

Ackleson, Jason, and Justin Krasner. 2006. "The Security and Prosperity Partnership of North America." *American Review of Canadian Studies* 36(2): 207–232.

Aiken, Sharryn. 2006. "Interdiction and the Post 9/11 Security Agenda: A Canadian Perspective." Le Centres d'etudes et de recherchés internationales. http://www.cerium.ca/article1932.html.

Amnesty International. 2009. "Mexico: New Reports on Human Rights Violations by the Military." http://www.amnesty.org/en/library/asset/AMR41/058/2009/en/e1a94ad6-3df1-4724-a545-f0b93f39af69/amr410582009en.pdf.

Andreas, Peter, and Nadelman. 2008. *Policing the Globe: Criminalization and Crime Control in International Relations.* New York: Oxford University Press.

Andreas, Peter, and Timothy Synder, eds. 2000. *The Wall Around the World: State Borders and Immigration Controls in North America and Europe.* Lanham, MD: Rowan and Littlefield.

Armitrage, David T. 2007. "The European Union: Measuring Counter-Terrorism Cooperation. Strategic Forum." http://www.ndu.edu/inss/Strforum/SF229/SF229.pdf.

Asbury, John. 2008 "Guns Move South via Inland Gangs." *Press-Enterprise*, September 28. http://www.pe.com/localnews/inland/stories/PE_News_Local_S_guns29.214203b.html.

Bach, Robert L. 2003. "Global Mobility, Inequality, and Security." *Journal of Human Development* 4 (2): 227–245.

Baker, Edwin. 2007. "Jihadi Terrorists in Europe, Their Characteristics and Circumstances in Which They Joined the Jihad: An Exploratory Study." Clingendael Institute. http://www.clingendael.nl/publications/2006/20061200_cscp_csp_bakker.pdf.

Banco de México. 2009. "SE27803: Remesas Familiares, Total." www.banxico.org.mx.

Beare, Margaret E. 2003. "Organized Corporate Criminality: Corporate Complicity in Tobacco Smuggling." In *Critical Reflections on Transnational Organized Crime, Money Laundering and Corruption*, ed. Beare, 183–206. Toronto: University of Toronto Press.

Beittel, June S. 2009. "Congressional Research Report for Congress: Mexico's Drug Related Violence." Washington DC: Congressional Research Service. http://www.fas.org/sgp/crs/row/R40582.pdf.

Berrong, Stephanie. 2009. "Cooperation on the Border: Security Management." *The Magazine*. http://www.securitymanagement.com/article/cooperation-border-005427.

Blumenthal, Ralph. 2005. "Texas Town Is Unnerved by Violence in Mexico." *New York Times*, August 11. http://www.nytimes.com/2005/08/11/national/.

Bunker, Pamela L., Lisa J. Campbell, and Robert J. Bunker. 2010. "Torture, Beheadings and Narcocultos." *Small Wars and Insurgencies* 21(1): 145–178.

Casteel, Steven W. 2003. "Narco-Terrorism, International Drug Trafficking and Terrorism—A Dangerous Mix." Statement before the U.S. Senate Judiciary Committee, May 20. http://www.usdoj.gov/dea/pubs/cngrtest/ct052003.html.

Castillo, Eduardo. 2010. "22,700 killed in Drug Related Violence in Mexico Since '06." *Houston Chronicle*, April 13. http://www.chron.com/disp/story.mpl/ap/latinamerica/6957687.html.

CONEVAL. 2009. "Reporta CONEVAL cifras de pobreza por ingresos 2008." El Consejo Nacional de Evaluación de la Política de Desarrollo (CONEVAL), July 18.

Cook, Colleen W. 2007. *Congressional Research Service Report: Mexico's Drug Cartels*. http://ftp.fas.org/sgp/crs/row/RL34215.pdf.

Cook, Philip J., and Anthony A. Braga. 2001. "Comprehensive Firearms Tracing: Strategic and Investigative Uses of New Data on Firearms Markets." *Arizona Law Review* 43 (2): 277–309.

Cook, Philip J., Wendy Cukier, and Keith Krause. 2009. "The Illicit Firearms Trade in North America." *Criminology and Criminal Justice* 9 (3): 265–286.

CTV News. 2009. "Cops in Metro Vancouver Struggle to End Gun Violence." http://www.ctvbc.ctv.ca/servlet/an/local/CTVNews/.

Diez, Jordi. 2007. "North America's Security Perimeter." *Security and Defense Studies Review* 7(1). http://www.ndu.edu/chds/Journal/PDF/2007/Diez_Article-formatted.pdf.

Dunn, Timothy. 1996. *The Militarization of the Border, 1978–1992: Low Intensity Conflict Doctrine Comes Home*. Austin, TX: CMAS Books, Center for Mexican American Studies, University of Texas.

Europa. 2009. "Summaries of EU Legislation: The Schengen Area and Cooperation." http://europa.eu/legislation_summaries/justice_freedom_security/free_movement_of_persons_asylum_immigration/l33020_en.htm.

Europol. 2009. "TE-SAT 2009: EU Terrorism Situation and Trend Report." http://www.scribd.com/doc/14818199/EuroPol-2009-report.

Farr, Kathryn. 2005. *Sex Trafficking: The Global Market in Women and Children.* New York: Worth Publishers.

Fernandez-Kelly, Patricia. "Borders for Whom? The Role of NAFTA in Mexico- U.S. Migration." *Annals of the American Academy of Political and Social Science* 610: 98–118.

GAO (Government Accountability Office). 2007. "Drug Control: U.S. Assistance Has Helped Mexican Counter-narcotics Efforts, but the Flow of Illicit Drugs into the United States Remains High."

GAO (Government Accountability Office). 2009. "Firearms Trafficking: U.S. Efforts to Combat Arms Trafficking to Mexico Face Planning and Coordination Challenges." http://www.gao.gov/htext/d09709.html.

Grayson, George W. 2009. *Mexico's Struggle with "Drugs" and "Thugs."* Foreign Policy Association, Headline Series No. 331, New York, NY, Winter.

Heyman, Josiah. 2004. "Ports of Entry as Nodes in the World System." *Identities: Global Studies in Culture and Power* 11: 303–327.

High, Travis Scott. 2009. "The Mexican Economy in 2009." Woodrow Wilson Mexico Institute. http://wilsoncenter.org/topics/docs/Mexican%20Economy%20in%202009.pdf.

Hussain, Imtiaz. 2008. "Mexico." In *PSI Handbook of Global Security and Intelligence,* vol. 1, ed. Stuart Farr, 64–97. Westport, CT: Praeger Security International.

ILO. 2008. "World of Work Report 2008: Income Inequalities in the Age of Financial Globalization." International Labor Organization. http://www.ilo.org/public/english/bureau/inst/download/world08.pdf.

Jane's Information Group. 2009. "Security-Mexico." February 20.

Johnson, Kevin. 2009. "Violence Drops in U.S. Cities Neighboring Mexico." *USA Today*, December 28. http://www.usatoday.com/news/nation/2009-12-27-Mexico-border-violence_N.htm?csp=34&utm_source=feedburner&utm_medium=feed&utm_campaign=Feed%3A+usatoday-NewsTopStories+%28News+-+Top+Stories%29.

Kleeman, Edward R. 2009. "Human Smuggling and Human Trafficking." In *Oxford Handbook of Crime and Public Policy*, ed. Michael Tonry, 209–327. New York: Oxford University Press.

Lacey, Marc. 2009a. "In Mexico, Ambivalence on a Drug Law." *New York Times*, August 23. http://www.nytimes.com/2009/08/24/world/americas/.

Lacey, Marc. 2009b. "In Mexican Drug War, Investigators Are Fearful." *New York Times,* October 16. http://www.nytimes.com/2009/10/17/world/americas/.

Lacey, Marc, and Ginger Thompson. 2010. "Two Drug Slayings in Mexico Rock U.S. Consulate." *New York Times,* March 14. http://www.nytimes.com/2010/03/15/world/americas/15juarez.html.

Lehti, M., and K. Aromaa. 2006. "Trafficking for Sexual Exploitation." In *Crime and Justice: A Review of Research* 34(1): 133–227

Li, Geoffrey. 2008. "Homicide in Canada 2007." *Juristat* 28 (9): 1–26. http://www.statcan.gc.ca/pub/85-002-x/2008009/article/10671-eng.pdf.

Lumpe, Lora. 1998. "The US Arms Both Sides of Mexico's Drug War." *Covert Action Quarterly* 61: 39–46.

Lumpe, Lora, ed. 2000. *Running Guns: The Global Black Market in Small Arms.* London: Zed Books.

Malkin, Elisabeth. 2009. "Leader Urges Cooperation Against Ills Mexico Faces." *New York Times,* September 2. http://topics.nytimes.com/top/news/international/countriesandterritories/mexico/drug_trafficking/index.html?offset=30&s=newest.

McKinley Jr., James C. 2009. "U.S. Arrests Hundreds in Raids on Drug Cartel." *New York Times,* October 22. http://www.nytimes.com/2009/10/23/us/23bust.html?_r=1&pagewanted=1.

Moore, Solomon. 2009. "Tougher Border Can't Stop Mexican Marijuana Cartels." *New York Times,* February 2. http://www.nytimes.com/2009/02/02/.

Moran, Terry. 2009. "Mexico President Vows to Win Drug War." *ABC News,* April 15. http://abcnews.go.com/Politics/story?id=7342256&page=1.

Napolitano, Janet. 2009. "Napolitano's Testimony before Senate Homeland Security and Governmental Affairs Committee, Southern Border Violence: Homeland Security Threats, Vulnerabilities, and Responsibilities." Council on Foreign Relations. http://www.cfr.org/publication/18945.

OECD (Organization for Economic Co-operation and Development). 2008. *Growing Unequal: Income Distribution and Poverty in OECD Countries.* Paris: Organization for Economic Cooperation and Development.

Office of the Attorney General. 2008. "Attorney General's Annual Report to Congress and Assessment of the U.S. Government's Activities to Combat Trafficking in Persons Fiscal Year 2007." http://www.justice.gov/ag/annualreports/tr2007/agreporthumantraffic-ing2007.pdf.

Office of the Inspector General of the Department of Defense, Department of Justice, Central Intelligence Agency, National Security Agency, Office of the Director of National Intelligence. 2009. *(U) Unclassified Report on the President's Surveillance Program*. July 10. http://documents.nytimes.com/federal-report-on-the-president-s-surveillance-program#p=1.

Olson, Eric. 2008. "Six Key Issues in U.S.-Mexico Security Cooperation." Woodrow Wilson Center Mexico Institute. http://www.wilsoncenter.org/news/docs/Olson%20Brief.pdf.

Olson, Eric L., and Robert Donnelly. 2009. "Report from the U.S.-Mexico-Security Cooperation Working Group and a Conference on International Experiences in Combating Organized Crime: Confronting the Challenges of Organized Crime in Mexico and Latin America." http://www.wilsoncenter.org/news/docs/Confronting%20Challenges%20of%20Organized%20Crime-%20Eric%20Olson%20Robert%20Donnelly.pdf.

Payan, Tony. 2006. *The Three U.S.-Mexico Border Wars: Drugs, Immigration, and Homeland Security*. Westport, CT: Praeger Security International.

Peters, Katherine McIntire. 2009. "DEA: Mexican Drug Violence Is a Sign of Progress, Not Failure." *Government Executive*, April 15. http://www.govexec.com/dailyfed/0409/041509kp1.htm.

Pierce, Glenn, and Anthony Braga. 2008. "US Illegal Firearms Markets: Potential Methods of Control." Unpublished paper presented at the New Directions in Drug and Crime Control conference, El Colegio de México, 28–9 April.

Presidency of the Republic. 2009. "Mexico's National Public Security System and Council." November 30. http://www.mexidata.info/id2480.html.

Rauschbaum, William K. "Revelations Begin in Routine Tax Inquiry." *New York Times,* March 11, 2008. http://www.nytimes.com/2008/03/11/nyregion/11inquire.html.

Richard, Stephanie. 2005. "State Legislation and Human Trafficking: Helpful or Hurtful?" *University of Michigan Journal of Law Reform* 38: 447–477.

Risen, James, and Eric Lichtblau. 2005. "Bush Lets U.S. Spy on Callers without Courts." *New York Times*, December 16, A1.

Risen, James, and Eric Lichtblau. 2009. "Court Affirms Wiretapping Without Warrants." *New York Times,* January 15. http://www.nytimes.com/2009/01/16/washington/16fisa.html?_r=1.

Royal Assent of Bill C-36. 2001. The Anti-Terrorism Act. http://www.justice.gc.ca/en/news/nr/2001/doc_28217.html.

Schengen Acquis. n.d. **eur-lex.europa.eu**/LexUriServ/LexUriServ.do?.

Seelke, Claire Ribando. 2009. "Congressional Research Service Report for Congress: Merida Initiative for Mexico and Central America: Funding and Policy Issues." http://www.wilsoncenter.org/news/docs/CRS%20Mérida%20Initiative%20for%20Mexico%20and%20Central%20America%20Funding%20Policy%20Issues.pdf.

Sele, Andrew. 2009. "Money, Guns and Drugs: Are U.S. Inputs Fueling Violence on the U.S.-Mexico Border?" Testimony by Andrew Sele to the House Subcommittee on National Security and Foreign Affairs. March 9. http://nationalsecurity.oversight.house.gov/documents/20090313115456.pdf.

Shifter, Michael. 2007. "Latin America's Drug Problem." *Current History*. February.

Stenersen, Anne. 2008. "The Internet: A Virtual Training Camp?" *Terrorism and Political Violence* 20 (2): 215–233.

Thompson, Ginger, and Marc Lacey. 2010. "U.S. and Mexico Revise Joint Anti-Drug Strategy." *New York Times*, March 23. http://www.nytimes.com/2010/03/24/world/americas/24mexico.html.

United Nations Office on Drugs and Crime. 2001. *United Nations Convention Against Transnational Organized Crime and the Protocols Thereto*. http://www.unodc.org/documents/treaties/UNTOC/Publications/TOC%20Convention/TOCebook-e.pdf.

United Nations Office on Drugs and Crime. 2006. *Trafficking in Persons: Global Patterns*. April. www.unodc.org/pdf/traffickinginpersons_report_2006ver2.pdf.

U.S. Attorney, Southern District of New York. 2008. "175 Alleged Gulf Cartel Members and Associates Arrested in Massive International Law Enforcement Operation." http://www.usdoj.gov/usao/nys/pressreleases/September08/projectreckoningpr.pdf.

U.S. Department of Justice National Drug Intelligence Center. 2006. "National Drug Threat Assessment, 2006." http://www.justice.gov/ndic/pubs11/18862/index.htm.

U.S. Department of Justice National Drug Intelligence Center. "National Drug Threat Assessment, 2009." http://www.usdoj.gov/ndic/pubs31/31379/index.htm.

U.S. Department of Justice National Drug Intelligence Center. 2009. National Drug Threat Assessment, 2010. http://www.justice.gov/ndic/pubs38/38661/38661p.pdf.

U.S. Department of Homeland Security. 2009. "Secretary Napolitano Announces Major SW Border Initiative." http://www.dhs.gov/ynews/releases/pr_1237909530921.shtm.

U.S. Department of State. 2008. Trafficking in Persons Report 2008. http://www.state.gov/g/tip/rls/tiprpt/2008.

U.S. Department of State. N.d. *Schengen Fact Sheet*. Accessed September 3, 2009. http://travel.state.gov/travel/cis_pa_tw/cis/cis_4361.html.

Clinton, Hillary Rodham, U.S. Department of State. 2009. "Remarks with Mexican Foreign Secretary Patricia Espinosa after Their Meeting." Mexico City, Mexico, March 25.

U.S. Joint Forces Command. 2008. "The Joint Operating Environment 2008: Challenges and Implications for the Future Joint Force." December. http://www.jfcom.mil/newslink/storyarchive/2008/JOE2008.pdf.

Victims of Trafficking and Violence Protection Act of 2000. Public Law 106-386-OCT 28, 2000. http://www.state.gov/documents/organization/10492.pdf.

Weinburg, Paul. 2009. "US-Canada: Shared Border, Unilateral Policy?" May 29. http://www.globalissues.org/news/2009/05/29/1664.

Winterdyck, John A., and Kelly W. Sundberg. 2010b. "Shifts in Canadian Border Security." In *Border Security in the Al-Qaeda Era*, ed. John A. Winterdyk and Kelly W. Sundberg, 3–36. New York: CRC Press.

Wintemute, Garen J. 2007. "Gun Shows across a Multistate American Gun Market: Observational Evidence of the Effects of Regulatory Policies." *Injury Prevention* 13: 150–155.

World Bank. 2001. *Development Cooperation and Conflict, Operational Policy 230*. Washington, DC: World Bank.

4

Chronology

Establishing the Geographical Boundaries of the United States through Frontier Expansion

1783	The Treaty of Paris ends the War of Independence between Great Britain and the 13 U.S. colonies and establishes the boundary with British Canada. The 13 colonies become the United States. The exact geographic coordinates are left unclear. The boundary becomes a source of conflict as both nations want territorial expansion.
1794	The Jay Treaty establishes an International Boundary Commission for the United States and British Canada.
1789	The Tariff Act creates U.S. Customs, whose job is to collect taxes on imports, known as customs duties. U.S. Customs is the primary source of federal revenue until an income tax law is passed in 1913.
1795	The Naturalization Act restricts citizenship eligibility to "free white persons" who have lived in the United States for longer than two years and are willing to renounce allegiance to the sending country.
1798	The Alien and Sedition Act allows for deportation of any foreigner considered dangerous. The Naturalization Act is revised to establish eligibility for citizenship after 14 years of residence.

1802	An act of Congress allows for citizenship eligibility after five years of residence.
1808	Congress prohibits the importation of slaves.
1812	War of 1812 involves armed conflict between the United States and Great Britain. The British occupy a majority of eastern Maine.
1818	A boundary agreement between Great Britain and the United States places the British America border at the 49th parallel from the Lake of the Woods to the Rockies. The Lake of the Woods is a body of water in the Canadian provinces of Ontario and Manitoba that border on the U.S. state of Minnesota. Great Britain and the United States agree to jointly occupy Oregon.
1819	Congress enacts a count of aliens entering the United States and requires shipmasters to provide a manifest of all aliens transported for immigration. The secretary of state is required to inform the Congress of the number admitted.
1821	Mexico wins its independence from Spain.
1824	The Mexican Constitution grants states considerable autonomy but places its territories under the authority of the Mexican Congress. The territory of Texas is placed with Coahuila. Tensions develop between the Mexican government and the frontier territories.
1836	The Texas Rebellion establishes Texas as independent from Mexico. Mexican outlawing of slavery and high taxation precipitate this conflict.
1837	A rebellion in Eastern British America results in U.S. discussions about its annexation. U.S. citizens assist rebels in Canada and some cross into Canada and enter into military conflict. Great Britain retaliates by crossing into the United States. An incident occurs involving the British destruction of an American-owned ship, the *Caroline*, used to supply the rebels, results in a U.S. request for an apology. Great Britain does not apologize.
1838	The United States and Great Britain enter into a dispute over the right to occupy the territory of Oregon. The area west of the Rockies in what is now Oregon is held jointly by the United States and Great Britain. In the United States, it is referred to as Oregon County, while it is known as the

	Columbia Department of the Hudson's Bay Company in British America.
1841	Canada passes the Customs Consolidation Act and places a tariff on imports.
1842	The Weber-Ashburton Treaty with Great Britain settles a dispute over territory in New Brunswick and the United States by allocating seven-twelfths to the United States. Lumberjacks enter into conflict over use of the tree resources.
1845	The United States annexes Texas.
1846–1848	The U.S.-Mexico War ends with the Treaty of Guadalupe Hidalgo in 1848. Mexico is forced to sell one-third of its territory to the United States. A pattern of asymmetrical relations in which the United States dominates its relationship with Mexico is established.

The Treaty of Guadalupe Hidalgo grants citizenship to Mexicans in the ceded territories.

1846	The Oregon Treaty between the United States and Great Britain gives control of the Oregon territory to the United States. It establishes the boundary between the United States and British America as at the 49th parallel with the exception of Vancouver Island. The British receive the right to navigate the Columbia River. The Strait of San Juan de Fuca is described as having a boundary through the middle of the channel. This treaty gives the United States control of the territories that become the states of Oregon, Washington, Idaho, and Montana.
1850–1859	Mass immigration of Chinese to the West Coast causes a nativist reaction. The Know Nothing political party advocates restriction on immigration and naturalization.
1853	The Gadsden Purchase of territory from Mexico is negotiated. Approximately 29,000 square miles of territory in what is present-day Arizona and parts of New Mexico are acquired. The land lost as a result of the U.S.-Mexico war expands to fully one-half of Mexico's prior territory.
1859	The "Pig War" results from conflict between the United States and Great Britain over the ownership of the San Juan Islands in the Strait of San Juan de Fuca. The Oregon treaty's maritime boundary, set

1859 (*cont.*)	as the middle of the channel, is vague. The blood-less dispute is named after an incident in which a pig was shot, becoming the only casualty.
1867	Canadian independence brings unification of the remaining British North American colonies. In the remainder of the 19th century, this border is unguarded and relatively unmonitored with few checkpoints.

The Peonage Abolition Act makes it a crime to force the labor of any man, woman, or child whether through debt or slavery. |
1868	Ratification of the Fourteenth Amendment stipulates that all individuals born or naturalized in the United States are under U.S. jurisdiction. No state is allowed to abridge citizens' right to due process of law or equal protection under the law. Citizenship rights are granted to former slaves and the phrase "free white persons" is removed from the Constitution to include blacks. The Fourteenth Amendment affirms the right of the federal government to regulate immigration and naturalized citizenship.
1870	The Naturalization Act is amended to restrict citizenship to "white persons and persons of African descent," thereby excluding Asians.
1875	The Page Law excludes certain social categories of persons from entrance including convicts and prostitutes. Immigration is made a matter of federal policy and all state immigration laws are declared unconstitutional.
1878	The Posse Comitas Act restricts but does not totally disallow military participation in domestic law enforcement. This act later permits the military to assist the U.S. Border Patrol at the U.S.-Mexico border in the prevention of drug trafficking and undocumented immigration.
1882	The Chinese Exclusion Act prohibits further Chinese immigration. This act is renewed in 1888, 1892, and 1904.

The Immigration Act of 1882 levies a "head tax" of 50 cents per immigrant and designates social categories of individuals who are restricted from coming, including "lunatics" and individuals "likely to become a public charge." |

1890–1899	A degree of monitoring is established by placing U.S. checkpoints with immigration inspectors at the Canadian border because European immigrants are crossing to avoid inspection and paying a head tax. Canadians are exempt from the head tax but subject to health, criminal history, and contract labor scrutiny.
1885	The Alien Contract Labor Law prohibits employers, companies, or individuals from bringing immigrants under contract to work in the United States while prepaying passage. Domestics and skilled workers needed for new trades or industries are an exception.
1886	U.S. Customs inspectors begin to patrol the Mexico border on horseback to prevent smuggling. Revenue cutters patrol at the maritime boundaries.
1888	The Scott Act rescinds reentry permits for Chinese laborers, preventing them from returning.
1891	Congress designates further social categories of individuals to be excluded from admission, including persons "suffering from a loathsome or contagious disease" or convicted of a "misdemeanor involving moral turpitude." The Immigration Act is revised to create a Bureau of Immigration within the Treasury Department. The position of "Superintendent of Immigration" is created.
1892	The Geary Act deprives Chinese immigrants of most legal rights and requires them to have a certificate of residence.
1894	Immigration inspectors are permitted to bar specified social categories of individuals from entrance, including Chinese persons.
1901	The assassination of President William McKinley by a Polish anarchist precipitates the Anarchist Exclusion Act. It restricts entrance of individuals based on their political beliefs.
1903	A joint tribunal involving the United States, Canada, and Great Britain clarifies northern water boundaries, including the Great Lakes.
	Congress designates immigration as a responsibility of the Department of Commerce and Labor.
1906	A Naturalization Act codifies naturalization practice.

1907	Congress passes the White Slave Traffic Act. It makes bringing girls and women for the purpose of prostitution or immorality a crime.
1911	The Dillingham Commission Report makes recommendations to restrict immigration. A Canadian Immigration Act creates an Immigration Department.
1908	The Gentleman's Agreement between the United States and Japan establishes that Japanese will no longer immigrate and that discrimination against Japanese present in the United States will end.
1910–1920	The Mexican Revolution begins in 1910 and causes refugee flows. The United States maintains its neutrality but seeks to protect its sovereignty and the security of citizens. The military and state and local law enforcement are used to protect U.S. interests.
1916	Pancho Villa crosses the border into Columbus, New Mexico, killing 17 U.S. citizens and burning and looting. The United States retaliates by invading with a force led by General John "Black Jack" Pershing.
1917	The United States enters World War I. Congress enacts an Immigration Act to exclude illiterates. Individuals are required to be able to read at least 40 words in any language. The Department of State and the Department of Labor enact a regulation requiring individuals to obtain a visa in their home country before appearing at a port of entry.

The Closing of the Nation's Borders to Immigration

1918	The president is given broad powers to restrict entry or departure at the borders during times of war. This policy is repeated in subsequent conflicts.
1919	The Covenant of the League of Nations stipulates that members should not intervene in the affairs of independent nations. National boundaries begin to be used to regulate the flow of people and goods.

	The "Red Scare" due to the Bolshevik Revolution in Russia results in the deportation of "radical" aliens considered a threat to security.
1920–1933	Prohibition outlaws the sale and consumption of alcohol in the United States. Smuggling of alcohol from Canada and Mexico becomes a problem. Many citizens cross to Canada or Mexico to drink.
1920	The Royal Canadian Mounted Police are organized. Together with customs, immigration inspectors, and police, they work to maintain border security.
1921	Negative public reaction to mass immigration from south and southeastern Europe, whose entrants are deemed "racially inferior," results in the Immigration Act of 1921 which restricted entrance to no more than 3% of the population from a particular country in the United States at the time of the 1910 Census.
1924	The Immigration Act (Johnson-Reed Act) resets the national origin quota to a maximum of 2% of the foreign-born population from that country as counted by the 1890 Census. This results in a shift in immigration from south and southeastern Europe to northwestern Europe. Most Asians are barred as ineligible for citizenship.
1924	The U.S. Border Patrol is established by Congress for the purpose of preventing unauthorized entry and smuggling. It is given the additional responsibility of interior enforcement through identification and deportation of undocumented immigrants and migrants. Its deployment establishes a trend in which the U.S.-Mexico border rather than the Canadian border or interior enforcement is the primary objective in control of immigration.
1940	A Registration Law is passed by Congress. Aliens are required to register their addresses every year. (This requirement ended in 1980.) The Immigration and Naturalization Service is unable to efficiently file the forms, which become backlogged or lost.
1941	The attack on Pearl Harbor brings the United States into World War II.
1942	The United States and Mexico begin the Bracero program, which allows Mexican nationals to enter as temporary workers to fill agricultural labor shortages.

1942 (*cont.*)	The program leads to the development of migratory networks which link sending and receiving communities. Gradually Mexicans begin to migrate without authorization for work.
1945	The United Nations Charter reaffirms the policy that independent nations should not intervene in each other's affairs. The sovereignty of states is considered to allow for regulation of people and goods crossing borders.
1949	The Agricultural Act is passed by Congress with a provision to recruit Mexican temporary workers for agriculture. The United Nations issues the Convention for the Suppression of the Traffic in Persons and the Exploitation of the Prostitution of Others.
1952	An immigration act (McCaron Walter Act) is passed by Congress. It ends racial restrictions on immigration but keeps a quota system and restricted entrance from specific countries. For the first time, familial relationships and skills are recognized as immigration selection criteria.
1954	Operation Wetback of the U.S. Border Patrol seeks to apprehend Mexican migrants in the Southwest who entered without authorization, primarily for agricultural work.
1956	The United Nations incorporates the International Criminal Police Organization (INTERPOL). It deals with migrant smuggling, human trafficking, and drugs and arms smuggling, among other transnational crimes.
1960–present	The United States begins a domestic and international campaign to prohibit illegal drugs and their trafficking.

Opening of the Nation's Borders to Immigration

1965	The Immigration and Nationality Act is passed by Congress. It ends the use of a quota system and

establishes a new system based on family relationships and skills preferences, standardizing the process of admission and establishing a country-specific limit of 20,000 for Eastern Hemisphere nations, allowed a total of 170,000. For the first time, Western Hemisphere nations are placed under a quota, set at 120,000. This places social constraints on the ability to legally migrate from Mexico and Central America, expanding unauthorized migration.

1973	President Nixon establishes the Drug Enforcement Administration (DEA).
1976	In *United States v. Martinez-Fuente* the Supreme Court rules that it is legal to place checkpoints within 100 miles of the border and to search vehicles for unauthorized entrants.
	Congress amends the visa system by extending the quota limits applied to Western Hemisphere countries.
1978– present	A process of militarization of the U.S.-Mexico border begins with the use of troops to stop drug trafficking. Each step toward militarization parallels an increase in relatively permanent unauthorized immigration.
1978	President Carter establishes a Select Committee on Immigration to issue recommendations about the growing unauthorized immigrant population.
1980– present	After the United States succeeds in limiting cocaine trafficking off the coast of Florida and takes action against Colombian cartel leaders, cocaine is increasingly trafficked across the Mexican border and Mexico develops major drug-trafficking organizations.
1981	During a recession, the Select Committee on Immigration issues its report. It recommends changes to the immigration system and border enforcement that are enacted in the Immigration Control and Reform Act of 1986 and continue to influence policy to the present.
1982	Congress begins a divisive debate about immigration reform.
1986	The Immigration Reform and Control Act (IRCA) is designed to control undocumented immigration through legalization and criminal and civil sanctions for employers hiring undocumented immigrants.

1986 (*cont.*)	IRCA allows amnesty for persons entering without authorization before January 1, 1981, who can provide documentation to prove their presence.
	IRCA fails to stop unauthorized migration because of a major loophole. Employers are not asked to verify employee documents, and an underground industry in false documentation develops.
	The Immigration and Naturalization Service, with the Department of Justice, does not initially apply criminal sanctions or devote sufficient personnel to interior enforcement of this IRCA. Instead the U.S. Border Patrol is repeatedly given increased funding for staff and equipment, and this effort is insufficient to prevent a large buildup in the unauthorized immigrant population. This buildup partly occurs because the difficulty in border crossing encourages migrants to stay permanently as immigrants.
1986	The United States and Canada reach a bilateral agreement to strengthen cross-border trade.

Expansion of Trade and Border Enforcement

1988	The 1988 Omnibus Anti-Drug Act stipulates that permanent resident aliens convicted of homicide, rape, drug trafficking, and/or arms trafficking, which are classified as aggravated felonies, must be immediately deported, referred to as expedited removal, after serving their sentence. This is to be done without access to a lawyer and with expanded exclusion from reentry.
	This law is applied retroactively and begins a process of increasing denial of due process rights under the law to noncitizens. The Institutional Removal Program (IRP) is begun to remove aliens who have committed an aggravated felony crime from the United States on completion of their sentence.
	The United States–Canada Free Trade Agreement reduces barriers to trade.

Three Syrians are arrested by U.S. Customs for attempting to cross the border in possession of explosives.

1990   The Immigration Act is passed by Congress. It establishes new hemispheric and worldwide quotas, redefines the familial and skills preferences, and adds a diversity criterion.

1993   The World Trade Center bombing involves a large explosive device placed in a vehicle which is placed below the North Tower. Six people are killed and 1,042 injured. This terrorist action is carried out by individuals with ties to al-Qaeda. The chief conspirator, Ramzi Yousef, had received explosives training in an al-Qaeda camp.

Operation Blockade, later renamed Operation Hold the Line, is begun in El Paso. U.S. Border Patrol agents are positioned in high-visibility positions along the borderline, a strategy called "line watching."

The North American Free Trade Agreement (NAFTA) between the United States, Canada, and Mexico opens the borders to economic trade but not immigration.

1994–2004   Estimates are that 2,978 migrants trying to enter without inspection have died trying to cross in more remote and dangerous regions due to U.S. Border Patrol line watching in urban zones. Deaths continue to occur.

1994   Operation Gatekeeper begins at the Imperial Beach Station in San Diego. The success of Operations Gatekeeper and Hold the Line in reducing unauthorized border crossing leads to its application in other locations, including McAllen, Texas. A debate about whether line watching deters or displaces potential undocumented crossers to riskier border zones begins.

The Violent Crime Control and Law Enforcement Act provides for enhanced penalties for alien smuggling, illegal reentry after deportation, and other immigration-related crimes.

1995   A Canada-U.S. Accord on Our Shared Border establishes that improvement of border infrastructure is a priority.

1995 (*cont.*)	President Clinton's Decision Directive 42 declares that international crime is a threat to the United States.
1996	The Anti-Terrorism and Effective Death Penalty Act contains provisions regarding the removal of terrorists and criminal aliens which limit judicial review.

The Illegal Immigration Reform and Immigrant Responsibility Act (IIRIRA) mandates the development of a data tracking system for foreign citizen arrivals and departure. (This would not be acted upon until after 9/11.)

IIRIRA classifies fifty categories of crime as aggravated felonies subject to removal upon sentence completion or retroactively. It further stipulates that any crime committed by an alien resulting in a sentence of more than one year, even if a misdemeanor, like drug possession, is to result in removal.

The International Crime Control Act is passed by Congress. It authorizes initiatives to stem drug trafficking, terrorism, and money laundering. Its provisions enable investigation, extradition, and prosecution of international criminals and provides for freezing of their assets and denial of entry over the U.S. borders.

1997	The shooting death of Ezequiel Hernandez, an American citizen of Mexican descent, by four Marines in a covert operation ends the direct use of the military in border enforcement.
1998	The United States and Mexico begin the Border Safety Initiative, a program to inform Mexican migrants about risks associated with crossing the border in remote regions and to establish rescue teams.
1999	A Canada-U.S. Partnership (CUSP), US INS-CIC Border Vision, and the Cross-Border Crime Forum are established to further trade and deal with security concerns.

Nongovernmental organizations dealing with immigration call for a reorganization of the Immigration and Naturalization Service to separate immigration enforcement from visa and citizenship functions.

Ahmed Ressam is arrested while attempting to cross the Canadian border and later charged with conspiring to bomb Los Angeles Airport at the millennium.

2000   Vincente Fox is elected president of Mexico and advocates a guest-worker program with the United States.

The United Nations Convention Against Transnational Organized Crime is signed.

2000   The Victims of Trafficking and Violence Protection Act (VTVPA) requires international cooperation with sending countries to identify human traffickers. Countries are ranked into three tiers based on the degree to which they have introduced antitrafficking initiatives and are attempting prevention and prosecution. Tier 3 countries are subject to sanctions. In the United States, the VTVPA makes it a crime to deceive or threaten harm to coerce work regardless of whether it is sex work or any other kind of labor. In addition, the act offers relief in the form of visas and support for victims willing to testify against traffickers. It is reauthorized in 2003, 2005, and 2008.

2000   The Immigration and Naturalization Service Data Management Act stipulates that an entrance-and-exit system should be established at the borders. This was not acted upon until after 9/11 and is still incomplete as it lacks a computerized exit system. This is significant because many undocumented immigrants are visa overstayers.

Terrorism and the Securitization of Immigration

2001   On September 11, the World Trade Center is destroyed and the Pentagon damaged by 19 al-Qaeda jet hijackers deploying four planes, one of

2001 (*cont.*)	which was brought down by passengers without reaching its target. The 19 suicidal jihadists and 2,976 victims, the vast majority of whom were civilians, died. The terrorist event caused massive shock and grief and precipitated the War on Terror and the war in Afghanistan. The United States first responds by closing its borders, and when they are reopened, intensified inspection causes major business and travel delays at the land border ports of entry.
2001	The Protocol to Prevent, Suppress and Punish Trafficking in Persons, Especially Women and Children (Palermo Protocol) is an international agreement to take action to prevent trafficking, prosecute traffickers, and provide victim protection.
2001	The Canada-U.S. Smart Border Accord harmonizes border screening, establishes sharing of intelligence databases, and initiates development of biometric identification technology in Canada.
2001	The Uniting and Strengthening America by providing Appropriate Tools Required to Intercept and Obstruct Terrorism Act (USA PATRIOT Act) greatly enhances the surveillance capacity of federal law enforcement in the area of communications by exempting the need for a warrant in terrorism-related investigations. This causes a civil liberties controversy. It also stipulates that noncitizens can be detained or removed without due process of law. This creates controversies over the duration of detention, removal, and access to lawyers or relations. The USA PATRIOT Act stipulates that more funding should be provided to create a U.S. Visit and Immigration Status Indicator Technology (U.S.-VISIT) system.
2002	Al-Qaeda names Australia, Canada, France, Germany, Great Britain, Italy, and the United States as targets for terrorist attacks due to their assistance of the United States. The Immigration and Naturalization Service informs certain deceased 9/11 hijackers that they

can enroll in U.S. flight-training schools. There is a call for removing immigration enforcement from the INS.

Attorney General John Ashcroft is allowed new authority for expedited removal.

Congress establishes a Department of Homeland Security and begins reorganization of the Immigration and Naturalization Service.

The Smart Border Declaration and 30 Point Action Plan to Enhance the Security of Our Shared Border While Facilitating the Legitimate Flow of People and Goods is entered into by the United States and Canada. This bilateral agreement addresses concerns about counterterrorism and border security while facilitating trade.

The Homeland Security Act joins 22 federal agencies and 180,000 employees into the same organization: the Department of Homeland Security (DHS). The DHS director becomes a member of the Cabinet. The Immigration and Naturalization Service is reorganized into U.S. Citizenship and Immigration Services, U.S. Immigration and Customs Enforcement, and U.S. Customs and Border Protection.

John Ashcroft initiates Operation Condor. All visa applications from men 16–45 from nations designated as terrorist sponsoring are to be screened. In the United States, the National Security Entrance-Exit Registration System (NSEERS) program requires Muslim men 16–45 to register. Approximately 140,000 people are registered and 13,000 deported for being "out-of status"—not having a valid visa. This program is criticized as an example of racial profiling.

The Enhanced Border Security and Visa Entry Reform Act again stipulates that more funding should be provided to create a U.S. Visit and Immigration Status Indicator Technology (U.S.-VISIT) system.

The Container Security Initiative introduces risk assessment to target containers to inspect and begins a trusted shippers program to expedite shipments that meet requirements. This is a part of the Customs-Trade Partnership Against Terrorism.

2003   Canada reorganizes its federal enforcement agencies into the Canadian Border Agency in a move parallel to the reorganization of like agencies into the Department of Homeland Security in the United States.

The Terrorist Threat Integration Center is authorized.

The Lateral Repatriation Program releases Mexican migrants apprehended while crossing the Arizona desert border in the heat of summer to Texas. It runs for 23 days.

Osiel Cárdenas Guillén, thought to be the leader of the Gulf cartel, is arrested in Mexico.

2004   The 9/11 Commission releases its report. It identifies failure to share intelligence between the FBI and the CIA as a major problem. The United States is viewed as slow to react to the destructive potential of international terrorism. Specifically, U.S. consulates and border inspectors are found to be limited in knowledge of how to screen for terrorist travel. Again the United States is found to lack an efficient entrance-and-exit tracking system.

The U.S. Visit and Intelligence Reform and Terrorism Act ends exemption from a passport requirement for Canadian citizens as a part of the Western Hemisphere Travel Initiative. It provides for expansion and increased funding of the U.S.-VISIT data system including biometric capability. It requires in-person interviews of visa applicants at U.S. consulates. Funding is provided for U.S. Border Patrol expansion and purchase and installation of electronic surveillance technology. The 9/11 Commission recommendations are funded for implementation.

A National Counterterrorism Center is created.

The Border Strategic Plan makes counterterrorism its most important initiative but focuses on the U.S.-Mexico border. The U.S. Border Patrol is given access to terrorist and criminal databases.

The U.S. Border Patrol releases data indicating that 460 migrants died while attempting unauthorized entry across the border in FY2004.

Congress authorizes building 40,000 detention beds for unauthorized entrants by 2010.

It is estimated that the unauthorized population has reached 11 million.

2005   The Security and Prosperity Agreement of the United States, Canada, and Mexico extends the original Canada-U.S. border declaration to Mexico. Intelligence will be shared between the three countries and Mexico will establish a trusted traveler program for expedited border crossing.

The Secure Border Initiative involves a billion-dollar investment in electronic surveillance technology for border security.

Operation Streamline of the U.S. Border Patrol changes the policy of releasing migrants apprehended for the first time without detention. To the extent that detention infrastructure allows, migrants are detained for two weeks to six months. This zero tolerance policy has been continued, although a shortage of detention facilities impedes its full implementation.

The Real ID Act, also called the Border Protection, Anti-Terrorism, and Illegal Immigration Control Act, mandates the states to develop improved driver's license identification but provides no funding for it. The states object and the law will face obstacles in implementation.

The governors of Arizona and New Mexico declare a "state of emergency" due to unauthorized migration.

The U.S. Border Patrol releases data indicating that over 500 migrants died while attempting unauthorized entry across the border in FY2005.

2006   Felipe Calderón is inaugurated as president of Mexico and declares he will take further action against drug traffickers and corrupt officials.

The U.S. Coast Guard arrests Francisco Javier Arellano Felix and other Tijuana cartel leaders and disrupts cartel operations. It is thought that he reaches an agreement with Osiel Cárdenas Guillén, the Gulf Cartel leader, while in Mexican prison and that they unify the two organizations.

2006
(cont.)
      The Secure Fence Act directs that two layers of secured fencing be built and additional physical barriers, roads, and surveillance technology be placed in five areas of Arizona, California, New Mexico, and Texas. The walls and fencing are for 850 miles. In response to protests by private landowners and environmentalists, Department of Homeland Security Secretary Michael Chertoff receives a waiver to begin building regardless of environmental and historic preservation laws. By 2009, 613 miles are constructed.

      New Mexico governor Bill Richardson and Arizona governor Janet Napolitano request National Guard troops to deal with undocumented entry and drug trafficking at the border. President Bush sends 6,000 National Guardsmen to the California, Arizona, New Mexico, and Texas borders. They are directed to assist the U.S. Border Patrol and are not directly involved in enforcement.

      The Border Tunnel Prevention Act increases criminal penalties for cross-border tunneling.

2007
The Protect America Act extends the provisions for federal access to communication established by the USA PATRIOT Act.

      The 9/11 Commission Act stipulates that 100% of air cargo must be physically inspected by 2010 and 100% of maritime containers must be physically inspected by 2012. Lack of infrastructure raises questions about feasibility of the timeline for implementation.

      Osiel Cárdenas Guillén is extradited to the United States and placed in maximum security. It is thought that he can no longer direct the Gulf drug organization.

      A turf war between rival Mexican drug-trafficking organizations leads to violence in Nuevo Laredo, Mexico, over control of trafficking routes between the Gulf and Sinaloa cartels.

      Calderón sends federal troops to Nuevo Laredo.

      Mexican newspaper *Reforma* reports 2,280 deaths from drug-related violence in 2007.

2007–2008	It is estimated that 183 migrants die attempting to enter the United States without authorization by crossing the border in remote regions in Arizona from October 2007 to October 2008.
2008	The Merida Initiative is signed and authorized by Congress. It is a security agreement involving the United States, Mexico, and Central American countries to provide intelligence, equipment, and training to combat drug trafficking.

Turf disputes between rival drug-trafficking organizations lead to increased violence in many regions of Mexico and in border cities such as Juarez, Mexico. Calderón sends federal troops to Juarez. Mexican citizens march to protest the violence.

Mexican newspaper *Reforma* reports 5,153 deaths from drug-related violence in 2008.

2008–2009	It is estimated that 238 migrants died attempting to enter the United States without authorization by crossing the border in remote regions of Arizona from October 2008 to October 2009.
2009	Governor Perry of Texas requests deployment of the National Guard to the Texas border but a funding dispute results in Texas Rangers being sent to assist the U.S. Border Patrol instead.

President Obama responds to criticism of immigrant detention by creating an Office of Immigrant Detention and Planning within Immigration and Customs Enforcement.

Secretary of Homeland Security Janet Napolitano expresses concern that Mexican drug-organization violence could have a spillover effect to U.S. border cities. In an effort to curb the violence, there is an increase in inspection of vehicles crossing to Mexico due to arms smuggling as the United States is the primary source of weapons.

Mexico passes a statute to decriminalize drug possession of small amounts to free prison space for more dangerous criminals.

A Mexican government report indicates 9,635 deaths due to drug-related violence in 2009.

2010
On March 14, 2010, a pregnant American consulate worker and her husband and the husband of another U.S. Consulate worker are killed due to what is believed to be drug-related violence in Ciudad Juarez, Mexico.

Secretary of Homeland Security Janet Napolitano announces that funding is being diverted from the electronic surveillance SBInet in favor of proven technology.

The United States and Mexico revise the Merida Initiative to emphasize civilian police rather than military assistance and strengthen efforts to rebuild Mexican communities with high poverty and crime rates.

On May 1, 2010, Faisal Shazad places a homemade explosive device left inside a car in Times Square, New York. It fails to detonate. Shazad is identified and placed on a no-fly list. He attempts to leave on an Emirates Airlines jet and is not detected because Emirates did not update its list. A second check of the passsenger list in the Department of Homeland Security database results in stopping the plane and Shazad's apprehension.

5

Biographical Sketches

Osama bin Laden (1957–)

The leader of the Muslim terrorist group al-Qaeda, Osama bin Laden was born to a wealthy family in Riyadh, Saudi Arabia. He grew up as a Wahhabi Muslim and attended the elite Al-Thager Model School. At King Abdulaziz University he studied economics and business administration. It is not known if he received a degree. In 1979, bin Laden went to Afghanistan to fight against the Soviet invasion and facilitated Muslim fighters, later establishing a camp. In 1990, Osama bin Laden returned to Saudi Arabia as a hero of jihad. Iraq invaded Kuwait, and when the Western powers engaged in the Persian Gulf War, he spoke out at his outrage at Saudi Arabia's cooperation, particularly its hosting of U.S. military forces. This antagonized the Saudis, who sought to silence him and revoked his citizenship.

In 1992, bin Laden moved to the Sudan and established a new Mujahideen base in Khartoum. In 1996, the Sudan came under pressure from Saudi Arabia, Egypt, and the United States to expel bin Laden and he returned to Jalalabad, Afghanistan. He befriended Mohammed Omar, who became head of the Taliban and raised money for his organization. At this point, al-Qaeda became involved in numerous worldwide terrorist actions, including some against civilians.

The United States responded to 9/11 with the War on Terror and sought to depose the Taliban in Afghanistan and capture or kill bin Laden and al-Qaeda members. In 2004, Osama bin Laden claimed responsibility for the 9/11 attacks which caused the deaths of 2,974 people.

Al-Qaeda is a loosely connected network of terrorist cells connected to participants in the 1993 World Trade Center bombing, the Los Angeles Airport Millennium bomb plot, and the 9/11 attacks on the World Trade Center and Pentagon. These are three major internationally planned terrorist activities meant to harm the United States.

David V. Aguilar

David Aguilar was chief of the Border Patrol from 7-1-2004 through 1-20-2010, when he was appointed the acting commissioner of U.S. Customs and Border Protection, a position he held until 3-27-2010. He earned an associate degree in accounting from Laredo Community College and attended Laredo State University (now Texas A&M International University) and the University of Texas at Arlington. In 1999, he graduated from the John F. Kennedy School of Government. In 1978, Aguilar began work with the U.S. Border Patrol in Laredo, Texas, serving as a U.S. Border Patrol agent, first-line supervisory agent, and assistant USBP agent-in-charge. During 1988–1996, he was USBP agent-in-charge of three Texas USBP stations in Dallas, Rio Grande City, and Brownsville, at varying points in time. The USBP stations in Dallas and Brownsville were both given the Commissioner's Award for Group Achievement while Aguilar was in charge.

From August 1996 through November 1999, Aguilar served as assistant regional director for the Border Patrol in the Central Region. He acted as the advisor to the regional director of the former Immigration and Naturalization Service and was involved in strategic planning. In late 1999, Aguilar became chief patrol agent of the Tucson-sector USBP with responsibility for administration and all operations. Two thousand–plus agents and 200 support personnel worked in the Tucson sector, which covers 261 miles of the Arizona-Mexico border. In 2004, Chief Aguilar was appointed the Border and Transportation Security Integrator for the Arizona Border Control Initiative. In 2003, Operation Safeguard was begun in areas at risk for migrant fatalities. The Tucson sector received the Customs and Border Protection Office of Anti-Terrorism Commissoner's Award for this operation. In 2005 David Aguilar received one of nine Department of Homeland Security Presidential Rank Awards for Meritorious Senior Professionals.

While in charge of the Border Patrol, Aguilar was subject to criticism by the National Border Patrol Council (NBPC). The NBPC is an affiliate of the AFL-CIO as a part of the American Federation of Government Employees. In February 2007 and on February 25, 2009, the NBPC unanimously issued a vote of ''no confidence'' in David Aguilar as chief of the Border Patrol. The reason for disapproval was that rank and file Border Patrol agents did not believe that senior management supported them.

John Ashcroft (1942–)

Ashcroft was president of his class at Hillcrest High in Springfield, Missouri. He was a captain and quarterback on the football team and received a football scholarship to Yale University. A knee injury kept him from football, but he engaged in intramural sports. After graduating with honors from Yale, Ashcroft went to the University of Chicago Law School on a scholarship. Upon receipt of his degree, Ashcroft returned to Springfield and opened a law practice. He started teaching at Southwest Missouri State University.

John Ashcroft's paternal grandfather was a Northern Irish immigrant who became a minister with the Christian evangelist Assembly of God church. He had a son, John, born to his wife Grace. Robert entered the footsteps of his father, becoming a minister and served as president of three colleges connected to the Assembly of God.

As an undergraduate at Yale, John Ashcroft interned one summer for his congressman. When the congressman did not seek reelection in 1972, Ashcroft ran as a replacement in the Republican primary, receiving almost 45% of the vote, but he lost. Instead, he was accepted as a replacement to fill an unexpired term as state auditor. Two years later, he again was not elected to Congress. Ashcroft was next hired as a legal assistant to state attorney general John Danforth. When Danforth was elected to the Senate in 1976, Ashcroft was elected to replace him as Missouri attorney general and won reelection in 1980. At that time he became chairman of the nonpartisan National Association of Attorneys General.

In 1984, Ashcroft was elected governor of Missouri and was chairman of the Education Commission for the states. In 1991, he was elected chairman of the nonpartisan National Governor's Association. In 1992, term limits prevented him from seeking reelection. In 1994, he successfully ran for Danforth's open seat. He served for six years on the by Senate Judiciary Committee and as chairman of the Constitution committee, where he became known for his conservative position on abortion and other issues. John Ashcroft ran for reelection, but his opponent, Mel Carnhan, died in an accident three weeks before the election, which was too late to change the ballot. McCarnhan won and his widow accepted a Senate appointment which Ashcroft left unchallenged.

In 2000 Ashcroft was nominated by President-elect George W. Bush to be U.S. Attorney General. His conservative views led to Senate opposition. He was confirmed by a vote of 68–42. After 9/11 Attorney General Ashcroft became very involved with the War on Terror. He used provisions of immigration law to hold noncitizens suspected of terrorism, including indefinite detention. Over 1,000 were detained on charges not publicly released and with little outside contact with relations or lawyers.

Kevin Bales

A leading antislavery expert, Kevin Bales received a Ph.D. from the London School of Economics. He is emeritus professor of sociology at Roehampton University in London, a visiting professor at the Wilberforce Institute for the Study of Slavery and Emancipation, University of Hull, and serves on the board of directors of the National Cocoa Institute. Bales's 1999 book *Disposable People: New Slavery in the Global Economy* was a Pulitzer Prize nominee and has been translated into 10 languages. Revised in 2005, this work received the designation as a top "World Changing Discovery" on a list of 100 created by an association of British universities. The Italian edition of this book was given a Premio Viareggio for humanitarian service in 2000. A documentary that Bales cowrote, *Slavery: A Global Investigation*, won a Peabody Award in 2000 and two Emmy awards in 2002. In 2004 Bales received the Judith Sargeant Murray Award for Human Rights, followed by the University of Alberta Human Rights Award in 2005.

Bales is president of Free the Slaves, an affiliate of Anti-Slavery International, at which he is a trustee. He is director of the Alliance to Stop Slavery and Stop Trafficking and a United Nations Global Program on Trafficking in Human Beings consultant. He has advised the U.S. government on slavery and human trafficking policy. Bales edited a United Nations antitrafficking toolkit and has authored a report on forced labor for the Human Rights Center at the University of California at Berkeley. For the National Institute of Justice, he researched human trafficking to the United States for two years. He is active in the international chocolate industry and seeks to end child labor. Additional books he has written include *New Slavery: A Reference Handbook* (revised 2nd edition, 2005) and *Ending Slavery: How We Free Today's Slaves* (2007). In 2008 *To Plead Our Cause: Personal Stories by Today's Slaves*, with Zoe Trod, and *Documenting Disposable People: Contemporary Global Slavery* with Magnum photographers, were published. In 2009 he coauthored *The Slave Next Door: Modern Slavery in the United States* with Ron Soodalter.

Sandra "La Reina del Pacifico (Queen of the Pacific)" Avila Beltran (1960–)

Sandra Avila Beltran was born in the state of Sinaloa, Mexico. Her uncle was Miguel Angel Felix Gallardo, a key Mexican drug trafficker. Her relationship with Juan Diego Espinoza Ramirez, a Colombian cocaine trafficker, is thought to have led to her drug-trafficking involvement. In 2001, nine tons of cocaine was found in the Manzanillo, Colima Pacific port. It was traced to Beltran and Juan Diego Espinoza. They were arrested on September 28, 2007. She is accused of organized criminal activity, trafficking in drugs, and money laundering in both Mexico and the United States, which has requested extradition. Beltran is considered the most successful female drug trafficker worldwide.

George Walker Bush (1946–)

The 43rd president of the United States, George Walker Bush, is the son of former president George H. W. Bush. He was born in

Connecticut, but raised in Texas, and later attended Phillips Academy in Andover, Massachusetts, and Yale University. Bush was a lieutenant in the Texas Air National Guard and then took several positions in Houston, including working with an underprivileged youth program called Pull for Kids. After attending Harvard Business School and receiving an MBA, George W. Bush became an oilman and ran for Congress at age 32, losing by six votes. After achieving financial success in the oil business, he started Bush Exploration, which did not do well in the soft energy market of the early 1980s. Bush Exploration was salvaged through a merger with Spectrum 7, a company that was later purchased by Harken Energy. Speculation exists that this deal only occurred because of Bush's father's influence. The deal was controversial because George W. Bush made money while Harken Energy lost millions. Bush worked for his father's 1988 presidential campaign and then returned to Texas, organizing a group of investors who bought the Rangers, an American League baseball team. He become a managing partner and increased the now–Texas Rangers' popularity.

In 1994 and 1998, Bush successfully ran for governor of Texas, which he used as a stepping stone to successfully run for president in 2000. The 2000 presidential election against Vice President Albert Gore was controversial because of a close vote and allegations of election fraud regarding the Florida vote count.

President George W. Bush has been associated with both the War on Terror and the criminalization of immigration. Bush initially favored an expansion of migration from Mexico through the establishment of a guest-worker program but the public and Congress failed to positively respond. As the sitting president at the time of the 9/11 attacks, Bush and his team crafted a series of external and internal responses to strengthen the United States and reduce the possibility of terrorist attack. Both the war in Afghanistan and the war in Iraq were presented as a means to strengthen national security. In Afghanistan, the Taliban regime was removed while in Iraq Saddam Hussein and his Sunni Muslim counterparts were taken from power. Both wars have persisted at great expense and lost a degree of support among the American public.

The War on Terror strategy involved a major reorganization of federal intelligence and law-enforcement agencies into the Department of Homeland Security. Policies of the War on Terror are very controversial because of their implication for loss of citizen's rights, such as protection from wiretapping without a judicial order.

Felipe de Jesús Calderón (1962–)

Felipe Calderón (**in full Felipe de Jesús Calderón Hinojosa**) was elected president of Mexico in 2006 for a six-year term. Born in Morelia, Michoacan, he received a degree from the Escuela Libre de Derecho in Mexico City and a master's degree in economics from the Instituto Technologico de Mexico (ITAM). Calderón attended the John F. Kennedy School of Government at Harvard University and received a master's in public administration.

Felipe Calderón's father cofounded the National Action Party (PAN), and he has been active in its politics during his career. He began his activities in the PAN youth movement and later served as national president of the party from 1996 to 1999. He won election to the legislative assembly as a local representative and twice was a member of the federal Chamber of Deputies. During Vincente Fox's presidency (2000–2006), Calderón was a federal deputy and secretary of energy.

Calderón is a strong supporter of free trade and immigration reform. He supports a road to legalization for unauthorized U.S. residents and is against the U.S.-Mexico border fence, which he believes harms bilateral relations. In turn, he authorized intensified law-enforcement efforts against Mexican drug-trafficking organizations (DTOs), which has led to the arrest of several high-ranking DTO members. These arrests have resulted in a continuation of turf wars between rival DTOs, and Calderón positioned federal police and troops in Mexican border cities. Escalation of drug-related violence has led to assignment of the Mexican Army to combat drug trafficking. Felipe Calderón has participated in the Merida Initiative, a regional agreement for cooperation among the United States, Mexico, and Central American countries to deal with drug trafficking and transnational crime. Unfortunately, as trafficking to the United States became more difficult, DTOs began selling their product in Mexico and addiction rates increased. Calderón is Catholic and believes that faith in God helps to prevent youth from trying drugs. He has advocated the harm reduction strategy of Mexican legalization of possession of small amounts of cocaine and drugs for addicts in treatment and stresses that the United States should take responsibility for easing its consumer drug demand.

Michael Chertoff (1953–)

Michael Chertoff, the second person appointed as secretary of Homeland Security, was born in Elizabeth, New Jersey. He received a bachelor's degree in history from Harvard University. In 1975, he went on to Harvard Law School, where he served as the editor of the *Harvard Law Review*, earned a J.D., and graduated magna cum laude in 1978. From 1978 to 1979, he served as a law clerk in Judge Murray Griffin's Second U.S. Circuit Court of Appeals and in 1979–1980, he worked for U.S. Supreme Court Justice William J. Brennan Jr. In 1980, Chertoff joined the firm of Latham and Watkins as an associate attorney. From 1990 to 1994, he was U.S. attorney for New Jersey and in 2001 went on to head the criminal division of the Department of Justice, where he was involved in developing the legal response to the 9/11 attacks. Chertoff advocated the detention of foreign nationals of Arab and Muslim ancestry, a position for which he was criticized. In 2003, he received a lifetime appointment as a judge to the Third U.S. Circuit Court of Appeals.

In 2005 Chertoff succeeded Tom Ridge to become the second secretary of the newly reorganized Department of Homeland Security. In this position, Chertoff sought to balance a need for homeland security with civil liberty concerns. During Chertoff's service as secretary, three major changes in policy were: (1) the Western Hemispheric Travel Initiative, which stopped the acceptance of oral declarations by U.S. and Canadian citizens in lieu of a passport; (2) the end of the "catch and release" of Mexican nationals back over the Mexican border without detention; and (3) active building of a border fence extension on the U.S.-Mexico border despite Environmental Protection Agency and civilian concerns.

Hillary Clinton (1947–)

Hillary Clinton received an undergraduate degree in political science from Wellesly College and attended Yale Law School, receiving a Juris Doctor degree in 1973. While at Yale, she served on the Board of Editors of the *Journal of Law and Social Action* and met Bill Clinton, whom she later married. Bill Clinton became governor of Arkansas and the 42nd president of the United States. Hillary Clinton was first lady of the United States from 1993 to 2001. As first lady, she took a more active political role than prior presidential spouses and was very involved with a failed national health care initiative but, in 1997, was successful in establishing a Children's Health Insurance Program.

Hillary Clinton's career path changed when Bill Clinton left office. She was elected the junior United States Senator from New York in 2000, the first time a first lady was elected to public office. In 2006 she was reelected, and Hillary Clinton became a Democratic candidate for president in the 2008 primaries, losing to Barack Obama. In 2009, Obama appointed her secretary of state.

David Cole (1958–)

David Cole is a legal advocate for the rights of immigrants and civil liberties. He received degrees from Yale University and Law School. His first position was as a law clerk for Judge Arlin M. Adams of the U.S. Court of Appeals for the Third Circuit. Next, he worked as a staff attorney for the Center for Constitutional Rights, where he remains as a volunteer and is on the board of directors. David Cole is a law faculty member at Georgetown University. He is a co-chairman of the Liberty and Security Committee of the Constitution Project.

Cole is *The Nation*'s legal affairs correspondent and a commentator on National Public Radio's *All Things Considered*. He publishes widely in the areas of civil liberties, civil rights, criminal justice, and constitutional law. His books include *Enemy Aliens: Double Standards and Constitutional Freedoms in the War on Terrorism* (2nd ed., 2005), and *Terrorism and the Constitution: Sacrificing Civil Liberties for National Security* (3rd ed., 2005). In 2004 he received an American Book award and the Hefner First Amendment prize for *Enemy Aliens*. Cole has received civil liberties and civil rights awards from the American Bar Association's Individual Rights and Responsibilities Section, the National Lawyers Guild, the Thomas Jefferson Center for the Protection of the Freedom of Expression, the American Arab Anti-Discrimination Committee, Trial Lawyers for Public Justice and the Political Asylum and Immigrant Rights Project, and the American Muslim Council.

Stockwell Day (1950–)

Canadian Public Safety Minister Stockwell Day is a member of the Conservative Party of Canada. He was born in Barrie, Ontario, but has lived in numerous Canadian locations including Ottawa. Day graduated from Westmount High School in Montreal and attended Ashbury College in Ottawa. From 1978 to 1975, Day was assistant pastor and school administrator at the Bentley Christian Center in Bentley, Alberta. From 1986 to 2000, he represented Red Deer North in the Legislative Assembly of Alberta as a Progressive Conservative. Concurrently, in 1992 Day was minister of labour in the Alberta Cabinet and in 1994 he became Government House Leader. In 1996, he was appointed Minister of Social Services and in 1997, Treasurer.

In 2000, Day joined the Canadian Alliance Party and was elected to the House of Commons in Parliament for the riding of Okanagan-Coquihalla in British Columbia. He sought party leadership but lost to Stephen Harper. When the Canadian Alliance and the Progressive Conservative Party merged as the Conservative Party of Canada, Day became the Conservative Foreign Affairs critic for the Conservative Party Caucus and was reelected to Parliament in 2004 and 2006.

After Stephen Harper was elected prime minister in 2006, Day became minister of public safety and joined the Privy Council. As the Minister of Public Safety, Day was responsible for national security advice and support, and he is a part of the Cross-Cultural Round Table on Security. Canada's national security policy reflects concerns about protecting Canadians and Canada, preventing Canada from being a base for international terrorism, and ensuring international security. In 2008, Day became the Minister of International Trade. One development Day is associated with is the creation of an electronic manifest cargo program to allow identification of high-risk shipments prior to arrival at the Canadian border.

Arellano Felix Brothers

The Arellano Felix brothers led the Tijuana cartel. On August 6, 2006, the U.S. Coast Guard arrested Francisco Javier Arellano Felix and other Tijuana cartel leaders on a boat off the coast of Mexico. His brother, Francisco Javier Arellano Felix, was extradited to the United States. He pled guilty to charges of running a criminal enterprise and money laundering and was sentenced to life imprisonment without the possibility of parole. In Mexico, Benjamin Arellano Felix was sentenced to 22 years for organized crime and drug-trafficking violations. The United States has requested his extradition on drug-trafficking, racketeering, and money-laundering charges. In September 2006, Francisco Rafael Arellano Felix was extradited to the U.S. and pled guilty to intent to distribute cocaine. He received a six-year sentence.

The Tijuana cartel operates in at least 15 states with an important base in Tijuana, Baja California. Additional bases are in Mexicali, Tecate, and Ensenada in Baja California and Sinaloa state. At its peak, the Tijuana cartel is considered to have supplied 40% of cocaine trafficked into the United States. The Tijuana cartel formed an alliance with the Gulf cartel after Francisco Javier Arellano Felix was imprisoned along with Osiel Cárdenas Guillén as a result of negotiations. Its major area of influence is the Mexican state of Baja California.

Ismael Higuera Guerrero and Gilberto Higuera Guerrero, high-ranking members of the Tijuana cartel, were extradited to the United States in January 2007. As of January 2006, 107 Tijuana cartel enforcers had been arrested. The weakening of this cartel through the loss of its leaders has led to attempts to defend control of its trafficking routes, corrupt Mexican law enforcement, and heightened violence. Despite arrests, the Tijuana cartel still controls the corridor between Tijuana and San Diego.

Michael J. Fisher

In January, 2010, Michael Fisher became the Acting Chief of the U.S. Border Patrol. On March 28, he became the Acting Comissioner of U.S. Customs and Border Protection. He holds undergraduate degrees in criminal justice and business administration and is a graduate of the Kennedy School of Government at Harvard University Senior Executive Fellows Program. He graduated first for physical efficiency in his Border Patrol class and began as a southwestern Border Patrol agent in 1987. His career progression included being selected for the Border Patrol Tactical Unit and becoming a field operations supervisor for El Paso, Texas, a position in which he directed U.S. and international operations. Next, he was appointed the deputy chief patrol agent of the Detroit Sector, serving as an administrative and operations officer. This was followed by assignment as assistant chief patrol agent of the Tucson Sector. In 2001, Michael Fisher received the "Manager of the Year" award for establishing a budgetary operational planning model in the Tucson Sector. Next he became deputy director for the U.S. Customs and Border Protection (CBP) Office of Anti-Terrorism in Washington, DC and was a liason to an inter-agency intelligence community for counterterrorism planning and operations. He became an associate chief patrol agent in Headquarters Border Patrol and was promoted as senior associate chief in 2004. Mr. Fisher established a Border Patrol Intelligence Division in its Washington, DC Operations Branch. In 2006, he became the deputy chief patrol agent in the San Diego Sector.

Miguel Angel Félix Gallardo (1946–)

In 1989, Félix Gallardo, a drug trafficking organization leader, was arrested. He was able to operate his organization by using a mobile phone in prison until the 1990s, when he was transferred to a maximum-security unit. After losing his leadership, his organization was divided by two factions which became the Tijuana cartel, led by the Arellano Felix brothers, and the Sinaloa cartel, run by Hector Palma Salazar, Adrian Comez Gonzalez, and Joaquin Guzman Loera.

Félix Gallardo began by working as a family bodyguard for Mexican governor Leopoldo Sanchez Celis. Celis was presented with the opportunity for corruption and it is believed that Félix Gallardo used Sanchez Celis's political connections to create his drug organization. He later partnered with the key Colombian cocaine trafficker, Pablo Escobar.

Miguel Angel Félix Gallardo was a godfather of Governor Sanchez Celis's son Rodolofo. Rodolfo Sanchez Celis was kidnapped, tortured, and assassinated. It is alleged that Hector Luis Palma Salazar and Joaquin Guzman Loera were responsible. In retaliation, Félix Gallardo kidnapped and decapitated Palma Salazar's wife. As a result, the Tijuana and Sinaloa cartels entered into conflict.

Vincente Carillo Fuentes (1962–)

Born in La Armitas, Zacatecas, Mexico, Vincente Carlos Fuentes is the leader of the Juarez cartel, a drug organization in control of a major U.S. interstate drug route. He is charged in the Western District of Texas with 46 counts of organized criminal activity, cocaine and marijuana importation and possession with intent to distribute, money laundering, witness tampering, and ordering assassinations to prevent communication with U.S. law. There is a $5 million reward offered by the Department of State for his arrest and/or conviction.

The founder of the Juarez cartel, Amado Carillo Fuentes, is Vincente Carlos Fuentes' brother. Amado brought in his six brothers and his son, Vincente Carillo Leyva, who was arrested on April 1, 2009. In 1999, Amado's death from a botched plastic surgery operation was a media sensation, and his passing set off a turf war over cartel leadership won by Vincente. After Amado Carillo Fuentes' death, this cartel has been less powerful. In the 1990s the "Maxiproceso" interdiction effort resulted in 110 arrest warrants for alleged cartel members and accomplices, 65 of which were executed.

After Amado's death, the Arellano Felix brothers became very powerful, but Vincente Carillo Fuentes avoided this conflict and strengthened his organization. In the late 1990s, tensions grew with the other cartels and some members defected to the Sinaloa cartel. In 2004, Rodolfo Carillo was murdered and the Sinaloa cartel was implicated. In retaliation, Guzman Loera's brother was killed in prison, setting off an intercartel turf war. The turf war between the Sinaloa cartel and the Gulf cartel in 2005–2006 led to a truce. The Juarez cartel contains factions loyal to the Carillos or to the Sinaloa cartel. In the first three months of 2008, intercartel conflict was connected to 200 murders. President Felipe Calderón of Mexico initially sent Mexican federal troops to Ciudad Juarez to curb the violence. Although the Juarez cartel is considerably less powerful, Vincente Carillo Fuentes is still very powerful.

The Juarez drug-trafficking cartel is active in 21 Mexican states, including Culiacan, Sinaloa, Monterrey, and Nuevo Leon. It has bases in Ciudad Juarez, Chihuahua; Ojinaga, Chihuahua; Mexico City; Guadalajara, Jalisco; Cuaernavaca, Morelos; and Cancun, Quintana Roo. It is the most geographically dispersed drug cartel operating in Mexico but is named after Ciudad Juarez, the Mexican sister city of El Paso, Texas. The Juarez cartel is predominant in the Mexican state of Chihuahua. This cartel is considered a member of the Federation Alliance, but this tie may have been weakened by murders committed by another federation member. As of January 2006, 66 Juarez cartel enforcers had been arrested.

Vincente Fox (1942–)

Vincente Fox was born in Mexico City and grew up on the San Cristobal ranch in the municipality of San Francisco del Rincon in the state of Guanajato, Mexico. He studied business administration at the Universidad Iberoamericana and received a top management diploma from the Harvard Business School. In 1964, he began work as a route supervisor for Coca-Cola and traveled throughout Mexico. In the 1980s he joined PAN, the Partido Accion Nacional. He became a federal congressman for the third district of Leon. In 1991, he ran for governor of Guanajuato, but Carlos Medina Plascencia was named interim governor. In 1995, he was elected Guanajuato's governor. Vincente Fox became the first member of the PAN party to be elected president of Mexico in 2000 and served a six-year term. In 2007, he became co-president of the Centrist Democrat International, an organization of Christian Democratic parties.

President Fox sought to improve trade relations with the United States and initiated bilateral efforts to curb drug trafficking and the government corruption associated with it. This effort resulted in arrest of certain drug-trafficking organization (DTO) leaders, and inter-DTO rivalry to take over lucrative drug-trafficking routes resulted in violence in Nuevo Laredo, Tamaulipas. Regarding immigration, Fox called for opening the borders and protecting the rights of Mexican undocumented workers. He discussed the prospect of a guest-worker program with President George W. Bush in 2000 but immigration reform was stalled by concerns about terrorism and negative U.S. public opinion. U.S. public sentiment was against admitting more Mexican workers and this initiative languished.

Alberto Gonzales (1955–)

Alberto Gonzalez is a corporate lawyer who became general counsel for George W. Bush in 1995 when Bush was governor of Texas. He was secretary of state of Texas from December 1997 to January 10, 1999. As secretary of state, Gonzales specialized in U.S.-Mexico border issues and developed immigration policy. In 2001, newly elected President Bush asked Gonzales to serve as general counsel to the White House. In 2005, Gonzalez became the first Hispanic American and Mexican American to be appointed attorney general when he succeeded John Ashcroft. In confirmation hearings before the Senate, all eight Democrats on the Judiciary Committee did not vote for him, but he was confirmed by a vote of 60 to 36.

Alberto Gonzales is the son of a migrant farm worker who was born in San Antonio, Texas. His parents did not finish elementary school and his father died in a work accident in 1982. Upon high school graduation, Gonzales joined the U.S. Air Force and served from 1973 to 1975. He was encouraged to enter the U.S. Air Force Academy but instead sought a career in law and enrolled at Rice University, graduating in 1979. He is the first to graduate from college in his family and went on to Harvard Law School before becoming a member of the Vinson and Elkins corporate law firm in 1982. He practiced law for 13 years. Alberto Gonzales has taught law as an adjunct professor at the University of Houston Law Center.

Gonzales was a distinguished alumnus of Rice University and later received the Harvard Law School Association Award. In his career, Gonzales has received the President's Awards from the U.S. Hispanic Chamber of Commerce and the League of United Latin American Citizens. In 1999, he was named Latino Lawyer of the Year by the Hispanic National Bar Association.

Alberto Gonzales pursued the policy of expedited removal and implementation of the USA PATRIOT Act, reorganization of federal agencies into the Department of Homeland Security, and the development of a law establishing a director of national intelligence. Gonzalez inherited many of the controversial policies of his predecessor, John Ashcroft, and while he was attorney general was embroiled in controversy. On April 9, 2007, he testified before Congress regarding the accusations that the Department of Justice and the Federal Bureau of Investigation used the USA PATRIOT Act electronic surveillance provisions in a manner not intended by the law. Subsequent intensification of controversy and calls from members of Congress for his resignation led him to step down on September 17, 2007.

Osiel Cárdenas Guillén (1967–)

The Gulf cartel operates in 13 states, including Monterrey, Nuevo Leon, and Morelia, Michoachan. Its center of activity is the Mexican state of Tamaulipus. Important bases are located in Nuevo Laredo, across from Laredo, Texas; Reynosa, across from McAllen, Texas; Matamoros, across from Brownsville, Texas; and Miguel Aleman. It is known as the Gulf cartel because of its bases along the Rio Grande River in southeastern Texas, which opens into the Gulf of Mexico at Matamoros and Brownsville. The Gulf cartel is known to be particularly violent, and it employed a paramilitary group known as the Zetas, which is now contesting leadership of their drug-trafficking territory (plaza). Through January 2006, 134 Gulf cartel enforcers have been arrested.

Osiel Cárdenas Guillén is thought to be the leader of the Gulf cartel, although he has been imprisoned since 2003. He was extradited to the United States in January 2007. Charges brought against him include drug trafficking and threatening to murder U.S. federal agents in Matamoros, Mexico. After entering prison, it is thought that he negotiated an alliance with the Tijuana cartel. Because of the impact of counter-trafficking enforcement on its leadership and drug profits, the Gulf cartel is thought to be expanding into human smuggling for profit. The attempts to cross people are thought to be attempts to divert attention from drug loads.

Joaquin Guzman Loera (1957–)

Joaquin Guzman Loera was born in the Mexican state of Sinaloa. In the 1980s, Guzman Loera was associated with Miguel Angel Félix Gallardo, a.k.a "El Padrino (the Godfather)," who headed Mexico's most active drug-trafficking organization. He left this organization to found his own international criminal enterprise. An early 1990s effort involved an under-border tunnel in Douglas, Arizona, used to smuggle cocaine. In May 1993, members of the Arellano-Felix organization attempted to assassinate Guzman Loera in Guadalajara, Jalisco, Mexico. The result was the heavily publicized murder of Catholic Cardinal Jan Jesus Posadas-Ocampo, who was traveling in the vehicle thought to hold Guzman Loera.

In 1993, Guzman Loera was connected to 7.3 tons of cocaine that was concealed in cans of chili peppers seized in Tecate, Baja California, Mexico. In the same time period, a very sophisticated tunnel was also discovered in Tijuana, Baja California, that ended in the Otay Mesa, California, area. Joaquin Guzman Loera was arrested in Mexico and convicted of criminal association and bribery. Joaquin Guzman Loera escaped from the maximum security Puente Grande prison in the Mexican state of Jalisco on January 19, 2001. He was serving a 20-year sentence for criminal association and bribery.

Guzman Loera is wanted for conspiracy to distribute cocaine, possession with intent to distribute, and money laundering by the U.S. and Mexican governments and INTERPOL. Drug trafficking has brought him great wealth, and Guzman Loera was listed as number 701 on Forbes' list of the world's wealthiest people in 2008 and number 47 of the world's most powerful people in 2009. The DEA has offered a $5 million reward for his capture.

The Sinaloa cartel smuggles multi-ton shipments of cocaine and operates in 17 Mexican states and Mexico City, Tepic, Nayarit, Toluca, and Cuautitlan, Mexico state; and most of Sinaloa state. As of January 2006, 98 Sinaloa enforcers have been arrested. The Negros and the Pelones are enforcer units. The Negros are thought to be responsible for many violent attacks against the Zetas in Nuevo Laredo in a fight to control drug routes and the local police. Certain agents of Mexico's Federal Investigative Agency (AFI) are thought to have been corrupted by the Sinaloa cartel. In 2005, nearly 1,500 of 7,000 agents were under investigation and 457 faced criminal charges.

Stephen Harper (1959–)

Born in Toronto, Stephen Harper is the 22nd prime minister of Canada and leader of the Conservative Party. He was elected in January 2006 after his party won the largest number of seats in the Canadian House of Commons. Previously, Harper attended Richview Collegiate Institute and went on to the University of Toronto, then dropped out. After working at Imperial Oil, he went to the University of Calgary and received a B.A. in economics. He later earned a master's degree in economics from the University of Calgary. In 1985, Harper began in politics as chief aide to Progressive Conservative MP Jim Hawkes but became disillusioned with that party and Brian Mulrony, the PC prime minister. Next, he became the Reform Party's chief policy officer. In 1992, he ran for MP and won, stepping down in 1997. Harper then became president of the National Citizen's Coalition, a conservative think tank.

In 2002, Harper became leader of the Canadian Alliance Party and was elected to the House of Commons and became leader of the opposition. He led efforts to merge the Canadian Alliance with the Progressive Conservative Party. They became the Conservative Party of Canada. In 2004, Harper resigned as leader of the opposition to run for leadership of the Conservative Party of Canada, winning the election. The Liberals were reelected as a minority government with the conservatives coming in second. In 2006, after a vote of no confidence in the scandal plagued liberal government, the Conservatives won the federal election and established a minority government with Harper as prime minister. In 2008, Harper and the Conservative Party were reelected. Harper received the Woodrow Wilson Award in 2006 for his Calgary public service. In 2008 he was awarded the Presidential Gold Medal for Humanitarianism by B'nai B'rith International.

Harper has stated, "Threats to the U.S. are threats to Canada" (Brennan 2009). He is fulfilling a campaign promise that Canada Border Service agents will be armed and that situations where they would need to work alone will be avoided. They are being provided with side arms to deal with transnational threats such as high-risk individuals, firearms, explosives, and drugs.

Eric H. Holder (1951–)

Eric Holder is a Columbia University and Columbia Law School graduate who began employment at the Department of Justice (DOJ). At the DOJ, he moved upward through the ranks and, in 1988, became an Associate Judge in the Superior Court of the District of Columbia. From 1993 to 1997, Eric Holder served as U.S. District Attorney for the District of Columbia by appointment of President Bill Clinton. He became Deputy Attorney General under Janet Reno from 1997 to 2001. Holder's actions in support of President Clinton's controversial pardon of Marc Rich, a financier who had fled the country due to criminal charges, were controversial. Eric Holder indicated that his opinion of the pardon was "neutral, leaning toward favorable" and Holder was accused of being too friendly with Rich's lawyer, Jack Quinn. After his appointment, he joined the corporate legal firm of

Covington & Burling from 2001 to 2008. After Barack Obama won the presidency, he nominated Holder to be Attorney General. Eric Holder was confirmed on 2-2-2009 and became the first African American to serve as Attorney General. In 2010, Holder began working with Congress on a law to permit law enforcement to delay giving Miranda warnings to terrorist suspects.

Edward Kennedy (1932–2009)

Edward Moore "Ted" Kennedy was born in Brookline, Massachusetts. He entered Harvard University in 1950, served in the U.S. Army beginning in 1951, and returned to Harvard in 1953, graduating in 1956. Kennedy attended the University of Virginia Law School and graduated in 1958. In 1960, he became an assistant district attorney in Suffolk County, Massachusetts. When his brother John F. Kennedy was elected president in 1960, Ted Kennedy stepped forward to run to fill his Massachusetts Senate seat in 1962. Despite lack of experience and criticism that he was using his brother's success, he won and then was reelected to a full term in 1964, serving through reelection until his death from brain cancer in 2009.

Kennedy was poised to run for president in 1972 when his actions became a national scandal. After a party on Chappaquiddick Island, Massachusetts, he drove away with Mary Jo Kopechne as a passenger. He had an accident in which his car fell off a narrow bridge and Kopechne was killed. Kennedy did not immediately report the accident and later pled guilty to a misdemeanor charge of leaving the scene. His presence, as a married man, in the company of a young, unmarried woman and his lack of responsible actions after the accident permanently impacted his political standing, and he did not run for president in 1972. He later ran for president in the Democratic primaries in 1980, but lost.

Kennedy was a strong advocate of social welfare legislation and a consistent supporter of legal immigration opportunities. He became the senior Democrat on the Immigration Subcommittee of the Judiciary Committee. He was the sponsor of the Enhanced Border Security Act of 2001 and was the coauthor of the 2007 Senate Immigration Reform Bill with John McCain, which was not passed. The bill was controversial because of its proposed path to legalization for undocumented residents and guest-worker program. For border security, it would have provided for an increase in U.S. Border Patrol agents, increased interior enforcement, strengthened electronic surveillance measures, and provided more border fencing.

Michele Marie Leonhart

Michele Leonhart is a 1978 graduate of Bemidji State University in Minnesota with a B.S. in criminal justice. She began her career as a police officer with the Baltimore Police Department, graduating from the Baltimore Police Academy and patrolling the Northwest District of Baltimore. In 1980, Leonhart became a Drug Enforcement Administration (DEA) special agent and began work in Minneapolis. In 1986, she was transferred to the Saint Louis field division and worked as a recruiter. Next, Leonhart was promoted as a GS-14 Group Supervisor in San Diego, working in the border region on intelligence and then enforcement. Her enforcement group dealt with a Bolivia cocaine cartel whose leader, Jorge Roca-Suarez, and co-defendants were arrested and convicted with $14 million in assets seized. She was acknowledged as group supervisor with a 1993 DEA Administrator's Award.

In 1993, Leonhart moved to DEA headquarters in Arlington, Virginia, working as an internal affairs inspector with the DEA Office of Professional Responsibility. Promoted to GS-15, she served on the DEA's Career Board until 1995, when she became assistant special agent in charge of the Los Angeles Field Division. In 1996, she was promoted to the Senior Executive Service and supervised the Special Agent Recruitment Program at headquarters. In 1997, she took charge of the San Francisco Field Division, commanding the heavily trafficked Los Angeles area, Nevada, Hawaii, Guam, and Saipan. In 2003, President Bush named her acting DEA deputy administrator. She was confirmed by the Senate in 2004. In 2008, she was nominated to become the next administrator of DEA. Leonhart is acting administrator of the DEA.

John McCain (1936–)

John McCain was born in the Panama Canal Zone and grew up on naval bases in the United States and internationally. His father, John McCain Jr., was an admiral who commanded the American navy in the Pacific during the Vietnam War. A graduate of Episcopal High School in 1954, McCain attended the U.S. Naval Academy in Annapolis, completing in 1958 and going on to become a naval aviator. On October 26, 1967, McCain was hit by an antiaircraft missile during a mission and ejected, receiving multiple broken bones. Held by the enemy, he received delayed medical care. Spending five and a half years as a prisoner of war, he was released on March 17, 1973. John McCain received the Silver Star, Bronze Star, Legion of Merit, Purple Heart, and Distinguished Flying Cross. Next, he attended the National War College in Washington, DC, in 1973–1974, but wished to fly. He became a training squadron commander in 1975 and was promoted to captain in 1977. In that year, the Navy made McCain its liaison to the U.S. Senate.

John McCain retired from the Navy in 1981 and was employed by his wife's father, a beer distributor. In 1982, he ran for the U.S. Congress as a Republican and won, keeping the seat with reelection. In 1986 McCain was elected to the Senate, a position he has consistently held through reelection. Throughout, McCain has been a Republican but is also known for taking stands with the Democrats. In 2008, McCain ran for president but lost to Barack Obama. John McCain was the cosponsor of the 2007 Secure America and Orderly Immigration Act. He prioritized border security but also favored a path to legalization for unauthorized immigrants and a guest-worker program.

Khalid Shaikh Mohammed (1964– or 1965–)

Khalid Shaikh Mohammed was born in Kuwait to parents from Baluchistan in Pakistan and spent some of his childhood in Kuwait, as did his nephew, Ramzi Yousef, a planner in the 1993 World Trade Center bombing. At age 16, Shaikh Mohammed joined the Muslim Brotherhood and subsequently went to Pakistan. Later, he went to the United States and attended the Baptist Chowan College in Murfreesboro, North Carolina, for one semester before transferring to North Carolina Agricultural and Technical State University. He received a degree in mechanical engineering in 1986.

In the late 1980s, Khalid Shaikh Mohammed went to Afghanistan and fought against the Soviet invasion. Afterward, he went to work for an electronics company, servicing communications equipment. Next, he worked with an organization helping Afghan fighters against the Soviets. In 1992, he went to fight with Muslims in Bosnia and Herzegovina. Afterward, he was a project engineer for the Qatari Ministry of Electricity through 1996, when he fled to Pakistan because he had become a U.S. terrorism suspect in the 1993 WTC bombing.

Beginning in 1999, he acted as a member of al-Qaeda, managing propaganda. The 9/11 Commission believes that he planned the 9/11 attacks. Khalid was captured in Pakistan on March 2003 and has been in U.S. custody since, including at Guantanamo Bay. There are allegations that the United States tortured him. CIA Director Michael Hayden stated before a Senate Committee on February 5, 2008, that waterboarding had been used. His subsequent confessions include a statement that he masterminded the 9/11 attacks, among other actions.

Khalid Shaikh Mohammed is a U.S. prisoner alleged to have committed acts of terrorism, including mass murder of civilians. On February 11, 2008, a military tribunal charged him with war crimes and murder and he faces the death penalty. In November 2009, it was announced that he will stand trial in a civilian federal court in New York City. The decision to hold the trial in a civilian court and locate it in New York City resulted in controversy and subsequent postponements of the trial.

Janet Ann Napolitano (1957–)

Born in New York City, Janet Napolitano was raised in Pittsburgh, Pennsylvania, and Albuquerque, New Mexico. She graduated from Sandia High School in Albuquerque and was voted "mostly likely to succeed." Napolitano was valedictorian of her class at Santa Clara University in Santa Clara, California, where she received a Truman Scholarship. She went on to the University of Virginia School of Law, and her first position was as a law clerk for Judge Mary M. Schroeder, who served on the U.S. Court of Appeals for the Ninth Circuit. Next, Napolitano joined the firm of Lewis and Roca in Phoenix, Arizona. In 1991 she was an attorney for Anita Hill, who testified before the Senate that she had been sexually harassed by Clarence Thomas when she was working for him at the Equal Employment Opportunity Commission.

In 1993, Janet Napolitano was appointed as U.S. attorney for the District of Arizona by President Bill Clinton. She was elected Arizona attorney general in 1998. In 2002, she was elected governor of Arizona and she won reelection in 2006. In 2006, Napolitano received the Woodrow Wilson Award for Public Service. She is a past member of the Democratic Governors Association and served as chair of the Western Governors Association and National Governors Association from from 2006 to 2007.

In 2009, Janet Napolitano began as the new Director of Homeland Security. Her initial duties have included dealing with the possibility that drug-related violence in Mexico will spill over to the United States and taking steps to prevent arms smuggling to Mexico.

Barack Hussein Obama (1961–)

The first African American or member of any minority to be elected president of the United States, Barack Obama was born in Honolulu, Hawaii, but grew up in both the United States and Indonesia. In 1979, he attended Occidental College in Los Angeles but transferred to Columbia University in New York City, majoring in political science with a specialization in international relations and receiving a B.A. Obama worked for the Business International Corporation and the New York Public Interest Research Group. Next, he moved to Chicago and was a director of the Developing Communities Project, a church-based community organization, from 1985 to 1988. In 1988, Obama went to Harvard Law School, where he was editor and then president of the *Harvard Law Review* before graduating with a Juris Doctorate magna cum laude.

In 1992, Obama structured the Project Vote registration drive in Illinois. Next he joined the Davis, Miner, Barnhill and Galland law firm, which specialized in civil rights and neighborhood economic development litigation. He was an associate from 1993 to 1996 and worked as counsel until 2004. Concurrently, he was a lecturer at the University of Chicago Law School from 1992 to 1996 and a senior lecturer from 1996 to 2004. From 1997 to 2004, Obama served in the Illinois Senate for the 13th District for three terms. He was defeated when running for the House of Representatives in 2000 and ran successfully for the U.S. Senate in 2004. In the Senate, Barack Obama supported the Secure America and Orderly Immigration Bill, which was not passed by Congress, and voted for the Secure Fence Act of 2006. In 2005–2006, Obama served on the Foreign Relations Committee and in 2007 he joined the Homeland Security and Governmental Affairs Committee.

In 2006 and 2008, Obama won Best Spoken Word Album Grammy Awards for the abridged audiobook version of *Dreams from My Father* (1995) and *The Audacity of Hope* (2008). Barack Obama's "Yes We Can" speech was set to music by independent artists and received a Daytime Emmy Award. In 2008, Obama was elected president of the United States and named *Time* magazine's Person of the Year, and in 2009, he received the Nobel Peace Prize.

Action taken by President Obama against Mexican drug-trafficking organizations (DTOs) include presidential authorization of seizure of any DTO assets in the United States and intensified enforcement efforts to apprehend U.S. citizens involved in drug or arms smuggling and money laundering. Regarding immigration, Obama believes that the U.S. system is broken and that it needs to be reformed. He backs a path to legalization for unauthorized immigrants. Obama's border-security policy follows that of his predecessor George W. Bush in authorizing increased funding for border-security inspections, trade facilitation at ports of entry (POEs), an increase in operational control in between POEs, and increases in air and marine operations, border fencing, infrastructure, and technology.

Nancy Pelosi (1940–)

Nancy Pelosi was born in Baltimore, Maryland, the daughter of a five-term congressman, Thomas D'Alesandro Jr. She attended Trinity College in Washington, DC, where she met her future husband, Paul Pelosi. Paul Pelosi was from San Francisco and they moved there and raised a family. Her first political position was as the Northern California Party chairwoman. She ran for Congress in 1987 and has been reelected every two years from California's Eighth District, a left-oriented constituency located in San Francisco. She served on the Appropriations and Intelligence Committee for 10 years as the ranking Democrat. Following the 9/11 terrorist attacks, she authored the bill creating the independent 9/11 Commission to investigate U.S. strategic intelligence failures.

In 2001, Pelosi became House minority whip, the first woman so selected. She replaced Richard Gephart as the House minority leader in 2004. She led Democratic criticism of the George W. Bush administration and was key to the reunification of Democrats prior to their taking control of both the House and Senate in the 2008 elections. Pelosi became Speaker of the House in 2009. She has been a co-sponsor of the Secure America and Orderly Immigration Act that would provide a path to legalization and start a guest-worker program. She voted against the Secure Fence Act of 2006 and in favor of the Border Tunnel Protection Act of 2006, which increased criminal penalties for tunneling. She later reversed her position and in 2007 voted for an amendment to increase border-fence funding.

Ahmed Ressam (1967–)

Labeled the "Millennium Bomber" by the media, Ahmed Ressam was born in Algeria. In 1994, he used a forged French passport to gain entrance to Canada by claiming political asylum from persecution in Algeria. Surviving through criminal activity, he was recruited to al-Qaeda. When he failed to appear for an asylum hearing, his asylum application was turned down and a warrant issued for his arrest. At that time he obtained a passport under the name "Benni Noris" and used it to travel to Afghanistan for military training for jihadists. In 1999, Ressam returned to Canada with plans for making an explosive weapon to attack a U.S. target. He decided to attack the Los Angeles Airport on the eve of the millennium, known as the "millennium attack plot."

On December 14, 1999, Ressam boarded the M/V Coho at Victoria on Vancouver Island, Canada, and attempted to pass border security at Port Angeles, Washington. Under suspicion, he had been monitored by Canadian intelligence for two years in Montreal. He disappeared and was traced to a motel room in British Columbia where bomb-making materials were left behind. The Royal Canadian Mounties notified U.S. Customs of a possible bomb threat. Ressam was cleared by U.S. immigration in Victoria. Ressam was uneasy and attempted to flee border inspection in Port Angeles, Washington. Diana Dean, a border agent, decided to search Ressam's car and found explosives meant for a bombing of LAX.

After conviction, Ressam eventually received 22 years plus 5 years supervision after release. The sentencing was delayed to win his cooperation in providing intelligence about terrorism. In 2001, Ressam cooperated with U.S. investigators and told them that al-Qaeda had sleeper cells in the United States. The President's Daily Briefing given to George Bush on August 6, 2001, contained information from Ressam and was titled "Bin Laden Determined to Strike in U.S." In 2007, the U.S. Court of Appeals for the Ninth Circuit in Seattle reversed one of the charges on which he was convicted and assigned him for resentencing. The Supreme Court overturned this decision in 2008 and restored the original conviction and sentence. The FBI projects that he will be released on July 6, 2019, when Ressam will be subject to removal for commission of an aggravated felony.

Silvestre Reyes (1944–)

Silvestre Reyes, a Mexican American, was born in Canutillo, Texas, a rural community located five miles from El Paso, Texas. Raised on a farm, Reyes first spoke Spanish and learned English in grade school. As a youngster, he watched for agents from the Border Patrol in order to warn unauthorized workers on the farm to hide. During summers, Reyes was a migrant farm worker in the Lower Rio Grande Valley of Texas and California. In 1966 he joined the military and fought in Vietnam for two years. Afterwards, GI benefits enabled him to attend El Paso Community College, from which he graduated in 1977, and then the University of Texas at El Paso and Austin, while working to support a family. He received the Outstanding Alumnus Award of the American Association of Community Colleges, 2001.

In 1969 Silvestre Reyes joined the Immigration and Naturalization Service (INS). He was promoted to be assistant regional commissioner in Dallas, Texas, where he had responsibility for 13 states and a $100 million budget. From 1984 to 1995, he was the Border Patrol chief for El Paso, Texas, supervising 900 employees and McAllen, Texas, with 500 employees. Prior to Reyes' supervision, the Border Patrol was viewed as largely ineffective, but Reyes introduced changes including the Canine Program. He has received national recognition for starting

Operation Hold the Line in 1993. Instead of using Border Patrol agents to catch undocumented migrants in the United States, which often involved harassment of Hispanic U.S. citizens, he strengthened enforcement to deter them from trying by visibly stationing agents at the border. This operation caused a major decline in migrants' attempts to cross at El Paso. Operation Hold the Line has been criticized for displacing attempts to enter without authorization to more dangerous rural regions, which has led to deaths. El Paso itself is considered to have suffered because of loss of unauthorized laborers and their consumer purchases. Finally, Reyes was criticized as a Mexican American who policed Mexicans, an accusation that offended him.

Upon retirement from the Border Patrol, he was elected as a Democrat to the U.S. Congress 16th District, representing El Paso County in Texas, a position he has served in through 2010. After the 9/11 attacks, Reyes focused on border security and was appointed to the Democratic Caucus Homeland Security Task Force. As a member of Congress, Reyes received the National Legislative Award, League of United Latin American Citizens in 2002. He is the chair of the House Permanent Select Committee on Intelligence and a member of the House Armed Services Committee, the Veterans Affairs Committee, and the Special Oversight Panel on Terrorism. Reyes opposed the Secure Border Act of 2006 and has promoted electronic surveillance to achieve a "virtual fence."

He is a past chair of the Congressional Hispanic Caucus and active in many congressional caucuses, including the Law Enforcement Caucus, the National Security Caucus, the Congressional Human Rights Caucus, the Older Americans Caucus, the Urban Caucus, and the Democratic Caucus Task Force on Education. In addition, he is a member of the Air Force Academy Visitors Board, American Legion, Association of the U.S. Army, AMVETS, Disabled American Veterans, Transatlantic Learning Community, US/Mexico Interparliamentary Group, Veterans of Foreign Wars, and Vietnam Veterans of America.

Tom Ridge

Tom Ridge was born August 26, 1945, in Munhill, Pennsylvania, and grew up in a housing project in Erie, Pennsylvania. He graduated from Harvard University in 1967 and began at the Dickinson

School of Law before being drafted and serving for two years as an infantryman in Vietnam. Ridge received the Bronze Star for Valor. He returned to law school and received a J.D. in 1972. He began in private practice and then served as a public defender. From 1979 to 1982, he was Erie County assistant district attorney. Ridge was elected as a Republican to the U.S. House of Representatives in 1982 and served until 1994, when he was elected governor for two terms.

Following the September 11, 2001, attacks, Tom Ridge became the first director of the Office of Homeland Security and transitioned to be the secretary of the Homeland Security Department in charge of 22 agencies and 180,000 employees. In 2003, the DHS sustained criticism from Congress and the public over its expensive planning, which it lacked the funding to carry through. In 2004, the United States began the war in Iraq and concern about terrorist attacks again increased. In December 2004, Tom Ridge resigned, citing job stress and personal financial issues. He is the author with Larry Bloom of *The Test of Our Times: America Under Siege . . . And How We Can Be Safe Again* (2009).

James Sensenbrenner (1943–)

James Sensenbrenner was born in Chicago and raised in Shorewood, Wisconsin, where he attended the private Milwaukee County Day School, graduating in 1961. He attended Stanford University, graduating with a B.A. in political science in 1965. In 1968, he received a J.D. from the University of Wisconsin Law School.

In 1968, Sensenbrenner, a Republican, was elected to the Wisconsin State Assembly and served until 1975, when he was elected to the Wisconsin State Senate, a position he served in until early 1979. In 1979, he was elected in Wisconsin's 9th District (now reapportioned as the 5th) to Congress and has been reelected 14 times. His congressional activities include service on the Committee of the Judiciary, including its subcommittee on the Constitution, Civil Rights, and Civil Liberties, where he is the ranking member. After Democrats became the majority in Congress in 2009, he finished his term as chairman of the House Judiciary committee.

On October 23, 2001, James Sensenbrenner introduced the USA PATRIOT Act, which he did not author. He is a strong advocate of the Bush administration's War on Terror policies. He has authored the Real ID Act of 2005, which would require proof of citizenship when issuing licenses and authorizes a federal driver's license database. Beginning in 2004, Sensenbrenner has repeatedly supported bills that would eliminate the immigration visa lottery. In 2005, Sensenbrenner sponsored H.R. 4437, a bill that would increase criminal penalties for aiding and abetting unauthorized entry to the United States.

September 11 Commission/ 9/11 Commission

The National Commission on Terrorist Attacks upon the United States (9/11 Commission) was established by legislative act of Congress on November 27, 2002 to investigate the details of the September 11, 2001, attacks, including the degree to which the United States was prepared and how it responded. It had a mandate to develop recommendations to prevent future terrorist attacks.

The cochairs were Thomas Kean and Lee H. Hamilton. Other members were Richard Ben-Veniste, Max Cleland, Fred F. Fielding, Jamie Gorlick, Slade Gorton, Bob Kerrey, John F. Lehman, Timothy J. Roemer, and James R. Thompson. The massive final report was based on numerous interviews and testimony. The 9/11 Commission concluded that the lack of intelligence sharing between the Central Intelligence Agency and the Federal Bureau of Investigation permitted the attack to be carried out and that it could possibly have been prevented. Major points of the report that have shaped border security policy include the development of a system to monitor terrorists' travel and prevent their entrance, integration of the U.S. border-security system into a larger network of screening points including international airports, development of a biometric entry-exit system, development of a secure identification system, and creation of a Department of Homeland Security with information-sharing capacity. Afterwards, co-chairs Kean and Hamilton wrote *Without Precedent: The Inside Story of the 9/11 Commission* about problematic issues faced in the investigation, including their skepticism about whether they were told the full story by U.S. government officials.

Arlen Specter (1930–)

Born in Wichita, Kansas, Arlen Specter graduated Phi Beta Kappa with a major in international relations from the University of Pennsylvania in 1951. He served in the U.S. Air Force in the Office of Special Investigations from 1951 to 1953 and then attended Yale Law School, graduating in 1956. He opened a Pennsylvania law practice with Marvin Katz and became an assistant district attorney under District Attorney James Crumlish as a Democrat. Arlen Specter was a member of the Warren Commission, investigating the assassination of President John F. Kennedy.

In 1965, Specter ran for district attorney as a Republican and won, ultimately serving two terms. In 1976, he was defeated in the Republican primary for a Senate seat and in 1978 he was defeated running for governor. After working in the firm of Dechert, Price and Rhoads, he ran for the Senate successfully in 1980. He became chairman of the House Judiciary Committee from 2005 to 2007. Arlen Specter is a member of the Committee on Appropriations, including the Subcommittee on Homeland Security; and the Committee on the Judiciary, including the Subcommittee on the Constitution, the Subcommittee on Crime and Drugs (past chair), and the Subcommittee on Human Rights and the Law.

Specter was critical of warrantless wiretapping. Nevertheless, he voted for the 2008 amendments to the Foreign Intelligence Surveillance Act, which places authority for electronic searches with the federal executive branch. He is considered conservative on national and border-security issues. Specter introduced Senate Bill 2611, the Comprehensive Immigration Reform Act of 2006, and supports both a pathway to citizenship for unauthorized immigrants and a guest-worker program. S. 2611 was passed by the Senate and stalled in the House. His view on immigration is liberal. Specter switched parties and ran for the Senate in the Democratic in 2010, but was defeated.

Tom Tancredo (1945–)

Born in Denver, Colorado, Tom Tancredo attended Holy Family High School. He has a B.A. in political science from the University of Northern Colorado. His professional career began as a history teacher at Drake Junior High School in Denver. In 1976 he ran for the Colorado House of Representatives and won, serving until 1981. In 1981, he was appointed by Ronald Reagan to be regional representative for the Department of Education. In 1993, he became president of the Independence Institute, a conservative think-tank in Golden, Colorado.

In 1998, he ran for Congress in the 6th District and won, serving for four terms. In Congress he served on the Foreign Affairs Committee and Subcommittee on Terrorism, Nonproliferation, and Trade. Tancredo is noted for his position on immigration and was critical of the Bush administration's border-security policy. He introduced the Mass Immigration Reduction Act in 1999 (H.R. 41), 2001 (H.R. 2712), and 2003 (H.R. 946). This bill would have placed an indefinite moratorium on U.S. immigration except for spouses and children of American citizens. The five-year moratorium would be extended until it was estimated that fewer than 10,000 unauthorized migrants were entering the U.S. each year and at a level that would not negatively impact the legal population. In 2006, Tancredo authored *In Mortal Danger: The Battle for America's Border and Security*. A controversial strategy for reducing U.S.-Mexico border and interior violence that he has promoted is the legalization of marijuana. In 2008, Tom Tancredo introduced H.R. 6975, the Jihad Prevention Act. The legislation would require aliens seeking admission to state that they would not advocate establishing a Sharia (Muslim) legal system in the United States. Potential entrants refusing to attest would be denied while visitors would have their visas revoked.

Tancredo was an early Republican candidate for president in 2007–2008, announcing that his participation was contingent on failure to address illegal immigration, which he viewed as a major threat to national security. He stood for strict enforcement of immigration law, a border fence, deportation of unauthorized immigrants, and ending sanctuary policies protecting the unauthorized entrants.

Ramzi Yousef

Born in Kuwait of Pakistani descent, Ramzi Yousef was partly educated in England, where he graduated from the Swansea Institute in Wales, majoring in electrical engineering. Later

Yousef attended an al-Qaeda training camp and learned bomb-making. He has a history of terrorist planning other than the first World Trade Center bombing: (1) the 1993 Benazir Bhutto assassination attempt; (2) carrying out the 1994 Imam Reza Shrine bombing; (3) preplanning for the failed Bojinka multiple airline hijacking plot; and (4) creation and placing of a bomb which exploded on 1994 Philippine Airlines Flight 434.

Ramzi Yousef was able to enter the United States with a passport and was taken into custody by the Immigration and Naturalization Service. A traveling companion was arrested with false immigration documents and terrorist materials in his luggage. It is considered that this served as a smokescreen. Yousef claimed political asylum and was interrogated while held, but he was released because of overcrowding in detention. Because he stated that he was a Pakistani national who had lost his passport, the New York Pakistani Consulate issued him a temporary document.

With the assistance of terrorist conspirators, Yousef assembled a 1,500-pound urea, nitrate, and hydrogen gas bomb to be delivered to the World Trade Center on February 26, 1993. The bombing was carried out by detonating a bomb inside a car under Tower One. It was intended to undermine Tower One and have it fall on Tower Two, destroying both towers and killing thousands of civilians. Instead, six people were killed and 1,042 injured. The *New York Times* printed a letter sent by Yousef which stated, "We declare our responsibility for the explosion on the mentioned building. This action was done in response for the American political, economic, and military support for Israel, the state of terrorism and to the rest of the dictator countries in the region."

Yousef was captured in Islamabad, Pakistan, in 1995 and extradited to the United States. On trial, Yousef said, "Yes, I am a terrorist, and proud of it as long as it is against the U.S. government and against Israel, because you are more than terrorists; you are the one who invented terrorism and using it every day. You are butchers, liars and hypocrites." In 1996, Yousef was one of three conspirators convicted for the Bojinka plot and sentenced to life in prison with no parole. In 1997, Yousef was convicted of planning the 1993 WTC bombing and in 1998 was also convicted of seditious conspiracy in the WTC case. Ramzi Yousef is in detention at the Supermax prison ADX Florence in Florence, Colorado.

6

Data and Documents

Border Security

A limited, solely terrorism-focused definition of border security focuses on "all efforts by the United States and other actors to interdict terrorists and their weapons of destruction at the U.S. border" (Lake 2007, 2). Yet, in the process of looking at all aspects of the maintenance of border security, one finds that:

> Initially it [border security] starts with direct intervention to prevent threats and interdict dangerous people and goods at the U.S. border itself (in terms of ports of entry at land, sea or air terminals). Protection efforts at the border are extended to encompass both such *extra*-border activities as targeting and pre-inspection of people and cargo in originating ports around the world, *cross-border efforts between ports of entry* by the Border Patrol, as well as *intra*-U.S. efforts to intercept people and goods as they are shipped inland from their initial port of arrival (or from internal U.S. sites). The latter involves using the internal enforcement tools of the Federal Bureau of Investigation (FBI), Immigration and Customs Enforcement (ICE), and other law enforcement agents. (Lake 2007, 2)

A more comprehensive definition of *border security* refers to more than the process of maintaining orderly entrance and exit of people and goods at a nation's borders (land, sea, or air). It involves

209

the externalization of the border through pre-inspection of travelers and cargo at ports outside the United States and the internalization of monitoring goods and people to detect proscribed goods and unauthorized entrants after they have passed through a border and into the interior. This process of monitoring, "inside and out," is based on the external checks abroad of visas and passports of travelers or cargo documentation at exiting countries, inspection of people and cargo at the U.S. borders and payment of any tariff fees, and a process of search for contraband such as drugs or unauthorized entrants in the interior.

In order to prevent terrorist acts, the process of effecting border security involves five missions:

1. Discovery and Interdiction of Terrorist Action Emanating from Abroad
2. Interdiction at the Border
3. Defending Against Catastrophic Terrorism Inside the United States
4. Protection of Critical Infrastructure and Populations
5. Emergency Preparedness and Response (Lake 2007, 3–4)

Other missions that have traditionally involved border enforcement and that became intertwined with prevention of terrorism, which became the *primary* mission, are:

1. Prevention of unauthorized entry by migrants into the United States.
2. Prevention of the smuggling of contraband, such as drugs, into the United States and interdicting the smuggling of arms or other *external* contraband to countries outside of the United States such as Mexico.
3. Tracking of unauthorized migrants and immigrants and contraband inside the United States and arrest or seizure of people and goods.

The complexity of merging the new priority to stop terrorism with the traditional activity of interdicting unauthorized entrants and contraband will result in the development of new strategies and means of border control and interior enforcement. These *transboundary* efforts are in their infancy and such elements as the internal and external security nexus are incompletely understood (Eriksson and Rhinard 2009, 243).

Documents

Eriksson, Johan, and Mark Rhinard. 2009. "The Internal-External Security Nexus: Notes on an Emerging Research Agenda." *Cooperation and Conflict* 44 (3): 243–267.

Lake, Jennifer E. 2007. "Border Security: The Complexity of the Challenge." Washington, DC: Congressional Research Service. http://fpc.state.gov/documents/organization/80215.pdf.

Ports of Entry

Ports of entry are locations where people and goods can be authorized for entrance into a country. Individual passports and visas or cargos are inspected to prevent passage of fraudulent entrants and smuggled goods. There are 327 designated ports of entry, including 15 preclearance stations, for international travelers and cargo to enter the United States. Roads, railroads, and international airports which cross boundaries are typically designated ports of entry. Certain land ports of entry are designated as bridges because they cross rivers or other bodies of water to connect two bordering countries. In 2008, 29 million trade entries were processed and $34.5 billion in revenue was collected (USCBP 2009).

Typically, immigration inspectors and U.S. Customs officers are present at ports of entry. In 2008, 409 million pedestrians and passengers were processed. Whether or not an air or sea port is classified as a port of entry for persons is a decision left to the civil authority controlling it. Many non-land border ports choose not to grant international entry.

Source: http://www.cbp.gov/.

The Department of Homeland Security (DHS)

The prioritization of prevention of terrorism resulted in the reorganization of federal law enforcement in order to consolidate intelligence from external, border, and interior sources. One major change was the dissolving of the Immigration and Naturalization Service (INS). In the DHS, U.S. Customs and the U.S. Border

FIGURE 6.1
Department of Homeland Security organization chart

U.S. DEPARTMENT OF HOMELAND SECURITY

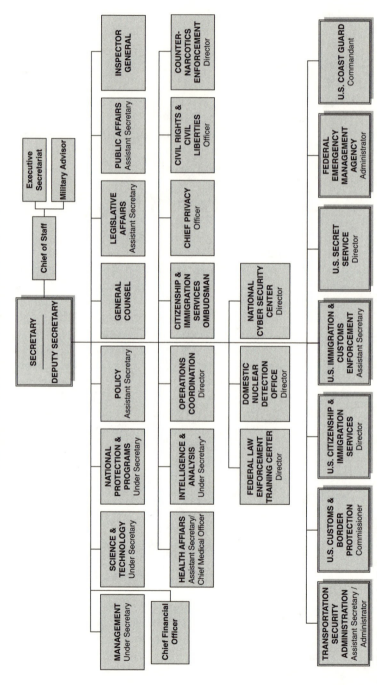

*Under Secretary for Intelligence & Analysis title created by Public Law 110-53, Aug. 3rd, 2007
Approved 3/20/2008

Patrol were subsumed as U.S. Customs and Border Patrol, which included the U.S. Border Patrol (USBP) and Immigration and Customs Enforcement (ICE). The Bureau of Citizenship and Immigration Services (CIS) took over the remainder of INS activity. Whether or not this effort has improved national and border security will not been known in such a short period of time.

As can be seen in the Department of Homeland Security chart, the United States has created one of the largest law enforcement and regulatory bureaucracies in the world. The complexity of law-enforcement cooperation is increased when one considers that inter-federal agency law enforcement and intelligence cooperation is expected despite a history of competitiveness between these agencies.

U.S. Border Patrol

Expansion of budget and personnel for the U.S. Border Patrol has been recurrent despite controversy over its effectiveness at controlling unauthorized immigration and human rights issues. In FY1992, their budget was $326 million and a steady rate of

TABLE 6.1
U.S. Border Patrol budget, FY1992–2009

Fiscal Year	Millions ($)
1992	326
1993	363
1994	400
1995	452
1996	568
1997	717
1998	877
1999	917
2000	1,055
2001	1,146
2002	1,416
2003	1,515
2004	1,409
2005	1,525
2006	2,115
2007	2,278
2008	2,245
2009	2,656

Source: U. S. Border Patrol Headquarters, Office of Public Affairs, September 25, 2009.

TABLE 6.2
U.S. Border Patrol agents stationed along the southwest border, FY1992–2009

Fiscal Year	Number of Agents
1992	3,555
1993	3,444
1994	3,747
1995	4,388
1996	5,333
1997	6,315
1998	7,357
1999	7,706
2000	8,580
2001	9,147
2002	9,239
2003	9,840
2004	9,506
2005	9,891
2006	11,032
2007	13,297
2008	15,442
2009	17,415

Source: U.S. Border Patrol Headquarters, Department of Public Affairs, September 25, 2009.

TABLE 6.3
U.S. Customs and Border Patrol and Immigration
and Customs Enforcement budgets, 2003–2009

Fiscal Year	CBP Budget (in billion $)	ICE Budget (in billion $)
2003	6.00	3.67
2004	6.34	3.13
2005	7.11	3.87
2006	7.75	4.70
2007	9.31	5.05
2008	10.94	5.68
2009	11.27	5.93

Source: U. S. Department of Homeland Security, budget in brief for FY2003–2009.

increase brought operating costs to $2,656 billion in FY2009 with further increases likely.

Increases in U.S. Border Patrol funding have largely gone to hire an increasing number of agents at the U.S.-Mexico border. In 1992 there were 3,555 agents. By 2009, 17,415 agents and staff were employed by the USBP and it was being repeatedly augmented by National Guardsmen or, in Texas, Texas Rangers. This degree of growth in personnel involves a major expansion of law enforcement on the southern border.

The increase in U.S. Border Patrol funding is not matched by increases in Immigration and Customs Enforcement (ICE) staffing. The focus has been on stationing USBP agents on line watch at the border to deter entry in urban areas and increasing agents on duty in rural regions, which have also been augmented by walls, fencing, and remote surveillance technology.

Low-Intensity Conflict Doctrine and the Militarization of the Border

Historically, the Canadian and Mexican borders have been among the most peaceful worldwide because of the absence of any military threat. In the 1970s, the United States and, to a lesser degree, Mexico began the use of military tactics and technology to control civilian cross-border activities such as unauthorized immigration and drug trafficking. Timothy J. Dunn (1996), a social scientist, introduced the concept of the militarization of the

TABLE 6.4
Spectrum of militarization of the U.S.-Mexico border, less militaristic
(1) to most militaristic (11)

1. Military gives or loans equipment to the Border Patrol (BP) and Law Enforcement Agencies (LEA)
2. Military troops operate and/or maintain loaned equipment
3. Military provides "expert advice" to BP and LEAs
4. Military construction for BP/LEAs
5. Military provides advisors and training for BP/LEAs
6. Military transports supplies, personnel, and equipment for BP and LEAs
7. Military aerial reconnaissance and surveillance for BP and LEAs
8. Military ground troops deployed on a small scale at or near border, mainly recon for BP/LEAs
9. "Improved integration"—"Total Integration" of military and BP/LEA efforts. Blurring of institutional lines between military and BP/LEAs
10. Massive deployment of military troops at or near border to perform variety of border enforcement roles
11. Military granted authority to arrest, search, seize civilians and property

Note: Sections 1 through 3: Allowed by the 1982 DOD Defense Authorization law; added new chapter to U.S. law, *Military Cooperation with Civilian Law Enforcement Officials*. This support is allowed for police bodies with jurisdiction to enforce drug, contraband, and immigration laws.
Sections 4 through 9: Allowed by 1989–1981 Defense Authorization Laws, amending 1982 provisions, specific to drug enforcement (broader in practice, however).
Sections 10 and 11: Bills filed and debated in Congress; no laws passed.
Source: Dunn, Timothy J. 2001. "Border Militarization Via Drug and Immigration Enforcement: Human Rights Implications." *Social Justice* 28 (2): 24.

U.S.-Mexico border. It refers to the use of low-intensity conflict doctrine, military tactics for guerrilla warfare, and military occupation to deal with armed insurgency and drug trafficking in Central and South America. Dunn (1996, 2001) classified the degree of military involvement on a scale from 1 (less) to 11 (most) as the type of military assistance and the degree of military involvement in direct interaction with civilian populations increased.

The militarization of the border peaked on May 20, 1997, when a Marine shot and killed Esequiel Hernandez, a U.S. citizen who was herding goats near Redford, Texas (Dunn 2001). Recently, military troops or the National Guard have been sent to assist the U.S. Border Patrol, but they have not been deployed as armed troops with the purpose of civilian law enforcement.

Traveler and Cargo Inspection Programs at the Borders

On average, U.S. Customs and Border Patrol handles processing of millions of travelers and tens of thousands of truck, rail, and sea containers. A variety of risk assessment and documentation procedures, listed alphabetically below according to whether travelers or cargo are inspected, have been set up for this:

Travelor Processing and Inspection
Cross-Border Advanced Traveler Information System (ATIS): Flashing variable message road signs, Web sites, and other means are used to provide travelers with real-time transportation updates.
Electronic Advanced Passenger Information System (eAPIS): This computerized system allows entry of passenger and crew manifests for prescreening and tracking purposes. After the 9/11 attacks, international airlines and other carriers were asked to provide such information.
Electronic System for Travel Authorization (ESTA): This automated system confirms traveler eligibility for visa waiver in the case of approved countries. Processing is done before boarding a carrier.
International Global Entry: A trusted-traveler program in which risk assessment is used to allow quicker processing of preapproved U.S. citizens, U.S. nationals, lawful permanent residents of the United States, and citizens of cooperating countries. Frequent international travelers who undergo a background check can use

an automated kiosk for examination of a machine-readable passport and pass through an expedited CBP processing lane.

Student Exchange Visitor Information System (SEVIS): A Web-based program to track and monitor students, schools, exchange visitors, and their dependents through the duration of their U.S. education. SEVIS by the Numbers provides a breakdown of trends in participation by foreign students.

United States Visitor and Immigrant Status Indicator Technology (U.S.-VISIT): A biometric inspection system operating to process entrance of international visitors and immigrants at the air, land, and sea borders. Its purpose is to track people and protect against terrorist entry and attacks by increasing border security. The system is not yet able to track exit.

U.S.-Canada NEXUS. The NEXUS card allows American and Canadian citizens to receive preapproval before crossing the shared border. It satisfies the Western Hemisphere Travel Initiative requirement for verification of identity and citizenship and substitutes for a passport. The NEXUS card is used at a land border crossing for scanning and at airport kiosks for retinal scanning. The scan takes 10 seconds. At land borders, special NEXUS lanes allow faster processing meaning of "as to" unclear kiosks at airports. All citizens of Canada and the United States with no criminal history are eligible for the card. Currently NEXUS has 255,000 members.

U.S.-Mexico Border Crossing Card (BCC): The Illegal Immigration Reform and Immigrant Responsibility Act of 1996 authorized Border Crossing Cards for the United States and Mexico. The "laser visa" is equivalent to a B1/B2 visa. Cards issued after 2008 have more advanced graphics and technology. Mexican citizens must prove that they have the economic and family ties to Mexico indicating a strong potential to return before a card is issued. All applicants must previously have been issued a Mexican passport.

U.S.-Mexico SENTRI: The SENTRI card allows preapproved low-risk American and Mexican travelers a secure and verifiable citizenship document for expedited entry. It meets the standards of the Western Hemispheric Travel initiative requirement for a passport or other approved document. SENTRI has been established at 16 lanes of the 9 most used ports of entry. At non-SENTRI U.S.-Mexico ports, a border crossing card is needed.

Z-Portal Passenger Imaging System: This system allows drive-through passenger vehicles to be safely scanned for human stowaways, drugs, and security threats. It produces left, right, and top-down security scanning images of suspicious items while allowing quick vehicle inspection to facilitate travel. Vehicles waived from a primary to a secondary inspection line are examined with Z-Portal. Passengers can safely remain in their vehicle.

Cargo Crossing and Inspection

Automated Commercial Equipment (ACE): A computerized commercial trade processing system. It is a part of the automated commercial environment.

Canada's Partners in Protection (PIP): A Canadian Border Services Agency program involving cooperation with private industry to combat terrorism, organized crime, and smuggling. It concentrates on trade chain security, including assessment of infrastructure and procedures. It is a prerequisite to participation in the FAST program.

Canada and Mexico Customs Trade Partnership Against Terrorism (C-TPAT): A bilateral agreement between the United States and Canada for mutual security standards for trade goods being exported or imported.

Canada and Mexico Free and Secure Trade (FAST) program: The FAST program seeks to identify low-risk shippers and shipments using integrated technology to link trade at 55 of 105 ports handling truck traffic. Carriers and importers have a past history of customs compliance and agree to use procedures that minimize exposure to criminal opportunity. Importers, drivers, and carriers have reduced information requirements if they use sound and secure business procedure. Currently, 87,000 drivers are enrolled in FAST.

This program uses electronic data sent by preauthorized participants in advance of arrival at the border. In return, qualified participants receive expedited clearance of low-risk transborder shipments with limited physical inspection and the use of dedicated border-crossing lanes. Barcodes and transponder technology identify the driver, carrier, importer, and shipment, permitting fast processing. Typically, precleared shipments will not be examined and, if they are, it will be at a reduced rate compared to non-FAST shipments.

Canada and Mexico Automated Commercial System (ACS): The ACS for Canada and Mexico imports and exports is comprised of the following components.

> **Automated Broker Interface (ABI) and Contact Information:** A system operated by U.S. Customs to track, control, and process commercial goods being imported into the

United States. Data on goods to be imported is filed electronically with CBP. This voluntary program is open to brokers, importers, carriers, port authorities, and independent border service centers. ABI is used by 96% of all commercial goods being processed through the borders.

Automated Line Release (ALR) or Border Release Advanced Screening and Selectivity (BRASS) program: A CBP-expedited release program that uses a periodic "blanket" declaration and file any needed subsequent reconciliation reports.

Automated Manifest System (AMS): A cargo inventory control and release notification system connected to Customs Cargo Selectivity and In-Bond Systems and indirectly with ABI to allow faster identification and release of low-risk shipments by CBP. It is open to carriers, port authorities, service bureaus, freight forwarders, and container freight systems. Cargo is moved and tracked faster and Customs service is improved.

Border Cargo Selectivity System: A computerized means of risk assessment to determine the need for examination of cargo at high-volume borders. The system uses the same editing process as the Cargo Selectivity System. The Border Cargo Selectivity System will soon be enhanced to allow ABI filers to transmit manifest information.

Customs Cargo Selectivity: This system differentiates low-risk cargo from high-risk cargo and assigns it to an intensive or less rigorous examination. It accepts data from the Automated Broker Interface (ABI) and uses established risk criteria to make an inspection determination and to post a bill of lading. It allows cargo processing to be faster. The Border Cargo Selectivity System is a system using the same risk criteria to indicate need for examination at high-volume ports of entry.

Entry Summary Selectivity: This advanced risk analysis system matches local and national selectivity criteria with the entry summary data to access risk using information on importer, manufacturer, country of origin, value, and tariff number. It uses paperless summary activity and produces summary findings of discrepancies for possible inspection.

National In-Bond System: An automated system for tracking of cargo being sent to the United States with departure, arrival, and closure data. This is done with conventional paperwork or the Paperless Master In-Bond program. Paperless Entry allows ABI importers and exporters to do without a Customs Form 3461 Entry/Immediate Delivery if the cargo meets CBP criteria and the merchandise is classified as low risk and not needing examination. Electronic notification is sent when the goods are released.

Quota: A system that tracks the quantity of imported goods in relation to visas from sending countries. This is because visas determine export limits. Quantity is matched to the number of visas, and the information is sent to the country of origin to reconcile the amount of exports and imports.

U.S. Customs and Border Protection Secure Border Initiative (SBI)

The Secure Border Initiative involved development of the SBI Tactical Infrastructure Program. This was to establish electronic surveillance for a virtual border with Canada and Mexico until funding was canceled in March, 2010 due to problems in equipment functioning. The southwestern border is also being fenced. The trial video and mobile systems relied on day and night cameras, radar, and unattended ground sensors. SBI programs included:

SBI*net* Technology Program: This program was to develop, test, and deploy high-tech border surveillance gear to detect and track unauthorized migrants, drug smuggling, and other activities outside of the law. The objective was to develop situational awareness to detect and enable front-line personnel to respond to illegal cross-border activity.

Command, Control, Communications, and Intelligence (C3I) Common Operating Picture (COP) Program: This program was expected to provide real-time monitoring of the border to facilitate the use of agents to cover widespread areas by controlling and integrating sensors and providing the means to identify and classify border entries. It attempted to provide a display of border activity to initiate a tactical response in a situation in which multiple missions are carried out. The system was being built by the Boeing Corporation and its partners and had major cost overruns subject to U.S. Government Accountability Office criticism.

Tactical Infrastructure (TI) Program: A variety of pedestrian and vehicle fencing materials have or are being installed to slow, and present an obstacle to, illegal activity. Roads and lights are also being deployed. This is not discontinued.

Northern Border Project: Common Operating Picture electronic surveillance technology was being placed along the Canadian border to integrate air, land, and also marine capability on the

Great Lakes and the Strait of San Juan de Fuca. The hardware included remote video and mobile surveillance systems. The primary locations are Detroit, Buffalo, New York, Swanton, Vermont, and Champlain, New York.

Marine Domain Awareness

The "National Plan to Achieve Maritime Domain Awareness" is meant to develop regular global monitoring of vessels, craft, cargo, vessel crews and passengers, and other activities of interest in the marine domain. This intelligence will be collected, analyzed, and given to public officials to take any needed action regarding the security and safety of the United States. It will integrate Global Maritime Intelligence and Global Situational Awareness.

Port Modernization Project: The American Recovery and Reinvestment Act of 2009 provides funding to upgrade port infrastructure.

Office of National Drug Policy Drug Interdiction Program

High Intensity Drug Trafficking Area Program (HIDTA): The High Intensity Drug Trafficking Areas program integrates federal, state, and local law-enforcement drug-interdiction efforts. It provides training and equipment while integrating law-enforcement efforts in areas where drug-trafficking problems are intense. The Director of National Drug Control Policy is responsible for designating HIDTA areas, many of which are located along the Mexico-U.S. border and the coasts.

Facts and Figures

Trade

In 2008, 29 million trade entries were processed and subject to inspection by U.S. Customs and Border Patrol as a security precaution. North American Free Trade Agreement partners, Canada and Mexico, are the nation's largest import and export partners. In both cases, the United States imports more goods from Canada and Mexico than it exports. The United States has a trade deficit with both Canada and Mexico. The deficit was

TABLE 6.5

Top U.S. trade partners ranked by 2008 U.S. total export value for goods (in millions of U.S. dollars)

Rank	Country	Exports						Imports					
		2007	2008	% Change	Through Oct. 2008	Through Oct. 2009	% Change	2007	2008	% Change	Through Oct. 2008	Through Oct. 2009	% Change
1	Canada	248,888	261,150	4.9%	225,065	167,933	−25.4%	317,057	339,491	7.1%	297,178	183,534	−38.2%
2	Mexico	135,918	151,220	11.3%	129,135	105,186	−18.5%	210,714	215,942	2.5%	186,201	142,358	−23.5%
3	China	62,937	69,733	10.8%	59,441	53,887	−9.3%	321,443	337,773	5.1%	284,428	242,351	−14.8%
4	Japan	61,160	65,142	6.5%	55,591	42,016	−24.4%	145,463	139,262	−4.3%	119,350	76,743	−35.7%
5	Germany	49,420	54,505	10.3%	46,319	35,670	−23.0%	94,164	97,497	3.5%	83,209	57,485	−30.9%
6	United Kingdom	49,981	53,599	7.2%	46,470	38,180	−17.8%	56,858	58,587	3.0%	50,565	39,090	−22.7%
7	Netherlands	32,837	39,719	21.0%	33,186	26,788	−19.3%	18,403	21,123	14.8%	18,288	13,165	−28.0%
8	Korea	34,402	34,669	0.8%	30,434	23,200	−23.8%	47,562	48,069	1.1%	41,167	32,538	−21.0%
9	Brazil	24,172	32,299	33.6%	27,365	21,385	−21.9%	25,644	30,453	18.8%	26,385	16,412	−37.8%
10	Belgium	25,259	28,903	14.4%	24,837	17,891	−28.0%	15,281	17,308	13.3%	15,114	10,578	−30.0%

Source: Top Trade Partners (December 2009), Industry Trade Data and Analysis, Office of Trade and Industry Information, International Trade Administration, http://ita.doc.gov/td/industry/otea/ftp/Top_Trade_Partners.pdf.

$143.1 billion in 2008. The U.S. goods trade deficit with NAFTA countries accounted for 17.5% of the overall U.S. goods trade deficit in 2008, up from 8.7% in 1994, the year that NAFTA began. The United States has a service trade surplus of $26.5 billion with Canada and Mexico. Imported goods are a source of tariff revenue. In 2008 U.S. Customs collected approximately $34.5 billion in Customs revenue.

Drug Trafficking

The drug trade is considered a dual national security threat. Besides the impact of drug use and addiction on the public, drug-trafficking organizations (DTOs) can reach the capacity of destabilizing foreign governments through corruption and a major decline in public safety. In addition, one form of narco-terrorism occurs when terrorist organizations become involved in drug trafficking as a money-raising activity.

Land-border drug interdiction is undertaken by the Drug Enforcement Administration and U.S. Customs and Border Patrol (USCBP). The U.S. Coast Guard intercepts maritime drug shipments, and Immigration and Customs Enforcement has air and maritime drug operations. In 2009, USCBP confiscated 4.75 million pounds of drugs, an increase from 3.1 million in 2008. Marijuana shipments are the most frequently taken, followed by cocaine and heroin. The United States has substantial domestic marijuana production, and most externally produced marijuana comes from Mexico with some high-quality marijuana grown in Canada. In recent years, Mexico has had greater involvement in methamphetamine production.

Drugs are routed to the United States over the Mexican and Canadian borders and by boat from the Caribbean and international destinations. Cocaine is transshipped from Colombia, Venezuela, and Andean nations while heroin originates from Mexico and internationally. The amount of drugs seized in any year depends on changes in drug-trafficking routes and the innovative approaches taken by both U.S. law enforcement and the traffickers. Although drug seizures are a performance evaluation measure, the principal objective of law enforcement is the disruption and dismantlement of DTOs. DTOs are the principal sources of the drug supply, and hampering their efforts is associated with market disruption, a decline in

TABLE 6.6
Drug seizures by the U.S. Customs and Border Patrol

Fiscal Year	Substance (pounds)			
	Marijuana	Cocaine	Heroin	Methamphetamine
2008	2,471,931	178,770	2,178	2,270
2007	N/A			
2006	489,300	53,700	2,500	
2005	531,700	42,800	2,300	
2004	653,000	44,600	2,800	

Source: Performance and Accountability Reports, 2008, 2006, U.S. Customs and Border Patrol, http://www.cbp.gov/xp/cgov/newsroom/publications/admin/.

TABLE 6.7
DEA drug seizures, 2001–2008

Calendar Year	Cocaine (kgs)	Heroin (kgs)	Marijuana (kgs)	Methamphetamine (kgs)	Hallucinogens (dosage units)
2008	49,823.3	598.6	660,969.2	1,540.4	9,199,693
2007	96,713	625	356,472	1,086	5,636,305
2006	69,826	805	322,438	1,711	4,606,277
2005	118,311	640	283,344	2,161	8,881,321
2004	117,854	672	265,813	1,659	2,261,706
2003	73,725	795	254,196	1,678	2,878,594
2002	63,640	710	238,024	1,353	11,661,157
2001	59,430	753	271,849	1,634	13,755,390

Source: DEA (STRIDE), U.S. Department of Justice, http://www.justice.gov/dea/statistics.html#seizures.

shipments that reach the U.S. interior for sales. The United States is cooperating with Mexico in an effort to target the Gulf, Juarez, and Sinaloa DTOs, and the Arellano Felix organization. In 2008 Eduardo Arellano-Felix, Jaime Gonzalez (Gulf DTO), and Alfredo Beltran Leyva (Sinaloa DTO) were arrested.

In Mexico, narcoterrorism involves violence due to conflicts between drug-trafficking organizations for control of territory and routes. The Bureau of Alcohol, Tobacco, and Firearms is enacting Project Gunrunner to stop smuggling of arms into Mexico. As part of the effort, it is providing e-trace technology for Mexican officials to trace confiscated weapons.

Terrorism

The Federal Bureau of Investigation uses a definition of *terrorism* from the Code of Federal Regulations. Terrorism is

> the unlawful use of force and violence against persons or property to intimidate or coerce a government, the civilian population, or any segment thereof, in furtherance of political or social objectives. (28 C.F.R. Section 0.85)

To define international acts of terrorism, the FBI states that it:

> involves violent acts or acts dangerous to human life that are a violation of the criminal laws of the United States or any state. These acts appear to be intended to intimidate or coerce a civilian population; influence the policy of a government by intimidation or coercion; or affect the conduct of a government by mass destruction, assassination or kidnapping and occur primarily outside the territorial jurisdiction of the United States or transcend national boundaries in terms of the means by which they are accomplished, the persons they appear intended to intimidate or coerce, or the locale in which their perpetrators operate or seek asylum. [18 U.S.C. § 2331(1)]

The 9/11 Hijackers: Why They Were Not Caught

The 9/11 Commission identified a host of reasons about why the 9/11 hijackers were not stopped (Eldridge et al. 2004). One reason was connected to terrorist travel. Consular officials were not sufficiently trained in how to detect fraudulent documents or to identify terrorist travel patterns. Al-Qaeda trained terrorists in methods of fraudulent travel-document preparation. This was partly to give the organization the means to alter passports and visas but also to give the operatives the ability to modify their own documents while in the field. Tampering often occurred to delete or avoid evidence of travel to countries with terrorist involvement such as Afghanistan and Pakistan. In addition, passport and visa alteration was easier before the post 9/11 advent of biometric identification systems. A second reason that the hijackers were able to proceed is constraints upon U.S. law enforcement. In several instances, a hijacker was stopped for speeding and immigration status was not examined.

Selected 9/11 Commission Recommendations
12.4 Protect Against and Prepare for Terrorist Attacks

Terrorist Travel. Targeting travel is at least as powerful a weapon against terrorists as targeting their money. The United States should combine terrorist travel intelligence, operations, and law enforcement in a strategy to intercept terrorists, find terrorist travel facilitators, and constrain terrorist mobility.

A Biometric Screening System. The U.S. border-security system should be integrated into a larger network of screening points that includes our transportation system and access to vital facilities, such as nuclear reactors. The president should direct the Department of Homeland Security to lead the effort to design a comprehensive screening system, addressing common problems and setting common standards with system-wide goals in mind. Extending these standards among other governments could dramatically strengthen America and the world's collective ability to intercept individuals who pose catastrophic threats.

The U.S. Border Screening System. The Department of Homeland Security, properly supported by Congress, should complete, as quickly as possible, a biometric entry-exit screening system, including a single system for speeding qualified travelers. It should be integrated with the system that provides benefits to foreigners seeking to stay in the United States. Linking biometric passports to good data systems and decisionmaking is a fundamental goal. No one can hide his or her debt by acquiring a credit card with a slightly different name, yet today, a terrorist can defeat the link to electronic records by tossing away an old passport and slightly altering the name in a new one.

International Intelligence Exchange on Terrorism. The U.S. Government cannot meet its own obligations to the American people to prevent the entry of terrorists without a major effort to collaborate with other governments. We should do more to exchange terrorist information with trusted allies and raise U.S. and global border-security standards for travel and border crossing over the medium and long term through extensive international cooperation.

Immigration Law and Enforcement. Secure Identification should begin in the United States. The federal government should set standards for the issuance of birth certificates and sources of identification, such as driver's licenses. Fraud in identification documents is no longer just a problem of theft. At many entry points in vulnerable facilities, including gates for boarding aircraft, sources of identification are the last opportunity to ensure that people are who they say they are and to check whether they are terrorists.

Strategies for Aviation and Transportation Security. Hard choices must be made in allocating limited resources. The U.S. government should identify and evaluate the transportation assets that need to be protected, set risk-based priorities for defending them, select the most practical and cost-effective ways of doing so, and then develop a plan, budget, and funding to implement the effort. The plan should assign roles and missions to the relevant authorities (federal, state, regional, and local) and to private stakeholders. In measuring effectiveness, perfection is unattainable. But terrorists should perceive that potential targets are defended. They may be deterred by a significant chance of failure.

A Layered Security System. Improved use of "no-fly" and "automatic selectee" lists should not be delayed while the argument about a successor to CAPPS continues. This screening function should be performed by TSA, and it should utilize the larger set of watchlists maintained by the federal government. Air carriers should be required to supply the information needed to test and implement this new system.

Explosive Screening of Passengers. The TSA and Congress must give priority attention to improving the ability of screening checkpoints to detect explosives on passengers. As a start, each individual selected for special screening should be screened for explosives. Further, the TSA should conduct a human factors study, a method often used in the private sector to understand problems in screener performance and set attainable objectives for individual screeners and for the checkpoints where screening takes place.

Source: Eldridge, Thomas R., Susan Ginsberg, Walter T. Hempel II, Janice L. Kephart, and Kelly Moore. 2004. 9/11 and Terrorist Travel. Staff Report of the National Commission on Terrorist Attacks upon the United States. http://govinfo.library.unt.edu/911/staff_statements/911_TerrTrav_Monograph.pdf.

Bioterrorism
Biological Weapons of Mass Destruction
The Center for Disease Control (2008) defines a bioterrorism attack as the: "deliberate release of viruses, bacteria or other germs (agents) used to cause illness or death in people, animals or plants." Previously referred to

as biological warfare or germ warfare, it has the capacity for producing mass casualties while being unpredictable and potentially uncontrollable. Unlike nuclear weapons, bioterrorism is a tactical weapon, not strategic, because a large quantity is not required to cause great harm. In 1972, the United Nations issued the Convention on the Prohibition of the Development, Production and Stockpiling of Bacteriological and Toxin Weapons. The major signatories were the United States, Soviet Union, and Great Britain, who are cooperating in countering terrorism.

To combat a limited and dispersed force of terrorists, a preventative search occurs that is like looking for a needle in a haystack because of the massive extent and geographical complexity of the U.S. borders. Biological weapons are thought to be most available and more likely to be used by terrorists. Individuals planning terrorist attacks may carry plans or ingredients for making such weapons when crossing borders.

In real-time bio-terrorism events, certain warning signs occur:

- Gas, mist, or liquid which is being dispensed in an explosion
- Spraying activity that is not expected
- A parcel or package that explodes
- Unattended spraying equipment
- Scattered dead birds, fish, or other animals
- Mass casualties without a known cause of injury or death
- A pattern of symptoms, injury, or death
- Mass casualties at a location considered a terrorist target such as mass transport, hotels, sports arenas, or government buildings

Chemical agents that can injure and/or cause mass death include:

Nerve agents: A chemical that attacks the human central nervous system and can cause convulsions and death. These agents are liquid at normal temperatures and pose great risk. They include GA (Tabun), GB (Sarin), GD (Soman), and VX (V agents). The nerve agent Sarin was used in the Aum attack on the Tokyo subway system.

Humans who have been exposed to a nerve gas attack display the following symptoms:

- Pinpoint pupils
- Vision blurring

- Eyes irritated by light
- Unusual sweating
- Nasal mucous and congestion
- Coughing
- Breathing difficulty
- Nausea
- Vomiting
- Anxiety

Vesicants or blistering agents: Heavy, oily liquids without color or odor that easily penetrate clothing and enter the blood stream through the skin. In World War I mustard gas, when inhaled, caused severe skin burns and eye and respiratory damage. Blistering agents include H (mustard), HD (distilled mustard), HN (nitrogen mustard), CX (phosgene oxime), and L (lewsite). Although less lethal than nerve agents, a few drops on the skin will result in serious injury and three grams will kill.

The symptoms of vesicant poisoning are:

- Red eyes
- Tearing and eye soreness
- Eyelid pain and spasm
- Itching and redness of the skin followed by pain and tenderness
- Fluid-filled blisters in normally moist skin areas such as armpit and groin
- Burning feeling in nose and throat
- Coughing
- Shortness of breath

Blood agents: Derivatives of cyanide compounds that cause death by stopping the blood's delivery of oxygen to cells, which leads to asphyxiation. Blood agents include AC (hydrogen cyanide) and CK (cyanogen chloride). These agents are common industrial chemicals, and information on them is readily available.

The indicators of blood agent poisoning are:

- Mass casualties with no trauma indicator
- Peach or almond odor

Choking agents: Chemicals that destroys respiratory track cells and cause internal fluid to build up, producing asphyxiation.

They include chlorine, phosgene, and chloropicrin. The signs are the smell of chorine or hay, which is an odor associated with phosgene. Chlorine is readily used and available for home and swimming pools.

The symptoms of choking agent poisoning are:

- Choking
- Coughing

Irritating agents: The most commonly used irritant is tear gas for riot control. The varieties used include CN (standard tear gas), CS (stronger tear gas, induces vomiting), and DM (adamsite vomiting agent). It is not lethal and smells of pepper. It causes tearing and respiratory distress.

Biological Weapons   The threat of bioterrorism is a major international concern. The Center for Disease Control classifies agents with bioterrorism capacity at three levels of severity. Category A agents include ones that:

- pose the greatest possible threat for a bad effect on public health
- may spread across a large area or need public awareness
- need a great deal of planning to protect the public's health

Anthrax: The *Bacillus anthracis*, anthracis, a one-celled organism, forms spores, dormant cells which can later activate. Humans can contract anthrax by breathing in spores from infected animal products, such as wool. It can also be spread as a weapon, as when letters with powder were mailed through the postal system to prominent people in 2001. This caused 22 cases of anthrax.

There are three types of anthrax: (1) skin (cutaneous); (2) lung (inhalation); and (3) digestive (gastrointestinal). The CDC identifies the symptoms of each as follows:

- Cutaneous: The first symptom is a small sore that develops into a blister. The blister then develops

into a skin ulcer with a black area in the center.
The sore, blister, and ulcer do not hurt.
- Gastrointestinal: The first symptoms are nausea,
loss of appetite, bloody diarrhea, and fever,
followed by bad stomach pain.
- Inhalation: The first symptoms of inhalation
anthrax are like cold or flu symptoms and can
include a sore throat, mild fever, and muscle aches.
Later symptoms include cough, chest discomfort,
shortness of breath, tiredness, and muscle aches.
(Caution: Do not assume that just because a person
has cold or flu symptoms that he or she has
inhalation anthrax.)

Symptoms could appear within seven days of exposure. Inhalation anthrax symptoms may develop over a week to 42 days. The
Center for Disease Control classifies anthrax as a Category A
agent. Early antibiotic treatment can cure cutaneous anthrax,
which 80% of those infected survive. Between 25% to 50% of gastrointestinal cases of anthrax cause death, while half of inhala-
tional anthrax cases result in death. Fortunately, a vaccine is being
developed for anthrax, but it is not yet available for the public.

Smallpox: Smallpox was eradicated worldwide as the result
of an international vaccination campaign. Two approved labs
in the United States and Russia keep the only extant smallpox
virus samples. Nevertheless, there is credible concern that the
virus may have been made into a weapon and that terrorists
could obtain it. Smallpox is a Category A health threat that can
cause death. Methods of smallpox infection include prolonged
face-to-face contact with a person who has smallpox, contact
with infected body fluids or objects such as bed sheets, or exposure to a smallpox aerosol. There is no proven treatment for
smallpox, and the best way to control it has been vaccination. The
CDC has developed a public health program for response to any
terrorist smallpox threat and has enough vaccine for everyone.

Botulism: This muscle-paralyzing disease is caused by a toxin
secreted by the *Clostridum botulin* toxin. This toxin may form
in contaminated food or be transmitted in an infected wound.
The CDC indicates that: With foodborne botulism, symptoms
begin within 6 hours to 10 days (most commonly between

12 and 36 hours) after eating food that contains the toxin. Symptoms of botulism include double vision, blurred vision, drooping eyelids, slurred speech, difficulty swallowing, dry mouth, and muscle weakness that moves down the body, usually affecting the shoulders first, then the upper arms, lower arms, thighs, calves, etc. Paralysis of breathing muscles can cause a person to stop breathing and die, unless assistance with breathing (mechanical ventilation) is provided.

Tularemia: The bacterium *Francisella tularensis* is carried by such animals as rodents, rabbits, and hares. It can cause serious illness and presents some of the following symptoms: sudden fever, chills, headaches, diarrhea, muscle aches, joint pain, dry cough, and progressive weakness. People can contract tularemia by:

- being bitten by an infected tick, deerfly, or other insect
- handling infected animal carcasses
- eating or drinking contaminated food or water
- breathing in the bacteria, *F. tularensis*

Symptoms typically appear in 3 to 5 days, but can take as long as 14 days. Because the bacterium is very infectious, as few as 10–50 organisms can make a person sick. As a weapon, it would likely be delivered in an infectious aerosol. People with tularemia infection develop severe respiratory illness, including pneumonia and infection. The CDC is responding by stockpiling antibiotics.

Source: http://www.bt.cdc.gov/agent/agentlist.asp#b

Incidents of Terrorism Worldwide

The United States is fortunate that it has not experienced a terrorist attack since September 11, 2001 although terrorist plots have been detected and stopped. In 2008, 11,800 terrorist attacks, which caused 54,000 deaths, injuries, and/or kidnappings, occurred. Methods of attack included coordinated arms strikes and improvised explosive devises. About 50,000 individuals were killed or injured worldwide. Sixty-five percent of these victims were civilians.

It is often difficult to get accurate information on attackers. Iraq, Afghanistan, and Pakistan were the locales of approximately

TABLE 6.8
Incidents of terrorism worldwide

	2005	2006	2007	2008
Attacks				
Worldwide	11,157	14,545	14,506	11,770
Resulting in death, injury, or kidnapping of at least 1 person	8,025	11,311	11,123	8.438
Resulting in the death of at least 1 individual	5,127	7,428	7,255	5,067
Resulting in the death of zero individuals	6,030	7,117	7,251	6,703
Resulting in the death of only 1 individual	2,880	4,139	3,994	2,889
Resulting in the death of at least 10 individuals	226	293	353	235
Resulting in the injury of at least 1 individual	3,842	5,796	6,256	4,888
Resulting in the kidnapping of at least one individual	1,475	1,733	1,459	1,125
People				
Worldwide				
Killed, injured, or kidnapped as a result of terrorism	74,280	74,709	71,608	54,747
Killed as a result of terrorism	14,560	20,468	22,508	15,765
Injured as a result of terrorism	24,875	38,386	44,118	34,124
Kidnapped as a result of terrorism	34,845	15,855	4,982	4,858

Source: U.S. Department of State, National Counter-Terrorism Center: Annex of Statistical Information. 2009. Country Reports on Terrorism, 2008. http://www.state.gov/s/ct/rls/crt/2008/122452.htm#*

55% of attacks. In Afghanistan, the Taliban claimed credit for the most attacks and highest death tolls. The al-Qaeda organization is thought to be planning attacks from northwest Pakistan and claimed attacks made in Algeria and Yemen.

The Secretary of State, under section 219 of the amended Immigration and Nationality act (INA), designates foreign terrorist organizations (FTOs). This is an international list which includes many organizations not known to be active in the United States.

Current List of Designated Foreign Terrorist Organizations

> Abu Nidal Organization (ANO)
> Abu Sayyaf Group
> Al-Aqsa Martyrs Brigade
> Al-Shabaab
> Ansar al-Islam
> Armed Islamic Group (GIA)
> Asbat al-Ansar
> Aum Shinrikyo
> Basque Fatherland and Liberty (ETA)

Communist Party of the Philippines/New People's Army
(CPP/NPA)
Continuity Irish Republican Army
Gama'a al-Islamiyya (Islamic Group)
HAMAS (Islamic Resistance Movement)
Harakat ul-Jihad-i-Islami/Bangladesh (HUJI-B)
Harakat ul-Mujahidin (HUM)
Hizballah (Party of God)
Islamic Jihad Group
Islamic Movement of Uzbekistan (IMU)
Jaish-e-Mohammed (JEM) (Army of Mohammed)
Jemaah Islamiya organization (JI)
al-Jihad (Egyptian Islamic Jihad)
Kahane Chai (Kach)
Kata'ib Hizballah
Kongra-Gel (KGK, formerly Kurdistan Workers' Party,
PKK, KADEK)
Lashkar-e Tayyiba (LT) (Army of the Righteous)
Lashkar i Jhangvi
Liberation Tigers of Tamil Eelam (LTTE)
Libyan Islamic Fighting Group (LIFG)
Moroccan Islamic Combatant Group (GICM)
Mujahedin-e Khalq Organization (MEK)
National Liberation Army (ELN)
Palestine Liberation Front (PLF)
Palestinian Islamic Jihad (PIJ)
Popular Front for the Liberation of Palestine (PFLF)
PFLP-General Command (PFLP-GC)
Tanzim Qa'idat al-Jihad fi Bilad al-Rafidayn (QJBR)
(al-Qaida in Iraq) (formerly Jama'at al-Tawhid
wa'al-Jihad, JTJ, al-Zarqawi Network)
al-Qa'ida
al-Qaida in the Islamic Maghreb (formerly GSPC)
Real IRA
Revolutionary Armed Forces of Colombia (FARC)
Revolutionary Nuclei (formerly ELA)
Revolutionary Organization 17 November
Revolutionary People's Liberation Party/Front (DHKP/C)
Shining Path (Sendero Luminoso, SL)
United Self-Defense Forces of Colombia (AUC)

Terrorist Exclusion List   Section 411 of the USA PATRIOT Act of 2001 (8 U.S.C. § 1182) authorized the Secretary of State, in consultation with or upon the request of the Attorney General, to designate terrorist organizations for immigration purposes. This authority is known as the "Terrorist Exclusion List (TEL)" authority. A TEL designation bolsters homeland security efforts by facilitating the USG's ability to exclude aliens associated with entities on the TEL from entering the United States.

Designation Criteria   An organization can be placed on the TEL if the Secretary of State finds that the organization:

- commits or incites to commit, under circumstances indicating an intention to cause death or serious bodily injury, a terrorist activity;
- prepares or plans a terrorist activity;
- gathers information on potential targets for terrorist activity; or
- provides material support to further terrorist activity.

Under the statute, "terrorist activity" means any activity that is unlawful under U.S. law or the laws of the place where it was committed and involves: hijacking or sabotage of an aircraft, vessel, vehicle, or other conveyance; hostage taking; a violent attack on an internationally protected person; assassination; or the use of any biological agent, chemical agent, nuclear weapon or device, or explosive, firearm, or other weapon or dangerous device (other than for mere personal monetary gain), with intent to endanger, directly or indirectly, the safety of one or more individuals or to cause substantial damage to property. The definition also captures any threat, attempt, or conspiracy to do any of these activities.

Legal Ramifications   Individual aliens providing support to or associated with TEL-designated organizations may be found "inadmissable" to the United States; that is, such aliens may be prevented from entering the United States or, if already in U.S. territory, may in certain circumstances be deported. Examples of activity that may render an alien inadmissible as a result of an organization's TEL designation include:

- membership in a TEL-designated organization;
- use of the alien's position of prominence within any country to persuade others to support an organization on the TEL list;
- solicitation of funds or other things of value for an organization on the TEL list;
- solicitation of any individual for membership in an organization on the TEL list; and
- commission of an act that the alien knows, or reasonably should have known, affords material support, including a safe house, transportation, communications, funds, transfer of funds or other material for financial benefit, false documentation or identification, weapons (including chemical, biological, or radiological weapons), explosives, or training to an organization on the TEL list.

(It should be noted that individual aliens may also found inadmissible on the basis of other types of terrorist activity unrelated to TEL-designated organizations; see 8 U.S.C. §1182(a)(3)(B).)

Other Effects of a Terrorist Exclusion List

1. Deters donation or contributions to named organizations.
2. Heightens public awareness and knowledge of terrorist organizations.
3. Alerts other governments to U.S. concerns about organizations engaged in terrorist activities.
4. Stigmatizes and isolates designated terrorist organizations.

Tables and Figures on Legal and Unauthorized Immigration

Conservatives and liberals express concern that our immigration system is broken. If that is the case, it is broken in many ways. Liberals express concern that the United States is the world's major immigrant-receiving nation, but its immigrants must be respected. Conservatives espouse cutting back on legal immigration, which is over a million per year, the largest rate of entrance since the early 20th century. Then as now, the cultural and perceived racial-ethnic differences of immigrants raise questions about their acceptance and cultural and economic incorporation into this society.

Although 19th- and early 20th-century immigration was predominately from southern and southeastern Europe, late 20th-century immigration was globalized. The greatest demand occurs from Mexico, which, along with Canada and the Caribbean, is placed in the North American region. After the racial-ethnic quotas of the 1924 Johnson Reed Act were abolished by the Immigration and Nationality Act of 1965, Asian immigration became very prominent. In the late 20th century, the Diversity Lottery and globalization are fostering the beginning of mass migration from South America and Africa.

Asia is catching up with Mexico and the Caribbean nations and may soon be the major sending region for legal U.S. immigrants. Mexico has been and by and far will be the major sending nation for U.S. legal permanent residents. If the rate of acceptance of Mexican nationals as permanent resident aliens follows the pattern of a high rate of admission, over 2 million will be legally admitted to the United States in the first decade of the 21st century.

The large numbers of individuals being legally admitted to the United States are augmented by unauthorized entrants. During the 2008–2010 Recession, which was only beginning to moderate in mid-2010, U.S. Border Patrol apprehensions declined. How much of this decline was due to staffing and technology and to what extent it was caused by lack of economic opportunity in the United States drawing people from Mexico and Central America is not known.

Interior Enforcement

Even prior to the War on Terror, the criminalization of permanent resident aliens who committed crimes designated as "aggravated felonies" increased deportation. Many individuals ordered removed, however, did not commit a conventional crime, but were in violation of immigration law through first-time unauthorized entry—a civil offense. This artificially increases the number of "criminal aliens" removed.

TABLE 6.9

Persons obtaining legal permanent resident status by region, FY1910–1999

	1910–1919	1920–1929	1930–1939	1940–1949	1950–1959	1960–1969	1970–1979	1980–1989	1990–1999
North America	1,070,539	1,591,278	230,319	328,435	921,610	1,674,172	1,904,355	2,695,329	5,137,743
Asia	269,736	126,740	19,231	34,532	135,844	358,605	1,406,544	2,391,356	2,859,899
Europe	4,985,411	2,560,340	444,399	472,524	1,404,973	1,133,443	825,590	668,886	1,348,612
South America	39,938	43,025	9,990	19,662	78,418	250,754	273,608	399,862	570,634
Africa	8,867	6,362	2,120	6,720	13,016	23,780	71,408	141,990	346,416
Oceania	12,339	9,860	3,306	14,262	11,353	23,630	39,980	41,432	56,800

Source: Yearbook of Immigration Statistics, 2008.

TABLE 6.10
Persons obtaining legal permanent resident status by region, FY2001–2008

	2001	2002	2003	2004	2005	2006	2007	2008
North America	405,638	402,949	249,968	342,468	345,561	414,075	339,375	393,253
Asia	348,256	340,494	243,918	334,540	400,098	422,284	383,508	383,608
Europe	174,411	173,524	100,434	133,181	176,516	166,244	120,821	119,138
South America	67,880	73,082	53,946	69,425	100,803	136,134	102,616	96,178
Africa	50,009	56,002	45,559	62,623	79,697	112,100	89,277	100,881
Oceania	7,201	6,495	5,076	6,954	7,432	8,000	6,639	5,926

Source: Yearbook of Immigration Statistics, 2008.

TABLE 6.11
Persons obtaining legal resident status from Mexico

Fiscal Year	Number of Persons
1910–1919	185,334
1920–1929	498,945
1930–1939	32,709
1940–1949	56,158
1950–1959	273,847
1960–1969	441,824
1970–1979	621,218
1980–1989	1,009,586
1990–1999	2,757,418
2000	171,445
2001	204,032
2002	216,924
2003	114,758
2004	173,711
2005	157,992
2006	170,042
2007	143,180
2008	188,015

Source: Yearbook of Immigration Statistics, 2008.

Since the late 19th century, the United States has deported noncitizens considered to present a problem, such as commission of a crime of moral turpitude. After 1970, the number of unauthorized entrants returned (given voluntary departure)

TABLE 6.12
Leading crime categories of criminal aliens removed, FY2008

Crime Category	Number Removed	Percent of Total
Total.	97,133	100.0
Dangerous drugs.	34,882	35.9
Immigration.	17,542	18.1
Assault.	7,485	7.7
Burglary.	3,292	3.4
Larceny.	3,282	3.4
Robbery.	3,101	3.2
Sexual assault.	2,929	3.0
Family offenses.	2,343	2.4
Fraudulent activities.	2,059	2.1
Weapon offenses.	2,048	2.1
Other.	18,170	18.7

Source: Department of Homeland Security, Office of Immigration Statistics Policy Directorate, 2009. Immigration Enforcement Actions, 2008, p. 4.

began to greatly increase, reaching over 1 million in the year before passage of the Immigration Reform and Control Act of 1986. Despite passage of a series of immigration laws, the rate of removals and returns has remained consistently high and an expense for taxpayers. These statistics indicate that the USBP and ICE have a certain degree of success, but the fact of entrance in such high numbers must be interpreted as meaning that many individuals were *not* deterred from coming by the threat of apprehension.

Table 6.14 indicates the breakdown of criminal versus noncriminal deportations in 2008. The criminal deportation statistics refer to both individuals deported after serving time for an aggravated felony and those retroactively deported after previously serving time and being released into the population. The North American region, which contains Mexico and Central America, accounts for the largest number of undocumented and legal immigrants, a fact which correlates with their rate of criminal and noncriminal removal.

The ultimate measure of the success of border interdiction efforts is the size of the undocumented population. At an estimated 11 million, it is far greater than at any prior historical period.

TABLE 6.13
Aliens removed or returned, FY1892–1930

Year	Removals[a]	Returns[b]	Year	Removals[a]	Returns[b]	Year	Removals[a]	Returns[b]
1892	2,801	NA[c]	1931	27,886	11,719	1970	17,469	303,348
1893	1,630	NA	1932	26,490	10,775	1971	18,294	370,074
1894	1,806	NA	1933	25,392	10,347	1972	16,883	450,927
1895	2,596	NA	1934	14,263	8,010	1973	17,346	568,005
1896	3,037	NA	1935	13,877	7,978	1974	19,413	718,740
1897	1,880	NA	1936	16,195	8,251	1975	24,432	655,814
1898	3,229	NA	1937	16,905	8,788	1976	38,471	955,374
1899	4,052	NA	1938	17,341	9,278	1977	31,263	867,015
1900	4,602	NA	1939	14,700	9,590	1978	29,277	975,515
1901	3,879	NA	1940	12,254	8,594	1979	26,825	966,137
1902	5,439	NA	1941	7,336	6,531	1980	18,013	719,211
1903	9,316	NA	1942	5,542	6,904	1981	17,379	823,875
1904	8,773	NA	1943	5,702	11,947	1982	15,216	812,572
1905	12,724	NA	1944	8,821	32,270	1983	19,211	931,600
1906	13,108	NA	1945	13,611	69,490	1984	18,696	909,833
1907	14,059	NA	1946	17,317	101,945	1985	23,105	1,041,296
1908	12,971	NA	1947	23,434	195,880	1986	24,592	1,586,320
1909	12,535	NA	1948	25,276	197,184	1987	24,336	1,091,023
1910	26,965	NA	1949	23,874	276,297	1988	25,829	911,790
1911	25,137	NA	1950	10,199	572,477	1989	34,427	830,890
1912	18,513	NA	1951	17,328	673,169	1990	30,039	1,022,533
1913	23,399	NA	1952	23,125	703,778	1991	33,189	1,061,105
1914	37,651	NA	1953	23,482	885,391	1992	43,671	1,105,829
1915	26,675	NA	1954	30,264	1,074,277	1993	42,542	1,243,410
1916	21,648	NA	1955	17,695	232,769	1994	45,674	1,029,107
1917	17,881	NA	1956	9,006	80,891	1995	50,924	1,313,764
1918	8,866	NA	1957	5,989	63,379	1996	69,680	1,573,428
1919	11,694	NA	1958	7,875	60,600	1997	114,432	1,440,684
1920	14,557	NA	1959	8,468	56,610	1998	174,813	1,570,827
1921	18,296	NA	1960	7,240	52,796	1999	183,114	1,574,863
1922	18,076	NA	1961	8,181	52,383	2000	188,467	1,675,876
1923	24,280	NA	1962	8,025	54,164	2001	189,026	1,349,371
1924	36,693	NA	1963	7,763	69,392	2002	165,168	1,012,116
1925	34,885	NA	1964	9,167	73,042	2003	211,098	945,294
1926	31,454	NA	1965	10,572	95,263	2004	240,665	1,166,576
1927	31,417	15,012	1966	9,680	123,683	2005	246,431	1,096,920
1928	30,464	19,946	1967	9,728	142,342	2006	280,974	1,043,381
1929	31,035	25,888	1968	9,590	179,952	2007	319,382	891,390
1930	24,864	11,387	1969	11,030	240,958	2008	358,886	811,263

Source: Yearbook of Immigration Statistics, 2008, 95.

[a]Removals are the compulsory and confirmed movement of an inadmissible or deportable alien out of the United States based on an order of removal. An alien who is removed has administrative or criminal consequences placed on subsequent reentry owing to the fact of the removal.

[b]Returns are the confirmed movement of an inadmissible or deportable alien out of the United States not based on an order or removal. Most of the voluntary returns are of Mexican nationals who have been apprehended by the U.S. Border Patrol and are returned to Mexico.

[c] NA = Not available.

TABLE 6.14
Aliens removed by criminal status and region, FY2008

Region and Country and Nationality	Total	Criminal	Noncriminal
Total	358,886	97,133	261,753
Africa	1,999	626	1,373
Asia	5,338	1,288	4,050
Caribbean	7,361	4,343	3,018
Central America	79,823	14,634	65,189
Europe	4,095	1,168	2,927
North America	248,176	72,126	176,050
Oceania	301	177	124
South America	11,704	2,745	8,959
Unknown	89	26	63

Source: Yearbook of Immigration Statistics, 2008.

TABLE 6.15
Unauthorized immigrant population, 2000–2008

Year	Millions
2000	8.5
2001	–
2002	–
2003	–
2004	–
2005	10.5
2006	11.3
2007	11.8
2008	11.6

Source: Michael Hoeffer, Nancy Rytina, and Bryan C. Baker. 2009. Estimates of the Immigrant Population Residing in the United States: January, 2008. Department of Homeland Security, Office of Immigration Statistics Policy Directorate, 2. http://www.dhs.gov/xlibrary/assets/statistics/publications/ois_ill_pe_2008.pdf.
Note: DHS estimates not produced for 2001–2004.

TABLE 6.16
Region of birth of the unauthorized immigrant population, January 2008 and 2000 (in millions)

	2000	2008
North America	6.1	8.8
Asia	1.2	1.2
South America	0.6	0.8
Europe	0.3	0.4
Other	0.2	0.4

Source: Michael Hoeffer, Nancy Rytina, and Bryan C. Baker. 2009. Estimates of the Immigrant Population Residing in the United States: January, 2008. Department of Homeland Security, Office of Immigration Statistics Policy Directorate, 4. http://www.dhs.gov/xlibrary/assets/statistics/publications/ois_ill_pe_2008.pdf.

TABLE 6.17

Country of birth of the unauthorized immigrant population, January 2008 and 2000

Country of Birth	Estimated Population in January		Percent of Total		Percent Change	Average Annual Change
	2008	2000	2008	2000	2000 to 2008	2000 to 2008
All countries	11,600,000	8,460,000	100	100	37	390,000
Mexico	7,030,000	4,680,000	61	55	50	290,000
El Salvador	570,000	430,000	5	5	35	20,000
Guatemala	430,000	290,000	4	3	48	20,000
Phillippines	300,000	200,000	3	2	51	10,000
Honduras	300,000	160,000	3	2	81	20,000
Korea	240,000	180,000	2	2	37	10,000
China	220,000	190,000	2	2	14	—
Brazil	180,000	100,000	2	1	72	10,000
Ecuador	170,000	110,000	1	1	50	10,000
India	160,000	120,000	1	1	29	—
Other countries	2,000,000	2,000,000	17	24	0	—

Source: Michael Hoeffer, Nancy Rytina, and Bryan C. Baker. 2009. *Estimates of the Immigrant Population Residing in the United States: January, 2008.* Department of Homeland Security, Office of Immigration Statistics Policy Directorate, 4. http://www.dhs.gov/xlibrary/assets/statistics/publications/ois_ill_pe_2008.pdf.

Documents

Initial Immigration Reform (1986)

After the passage of the Immigration and Nationality Act of 1965, legal immigration to the United States from Asia and other non-European world regions greatly increased. The act also placed a quota on Western Hemisphere immigrants (Mexican, Central America, Canada, etc.) which limited legal access, and, in the 1970s, the size of the unauthorized population began to grow. Many of the concerns about unauthorized immigration and its consequences that are aired in public today were first voiced in the 1970s and became a source of congressional debate in the 1980s. After repeated attempts at immigration reform, the Immigration Reform and Control Act (IRCA) set a basis for many policies followed today. It provided increased funding for the U.S. Border Patrol, established civil and criminal sanctions for employers who knowingly hire unauthorized workers, and established an amnesty: a process of legalization with no fines or necessity to return to the sending country before being readmitted.

Immigration Reform and Control Act of November 6, 1986 (100 Stat. 3360)
TITLE I—Control of Illegal Immigration
PART A—Employment

Sec. 101. Control of Unlawful Employment of Aliens.— Made it unlawful for employers to hire (including through subcontractors), recruit, or refer for a fee any alien knowing that the person is unauthorized to work or any person without verifying his or her employment status. It also made continued employment of unauthorized or unverified illegal.

Establishes an employment verification system requiring that the employee's birth certificate, Social Security card, employment verification papers, and passport be examined. Compliance with verification without checking for fraudulent documentation was considered sufficient.

Directs the Attorney General to establish both hiring violation complaint and investigation procedures.

Provides for employer sanctions including first and graduated subsequent civil penalties, criminal penalties, and injunctive remedies.

Sec. 102—Makes it an unfair immigration-related employment practice for any employer to discriminate against any individual other than an unauthorized alien with respect to hiring, recruitment, firing, or referral for fee because of individual origin or citizenship (or intended citizenship) status and states that it is not a violation to hire an equally qualified U.S. citizen or national over an equally qualified alien.

Sec. 103—Makes fraud and misuse of certain immigration-related documents illegal.

PART B—Improvement of Enforcement and Services

Sec. 111—Authorized increased appropriations for enforcement and service activities of the Immigration and Naturalization Service, the Executive Office of Immigration Review, the Border Patrol and other appropriate federal agencies. Authorizes additional appropriations for wage and hour enforcement.

Sec. 112—Revised penalties for unlawful transportation of aliens to the United States.

Sec. 113—Authorized a $35-million immigration emergency fund for enforcement costs and state and local reimbursement.

Sec. 114—Permits owners and operators of international bridges and toll roads to request the assistance of the Attorney General to inspect and approve measures to prevent the unauthorized crossing of aliens into the United States.

Sec. 115—Expressed the sense of Congress that the immigration laws of the United States should be vigorously enforced while protecting the rights and safety of U.S. citizens.

Sec. 116—Requires the INS to have the owner's consent or a warrant, restricting warrantless entry in the case of outdoor agricultural operations to interrogate persons to see if unauthorized aliens are present.

Sec. 117—Prohibits the adjustment of status to permanent resident for visa violators.

TITLE V—State Assistance for Incarceration Costs of Illegal Aliens and Certain Cuban Nationals

Sec. 501—Directs the Attorney General to reimburse states for the costs of incarcerating illegal aliens and certain Cuban nationals convicted of felonies.

TITLE VII—Federal Responsibility for Deportable and Excludable Aliens Convicted of Crimes

Sec. 701—Provides for the expeditious deportation of aliens convicted of crimes.

Sec. 702—Provides for the identification of Department of Defense facilities to incarcerate deportable or excludable aliens.

Era of Criminalization of Immigration

Negative public reaction to unauthorized immigration became interconnected with the "War on Crime" and the "War on Drugs." One result was that the Omnibus Anti-Drug Abuse Act of 1988 created the "aggravated felony": a crime for which a permanent resident alien (or an unauthorized immigrant) would be deported and denied reentry on a permanent basis.

Omnibus Anti-Drug Abuse Act of 1988
H.R. 5210, November 18, 1988
Subtitle J—Provisions Relating to the Deportation of Aliens Who Commit Aggravated Felonies

Directs the Attorney General to: (1) take into custody any alien convicted of an aggravated felony (murder, drug-trafficking crimes, or illicit trafficking in firearms or destructive devices) upon completion of the relevant sentence; (2) establish a system to maintain records of such aliens and train Immigration and Naturalization Service (INS) personnel to act as a liaison to other law enforcement entities with respect to such aliens; and (3) report to the congressional Judiciary Committees on reports in these areas.

Prohibits the voluntary departure of aliens convicted of an aggravated felony. Includes within a class of deportable aliens any alien convicted: (1) of an aggravated felony at any time after entry into the United States; or (2) of possessing or carrying unlawfully any firearm, destructive device, or revolver.

Establishes criminal penalties to apply to persons deported subsequent to a felony or aggravated felony conviction who reenter the United States, as well as for persons who assist certain deportees in their reentry.

During a period in which unauthorized immigration was re-emerging as a social issue, the North American Free Trade Agreement was passed, easing tariff fees on goods crossing the borders. Public reaction against admission of unskilled labor meant that immigration was restricted while trade was opened. The failure to increase legal immigration opportunities, in relation to labor market demand in the United States, led to increased unauthorized immigration and a new population buildup as employers in less skilled labor industries sought to hire these willing workers.

North American Free Trade Agreement of 1994
Signatories: United States, Canada, and Mexico
NAFTA PART TWO—Trade in Goods
Article 302: Tariff Elimination

1. Except as otherwise provided in this Agreement, no Party may increase any existing customs duty, or adopt any customs duty, on an originating good.
2. Except as otherwise provided in this Agreement, each Party shall progressively eliminate its customs duties on originating goods in accordance with its Schedule set out in Annex 302.2 or as otherwise indicated in Annex 300-B.
3. At the request of any Party, the Parties shall consult to consider accelerating the elimination of customs duties set out in their Schedules. An agreement between any two or more Parties to accelerate the elimination of a customs duty on a good shall supersede any prior inconsistent duty rate or staging category in their Schedules for such good when approved by each such Party in accordance with Article 2202(2) (Amendments).

Subchapter C—Non-Tariff Measures
Article 309: **Import and Export Restrictions**
1. Except as otherwise provided in this Agreement, no Party shall adopt or maintain any prohibition or restriction on the importation of any good of another Party or on the exportation or sale for export of any good destined for the territory of another Party, except in accordance with Article XI of the GATT, including its interpretative notes, and to this end Article XI of the GATT and its interpretative notes, or any equivalent provision of a successor agreement to which all Parties are party, are incorporated into and made part of this Agreement.
Article 315: **Export Taxes**
Except as set out in Annex 315 or Article 604 (Energy-Export Taxes), no Party may adopt or maintain any duty, tax,

or other charge on the export of any good to the territory of another Party, unless such duty, tax, or charge is adopted or maintained on: (a) exports of any such good to the territory of all other Parties; and (b) any such good when destined for domestic consumption.

The Antiterrorism and Effective Death Penalty Act of 1996 reinforced the criminalization of unauthorized immigration by increasing the number of offenses classified as "aggravated felonies" and specified that deportation would be retroactive. In other words, an individual who has served time for an aggravated felony could be deported years or decades afterwards. This step was taken due to concerns raised by the bombing of the World Trade Center by terrorists in 1993 and the Oklahoma City bombing in 1995, at first attributed to external terrorists, but later found to have been carried out by Timothy McVeigh, a U.S. citizen.

Antiterrorism and Effective Death Penalty Act of 1996
Senate 735, April 24, 1996
Title IV—Terrorist and Criminal Alien Removal and Exclusion
Subtitle A—Removal of Alien Terrorists
Section 401—Alien Terrorist Removal

Subtitle B—Exclusion of Members and Representatives of Terrorist Organizations
Sec. 411—Exclusion of alien enemy terrorists. Establishes membership in or representation of a terrorist organization as a ground for denying an alien entry into the United States. . . .

Sec. 412—Waiver of authority concerning notice of denial of application for visas. Allows the Attorney General to waive notice of visa application denials . . . to any individual or class of excludable individuals, except in cases of visas sought with the intent to immigrate.

Sec. 413—Denial of other relief for alien terrorists. Limits the discretion of the Attorney General with respect to those who have engaged in terrorist activities to: withhold deportation . . ., suspend deportation . . ., permit voluntary departure . . ., adjust status of nonimmigrant to that of resident alien . . ., or enter a record of lawful admission for alien who entered the U.S. prior to January 1, 1972. . . . The Attorney General may stay deportation upon a determination that otherwise the alien may be persecuted and would be contrary to the U.N. protocol on refugees. . . .

Sec. 414—Exclusion of aliens who have not been inspected and admitted. ". . .by operation of law, returns 'to the border' any alien who has entered the United States unlawfully, regardless of the duration of his or her presence In the United States,". . . The Attorney General, however, is required to establish a procedure whereby aliens citied under this section have the opportunity to demonstrate that they were in fact lawfully admitted. . . ."

Subtitle D—Criminal Alien Procedural Improvements

Sec. 432—Criminal alien identification system—. . . adjusts the provisions calling for a criminal alien tracking station to authorize the creation of a criminal alien identification system to assist in identifying and locating aliens deportable by virtue of their conviction for aggravated felonies. . . .

Sec. 434—. . . adds a number of immigration offenses to the list of RICO predicate Offenses. . . . The Racketeer Influenced and Corrupt Organization (RICO) provisions . . . prohibit (1) the acquisition or conduct of the affairs of (2) an enterprise whose activities affect interstate or foreign commerce (3) through the patterned commission of predicate crimes. RICO violations are punishable by imprisonment for not more than 20 years, by criminal forfeiture of any proceeds of the offense, and may result in civil liability to injured parties. The new predicate offenses include: 18 U.S.C. 1028 (relating to fraud concerning identification documents) when committed for financial gain; 18 U.S.C. 1542 (relating to false statement to secure a passport) when committed for financial gain; 18 U.S.C. 1543 (relating to forgery or false use of a passport) when committed for financial gain; 18 U.S.C. 1544 (relating to misuse of a passport) when committed for financial gain; 18 U.S.C. 1546 (relating to fraud and misuse of immigration entry documents) when committed for financial gain; 18 U.S.C. 1581–1588 (relating to peonage and slavery); 8 U.S.C. 1324 (relating to bringing in, transporting, or harboring illegal aliens); 8 U.S.C. 1327 (relating to aiding illegal reentry by aliens excludable as terrorists or for conviction of aggravated felonies); and 8 U.S.C. 1328 (relating to importing aliens for immoral purposes) when committed for financial gain.

Sec. 435 . . . enables law enforcement officials to use court ordered wiretapping to investigate various immigration offenses, 18 U.S.C. 2516, i.e.: 18 U.S.C. 1028 (relating to fraud concerning drivers' licenses, social security cards and other forms of identification); 18 U.S.C. 1542 (relating to false statements made to secure a passport); 18 U.S.C. 1546 (relating to forgery or false statements concerning immigration cards or other documents); 8 U.S.C. 1324 (relating to bringing in, transporting, or harboring illegal aliens); 8 U.S.C. 1327 (relating to aiding illegal reentry by aliens excludable as terrorists or for conviction of aggravated felonies); and 8 U.S.C. 1328 (relating to importing aliens for immoral purposes).

Sec. 436—Expansion of criteria of deportation for crimes of moral turpitude. . . . Amends the description of the crimes of moral turpitude which render an alien deportable, 8 U.S.C. 1251(a)(2)(A)(i)(II), to make it clear that "crimes of moral turpitude" refers to those punishable by imprisonment for one year or more rather than those for which the alien is actually sentenced to imprisonment for one year or more.

Sec. 437—. . . permits, with the agreement of the parties, deportation proceedings to be conducted by telephone conference call or in the absence of the alien. . . .

Sec. 438—Deportation of nonviolent offenders prior to completion of sentence of imprisonment. . . . directs the development and implementation within 180 days of a plan to relocate at least 500 kilometers from the U.S. border any alien who has entered the U.S. illegally and been returned to a contiguous country at least 3 times.

. . . permits the deportation before complete service of sentence of aliens convicted of nonviolent crimes (but excluding alien smuggling) under federal or state law; aliens who subsequently reenter the U.S. unlawfully would be required to serve the remainder of their sentences in addition to any other penalties that might be imposed.

Sec. 439—Authorizing State and local law enforcement officials to arrest and detain certain illegal aliens. . . . authorizes state and local law enforcement officers, unless contrary to state law, to arrest and detain aliens unlawfully reentering the U.S., 8 U.S.C. 1252c.

Sec. 440—Criminal alien removal. . . . provides for more expeditious deportation of certain criminal aliens. It adds to the list of "aggravated felon[ies]," 8 U.S.C. 1101(a)(43), conviction for which constitutes grounds for deportation: violations of 18 U.S.C. 1084 (other than a first offense relating to transportation of wagering information) or 18 U.S.C. 1955 (running a gambling business), 18 U.S.C. 2421, 2422, 2423 (relating to transportation in interstate or foreign commerce for purposes of criminal sexual activity) for commercial purposes; 8 U.S.C.1324(a)(2) bringing aliens into the U.S. in reckless disregard of their authority to enter if the offender has been previously convicted, the arrangement is commercial, or the alien is not presented to immigration officials upon entry (existing law includes knowingly smuggling, transporting, or harboring illegal aliens); 18 U.S.C. 1543 (relating to forgery of a passport) or 18 U.S.C. 1546(a) (relating to fraud, false impersonation, or false statements in connection with documents for entry into the U.S.), when a sentence of at least 18 months imprisonment is imposed; previous law included violations of 1546 (relating to trafficking in forged entry documents) punishable by imprisonment for at least 5 years; failure to appear to serve a sentence for an offense punishable by imprisonment for a term of 5 years or more; prior law included failure to appear to serve a sentence for an offense punishable by imprisonment for a term of 15 years or more; when committed by an alien previously deported on the bases of a conviction for an aggravated felony, 8 U.S.C. 1325(a) (relating to improper entry by an alien) or 1326 (relating to reentry by a deported alien); when punishable by imprisonment for 5 years or more, commercial bribery, counterfeiting, forgery, or trafficking in vehicles with altered identification numbers; when punishable by imprisonment for 5 years or more, obstruction of justice, perjury, subornation of perjury, or bribery of a witness; and failure to comply with a court order to appear to answer or dispose of a felony charge punishable by imprisonment for 2 years or more.

The section provides expedited procedures for aliens who commit aggravated felonies or violate the drug laws, the firearms laws, the espionage, sabotage, selective service, trading with the enemy, or sedition laws, or threaten the President, or launch an invasion from the United States or commit a second crime of moral turpitude. Expedited procedures in such cases include: no judicial review after the Board of Immigration Appeals (prior law permitted subsequent review under habeas provisions or appeal to the U.S. court of appeals), 8 U.S.C. 1105a(a)(10), 1101(a)(47); arrest for expeditious deportation following release from incarceration (prior law applied only to those convicted of aggravated felonies), 8 U.S.C. 1252(a)(2); exclusion of permanent resident aliens who commit such offenses, then leave the country temporarily and seek to reenter (prior law applied only to those convicted of aggravated felonies), 8 U.S.C. 1182(c); conducting deportation proceedings at correctional institutions prior to the alien's release from incarceration (prior law applied only to those convicted of aggravated felonies), 8 U.S.C. 1252a; requires the Attorney General to effect deportation within 30 days of the final order rather than 6 months afforded in other cases, 8 U.S.C. 1252(c).

Sec. 441—Limitation on Collateral Attacks on Underlying Deportation Order modifies the section outlawing illegal reentry by deported aliens to bar challenges to the underlying deportation order unless—the alien has exhausted administrative review; was previously denied the opportunity for judicial review; and can show that the deportation order was fundamentally unfair, 8 U.S.C. 1326(d).

Sec. 442—Deportation procedures for certain criminal aliens who are not permanent residents. Modifies the expedited procedures for deportation of aliens (other than permanent resident aliens) convicted of aggravated felonies, 8 U.S.C. 1252a to: exclude from application of the procedure those under conditional permanent resident alien status rather than, as is now the case, those who are entitled to deportation relief under immigration law; shorten the notice period from 30 to 14 days; provide for the translation of the proceedings into a language the alien understands; require an explicit determination as to whether the alien appearing at the proceedings is the alien against whom the proceedings were brought and whether he or she is appropriately subject to the procedure; bar the exercise of discretionary relief from deportation by the Attorney General; limit habeas corpus or other review of a final deportation order for criminal aliens to identification of the alien, 8 U.S.C. 1105a(c); and establishes a "conclusive" presumption that an alien convicted of an aggravated felony is deportable, 8 U.S.C. 1252a(c).

Research indicating that human trafficking for purpose of prostitution or enslavement had become a global problem led to the passage of harsher criminal penalties for traffickers. Nevertheless, the Victims of Trafficking and Violence Protection Act of 2000 provided visas for victims willing to testify against traffickers and enacted a system of sanctions for sending countries which did not take steps to protect their citizens.

Victims of Trafficking and Violence Protection Act of 2000
H.R. 3244

Amends the Foreign Assistance Act of 1961 (FAA) to require the Secretary of State (the Secretary) to include as part of required reports on human rights and development assistance and human rights and security assistance: (1) a description of the nature and extent of severe forms of trafficking in persons in each foreign country; and (2) with respect to each country that is a country of origin, transit, or destination for victims of severe forms of trafficking in persons, an assessment of the efforts by such countries' governments to combat such trafficking.

Section 105—Requires the President to establish an Interagency Task Force to Monitor and Combat Trafficking, chaired by the Secretary. Authorizes the Secretary to establish within the Department of State an Office to Monitor and Combat Trafficking, which shall assist the Task Force and be administered by a Director. Requires the Director to consult with domestic organizations, international nongovernmental organizations, and multilateral organizations, including the Organization of American States, the Organization for Security and Cooperation in Europe (OSCE), and the United Nations, and with trafficking victims or other affected persons.

Directs the Task Force to: (1) coordinate the implementation of this division; (2) measure and evaluate progress of the United States and other countries in trafficking prevention, provision of assistance to and protection of trafficking victims, and prosecution of and enforcement against traffickers; (3) assist the Secretary in the preparation of the reports under section 110, below; (4) expand interagency procedures to collect and organize data and to respect the confidentiality of trafficking victims; (5) engage in efforts to facilitate cooperation among countries of origin, transit, and destination; (6) examine the role of the international "sex tourism" industry in the trafficking of persons and in the sexual exploitation of women and children around the world; and (7) engage in consultation and advocacy with governmental and nongovernmental organizations, among other entities, to advance the purposes of this division.

Sec. 106—Directs the President: (1) to establish and carry out initiatives to enhance economic opportunity for potential victims of trafficking as a method to deter trafficking; (2) acting through the Secretaries of Labor, Health and Human Services (HHS), and State and the Attorney General, to establish and carry out programs to increase public awareness, particularly among potential victims, of the dangers of trafficking and the protections that are available for victims; and (3) to consult with appropriate nongovernmental organizations with respect to the establishment and conduct of initiatives under this section.

Sec. 107—Requires the Secretary and the Administrator of the Agency for International Development (AID) to establish and carry out programs and initiatives in foreign countries to assist in the safe integration, reintegration, or resettlement of victims of trafficking and their children and to take appropriate steps to enhance cooperative efforts among foreign countries, including countries of origin of victims, to assist in such integration, reintegration, or resettlement.

Directs the Secretaries of HHS and Labor, the Board of Directors of the Legal Services Corporation (LSC), and the heads of other Federal agencies to expand benefits and services to victims of severe forms of trafficking in persons within the United States, without regard to the immigration status of such victims. Makes an alien who is such a victim eligible for benefits and services to the same extent as an alien who is admitted to the United States as a refugee under the Immigration and Nationality Act (INA). Sets forth reporting and certification requirements. Directs the Attorney General and the Secretary to promulgate regulations for law enforcement personnel, immigration officials, and State Department officials to provide that: (1) such victims, while in Federal custody, shall not be detained in facilities inappropriate to their status as crime victims, shall receive necessary medical care and other assistance, and shall be provided protection if a victim's safety is at risk or if there is danger of additional harm by recapture by a trafficker; (2) such victims shall have access to information about their rights and translation services; (3) Federal law enforcement officials may act to ensure an alien's continued presence in the United States if it is determined that such individual is a victim of trafficking and a potential witness to the prosecution of those responsible; (4) such officials, in investigating and prosecuting traffickers, shall protect the safety of trafficking victims; and (5) appropriate personnel of the Departments of State and Justice shall be trained in identifying such victims and providing for their protection.

Amends the INA to create a new non-immigrant "T" visa for: (1) an alien who the Attorney General determines is a victim of a severe form of trafficking in persons, who is in the United States, American Samoa, the Commonwealth of the Northern Mariana Islands, or a U.S. port of entry on account of such trafficking, who has complied with any reasonable request for assistance in the investigation or prosecution of acts of trafficking or has not attained age 15, and who would suffer extreme hardship involving unusual and severe harm upon removal from the United States; (2) the spouse, children, and parents of such an alien who is under 21 if the Attorney General considers it necessary to avoid extreme hardship; or (3) the minor children of such an alien who is 21 years of age or older if they are accompanying or following to join such alien. Limits the total number of aliens who may be issued visas or otherwise provided non-immigrant status during a fiscal year to 5,000. Makes this numerical limitation applicable only to principal aliens and not to the spouses, sons, daughters, or parents of such aliens.

Directs the Attorney General and other government officials to refer such non-immigrant aliens to nongovernmental organizations that would advise the aliens regarding their options and the resources available to them. Requires the Attorney General, during the period those aliens are in lawful temporary resident status, to grant them authorization to engage in employment in the United States and to provide them with an "employment authorized" endorsement or other appropriate work permit.

Permits the Attorney General to adjust the status of a "T" visa holder to that of a permanent resident if the alien: (1) has been physically present in the United States for a continuous period of at least three years since the date of admission; (2) has been a person of good moral character throughout such period; and (3) has complied with any reasonable request for assistance in the investigation or prosecution of trafficking acts throughout such period, or would suffer extreme hardship upon removal from the United States. Permits the Attorney General to adjust the status of any other alien admitted under that section, with an exception.

Sec. 108—Establishes minimum standards for the elimination of trafficking applicable to the government of a country of origin, transit, or destination for a significant number of victims of severe forms of trafficking. Urges such countries to prohibit such trafficking, to punish such acts, and to eliminate such trafficking.

Sec. 109—Amends the FAA to authorize the President to provide assistance to foreign countries directly or through nongovernmental, intergovernmental, and multilateral organizations for programs and activities designed to meet the minimum standards for the elimination of trafficking, including the drafting of laws to prohibit and punish acts of trafficking, the investigation and prosecution of traffickers, the creation and maintenance of facilities, programs, and activities for the protection of victims, and the expansion of exchange programs and international visitor programs for governmental and nongovernmental personnel to combat trafficking.

Sec. 110—Declares that it is U.S. policy not to provide non-humanitarian, non-trade-related foreign assistance to any government that does not comply with minimum standards for the elimination of trafficking and that is not making significant efforts to comply with such standards.

Requires the Secretary to submit to the appropriate congressional committees reports with respect to the status of severe forms of trafficking and those countries to which the minimum standards for the elimination of trafficking are applicable whose governments: (1) fully comply with such standards; (2) do not yet fully comply but are making significant efforts to comply; and (3) do not fully comply and are not making significant efforts to do so. Specifies possible presidential determinations with respect to: (1) the withholding of non-humanitarian, non-trade-related assistance; (2) ongoing, multiple, broad-based restrictions on assistance in response to human rights violations; (3) subsequent compliance; and (4) continuation of assistance in the national interest and waiver authority.

Securitization of Immigration

The 9/11 attacks led to the rapid passage of the USA PATRIOT Act of 2001 as a part of the initiative known as the "War on Terror." The 21st-century legislative emphasis on dealing with visitors from abroad, legal immigrants, and unauthorized entrants has emphasized protecting the American population from terrorists. This act is controversial for the degree of surveillance of both citizens and noncitizens which was authorized. Certain portions of the act are due to "sunset," but in 2010 most of the surveillance provisions were still in effect and sustaining legal challenge. Regarding security at the borders, this act sought to enhance Canadian border personnel and surveillance technology. It is also noted for its antimoney-laundering provisions, authorization of mandatory detention without judicial review for terrorism suspects, and enhanced penalties for terrorists. It has provided that all individuals, citizen or noncitizen, seeking to enter or exit the United States must provide enhanced documentation, including biometric technology.

USA PATRIOT Act of 2001
HR 3162, October 24, 2001
Title I—Enhancing Domestic Security Against Terrorism

Sec. 102—Sense of Congress condemning discrimination against Arab and Muslim Americans and Americans from South Asia.

(a) FINDINGS—Congress makes the following findings:

(1) Arab Americans, Muslim Americans, and Americans from South Asia play a vital role in our Nation and are entitled to nothing less than the full rights of every American.

(2) The acts of violence that have been taken against Arab and Muslim Americans since the September 11, 2001, attacks against the United States should be and are condemned by all Americans who value freedom.

(3) The concept of individual responsibility for wrongdoing is sacrosanct in American society, and applies equally to all religious, racial, and ethnic groups.

(4) When American citizens commit acts of violence against those who are, or are perceived to be, of Arab or Muslim descent, they should be punished to the full extent of the law.

(5) Muslim Americans have become so fearful of harassment that many Muslim women are changing the way they dress to avoid becoming targets.

(6) Many Arab Americans and Muslim Americans have acted heroically during the attacks on the United States, including Mohammed Salman Hamdani, a 23-year-old New Yorker of Pakistani descent, who is believed to have gone to the World Trade Center to offer rescue assistance and is now missing.

(b) SENSE OF CONGRESS—It is the sense of Congress that—

    (1) the civil rights and civil liberties of all Americans, including Arab Americans, Muslim Americans, and Americans from South Asia, must be protected, and that every effort must be taken to preserve their safety;

    (2) any acts of violence or discrimination against any Americans be condemned; and

    (3) the Nation is called upon to recognize the patriotism of fellow citizens from all ethnic, racial, and religious backgrounds.

Title II—Enhanced Surveillance Procedures

Sec. 201—Authorizes interception of wire, oral, and electronic communications relating to terrorism or production and dissemination of chemical weapons from both citizens and noncitizens.

Sec. 202—Establishes authority to intercept wire, oral, and electronic communications relating to felony fraud and abuse offenses against computers.

Sec. 203—Allows warrantless interception and sharing of criminal investigative information disclosed to a grand jury among federal agencies if it involves foreign intelligence or counterintelligence.

Sec. 204—Extends intelligence exceptions for interception and disclosure of wire, oral, and electronic communications.

Sec. 206—Establishes roving wiretap authority allowing surveillance of any communications made to an intelligence target under the Foreign Intelligence Surveillance Act (FISA) of 1978.

Sec. 207—Extends duration of FISA surveillance of non–United States persons who are agents of a foreign power.

Sec. 209—Authorizes seizure of voice mail messages after obtaining warrants.

Sec. 210—Extends use of subpoenas, rather than court orders for an expanded variety of records of electronic communications and does not limit use to suspected terrorism investigations.

Sec. 212—Authorizes emergency disclosure of electronic communications to protect life and limb.

Sec. 213—Delineates authority for notice of the execution of a warrant which permits delay until after surveillance occurs. [Referred to as "sneak and peak"]

Sec. 214—Removes statutory requirement that the government must prove an individual is "an agent of a foreign power" and extends pen register and trap and trace authority to the Internet under FISA.

Sec. 215—Authorizes FBI ability to request an order "requiring the production of any tangible things" (records, books, documents, etc.) under the Foreign Intelligence Surveillance Act to investigate terrorism.

Sec. 216—Expands court jurisdiction to place wiretaps and pen register/trap and trace outside of geographic jurisdiction.

Sec. 217—Authorizes interception of computer trespasser communications.

Sec. 218—Allows collection of foreign intelligence information as a significant and not necessarily the sole purpose of an investigation.

Sec. 219—Expands court jurisdiction to place wiretaps and pen trap and trace outside of geographic jurisdiction in investigations of international or domestic terrorism.

Sec. 220—Authorizes nationwide service of search warrants for electronic evidence.

Sec. 223—Establishes civil liability for unauthorized and improper disclosures violating communications privacy made by government officials or the courts.

Sec. 224—Provides for sunset of many enhanced surveillance and foreign intelligence Amendments (201, 202, 203b, 204, 206, 207, 209, 212, 214, 215, 217, 218, 220, 223, 225) on December 31, 2005.

Sec. 225—Authorizes immunity to providers for compliance with FISA wiretaps.

Title IV—Protecting the Border
Subtitle A—Protecting the Northern Border

Sec. 401—Ensures adequate personnel on the northern border. There are authorized to be appropriated—

(1) such sums as may be necessary to triple the number of Border Patrol personnel (from the number authorized under current law), and the necessary personnel and

facilities to support such personnel, in each State along the Northern Border;

(2) such sums as may be necessary to triple the number of Customs Service personnel (from the number authorized under current law), and the necessary personnel and facilities to support such personnel, at ports of entry in each State along the Northern Border;

(3) such sums as may be necessary to triple the number of INS inspectors (from the number authorized on the date of the enactment of this Act), and the necessary personnel and facilities to support such personnel, at ports of entry in each State along the Northern Border; and

(4) an additional $50,000,000 each to the Immigration and Naturalization Service and the United States Customs Service for purposes of making improvements in technology for monitoring the Northern Border and acquiring additional equipment at the Northern Border.

Sec. 403—Grants access by the Department of State and the INS to certain identifying records in the criminal history records of visa applicants and applicants seeking admission to the United States.

(b)(1) The Attorney General and the Director of the Federal Bureau of Investigation shall provide the Department of State and the Service access to the criminal history record information contained in the National Crime Information Center's Interstate Identification Index (NCIC-III), Wanted Persons File, and to any other files maintained by the National Crime Information Center that may be mutually agreed upon by the Attorney General and the agency receiving the access, for the purpose of determining whether or not a visa applicant or applicant for admission has a criminal history record indexed in any such file.

(2) Such access shall be provided by means of extracts of the records for placement in the automated visa lookout or other appropriate database, and shall be provided without any fee or charge.

(3) The Federal Bureau of Investigation shall provide periodic updates of the extracts at intervals

mutually agreed upon with the agency receiving the access. Upon receipt of such updated extracts, the receiving agency shall make corresponding updates to its database and destroy previously provided extracts.

(4) Access to an extract does not entitle the Department of State to obtain the full content of the corresponding automated criminal history record. To obtain the full content of a criminal history record, the Department of State shall submit the applicant's fingerprints and any appropriate fingerprint processing fee authorized by law to the Criminal Justice Information Services Division of the Federal Bureau of Investigation.

(c) The provision of the extracts described in subsection (b) may be reconsidered by the Attorney General and the receiving agency upon the development and deployment of a more cost-effective and efficient means of sharing the information.

(d) For purposes of administering this section, the Department of State shall, prior to receiving access to NCIC data but not later than 4 months after the date of enactment of this subsection, promulgate final regulations—

(1) to implement procedures for the taking of fingerprints; and

(2) to establish the conditions for the use of the information received from the Federal Bureau of Investigation, in order—

(A) to limit the redissemination of such information;

(B) to ensure that such information is used solely to determine whether or not to issue a visa to an alien or to admit an alien to the United States;

(C) to ensure the security, confidentiality, and destruction of such information; and

(D) to protect any privacy rights of individuals who are subjects of such information.

(b) REPORTING REQUIREMENT—Not later than 2 years after the date of enactment of this Act, the Attorney General and the Secretary of State jointly shall report to

Congress on the implementation of the amendments made by this section.

(c) TECHNOLOGY STANDARD TO CONFIRM IDENTITY—

    (1) IN GENERAL—The Attorney General and the Secretary of State jointly, through the National Institute of Standards and Technology (NIST), and in consultation with the Secretary of the Treasury and other Federal law enforcement and intelligence agencies the Attorney General or Secretary of State deems appropriate and in consultation with Congress, shall within 2 years after the date of the enactment of this section, develop and certify a technology standard that can be used to verify the identity of persons applying for a United States visa or such persons seeking to enter the United States pursuant to a visa for the purposes of conducting background checks, confirming identity, and ensuring that a person has not received a visa under a different name or such person seeking to enter the United States pursuant to a visa.

    (2) INTEGRATED—The technology standard developed pursuant to paragraph (1), shall be the technological basis for a cross-agency, cross-platform electronic system that is a cost-effective, efficient, fully integrated means to share law enforcement and intelligence information necessary to confirm the identity of such persons applying for a United States visa or such person seeking to enter the United States pursuant to a visa.

    (3) ACCESSIBLE—The electronic system described in paragraph (2), once implemented, shall be readily and easily accessible to—

        (A) all consular officers responsible for the issuance of visas;

        (B) all Federal inspection agents at all United States border inspection points; and

        (C) all law enforcement and intelligence officers as determined by regulation to be responsible for investigation or identification of aliens admitted to the United States pursuant to a visa.

   (4) REPORT—Not later than 18 months after the date
of the enactment of this Act, and every 2 years
thereafter, the Attorney General and the Secretary
of State shall jointly, in consultation with the
Secretary of Treasury, report to Congress
describing the development, implementation,
efficacy, and privacy implications of the technology
standard and electronic database system described
in this subsection.

   (5) FUNDING—There is authorized to be appropriated
to the Secretary of State, the Attorney General, and
the Director of the National Institute of Standards
and Technology such sums as may be necessary to
carry out the provisions of this subsection.

(d) STATUTORY CONSTRUCTION—Nothing in this
section, or in any other law, shall be construed to limit
the authority of the Attorney General or the Director
of the Federal Bureau of Investigation to provide access
to the criminal history record information contained in
the National Crime Information Center's (NCIC)
Interstate Identification Index (NCIC-III), or to any
other information maintained by the NCIC, to any
Federal agency or officer authorized to enforce or
administer the immigration laws of the United States,
for the purpose of such enforcement or administration,
upon terms that are consistent with the National Crime
Prevention and Privacy Compact Act of 1998 (subtitle
A of title II of Public Law 105-251; 42 U.S.C. 14611-16)
and section 552a of title 5, United States Code.

SEC. 405. REPORT ON THE INTEGRATED AUTO-MATED FINGERPRINT IDENTIFICATION SYSTEM FOR PORTS OF ENTRY AND OVERSEAS CONSULAR POSTS.

Sec. 405—Establishes the integrated automated fingerprint
identification system for ports of entry and overseas consular posts.

(a) IN GENERAL—The Attorney General, in consultation
with the appropriate heads of other Federal agencies,
including the Secretary of State, Secretary of the Treasury, and the Secretary of Transportation, shall report to
Congress on the feasibility of enhancing the Integrated
Automated Fingerprint Identification System (IAFIS) of

the Federal Bureau of Investigation and other identification systems in order to better identify a person who holds a foreign passport or a visa and may be wanted in connection with a criminal investigation in the United States or abroad, before the issuance of a visa to that person or the entry or exit from the United States by that person.

Subtitle B—Enhanced Immigration Provisions

Sec. 411—Defines new legal terms relating to terrorism.

Sec. 412—Mandatory detention of suspected terrorists, denial of habeas corpus under specified conditions and limits on judicial review.

Sec. 236A. (a) DETENTION OF TERRORIST ALIENS—

(1) CUSTODY—The Attorney General shall take into custody any alien who is certified under paragraph (3).

(2) RELEASE—Except as provided in paragraphs (5) and (6), the Attorney General shall maintain custody of such an alien until the alien is removed from the United States. Except as provided in paragraph (6), such custody shall be maintained irrespective of any relief from removal for which the alien may be eligible, or any relief from removal granted the alien, until the Attorney General determines that the alien is no longer an alien who may be certified under paragraph (3). If the alien is finally determined not to be removable, detention pursuant to this subsection shall terminate.

(3) CERTIFICATION—The Attorney General may certify an alien under this paragraph if the Attorney General has reasonable grounds to believe that the alien—

   (A) is described in section 212(a)(3)(A)(i), 212(a)(3)(A)(iii), 212(a)(3)(B), 237(a)(4)(A)(i), 237(a)(4)(A)(iii), or 237(a)(4)(B); or

   (B) is engaged in any other activity that endangers the national security of the United States.

(4) NONDELEGATION—The Attorney General may delegate the authority provided under paragraph (3) only to the Deputy Attorney General. The Deputy Attorney General may not delegate such authority.

(5) COMMENCEMENT OF PROCEEDINGS—The Attorney General shall place an alien detained under

paragraph (1) in removal proceedings, or shall charge the alien with a criminal offense, not later than 7 days after the commencement of such detention. If the requirement of the preceding sentence is not satisfied, the Attorney General shall release the alien.

(6) LIMITATION ON INDEFINITE DETENTION—An alien detained solely under paragraph (1) who has not been removed under section 241(a)(1)(A), and whose removal is unlikely in the reasonably foreseeable future, may be detained for additional periods of up to six months only if the release of the alien will threaten the national security of the United States or the safety of the community or any person.

(7) REVIEW OF CERTIFICATION—The Attorney General shall review the certification made under paragraph (3) every 6 months. If the Attorney General determines, in the Attorney General's discretion, that the certification should be revoked, the alien may be released on such conditions as the Attorney General deems appropriate, unless such release is otherwise prohibited by law. The alien may request each 6 months in writing that the Attorney General reconsider the certification and may submit documents or other evidence in support of that request.

(b) HABEAS CORPUS AND JUDICIAL REVIEW—

(1) IN GENERAL—Judicial review of any action or decision relating to this section (including judicial review of the merits of a determination made under subsection (a)(3) or (a)(6)) is available exclusively in habeas corpus proceedings consistent with this subsection. Except as provided in the preceding sentence, no court shall have jurisdiction to review, by habeas corpus petition or otherwise, any such action or decision.

(2) APPLICATION—

(A) IN GENERAL—Notwithstanding any other provision of law, including section 2241(a) of title 28, United States Code, habeas corpus proceedings described in paragraph (1) may be initiated only by an application filed with—

(i) the Supreme Court;

(ii) any justice of the Supreme Court;

> (iii) any circuit judge of the United States Court of Appeals for the District of Columbia Circuit; or
>
> (iv) any district court otherwise having jurisdiction to entertain it.
>
> (B) APPLICATION TRANSFER—Section 2241(b) of title 28, United States Code, shall apply to an application for a writ of habeas corpus described in subparagraph (A).
>
> (3) APPEALS—Notwithstanding any other provision of law, including section 2253 of title 28, in habeas corpus proceedings described in paragraph (1) before a circuit or district judge, the final order shall be subject to review, on appeal, by the United States Court of Appeals for the District of Columbia Circuit. There shall be no right of appeal in such proceedings to any other circuit court of appeals.
>
> (4) RULE OF DECISION—The law applied by the Supreme Court and the United States Court of Appeals for the District of Columbia Circuit shall be regarded as the rule of decision in habeas corpus proceedings described in paragraph (1).

(c) STATUTORY CONSTRUCTION—The provisions of this section shall not be applicable to any other provision of this Act.

(b) CLERICAL AMENDMENT—The table of contents of the Immigration and Nationality Act is amended by inserting after the item relating to section 236 the following:

Sec. 236A. Mandatory detention of suspected terrorist; habeas corpus; judicial review.

> (c) REPORTS—Not later than 6 months after the date of the enactment of this Act, and every 6 months thereafter, the Attorney General shall submit a report to the Committee on the Judiciary of the House of Representatives and the Committee on the Judiciary of the Senate, with respect to the reporting period, on—
>
> (1) the number of aliens certified under section 236A(a)(3) of the Immigration and Nationality Act, as added by subsection (a);

(2) the grounds for such certifications;
(3) the nationalities of the aliens so certified;
(4) the length of the detention for each alien so certified; and
(5) the number of aliens so certified who—
    (A) were granted any form of relief from removal;
    (B) were removed;
    (C) the Attorney General has determined are no longer aliens who may be so certified; or
    (D) were released from detention.

Sec. 413—Increases multilateral cooperation against terrorists.

Sec. 414—Expands visa integrity and security.

Sec. 415—Mandate for Office of Homeland Security to participate in Entry-Exit Task Force.

Sec. 416—Establishes a program for monitoring foreign students.

Sec. 417—Initiates machine readable passports.

Title VIII—Strengthening the Criminal Laws Against Terrorism

Sec. 801—Terrorist attacks and other acts of violence against mass transportation systems.

Sec. 803—Prohibits harboring terrorists.

Sec. 805—Material support of terrorism.

Sec. 807—Technical clarification relating to provision of material support to terrorism.

Sec. 808—Defines federal crime of terrorism.

Sec. 809—Removes statute of limitation for certain terrorism offenses.

Title X—Miscellaneous

Sec. 1003—Defines electronic surveillance.

Sec. 1008—Feasibility study of use of biometric identifier system with access to the FBI integrated automated fingerprint identification system at overseas consular posts and points of entry to the United States.

The trends established in the USA PATRIOT Act of 2001 were reinforced by the Enhanced Border Security and Visa Entry Reform Act of 2002 and the U.S. Visit and Intelligence Reform and Terrorism Act of 2004.

Enhanced Border Security and Visa Entry Reform Act of 2002

Title 1—Funding

Sec. 101—Authorization of Appropriations for Hiring and Training Governmental Personnel.

Sec. 102—Authorization of Appropriations for Improvements in Technology and Infrastructure.

Sec. 103—Machine Readable Visa Fees.

Title 2—Intragency Information Sharing

Sec. 202—Interoperable Law Enforcement and Intelligence Data System With Name Matching Capacity and Training

(a) Interoperable Law Enforcement and Intelligence Electronic Data System.—

(1) Requirement for integrated immigration and naturalization data system.—The Immigration and Naturalization Service shall fully integrate all databases and data systems maintained by the Service that process or contain information on aliens. The fully integrated data system shall be an interoperable component of the electronic data system described in paragraph (2).

(2) Requirement for interoperable data system.—Upon the date of commencement of implementation of the plan required by section 201(c), the President shall develop and implement an interoperable electronic data system to provide current and immediate access to information in databases of Federal law enforcement agencies and the intelligence community that is relevant to determine whether to issue a visa or to determine the admissibility or deportability of an alien.

(3) Consultation requirement.—In the development and implementation of the data system under this subsection, the President shall consult with the Director of the National Institute of Standards and Technology (NIST) and any such other agency as may be deemed appropriate.

(4) Technology standard.—

(A) In general.—The data system developed and implemented under this subsection, and the databases referred to in paragraph (2), shall utilize the technology standard established pursuant to section 403(c) of the USA PATRIOT Act, as amended by section 201(c)(5) and subparagraph (B).

(5) Access to information in data system.—Subject to paragraph (6), information in the data system under this subsection shall be readily and easily accessible—

(A) to any consular officer responsible for the issuance of visas;

(B) to any Federal official responsible for determining an alien's admissibility to or deportability from the United States; and

(C) to any Federal law enforcement or intelligence officer determined by regulation to be responsible for the investigation or identification of aliens.

Title 3—Visa Issuance

Sec. 302—Implementation of an Integrated Entry and Exit Data System

(a) Development of System.—In developing the integrated entry and exit data system for the ports of entry, as required by the Immigration and Naturalization Service Data Management Improvement Act of 2000 (Public Law 106-215), the Attorney General and the Secretary of State shall—

(1) implement, fund, and use a technology standard under section 403(c) of the USA PATRIOT Act (as amended by sections 201(c)(5) and 202(a)(3)(B)) at United States ports of entry and at consular posts abroad;

(2) establish a database containing the arrival and departure data from machine-readable visas, passports, and other travel and entry documents possessed by aliens; and (3) make interoperable all security databases relevant to making determinations of admissibility under section 212 of the Immigration and Nationality Act (8 U.S.C. 1182).

Sec. 303—Machine-readable Tamper-Resistant Entry and Exit Documents
 (b) Requirements.—
  (1) In general.—Not later than October 26, 2003, the Attorney General and the Secretary of State shall issue to aliens only machine-readable, tamper-resistant visas and travel and entry documents that use biometric identifiers. The Attorney General and the Secretary of State shall jointly establish biometric identifiers standards to be employed on such visas and travel and entry documents from among those biometric identifiers recognized by domestic and international standards organizations.
  (2) Readers and scanners at ports of entry.—
   (A) In general.—Not later than October 26, 2003, the Attorney General, in consultation with the Secretary of State, shall install at all ports of entry of the United States equipment and software to allow biometric comparison of all United States visas and travel and entry documents issued to aliens, and passports issued pursuant to subsection (c)(1).

Sec. 303—Improved Training for Consular Officers

 (a) Training.—The Secretary of State shall require that all consular officers responsible for adjudicating visa applications, before undertaking to perform consular responsibilities, receive specialized training in the effective screening of visa applicants who pose a potential threat to the safety or security of the United States.

Sec. 306—Restrictions on Issuance of Visas to Nonimmigrants From Countries That Are State Sponsors of International Terrorism

 (a) In General.—No nonimmigrant visa under section 101(a)(15) of the Immigration and Nationality Act (8 U.S.C. 1101(a)(15)) shall be issued to any alien from a country that is a state sponsor of international terrorism unless the Secretary of State determines, in consultation with the Attorney General and the heads of other appropriate United States agencies, that such alien does not pose a threat to the safety or national security of the United States. In making a determination under this subsection, the Secretary of State shall apply standards developed by the Secretary of State, in consultation with the Attorney General and the heads of other appropriate United States agencies, that are applicable to the nationals of such states.

(b) State Sponsor of International Terrorism Defined.—

(1) In general.—In this section, the term "state sponsor of international terrorism" means any country the government of which has been determined by the Secretary of State under any of the laws specified in paragraph (2) to have repeatedly provided support for acts of international terrorism.

U.S. VISIT and Intelligence Reform and Terrorism Act 2004
Subtitle B—Terrorist Travel and Effective Screening
SEC. 7201—COUNTERTERRORIST TRAVEL INTELLIGENCE.

(a) Findings.—Consistent with the report of the National Commission on Terrorist Attacks Upon the United States, Congress makes the following findings:

(1) Travel documents are as important to terrorists as weapons since terrorists must travel clandestinely to meet, train, plan, case targets, and gain access to attack sites.

(2) International travel is dangerous for terrorists because they must surface to pass through regulated channels, present themselves to border security officials, or attempt to circumvent inspection points.

(3) Terrorists use evasive, but detectable, methods to travel, such as altered and counterfeit passports and visas, specific travel methods and routes, liaisons with corrupt government officials, human smuggling networks, supportive travel agencies, and immigration and identity fraud.

(4) Before September 11, 2001, no Federal agency systematically analyzed terrorist travel strategies. If an agency had done so, the agency could have discovered the ways in which the terrorist predecessors to al Qaeda had been systematically, but detectably, exploiting weaknesses in our border security since the early 1990s.

(5) Many of the hijackers were potentially vulnerable to interception by border authorities. Analyzing their characteristic travel documents and travel

patterns could have allowed authorities to intercept some of the hijackers and a more effective use of information available in government databases could have identified some of the hijackers.

(6) The routine operations of our immigration laws and the aspects of those laws not specifically aimed at protecting against terrorism inevitably shaped al Qaeda's planning and opportunities.

(7) New insights into terrorist travel gained since September 11, 2001, have not been adequately integrated into the front lines of border security.

(8) The small classified terrorist travel intelligence collection and analysis program currently in place has produced useful results and should be expanded.

(b) Strategy.—

(1) In general.—Not later than 1 year after the date of enactment of this Act, the Director of the National Counterterrorism Center shall submit to Congress unclassified and classified versions of a strategy for combining terrorist travel intelligence, operations, and law enforcement into a cohesive effort to intercept terrorists, find terrorist travel facilitators, and constrain terrorist mobility domestically and internationally. The report to Congress should include a description of the actions taken to implement the strategy and an assessment regarding vulnerabilities within the United States and foreign travel systems that may be exploited by international terrorists, human smugglers and traffickers, and their facilitators.

(2) Coordination.—The strategy shall be developed in coordination with all relevant Federal agencies.

Sec. 7202—Establishment of Human Smuggling and Trafficking Center

(1) serve as the focal point for interagency efforts to address terrorist travel;

(2) serve as a clearinghouse with respect to all relevant information from all Federal Government

agencies in support of the United States strategy to prevent separate, but related, issues of clandestine terrorist travel and facilitation of migrant smuggling and trafficking of persons;

Sec. 7204—International Agreements to Track and Curtail Terrorist Travel Through the Use of Fraudulently Obtained Documents.

(1) International agreement on lost, stolen, or falsified documents.—The President should lead efforts to track and curtail the travel of terrorists by supporting the drafting, adoption, and implementation of international agreements, and relevant United Nations Security Council resolutions to track and stop international travel by terrorists and other criminals through the use of lost, stolen, or falsified documents to augment United Nations and other international anti-terrorism efforts.

(2) Contents of international agreement.—The President should seek, as appropriate, the adoption or full implementation of effective international measures to—

(A) share information on lost, stolen, and fraudulent passports and other travel documents for the purposes of preventing the undetected travel of persons using such passports and other travel documents that were obtained improperly;

(B) establish and implement a real-time verification system of passports and other travel documents with issuing authorities;

(C) share with officials at ports of entry in any such country information relating to lost, stolen, and fraudulent passports and other travel documents;

(D) encourage countries—

(i) to criminalize—

(I) the falsification or counterfeiting of travel documents or breeder documents for any purpose;

        (II) the use or attempted use of false documents to obtain a visa or cross a border for any purpose;

       (III) the possession of tools or implements used to falsify or counterfeit such documents;

       (IV) the trafficking in false or stolen travel documents and breeder documents for any purpose;

       (V) the facilitation of travel by a terrorist; and

       (VI) attempts to commit, including conspiracies to commit, the crimes specified in subclauses (I) through (V);

    (ii) to impose significant penalties to appropriately punish violations and effectively deter the crimes specified in clause (i); and

    (iii) to limit the issuance of citizenship papers, passports, identification documents, and similar documents to persons—

       (I) whose identity is proven to the issuing authority;

       (II) who have a bona fide entitlement to or need for such documents; and

       (III) who are not issued such documents principally on account of a disproportional payment made by them or on their behalf to the issuing authority;

(A) provide technical assistance to countries to help them fully implement such measures; and

(B) permit immigration and border officials—

    (i) to confiscate a lost, stolen, or falsified passport at ports of entry;

    (ii) to permit the traveler to return to the sending country without being in possession of the lost, stolen, or falsified passport; and

    (iii) to detain and investigate such traveler upon the return of the traveler to the sending country.

Sec. 7208—Biometric Entry and Exit Data System

(a) Finding.—Consistent with the report of the National Commission on Terrorist Attacks Upon the United States, Congress finds that completing a biometric entry and exit data system as expeditiously as possible is an essential investment in efforts to protect the United States by preventing the entry of terrorists. . . .

(d) Collection of Biometric Exit Data.—The entry and exit data system shall include a requirement for the collection of biometric exit data for all categories of individuals who are required to provide biometric entry data, regardless of the port of entry where such categories of individuals entered the United States.

(h) Entry-Exit System Goals.—The Department of Homeland Security shall operate the biometric entry and exit system so that it—

(1) serves as a vital counterterrorism tool;

(2) screens travelers efficiently and in a welcoming manner;

(3) provides inspectors and related personnel with adequate real-time information;

(4) ensures flexibility of training and security protocols to most effectively comply with security mandates;

(5) integrates relevant databases and plans for database modifications to address volume increase and database usage; and

(6) improves database search capacities by utilizing language algorithms to detect alternate names.

(k) Expediting Registered Travelers Across International Borders.—

(1) Findings.—Consistent with the report of the National Commission on Terrorist Attacks Upon the United States, Congress makes the following findings:

(A) Expediting the travel of previously screened and known travelers across the borders of the United States should be a high priority.

(B) The process of expediting known travelers across the borders of the United States can permit inspectors to better focus on identifying terrorists attempting to enter the United States.

Sec. 7209—Travel Documents

(a) Findings.—Consistent with the report of the National Commission on Terrorist Attacks Upon the United States, Congress makes the following findings:

   (1) Existing procedures allow many individuals to enter the United States by showing minimal identification or without showing any identification.

   (2) The planning for the terrorist attacks of September 11, 2001, demonstrates that terrorists study and exploit United States vulnerabilities.

   (3) Additional safeguards are needed to ensure that terrorists cannot enter the United States.

(b) Passports.—

   (1) Development of plan.—The Secretary of Homeland Security, in consultation with the Secretary of State, shall develop and implement a plan as expeditiously as possible to require a passport or other document, or combination of documents, deemed by the Secretary of Homeland Security to be sufficient to denote identity and citizenship, for all travel into the United States by United States citizens and by categories of individuals for whom documentation requirements have previously been waived under section 212(d)(4)(B) of the Immigration and Nationality Act (8 U.S.C. 1182(d)(4)(B)). This plan shall be implemented not later than January 1, 2008, and shall seek to expedite the travel of frequent travelers, including those who reside in border communities, and in doing so, shall make readily available a registered traveler program (as described in section 7208(k)).

   (2) Requirement to produce documentation.—The plan developed under paragraph (1) shall require all United States citizens, and categories of individuals for whom documentation requirements have previously been waived under section 212(d)(4)(B) of such Act, to carry and produce the documentation described in paragraph (1) when traveling from foreign countries into the United States.

Sec. 7210. Exchange of Terrorist Information and Increased Preinspection at Foreign Airports.

(a) Findings.—Consistent with the report of the National Commission on Terrorist Attacks Upon the United States, Congress makes the following findings:

   (1) The exchange of terrorist information with other countries, consistent with privacy requirements, along with listings of lost and stolen passports, will have immediate security benefits.

   (2) The further away from the borders of the United States that screening occurs, the more security benefits the United States will gain.

(b) Sense of Congress.—It is the sense of Congress that—

   (1) the Federal Government should exchange terrorist information with trusted allies;

   (2) the Federal Government should move toward real-time verification of passports with issuing authorities;

   (3) where practicable, the Federal Government should conduct screening before a passenger departs on a flight destined for the United States;

   (4) the Federal Government should work with other countries to ensure effective inspection regimes at all airports;

   (5) the Federal Government should work with other countries to improve passport standards and provide foreign assistance to countries that need help making the transition to the global standard for identification; and

   (6) the Department of Homeland Security, in coordination with the Department of State and other Federal agencies, should implement the initiatives called for in this subsection.

The REAL ID Act of 2005 was a House of Representatives rider to the Emergency Supplemental Appropriations Act for Defense, the Global War on Terror, and Tsunami Relief. Its purpose was to regulate people crossing borders and remove individuals over the border. It is not all about native-born citizens although they would need new identification; it concerns the monitoring of individuals who have crossed the borders in order to detect those who have undocumented status.

Emergency Supplemental Appropriations Act for Defense, the Global War on Terror, and Tsunami Relief

H.R. 1268, May 11, 2005
Division B: REAL ID Act of 2005 –
Title I: Amendments to Federal Laws to Protect Against Terrorist Entry—

Section 101—Preventing terrorists from obtaining relief from removal

Applications for relief or protection from removal—the alien applying has the burden of establishing that they (1) satisfy the applicable eligibility requirements; and with respect to any form of relief that is granted in the exercise of discretion, that the alien merits a favorable exercise of discretion.

Sustaining burden—The applicant must comply with the applicable requirements to submit information or documentation in support of the applicant's application for relief or protection as provided by law or by regulation or in the instructions for the application form. In evaluating the testimony of the applicant or other witness in support of the application, the immigration judge will determine whether or not the testimony is credible, is persuasive, and refers to specific facts sufficient to demonstrate that the applicant has satisfied the applicant's burden of proof. In determining whether the applicant has met such burden, the immigration judge shall weigh the credible testimony along with other evidence of record. Where the immigration judge determines that the applicant should provide evidence which corroborates otherwise credible testimony, such evidence must be provided unless the applicant demonstrates that the applicant does not have the evidence and cannot reasonably obtain the evidence.

Credibility determination—Considering the totality of the circumstances, and all relevant factors, the immigration judge may base a credibility determination on the demeanor, candor, or responsiveness of the applicant or witness, the inherent plausibility of the applicant's or witness's account, the consistency between the applicant's or witness's written and oral statements (whenever made and whether or not under oath, and considering the circumstances under which the statements were made), the internal consistency of each such statement, the consistency of such statements with other evidence of record (including the reports of the Department of State on country conditions), and any inaccuracies or falsehoods in such statements, without regard to whether an inconsistency, inaccuracy, or falsehood goes to the heart of the applicant's claim, or any other relevant factor. There is no presumption of credibility; however, if no adverse credibility determination is explicitly made, the applicant or witness shall have a rebuttable presumption of credibility on appeal.

Standard of Review for Orders of Removal—Limits judicial review of determinations regarding the availability of corroborating evidence.

Section 102—Waiver of legal requirements necessary for improvement of barriers at borders; federal court review. Authorizes the Secretary of Homeland Security at sole discretion, to waive all legal requirements as necessary to ensure expeditious construction of certain barriers and roads at the U.S. border. Makes the Secretary's decision effective upon publication in the Federal Register. Gives U.S. district courts exclusive jurisdiction to hear causes or claims arising from actions or decisions by the Secretary pursuant to this section. Limits such causes or claims to those alleging a violation of the Constitution. Authorizes appellate review only upon petition for a writ of certiorari to the Supreme Court.

Section 103—Inadmissibility due to terrorist and terrorist-related activities. Expands the grounds of inadmissibility and deportability due to terrorist or terrorist-related activity to include aliens who: (1) are representatives of terrorist organizations or political, social, or other groups that endorse or espouse terrorist activity; (2) are members of designated terrorist organizations; (3) are members of organizations that engage in specified acts of terrorism; (4) endorse or espouse any terrorist activity or persuade others to do so; or (5) have received military type training from or on behalf of any organization that at the time was a terrorist organization.

Expands the definition of terrorist organization to incorporate a broader range of underlying activities.

Makes this section applicable to removal proceedings instituted, and grounds of inadmissibility occurring before, on, or after this Act.

Section 104—Waiver for certain grounds of inadmissibility. Authorizes the Secretary of State or the Secretary to conclude at sole unreviewable discretion that specified terrorism-related grounds of inadmissibility shall not apply to an alien, including those grounds applicable to: (1) representatives of groups whose public endorsement of terrorist activities the Secretary of State has determined undermines U.S. efforts to reduce or eliminate terrorist activities; (2) spouses or children of aliens inadmissible on terrorist grounds for activities occurring in the last five years; (3) alilens providing material support to organizations or individuals that have engaged in terrorist activity; or (4) groups that fall within the definition of "terrorist organization" simply by virtue of having a subgroup consisting of two or more individuals that engages in a specified terrorist activity or related planning. Prohibits the Secretary of State from exercising such discretion after removal proceedings have been instituted.

Requires the Secretary of Homeland Security and the Secretary of State to report to Congress on the application of this section of legislation.

Section 105—Removal of terrorists. Expands the grounds of deportability due to terrorist activity to include aliens who would be inadmissible on terrorism-related grounds.

Makes this applicable to removal proceedings initiated before, on, or after the date of enactment of this Act; and (2) grounds of inadmissibility, excludability, deportation, or removal occurring or existing before, on, or after such date.

Section 106—Judicial review of orders of removal.

Bars inadmissible arriving aliens from seeking judicial review of removal orders through habeas corpus, mandamus, or other extraordinary petitions.

Imposes a similar bar on denials of discretionary relief and orders against criminal aliens, with an exception for petitions for review concerning constitutional claims or questions of law.

Establishes the INA's judicial review provisions as the sole avenue for reviewing claims arising under the United Nation's Convention Against Torture and Other Forms of Cruel, Inhuman, or Degrading Treatment or Punishment and for challenging removal orders.

Requires petitions for review filed under pre-IIRIRA law to be treated as if filed under the INA as amended by this section. States that such petitions shall be the sole and exclusive means for judicial review of orders of deportation and exclusion.

Title II: Improved Security for Driver's Licenses and Personal Identification Cards—

Section 202—Minimum document requirements and issuance standards for federal recognition. Prohibits Federal agencies from accepting State issued driver's license or identification cards unless such documents are determined by the Secretary of Homeland Security to meet minimum security requirements, including the incorporation of specified data, a common machine-readable technology, and certain anti-fraud security features.

Minimum issuance standards—

To meet the requirements of this section, a State shall require, at a minimum, presentation and verification of the following information before issuing a driver's license or identification card to a person:

(A) A photo identity document, except that a nonphoto identity document is acceptable if it includes both the person's full legal name and date of birth.

(B) Documentation showing the person's date of birth.

(C) Proof of the person's social security account number or verification that the person is not eligible for a social security account number.

(D) Documentation showing the person's name and address of principal residence.

(2) SPECIAL REQUIREMENTS.—

(A) IN GENERAL.—To meet the requirements of this section, a State shall comply with the minimum standards of this paragraph.

(B) EVIDENCE OF LAWFUL STATUS.—A State shall require, before issuing a driver's license or identification card to a person, valid documentary evidence that the person—

   (i) is a citizen or national of the United States;

   (ii) is an alien lawfully admitted for permanent or temporary residence in the United States;

   (iii) has conditional permanent resident status in the United States;

   (iv) has an approved application for asylum in the United States or has entered into the United States in refugee status;

   (v) has a valid, unexpired nonimmigrant visa or nonimmigrant visa status for entry into the United States;

   (vi) has a pending application for asylum in the United States;

> (vii) has a pending or approved application for temporary protected status in the United States;
> (viii) has approved deferred action status; or
> (ix) has a pending application for adjustment of status to that of an alien lawfully admitted for permanent residence in the United States or conditional permanent resident status in the United States.

Sets forth minimum issuance standards for such documents that require:

(1) verification of presented information;
(2) evidence that the applicant is lawfully present in the United States;
(3) issuance of temporary driver's licenses or identification cards to persons temporarily present that are valid only for their period of authorized stay (or for one year where the period of stay is indefinite);
(4) a clear indication that such documents may not be accepted for Federal purposes where minimum standards are not met; and
(5) electronic access by all other States to the issuing state's motor vehicle database.

Section 2003—Trafficking in authentication features for use in false identification documents. Amends the Federal criminal code to prohibit trafficking in actual as well as false authentication features for use in fake identification documents, document-making implements or means of identification.

Requires the Secretary of Homeland Security to enter into the appropriate aviation security screening database information regarding persons convicted of using false driver's licenses at airports.

Title III: Border Infrastructure and Technology Integration—
Section 301—Vulnerability and Threat Assessment
Directs the Under Secretary of Homeland Security for Border and Transportation Security to study the technology, equipment, and personnel needed to address security vulnerabilities within the United States for each Customs and Border Protection field office that has responsibility for U.S. borders with Canada and Mexico.

Section 302—Use of Ground Surveillance Technologies for Border Security

Directs the Under Secretary of Homeland Security for Science and Technology to develop and report to specified congressional committees on a pilot program to utilize or increase the utilization of ground surveillance technologies to enhance U.S. border security. Requires pilot program technologies to include video camera, sensor and motion detection technologies.

Technologies—the ground surveillance technologies . . . shall include:

(A) video camera technology
(B) sensor technology
(C) motion detection technology

Section 303—Enhancement of Communications Integration and Information Sharing on Border Security

Requires the Secretary of Homeland Security, acting through the Under Secretary for Border and Transportation Security, to develop and Implement a plan to: (1) improve communication systems of Federal agencies to facilitate integrated communications among such agencies, State and local government agencies, and Indian tribes on border security matters; and (2) enhance related information sharing among such entities.

In the absence of successful terrorist incidents attempted in the United States, concerns grew about the expanding unauthorized population. It was feared that terrorists might also use the Mexican border for entry and the public supported building a wall to enclose the United States which was authorized by the Secure Fence Act of 2006.

Secure Fence Act
H.R. 6061, January 3, 2006
Section 2—Securing operational control of the border
Authorizes the Secretary of Homeland Security to take necessary and appropriate actions to achieve and maintain operational control over the entire U.S. international land and maritime borders, including:

(1) systematic border surveillance through more effective use of personnel and technology, such as unmanned

aerial vehicles, ground-based sensors, satellites, radar coverage, and cameras; and

(2) physical infrastructure enhancements to prevent unlawful border entry and facilitate border by United States Customs and Border Protection, such as additional checkpoints, all weather access roads, and vehicle barriers.

Defines operational control as the prevention of all unlawful U.S. entries into the United States, including entries by terrorists, other unlawful aliens, instruments of terrorism, narcotics, and other contraband.

Requires the Secretary of Homeland Security to report annually to Congress on progress towards border control.

Section 3—Construction of fencing and security improvements in border area from Pacific Ocean to Gulf of Mexico.
Amends Section 102(b) of the Illegal Immigration Reform and Immigrant Responsibility Act of 1996 to direct the Secretary of Homeland Security to increase border security through:

Reinforced Fencing—. . . at least 2 layers of reinforced fencing, the installation of additional physical barriers, roads, lighting, cameras and sensors extending from: (1) 10 miles west of the Tecate, California port of to 10 miles east of the Tecate, California port of entry; (2) 10 miles west of the Calexio, California port of entry to 5 miles east of the Douglas, Arizona port of entry; (3) 5 miles west of the Columbus, New Mexico port of entry to 5 miles southeast of the Eagle Pass, Texas port of entry; and (4) 15 miles northwest of the Laredo, Texas port of entry to the Brownsville, Texas port of entry. States that if an area has an elevation grade exceeding 10% the Secretary may use other means to secure such area, including surveillance and barrier tools

Section 4—Northern border study
Directs the Secretary of Homeland Security to conduct a study on the necessity and feasibility of implementing a state-of-the-art infrastructure security system along the northern international land and maritime border of the United States and to include assessment of the economic impact that implementation of such a system would have on the northern border. A study report for the Committee on Homeland Security of the House of Representatives

and the Committee on Homeland Security and Governmental Affairs of the Senate was required within one year.

Section 5—Evaluation and report relating to customs authority to stop certain fleeing vehicles
Directs the Secretary of Homeland Security to: review the equipment and technology available and evaluate the authority (and consider its expansion) and the training of personnel of United States Custom and Border Protection to stop vehicles that enter the United States illegally and refuse to stop when ordered to do so and report back to the Congress.

War on Terrorism Documents

President George W. Bush set the tone for the War on Terrorism with Executive Order 13224:

Executive Order 13224 By the authority vested in me as President by the Constitution and the laws of the United States of America, including the International Emergency Economic Powers Act (50 U.S.C. 1701 et seq.)(IEEPA), the National Emergencies Act (50 U.S.C. 1601 et seq.), section 5 of the United Nations Participation Act of 1945, as amended (22 U.S.C. 287c) (UNPA), and section 301 of title 3, United States Code, and in view of United Nations Security Council Resolution (UNSCR) 1214 of December 8, 1998, UNSCR 1267 of October 15, 1999, UNSCR 1333 of December 19, 2000, and the multilateral sanctions contained therein, and UNSCR 1363 of July 30, 2001, establishing a mechanism to monitor the implementation of UNSCR 1333, I, GEORGE W. BUSH, President of the United States of America, find that grave acts of terrorism and threats of terrorism committed by foreign terrorists, including the terrorist attacks in New York, Pennsylvania, and the Pentagon committed on September 11, 2001, acts recognized and condemned in UNSCR 1368 of September 12, 2001, and UNSCR 1269 of October 19, 1999, and the continuing and immediate threat of further attacks on United States nationals or the United States constitute an unusual and extraordinary threat to the national security, foreign policy, and economy of the United States, and in furtherance of my proclamation of September 14, 2001, Declaration of National Emergency by Reason of Certain Terrorist Attacks, hereby declare a national emergency to deal with that threat. I also find that because of the pervasiveness and expansiveness of the financial foundation of foreign terrorists, financial sanctions may be appropriate for those foreign persons that support or otherwise associate with these foreign terrorists. I also find that a need exists for further consultation and cooperation with, and sharing of information by, United States and foreign financial institutions as an additional tool to enable the United States to combat the financing of terrorism.

I hereby order:

Sec. 1. Except to the extent required by section 203(b) of IEEPA (50 U.S.C. 1702(b)), or provided in regulations, orders, directives, or licenses that may be issued pursuant to this order, and notwithstanding any contract entered into or any license or permit granted prior to the effective date of this order, all property and interests in property of the following persons that are in the United States or that hereafter come within the United States, or that hereafter come within the possession or control of United States persons are blocked:

(a) foreign persons listed in the Annex to this order;

(b) foreign persons determined by the Secretary of State, in consultation with the Secretary of the Treasury and the Attorney General, to have committed, or to pose a significant risk of committing, acts of terrorism that threaten the security of U.S. nationals or the national security, foreign policy, or economy of the United States;

(c) persons determined by the Secretary of the Treasury, in consultation with the Secretary of State and the Attorney General, to be owned or controlled by, or to act for or on behalf of those persons listed in the Annex to this order or those persons determined to be subject to subsection 1(b), 1(c), or 1(d)(i) of this order;

(d) except as provided in section 5 of this order and after such consultation, if any, with foreign authorities as the Secretary of State, in consultation with the Secretary of the Treasury and the Attorney General, deems appropriate in the exercise of his discretion, persons determined by the Secretary of the Treasury, in consultation with the Secretary of State and the Attorney General;

(i) to assist in, sponsor, or provide financial, material, or technological support for, or financial or other services to or in support of, such acts of terrorism or those persons listed in the Annex to this order or determined to be subject to this order; or

(ii) to be otherwise associated with those persons listed in the Annex to this order or those persons determined to be subject to subsection 1(b), 1(c), or 1(d)(i) of this order.

Sec. 2. Except to the extent required by section 203(b) of IEEPA (50 U.S.C. 1702(b)), or provided in regulations, orders, directives, or licenses that may be issued pursuant to this order, and notwithstanding any contract entered into or any license or permit granted prior to the effective date:

(a) any transaction or dealing by United States persons or within the United States in property or interests in property blocked pursuant to this order is prohibited, including but not limited to the making or receiving of any contribution of funds, goods, or services to or for the benefit of those persons listed in the Annex to this order or determined to be subject to this order;

(b) any transaction by any United States person or within the United States that evades or avoids, or has the purpose of evading or avoiding, or attempts to violate, any of the prohibitions set forth in this order is prohibited; and

(c) any conspiracy formed to violate any of the prohibitions set forth in this order is prohibited. . . .

Sec. 6. The Secretary of State, the Secretary of the Treasury, and other appropriate agencies shall make all relevant efforts to cooperate and coordinate with other countries, including through technical assistance, as well as bilateral and multilateral agreements and arrangements, to achieve the objectives of this order, including the prevention and suppression of acts of terrorism, the denial of financing and financial services to terrorists and terrorist organizations, and the sharing of intelligence about funding activities in support of terrorism.

Sec. 7. The Secretary of the Treasury, in consultation with the Secretary of State and the Attorney General, is hereby authorized to take such actions, including the promulgation of rules and regulations, and to employ all powers granted to the President by IEEPA and UNPA as may be necessary to carry out the purposes of this order. The Secretary of the Treasury may redelegate any of these functions to other officers and agencies of the United States Government. All agencies of the United States Government are hereby directed to take all appropriate measures within their authority to carry out the provisions of this order.

. . . .
GEORGE W. BUSH
THE WHITE HOUSE,
September 23, 2001.

International Human Rights and Terrorism Related Documents

United Nations International Covenant on Civil and Political Rights

Article 9. Everyone has the right to liberty and security of person. No one shall be subject to arbitrary arrest and detention.

United Nations Security Council Resolution 1373

A resolution that called for international cooperation to prevent and eradicate acts of terrorism worldwide; unanimously adopted on September 28, 2001, under Chapter 7 of the U.N. General Assembly by consensus of the 189 member states.

Convention to Prevent and Punish Acts of Terrorism Taking the Form of Crimes Against Persons and Related Extortion That Are of International Significance

An Organization of American States treaty that defines attacks against internationally protected persons as a common crime. Its purpose was to protect the absolute inviolability of diplomatic missions.

7

Directory of Organizations and Government Agencies

National Government Agencies and Organizations

U.S. Department of Homeland Security
http://www.dhs.gov/index.shtm

This newly created organization leverages resources of the federal government to integrate the agencies protecting the United States. Among its components, the DHS contains the Office of Intelligence and Analysis (OIA), the Office of Operations Coordination (OOC), the Domestic Nuclear Detection Office (DND), the Transportation Security Administration (TSA), U.S. Customs and Border Protection (CBP), U.S. Citizenship and Immigration Services (CIS), U.S. Immigration and Customs Enforcement (ICE), the U.S. Coast Guard (USCG), the Federal Emergency Management Agency (FEMA), and the U.S. Secret Service. The Office of the Secretary within the DHS is concerned with border security, intelligence analysis, and protection of infrastructure, using science and technology to prevent use of weapons of mass destruction and establishing a response and recovery system. The operation of the immigrant admittance system and interdiction of unauthorized entrants are both contained in the same umbrella organization but separated in different agencies: CBP, ICE, and CIS. The Secretary of Homeland Security carries the chief responsibility for the control of unauthorized immigration, prevention of terrorism, and developing border-security measures.

U.S. Customs and Border Protection (USCBP)
http://www.cbp.gov/xp/cgov/home.xml

U.S. Customs and Border Protection is one of the Department of Homeland Security's largest and most complex components, with a priority mission of keeping terrorists and their weapons out of the United States (CBP.gov, 2010). It also has a responsibility for securing and facilitating trade and travel while enforcing hundreds of U.S. regulations, including immigration and drug laws.

CBP contains the first-line responders for border security and provides border law enforcement for DHS. It is the section of the former Immigration and Naturalization Service (INS) which combines the inspection and border authority of U.S. Customs, U.S. Immigration, the Animal and Plant Health Inspection Service, and the U.S. Border Patrol. It oversees cross-border travel and commerce. This involves the processing of visitors and immigrants for entry and inspection of goods, including agricultural produce. It is the security agency in place at the Canada and Mexico borders. A focus is the "one face at the border initiative." CBP officers are cross-trained to perform immigration, customs, and agricultural inspections. Its officers enforce immigration law by verifying travel documents and the right to enter the country.

Within the Department of Homeland Security, CBP protects our nation's borders from terrorism, human and drug smuggling, illegal migration, and agricultural pests while simultaneously facilitating the flow of legitimate travel and trade. As the nation's single unified border agency, CBP's mission is vitally important for the protection of the American people and the national economy. Nearly 52,000 CBP employees work in a variety of ways to secure the nation's borders both at and between the official ports of entry and also to extend our zone of security abroad through pre-clearance of travelors and inspection of cargo. Employees continually incorporate the core values of vigilance, service to country, and integrity into their actions.

CBP is responsible for guarding nearly 7,000 miles of land border the United States shares with Canada and Mexico and 2,000 miles of coastal waters surrounding the Florida peninsula and off the coast of Southern California. The agency also protects

95,000 miles of maritime border in partnership with the U.S. Coast Guard. To secure this vast terrain, more than 17,000 CBP Border Patrol agents, 1,000 CBP Air and Marine agents, and almost 22,000 CBP officers and agriculture specialists, together with the nation's largest law-enforcement canine program, stand guard along America's front line. Its activities are as follows:

- CBP Customs officers protect America's borders at official ports of entry, while CBP's Border Patrol agents prevent unauthorized entry into the United States of people and smuggling of contraband between the ports of entry.
- CBP Air and Marine, which manages the largest law-enforcement air force in the world, patrols the nation's land and sea borders to stop terrorists and drug smugglers before they enter the United States.
- CBP agriculture specialists prevent the entry of exotic plant and animal pests, and confront emerging threats from agro- and bioterrorism.

Counterterrorism is presented as CBP's top priority. It seeks to carry out two potentially conflicting goals: facilitating legitimate trade and travel while preventing terrorism and use of weapons of mass destruction. Both people and goods are subject to a multilevel inspection process when crossing the border at a port of entry. It operates the Advance Passenger Information System (APIS), U.S. Visitor and Immigrant Status Indication Technology (US-VISIT), the Student and Exchange Visitor System (SEVIS), and the Container Security Initiative (CSI). Within CBP, the U.S. Border Patrol seeks to secure the open border between ports of entry by deterring or stopping entrants attempting crossing the border without inspection and smugglers of contraband.

U.S. Citizenship and Immigration Services (USCIS)
http://www.uscis.gov/portal/site/uscis/

Formerly a part of the Immigration and Naturalization Service, CIS is now located in the Department of Homeland Security. CIS is a federal agency that admits and tracks legal immigrants. It is responsible for granting entrance, maintaining records of permanent residency, and conducting the process of naturalization to citizenship. It maintains the security of the immigration process and provides immigration information and services.

U.S. Immigration and Customs Enforcement (ICE)
http://www.ice.gov/

U.S. Immigration and Customs Enforcement (ICE) is the largest DHS investigative agency. Its primary mission is detection and interdiction of terrorists and criminals through targeting the persons, materials, and money used to support terrorist and criminal organizations. ICE handles investigations for interior enforcement of immigration and customs law to counter national security threats and contributes to border enforcement. It handles detention and removal of unauthorized entrants and noncitizen criminals, probes of immigration document fraud, air and marine drug interdiction operations, and federal protective services.

The ICE Office of Intelligence (INTEL) collects information from both the public and law enforcement inside and outside of the Department of Homeland Security on individuals who have entered without documentation and suspected threats or criminal activities. This intelligence is provided to the Office of Investigations (OI), which examines and enforces laws relating to terrorism, immigration fraud and crime, human smuggling, child pornography/exploitation, human rights violations, export and import enforcement issues, narcotics, weapons and other types of smuggling, cyber crimes, and financial crimes such as money laundering. In addition it seeks to protect infrastructure vulnerable to attack or sabotage. If undocumented entrants are taken into custody, they are referred to the Office of Detention and Removal (DRO), which apprehends, identifies, and removes noncitizens without legal documentation, fugitive aliens who did not present themselves at an immigration hearing or register, and criminal aliens. ICE also houses the Federal Air Marshalls program for passenger safety during flights.

U.S. Transportation Security Administration (TSA)
http://www.tsa.gov/index.shtm

TSA was created after 9/11 by the Aviation and Transportation Security Act (Public Law 107-71). It organized previously poorly paid airport baggage screeners and provided training and equipment for upgrading security. It has the task of securing the national land, air, and rail transport system against attack for the purpose of facilitating movement of people and goods. TSA checks passengers and baggage for explosive devices and is responsible for airport security.

U.S. Coast Guard (USCG)
http://www.uscg.mil/

The USCG provides border security by patrolling territorial and near international waters for the purpose of deterring and interdicting drugs, contraband, and unauthorized entry, including terrorist penetration. It is a stand-alone division within the Department of Homeland Security. The USCG evaluates, boards, and inspects commercial shipping. A participant in Operation Noble Eagle, it is on heightened alert to protect 361 ports and 95,000 miles of coastline.

U.S. Department of Justice Executive Office for Immigration Review (EOIR)
http://www.justice.gov/eoir/

EOIR has authority delegated from the Attorney General to interpret federal immigration laws and adjudicate immigration cases. It conducts immigration court proceedings and administrative hearings. Within EOIR, the Office of the Chief Immigration Judge manages geographically dispersed immigration courts with sitting immigration judges. The Board of Immigration Appeals conducts appellate review of immigration judges' decisions. The Office of the Chief Administrative Hearing Officers adjudicates immigration employment cases.

U.S. Drug Enforcement Administration (DEA)
http://www.justice.gov/dea/index.htm

The DEA enforces the Controlled Substances Act and drug regulations, particularly targeting drug-trafficking organizations (DTOs) and their members, including violent drug gangs, for criminal arrest and prosecution. They are involved with prevention of the growth, manufacture, or distribution of controlled substances in the illicit economy. DEA manages a national drug-intelligence program in cooperation with local, state, national, and international law enforcement and coordinates interdiction efforts with these officials. They have the authority to seize assets used in illegal drug trafficking. DEA provides training for Mexican law-enforcement officers and crop eradication or crop substitution. DEA is responsible for drug law-enforcement operations overseas. It cooperates with the United Nations, Interpol, and Europol on international drug-control efforts.

U.S. Office of National Drug Control Policy (ONDCP)
http://www.whitehousedrugpolicy.gov/

The White House ONDCP was established by the Anti-Drug Abuse Act of 1988. It sets national drug-control priorities and policy. It deals with drug trafficking–related concerns such as manufacturing and sales and related crime and violence. Unlike the Drug Enforcement Administration, it is concerned with the demand side of drug control and with reducing drug use and its health consequences. To meet the objective of dealing with both interdiction and demand, ONDCP produces the National Drug Control Strategy and establishes a program, budget, and guidelines for federal, state, and local organizations. The director also coordinates international and national antidrug efforts among federal agencies and ensures that these are complementary with state efforts. The ONDCP also distributes drug-related prevention information to the public.

U.S. Federal Bureau of Investigation (FBI)
http://www.fbi.gov/

The FBI has jurisdiction over more than 200 categories of federal law. Counterterrorism-related investigation includes both international and domestic terrorism as well as preventing the use of weapons of mass destruction. It conducts intelligence operations and is a primary enforcer against organized crime. Other investigative areas include money laundering and human trafficking.

U.S. Central Intelligence Agency (CIA)
www.cia.gov

The Director of National Intelligence is the head of the Central Intelligence Agency, heads the U.S. intelligence community, and acts as the principal intelligence advisor to the president on matters of national security. The CIA Director reports to the

Director of National Intelligence. The CIA has authorization to conduct intelligence but has no law-enforcement powers and does not conduct internal security operations. It collects intelligence outside the United States on matters of national security. Its high-priority concerns include nonproliferation of nuclear weapons, counterterrorism, transnational organized crime, drug trafficking, and arms-control intelligence.

U.S. Department of State
www.state.gov

The Department of State develops a national security strategy for dealing with transnational issues. Policy concerns include counterterrorism, democracy and human rights, energy security, food security, health, narcotics and trafficking in persons. Regarding counterterrorism, it publishes online Country Reports on Terrorism, State Sponsors of Terrorism Reports and Terrorist Designation lists. A chief border security concern is human trafficking. It publishes an annual Trafficking in Persons Report which is available online. The Department of State has become involved in diplomacy to develop a bilateral response to Mexican drug trafficking and related violence.

U.S. Government Accountability Office (GAO)
http://www.gao.gov/

The GAO is an independent, nonpartisan agency that works for Congress. Among its general activities, it has primary responsibility for evaluating the various federal administrative and law-enforcement efforts to provide border security. Congressional committees and subcommittees can request a report on how tax dollars are spent. GAO has carried out many studies of Mexican and Canadian border-security policy and operations to monitor effectiveness in deterring terrorists, technology being used for intelligence surveillance, and other security issues. GAO provides information for Congress and the federal government on how to be more efficient, ethical, and responsive to the public.

U.S. Census Bureau
http://www.census.gov/

The U.S. Census Bureau collects statistical data on the nation's population, including immigrants. The surveys include a Decennial

Population and Housing Census, an Economic Census every five years, and an annual American Community Survey. Data provided supplies the best estimate of the permanent resident immigrant and undocumented immigrant populations. This information allows for projection of changes in the immigrant population over time and allows measurement of how immigrants are becoming incorporated into mainstream institutions.

U.S. Census data on immigration is important for apportioning seats in the U.S. House of Representatives because the process is based on population counts in districts. Immigrant counts also impact the definition of state legislature districts, school districts, and decisions about federal fund allocation and community planning. Online information describing the population of any zip code is available at http://factfinder.census.gov/home/saff/main.html?_lang=en.

U.S. Commission on Civil Rights
http://www.usccr.gov/contact/contndx.htm

The USCCR is an independent agency within the federal branch established by the Civil Rights Act of 1957. It collects information on discrimination and denial of equal protection under the laws under the Constitution based on race, color, religion, sex, age, disability, or national origin, or in the administration of justice. It analyzes federal laws and policy for discriminatory impact and investigates complaints that citizens, including naturalized immigrants, are being deprived of the right to vote or subject to election fraud. It submits reports to the president and Congress on the civil rights of immigrants, including the human rights of unauthorized immigrants, and issues connected to immigration trends and civil rights.

U.S. Department of Health and Human Services
http://www.hhs.gov/

This department is the principal federal agency for protecting health and providing related services, particularly for those who are unable to afford care, including noncitizen immigrants who meet congressionally established program guidelines. It expends more than 25% of all federal outlays and provides national health care, such as Medicare and Medicaid. Its 11 operating divisions include the National Institutes of Health (NIH), the Centers for Disease Control and Prevention (CDC), the Health Resources and Services Administration (HRSA), the Substance Abuse and Mental Health Services Administration (SAMHSA), the Agency for Health Care Research and Quality (HCRQ), and Administration for Children and Families (ACF). After 9/11, a new initiative of the umbrella agency became medical preparedness for emergencies, including potential terrorist incidents. The CDC works with states and partners to monitor health and prevent disease outbreaks, including bioterrorism.

U.S. House Committee on the Judiciary
http://judiciary.house.gov/index.html

This House committee has two subcommittees of primary importance in legislating for border security. The Subcommittee on Immigration, Citizenship, Refugees, Border Security, and International Law has jurisdiction over immigration and naturalization, border security, treaties, international agreements and conventions, and nonborder enforcement. The Subcommittee on Crime, Terrorism, and Homeland Security has jurisdiction over the Federal Criminal Code and Federal Rules of Criminal Procedure, drug enforcement, terrorism, and prisons.

U.S. Senate Committee on the Judiciary
http://judiciary.senate.gov/

The subcommittees of the Senate Committee on the Judiciary include Immigration, Border Security and Citizenship; Terrorism, Technology and Homeland Security; and Human Rights and the Law.

U.S. Department of State Bureau of Population, Refugees, and Migration
http://www.state.gov/g/prm/

The Bureau of Population, Refugees, and Migration (PRM) promotes the United States' population and migration policies. It aids refugees, victims of conflict, and stateless persons (individuals who cannot establish homeland citizenship through documentation). It fosters repatriation to original homelands, local re-integration of displaced persons, and resettlement in the United States.

U.S. National Institute of Justice (NIJ)

The NIJ is the research, development, and evaluation agency of the Department of Justice. It provides objective evidence-based information on crime and justice issues, particularly at the state and local level. Its research priorities include drugs and crime and counterterrorism/critical incidents. It seeks to synthesize knowledge about terror-group networks and finances, develop tools to prevent, deter, and apprehend terrorists, improve tools and techniques for first responders, and refine and evaluate technologies, practices, and procedures to minimize harm to persons, properties, and communities from terrorism. It provides current crime statistics and publications on human trafficking, drug trafficking, and the relationship between immigration and crime.

Political Groups

Immigration Reform Caucus (IRC)
http://www.house.gov/bilbray/immreformmsg.shtml

The House of Representatives has a political suborganization with voluntary membership, which meets to discuss policy on unauthorized immigration. They seek to identify policy that can be the basis of a legislative solution.

Domestic Security Organizations

National Security Agency (NSA)/Central Security Service (CSS)
http://www.nsa.gov/index.shtml

The NSA/CSS has the mission of protecting U.S. national security systems and collecting foreign signals intelligence. It makes and breaks code. Information Assurance initiatives involve preventing foreign adversaries from gaining access to classified U.S. information. Intelligence is also collected from foreign signals and/or clandestinely and analyzed to prevent security threats. It authorizes Network Warfare operations for purposes of counterterrorism.

National Cyber-Security Division (NCSD)

http://www.dhs.gov/xabout/structure/editorial_0839.shtm

Located in the Department of Homeland Security, NCSD identifies, analyzes, and contains or removes cyber threats and vulnerabilities. It issues cyber-threat warnings, provides coordination of incident response, and technically assists continuity of computerized operations and recovery.

U.S. Office of the National Counterintelligence Executive (ONCIX)

http://www.ncix.gov/about/index.html

Led by the Director of National Intelligence, ONCIX provides counterintelligence, which involves identifying and dealing with foreign intelligence threats within the United States, including terrorist groups. It conducts foreign intelligence threat assessment and other intelligence activities.

U.S. National Counterterrorism Center (NCTC)

http://www.nctc.gov/

This office reports to the Director of National Intelligence at ONCIX. It is a center to facilitate joint operational intelligence between federal agencies, a recommendation of the 9/11 Commission. It is the primary agency to integrate counterterrorism intelligence.

International Security and Policing Organizations

Canadian Security Intelligence Service (CSIS)

http://www.csis-scrs.gc.ca/index-eng.asp

The premier national intelligence-gathering agency, CSIS gathers information on national security threats to take pre-emptive action. It reports to the Canadian government and advises it on security issues. Key threats are terrorism, weapons of mass destruction, espionage, foreign interference, and cyber tampering. Its Security Screening Program is meant to keep individuals connected to terrorism from entering Canada or receiving permanent resident status and citizenship. CSIS's top priority is countering terrorism, and it seeks to stop terrorist planning and actions in its own territory and abroad. It has a proactive role of preventing threats rather than a reactive role in investigating and prosecuting crime such as in law enforcement.

Centro de Información de Seguridad Nacional (CISEN)

Mexico's major national security agency, CISEN, is a civilian organization controlled by the Office of the Minister of the Interior. Its function is to collect intelligence for safeguarding Mexican national security. CISEN has its own budget and technical and operative autonomy although it is subject to the legislative and judicial branches of the Mexican government. It collects intelligence for national security decisions and seeks to maintain the stability of the Mexican state. It does not have jurisdiction over Mexican law-enforcement activities. It is not directly linked to U.S. counterpart agencies.

Consejo Nacional de Seguridad Privada de Mexico (CNSP)
http://www.cnsp.org.mx/

Mexico's CNSP, labeled in English as the National Security Council, coordinates federal government agencies and local and state and federal law enforcement. This organization is placed above the Centro de Información de Seguridad Nacional (CISEN).

Europol
http://www.europol.europa.eu/

This abbreviated term is used to refer to the European Police Office, a consortium of members of the European Union who engage in international police cooperation. Founded in 1992 and fully operational in 1999, Europol is the European Union's policing organization in charge of criminal intelligence. Its mission is to assist member states in combating organized crime and terrorism. Over 670 staff members work with police in the 27 member states of the European Union and partner with such countries as the United States and Canada. Europol does not have direct power of arrest but provides information and analysis for law enforcement and takes part in joint investigative teams. It produces regular assessments, including the European Organized Crime Threat Assessment (OCTA) about the structure and operations of European organized crime groups, and the European Terrorism Situation and Trend Report (TE-SAT). Europol has acquired extensive criminal intelligence on drug trafficking, illicit immigration networks, human trafficking, and international terrorist groups.

International Association for Counterterrorism and Security Professionals (IACSP)
Institute of Terrorism Research and Response (ITRR)
http://www.iacsp.com/

The Institute of Terrorism Research and Response (ITRR), within IACSP, is an American and Israeli nonprofit corporation. It provides training seminars and expertise in dealing with such issues as weapons of mass destruction. It has a Targeted Actionable Monitoring Center (TAM-C), which provides information and terrorist plans and actions, historical "red flag dates," and real-time alerts. Within TAM-C, the Ground Security Network receives information from the field for real-time intelligence.

Interpol
http://www.interpol.int/

The abbreviation "Interpol" is in reference to the International Criminal Police Organization. It originated in 1923 to assist in international police cooperation. The world's largest international policing organization, Interpol has 188 member countries. It provides four core services: (1) securing police communication services; (2) police operational databases and data services; (3) operational police support services; and (4) police training and development. A main activity is facilitating cross-border police cooperation and sharing of intelligence. I-24/7, Interpol's global police communications system, allows police in all member countries to request, submit, and access crime-related data in a secure environment. This database system contains information on known criminals, fingerprints, DNA profiles, and lost or stolen travel documents. Its Command and Coordination Center can deploy an incident-response team to crime or disaster scenes on a 24/7 basis. Interpol's priority crime investigation areas include drugs and criminal organizations, trafficking in human beings, and public safety and terrorism.

Policia Federal de Preventa (PFP)

The Federal Preventative Police of Mexico has jurisdiction over federal crimes and legal offenses. It has a special mandate to provide public security in border areas, coastlines, bridges, customs, immigration control points, the federal highways, railways, airports, and seaports authorized for international traffic. The PFP controls the Inter-Institutional Coordination Unit Gruppa Antiterrorista (UCIDGAT), the antiterrorism policing organization. Originally organized to deal with armed insurgent groups within Mexico, UCIDGAT is in charge of both border security and efforts to stop drug and arms trafficking and other organized crime.

Sistema Nacional de Seguridad Publica (SNSP)

Under direction of the Mexican president, the SNSP, known in English as the National Public Security System, coordinates and distributes public security functions between the Mexico City Federal District and other municipalities and the Federation states of Mexico. SNSP is in charge of public security and coordinated police departments, state prosecutors' offices, and penal institutions. Among its duties, it oversees public security policy and programs, establishes criteria for the technological modernization of public security, and establishes and controls intelligence databases on criminal activities. It was established in November, 2009.

International Organizations

Inter-American Development Bank
http://www.iadb.org/

In 1959, the Inter-American Development Bank was established to make loans for the purpose of development to qualifying Latin American countries. It has issued funds to the extent of $168 billion for novel technical cooperation programs, or economic and social development projects, and is a major source for multilateral financing. It promotes trade and regional integration in the Latin American and Caribbean region. Its projects, which are aimed at low-income populations, have become a model for other regional and subregional development institutions. Its current projects focus on poverty reduction, global competitiveness, state modernization, and regional integration. Success of its economic development projects can stabilize population and reduce international migration.

United Nations
http://www.un.org/

The United Nations Universal Declaration of Human Rights was issued by the General Assembly on December 10, 1948. It is one basis for the orientation referred to as the open border policy. The United Nations contains the Office of the High Commissioner for Human Rights and an Office on Drugs and Crime. It publishes online documents on counterterrorism, human trafficking, and a host of other international issues involving border security.

The World Bank
http://www.worldbank.org/

Established in 1944, the World Bank contains two development institutions: the International Bank for Reconstruction and Development (IBRD) and the International Development Association (IDA). The IBRD promotes inclusive and sustainable globalization through reduction of poverty in middle income and "credit-worthy" poorer countries. The IDA targets the poorest nations. These institutions are connected to the International Finance Corporation (IFC), the Multilateral Investment Guarantee Agency (MIGA), and the International Center for the Settlement of Investment Disputes (ICSID). Together, these institutions work to provide low-interest loans, interest-free credits, and grants to developing countries for agriculture, natural resources, environmental, education, infrastructure, financial, and private-sector development. Headquartered in Washington, DC, the World Bank has more than 10,000 employees and offices in over 100 countries. Its mission is to fight poverty through encouraging self-help and building capacity.

International Human Rights Advocacy Organizations

American Friends Service Committee (AFSC)
http://www.afsc.org/immigrant-rights

The American Friends Service Committee believes in the "worth and inherent dignity of every human being." Its current concerns include immigrant detention standards, secure community-based alternatives to detention, access to counsel, conducting a review of federal enforcement of immigration law, border policy, and advocacy for legalization. It conducts projects in various areas of the country, including a U.S.-Mexico border program that monitors the actions of law enforcement toward migrants.

Amnesty International USA (AIUSA)
http://www.amnestyusa.org/

Amnesty International is a Nobel Prize–winning grassroots activist organization with branches in over 150 nations and a worldwide membership of over 2 million supporters, activists, and volunteers. Amnesty International USA is one if its branches. It advocates that all peoples should receive the rights in the United Nation's Universal Declaration of Human Rights and that countries should meet other international standards for humane treatment. It seeks to have governments stop violations and to change law and practice. It supports research and action on all human rights.

Anti-Slavery International
http://www.antislavery.org/english/default.aspx

Founded in 1787, Anti-Slavery International is the world's oldest international human rights organization. This nonprofit works locally, nationally, and internationally to end all forms of slavery. Through research, lobbying, and the raising of awareness, it seeks to end trafficking, forced labor, child labor, and child domestic work. It stresses the connection between what people buy and the use of forced labor in its production. The organization has conducted many successful campaigns and works with the new Special Rapporteur on Slavery in the United Nations, the first new U.N. special mechanism on slavery in 30 years.

Human Rights Watch
http://www.hrw.org

Human Rights Watch is an independent nongovernmental organization (NGO) that seeks to defend and protect human rights. It investigates ongoing situations in which human rights may be violated and publicizes its findings. Its work is international in scope and includes investigations and targeted advocacy for a wide range of human rights, including those of immigrants. Its international work in protecting the rights of migrants and immigrants includes research on the exploitation of unauthorized immigrants in the workplace. Recent research has covered expedited removal, the rights of asylees, and detention conditions. Human Rights Watch has been critical of U.S. detention policy and is actively lobbying for reform. It publishes numerous reports on human rights in many nations, including the United States.

Witness
http://www.witness.org/

Witness records human rights violations on video to change stories of abuse into tools for justice. It envisions a just and equitable world in which all individual and community human rights are upheld. Its core partner program works with 12–15 human rights organizations for a period of 1–3 years to train and support them to use video as a tool for human rights campaigns with high visibility and impact. These videos have been used as evidence in domestic and international courts, in reports on human rights abuses and the media.

Domestic Advocacy Organizations

American Anthropological Association Committee on Human Rights
http://www.aaanet.org/cmtes/cfhr/index.cfm

This subcommittee of the American Anthropological Association seeks to protect the human rights of indigenous peoples and cross-border migrants. It consults on human rights issues and works with human rights organizations, foreign colleagues, and international policymakers. This group issues a series of statements on human rights issues.

American Conservative Union (ACU)
http://www.conservative.org/

Established in 1964, the ACU is the oldest grassroots conservative lobbying organization. It advocates a free market economy, the doctrine of original intent of the Constitution's architects, and traditional moral values. It is committed to a strong national defense. It sponsors town meetings on such issues as defending the homeland and opposition to immigration policy. Since 1971, it has published an annual rating of Congress that tallies how members voted on issues to evaluate the degree to which members support conservative principles. Since 1973, ACU has hosted CPAC, the annual Conservative Political Action Conference, which brings conservatives from across the country together to discuss issues and policy to set a conservative agenda. It has supported strengthening border security and suggested it should be a higher priority than other changes in immigration law.

American Immigration Control Foundation
http://www.aicfoundation.com/

Founded in 1983, the American Immigration Control Foundation is a nonprofit organization for education and research on regulating immigration to restrict it to meet the national interest and capacity for assimilation of newcomers. It considers that there is an immigration crisis and advocates immigration reform, particularly restriction of unauthorized Mexican migration, which it views as weakening the rule of law. Deeply committed to preserving the national heritage, it provides many books, pamphlets, monographs, and videos.

American Immigration Council (AIC)
http://www.americanimmigrationcouncil.org

Established in 1987, this tax-exempt, not-for profit organization (formerly the American Immigration Law Foundation) was started by the American Immigration Lawyer's Association (AILA). Its mission is to showcase American immigration history and to support immigration policies that honor constitutional and human rights. It works to promote the United States' prosperity and cultural richness through: (1) citizen education about immigrant contributions; (2) support of humane immigration policy reflective of American values; (3) enacting immigration law which reflects constitutional and human rights; and (4) work to achieve justice and fairness for immigrants. Its motto is "Honoring our immigrant past, shaping our immigrant future."

American Immigration Lawyers Association (AILA)
http://www.aila.org/

AILA is a national nonprofit association of more than 11,000 attorneys and law professors who teach about and practice immigration law. The association promotes justice, advocates for fairness in immigration law, and enhances professional development of members. Members represent both immigrants and businesses and offer services at a pro bono (no cost) basis for asylum seekers, foreign students, and others in need who are seeking to enter. The AILA also has a Legal Action Center. The Legal Action Center provides legal education, information, professional services, and expertise and has 36 chapters and over 50 national committees. AILA engages in public education and advocates before the Congress, Judiciary, federal agencies, and the media. It supports legalization, increasing legal opportunities to immigrate, and promoting border enforcement which allows the efficient flow of people and goods.

Business Roundtable
http://www.businessroundtable.org/

The Business Roundtable is a conservative group comprised of chief executives of major U.S. corporations with more than $5 trillion in annual revenues. The group promotes sustainable long-term economic growth that is not inflationary and maintains American competitiveness in a global economy. To this effect, it supports workplace policies for a flexible and available workforce, including high skilled (professionals and college educated) immigration. It has supported a guest-worker program for unskilled, less educated workers and "earned legalization." It is a part of the pro-immigration lobby.

Center for American Progress (CAP)
http://www.americanprogress.org/

CAP is headed by John Podesta, professor of law at Georgetown University and former chief of staff to President Bill Clinton. This progressive think-tank challenges conservative policy. Issues it focuses on include achieving immigration reform and sustainable national security. CAP stresses the linkage of economic globalization and immigration and stresses development in the sending countries as a part of the solution. Domestic policies supported include legalization of the unauthorized population, increasing family reunification visas, strengthening worker protections, making the visa allocation system more flexible to deal with the application backlog and responsive to labor market needs, working to socially and culturally integrate the immigrant population, and strengthening border and interior enforcement including through expansion of the Department of Homeland Security.

Center for Democracy and Technology
http://www.cdt.org/contact

The Center for Democracy and Technology is a nonprofit organization that seeks to keep the Internet "open, innovative, and free." It addresses civil liberties issues in law, technology, and policy and seeks to enhance free expression and privacy in communications technologies by finding practical and innovative solutions to public policy challenges while protecting civil liberties. The Center for Democracy and Technology has advocated restoring checks and balances on access to confidential information removed by the USA PATRIOT Act.

Coalition Against Trafficking in Women (CATW)
http://www.catwinternational.org/

Founded in 1988, CATW is a nongovernmental organization that promotes human rights by working internationally to prevent sexual exploitation of women and girls. It was the first international organization to focus on human trafficking, particularly sex trafficking. In 1989 it received Category II Consultative status with the United Nations Economic and Social Council. CATW considers that women and girls have a "right to sexual integrity and autonomy."

Deletetheborder.org
http://deletetheborder.org/

Deletetheborder.org is an online community seeking participation in a global movement to abolish borders. It provides open postings, news feed collection, media galleries, blogs, and forums.

Federal Immigration Reform and Enforcement Coalition (FIRE Coalition)
http://www.firecoalition.com/index.asp

The FIRE Coalition is a website devoted to grassroots organizing for immigration restriction. It has an extensive list of coalition partners including the American Border Patrol, Citizens for Immigration Law Enforcement, the Colorado Alliance for Immigration Reform, Limits to Growth, and Save Our State, among others. Its vision is to "end the invasion of illegal aliens to the United States." It operates "WeHireAliens.com" to expose employers of unauthorized immigrants and "Operation Fire and Ice," to educate the public about the 287(g) federal law-enforcement cooperation program with state and local police, among its many reporting programs. It is pro-enforcement of immigration law, seeks repatriation of the unauthorized immigrant population, advocates more effective implementation of employer sanctions, and provides immigration information and resources. It is self-described as a nonprofit grassroots coalition organization seeking to educate the public and politically campaign for its agenda.

Federation for American Immigration Reform (FAIR)
http://www.fairus.org

Founded in 1979, FAIR is a national nonprofit organization with 250,000 members. It advocates ending unauthorized immigration, securing the border, and reducing legal immigration. In particular, it seeks a moratorium on all legal immigration except spouses and children of U.S. citizens and a small quota of refugees. It exposes border control to reduce unauthorized immigration and is opposed to legalization. Internationally, it supports efforts at population stabilization, economic development, and alleviating poverty, particularly in high-migration countries.

The Heritage Foundation
http://www.heritage.org/research/immigration

Founded in 1973, the Heritage Foundation is a self-designated "conservative" public policy research institute. It supports principles of free enterprise, limitations on government, and traditional values. Regarding immigration, it seeks a reduction in the number admitted and expanded enforcement of immigration law. It is opposed to a path to legalization. The Heritage Foundation supports cross-border trade while maintaining border security, especially against international terrorism.

Humane Borders
http://www.humaneborders.org/

Established in June 2000, Humane Borders is a faith-based citizen-action group that seeks to promote a humane and just border environment. It works to provide humanitarian assistance to individuals seeking to cross the border without authorization in the remote Arizona desert. Its priorities include reducing migrant deaths, changing U.S. policy to permit increased legal migration through ports of entry, legalization of the unauthorized population, providing legal work for migrants, and giving economic relief of U.S. agencies involved in helping migrants. It maintains a network of water stations in the Arizona desert to prevent death by dehydration and provides maps and warning posters about dangers in Mexico to deter migrants from risking their lives through desert crossing. It has testified before Congress to promote a humane, non-militarized border.

International Immigrants Foundation
http://www.10.org/

In 1973 the International Immigrants Foundation was established to help immigrant families and children realize a "better life." It provides direct support to improve intercultural relations. It offers counseling and English, homebuyers, and citizenship classes. It sponsors the annual International Cultures celebration Expo-Fest and Parade in New York City.

Minuteman Civil Defense Corps
http://www.minutemanhq.com/hq/

The Minuteman Civil Defense Corps (MCDC), headed by Chris Simcox, split off from the Minuteman Project. It prioritized border enforcement and was opposed to legalization of the unauthorized population. This group organized citizen volunteers to "observe, report and direct" to the U.S. Border Patrol to suspected unauthorized entrants and illegal activities. It has conducted operations at both the southern and northern border. The organization stresses that its members "do not verbally contact, physically gesture to or have any contact" with unauthorized entrants.

In March, 2010, the Minuteman Civil Defense Corps Inc. corporate entity ceased operation because of increasing liability issues and concern for the safety of citizen watch volunteers. The Declaration Alliance, with Chris Simcox as Honorary Chairman, continues to support the MCDC Project and its Political Action Committee.

The Minuteman Project
http://www.minutemanproject.com

In 2004, the Minuteman Project was founded by Jim Gilchrist to enforce immigration law with a focus on volunteering to assist in monitoring the borders. Observers report and attempt to deter unauthorized migrants and drug smuggling. The Minuteman Project seeks to increase national awareness of unauthorized immigration and advocates for increased border enforcement, which it perceives as essential for national security, and immigration reform. It prioritizes U.S.-Mexico border enforcement over the Canadian border.

National Immigration Forum
http://www.immigrationforum.org

This organization advocates the value of immigrants and immigration for the nation. It seeks to develop an understanding of diverse views, provide pro-immigration information, analysis, and advocacy, and develop coalitions for change. It provides information on border enforcement, immigrants and crime, detention and enforcement, immigration and national security, and a broad range of other immigration issues.

National Network for Immigrant and Refugee Rights (NNIRR)
http://www.nnirr.org

NNIRR is a national organization that contains coalitions and various community, religious, labor, legal, civil rights, and immigrant organizations. It provides information for education and develops action plans on the immigration issue. It offers immigrant and refugee rights training, hosts the national community dialog for the border, and campaigns for fair and just immigration.

No More Deaths/No Más Muertes
http://www.nomoredeaths.org

This Arizona volunteer group believes that people of conscience must act to uphold civil rights. It advocates that it has a "right to provide humanitarian assistance" to men, women, and children attempting to enter the United States without authorization through the southern Arizona desert and mountains. It provides a humanitarian presence in the desert to provide food, water, and medical assistance to prevent migrant deaths. Its activities include maintaining water stations and camps for watching the border and providing outreach. No More Deaths follows medical and legal protocols to save lives.

Numbers USA

http://www.numbersusa.com/content/

Executive Director Roy Beck provides information on the impact of mass immigration on the environment, labor market, and local communities in the United States. Numbers USA advocates for securing the border, better enforcement of immigration law, arrest of smugglers and traffickers, streamlining and improvement of the process of workplace verification of work status, detention and removal of the unauthorized population, and denial of access to benefits and services for unauthorized entrants. It is opposed to legalization but works to allow those who return to the sending nation voluntarily the opportunity to return without penalty. It considers that the immigration situation has come by "accident or acquiescence" rather than deliberate action and that immigration-related actions should benefit the native-born citizens of the United States.

U.S. Border Watch

www.USborderwatch.com

The volunteer U.S. Border Watch is active at both the Mexican and Canadian borders. This citizen action group seeks to draw media attention to border security. The organization conducts day-labor site observations. It advocates a constitutional amendment to end unauthorized immigration and give power over immigration control to the states. It seeks action against employers of unauthorized immigrants and opposes legalization.

U. S. Chamber of Commerce

http://www.uschamber.com/default

The world's largest business lobby organization represents 3,000 businesses of all types, sizes, and regions, state and local chambers of commerce, and industrial associations. It advocates for free enterprise. The U.S. Chamber of Commerce supports immigration reform including an earned pathway to legalization, addressing backups in processing legal immigration, expansion of visas for skilled workers, and addressing delays, backlogs, and disruptions of the border management system impacting the flow of people and goods. The Chamber partners with the Americans for Better Borders Coalition to ensure the speedy passage of legitimate traffic at the border.

Civil Rights Legal Advocacy Organizations

American Civil Liberties Union (ACLU) Immigrant Rights Project
http://www.aclu.org/

The ACLU Immigrant Rights Project (IRP) undertakes class-action lawsuits and law-reform litigation on behalf of immigrants. It works with immigration advocates, community groups, the immigration bar, and legislatures to preserve the rights of individual citizens guaranteed in the U.S. Constitution and the civil liberties of noncitizens. It particularly focuses on equal protection rights, the right to due process, and the right to privacy. The ACLU IRP is involved with cases of unauthorized immigrants, legal immigrants, asylum applicants, and refugees. Many cases involve discrimination, workplace rights, due process rights, detention, and ICE or police abuse of immigrants. The Supreme Court cases in which it has been involved include *Demore v. Kim* and *INS v. St. Cyr*, which upheld the right to habeas corpus of noncitizens and reversed the retroactive deportation of longtime legal residents. It advocates that the right to equal protection under the law and due process is the right of all "persons" and not restricted to citizens.

Southern Poverty Law Center (SPLC) Immigrant Justice Project
http://www.splc.org

In 1971, a civil rights firm founded the nonprofit Southern Poverty Law Center to take legal action against hate and discrimination. The SPLC legal department has taken civil suits against hate groups, including to the Supreme Court. Its SPLC

Intelligence Project monitors the activities of hate groups and extremists, including their actions against immigrants, and publishes information on its research available at its website. It offers the Teaching Tolerance program for K-12 teachers to generate respect and offers anti-bias resources. Recently, its Immigrant Justice Project has taken civil suits against agribusiness and begun an antidiscrimination and sexual harassment educational project for immigrant women to notify them of their rights.

Research Centers

Brookings Institution
http://www.brookings.edu/

A nonprofit public policy organization, the Brookings Institution's mission is to conduct independent research to develop innovative, practical recommendations that (1) strengthen American democracy; (2) foster the economic and social welfare, security, and opportunity of all Americans; and (3) secure a more open, safe, prosperous, and cooperative international system. In January 2009 *Foreign Policy* magazine's Think Tank Index ranked Brookings as the number 1 think-tank and number 1 in the following categories: impact on public policy debates, international and security affairs, international development, international economic policy, health policy, domestic economic policy, and social policy. Topics researched include counternarcotics policy, globalization, homeland security, immigration, Mexico, migration, terrorism, the U.S. Department of Homeland Security, and weapons of mass destruction. It explores immigration in the United States, Europe, and the Middle East. Its Immigration Policy Roundtable recommended linking legalization with employment verification; restricting family reunification to nuclear family members, and increasing visas for highly skilled workers, while also increasing unskilled worker visas but making them unrenewable after five years, establishing an independent standing commission on immigration, and cooperating with Mexico on investment and law enforcement and interdiction.

Carnegie Endowment for International Peace
http://www.carnegieendowment.org/

Founded in 1910, this private nonprofit organization seeks to enhance cooperation between nations and international engagement of the United States. The Carnegie Endowment for International Peace is establishing overseas centers in an effort to become the first "multinational, truly global" think-tank. It now has operations in Moscow, Beijing, Beirut, and Brussels. It believes that single international outlooks are overly restrictive. In Latin America, Carnegie has been examining political and economic development, the impact of the North American Free Trade Agreement on Mexico, and the impacts of global financial crisis on migrants. Issues examined include the relationship of migration and globalization, fighting cross-border corruption, nuclear policy, and terrorism and cross-radicalization.

Cato Institute
www.//http://cato.org

Founded in 1977, the Cato Institute is a nonprofit public policy research foundation. It promotes libertarian principles of free markets, limits on the federal government, rule of law, and individual liberty. It generates policy proposals to achieve free and open civil society. In keeping with its orientation of market libertarianism, it advocates for immigration but focuses on expanding employment visas and legal immigration quotas. It seeks repeal of the cap on Hi-B cap visas for skilled workers and expansion of unskilled worker visas as a way to control unauthorized immigration. Regarding enforcement, it prioritizes keeping criminals and terrorists from entering the United States.

Center for Comparative Immigration Studies (CCIS)
http://www.ccis-ucsd.org

In 1999, sociologist Wayne Cornelius established CCIS under the auspices of the University of California–San Diego's Center for U.S.-Mexican Studies. It is a research center with a global network of research associates and 19 institutional affiliates. The center focuses on study of Mexican migration to the United States and Latin American/North African migration to Spain. It hosts the Mexican Migration Field Research program.

Center for Immigration Studies (CIS)
http://www.cis.org

CIS is an independent nonprofit organization researching immigration. The center has a "pro-immigrant, low immigration" orientation. The executive director is Mark Kirkorian. It covers legal and unauthorized immigration issues and national security.

Center for Migration Studies (CMS)
http://www.cmsny.org

Established in 1964, CMS is a nonprofit organization that conducts research on international migration and publishes the *International Migration Review*. It holds the annual National Legal Conference on Immigration and Refugee Policy in Washington, DC.

Center for Strategic and International Studies (CSIS)
http://csis.org/

A provider of strategic insights and policy solutions, CSIS is a bipartisan nonprofit organization. It assists government, business, and citizens with foreign policy and national security issues. In 2007 the CSIS Smart Power Commission developed an approach to shoring up the United States' declining world standing. It hosts a Homeland Security and Counterterrorism Program, the Global Strategy Institute, a Human Rights and Security Initiative, an International Security Program, and the Transnational Threats Project. The Transnational Threats Project assesses terror, insurgent, and criminal networks. It has examined drug, arms, and human trafficking in the Mesoamerican corridor (http://csis.org/event/trafficking-mesoamerican-corridor-threat-regional-and-human-security).

International Organization for Migration (IOM)
http://www.iom.int/jahia/Jahia/lang/en/pid/1

The IOM is an intergovernmental migration organization that assists governmental, nongovernmental, and intergovernmental partners. It has 127 member states, including the United States, 17 states with observer status, and over 100 offices in different countries. Seventy-six global and regional international governmental organizations (IGOs) and nongovernmental organizations (NGOs) are members. Over 6,000 staff members work on over 2,000 projects with more than $1 billion in expenditures. It promotes the "orderly and humane management of migration." Services are provided by IOM in the areas including migrant health, return assistance to migrants and governments, resettlement assistance, repatriation assistance, and emergency and postemergency operations assistance.

Jamestown Foundation

http://www.jamestown.org/

The Jamestown Foundation studies terrorism in Eurasia and its threat to the United States. It publishes the *Terrorism Monitor*, the *Eurasian Monitor*, *Terrorism Focus*, *China Brief*, and *North Caucasus Analysis*. It provides information on contact between Eurasian countries and Latin American governments.

Migration Policy Institute

http://www.migrationpolicy.org

A nonpartisan think-tank, the Migration Policy Institute looks at local, national, and international migration patterns. It seeks to develop migration policy that benefits immigrant families, sending and receiving communities, and the countries of origin and destination. International comparative research is presented for community leaders, immigrant advocacy groups, and policymakers. A variety of online subsites and reports provide information on U.S. immigration, European migration, international immigration, and development.

NYU Center on Law and Security

http://www.lawandsecurity.org/contact.cfm

In 2003, the Center on Law and Security was founded at New York University. It is an independent center seeking to network policymakers, academicians, journalists, and other experts to discuss issues of law and security. The center's programs focus on domestic security and global law and security. It hosts conferences, roundtables, and research groups and publishes the *NYU Review of Law and Security*, the *Bulletin on Law and Security*, and *Terrorist Trial Report Cards*, which provide statistics on post-9/11 terrorism-related court cases. The Report Cards give information on charges, plea bargains, and trial convictions and sentencing.

People for the American Way
http://site.pfaw.org/site/PageServer?pagename=homepagenew

The mission of People for the American Way is to promote equality, freedom of speech, freedom of religion, the right to seek justice in a court of law, and the right to vote. Although this organization is not focused on immigration, it critiques the conservative right.

PEW Hispanic Center
http://pewhispanic.org/

The PEW Hispanic Center is a division of the PEW Research Center, which conducts research on the Hispanic population and its impact on the United States. It is a nonpartisan think-tank that conducts scientific research on Hispanic population structure, identity, education, employment, politics, immigration, and remittances sent abroad. Findings of its research are published in reports available on the Internet.

The Protection Project
http://www.protectionproject.org/index.htm

This human rights center is contained within the Foreign Policy Institute at the Johns Hopkins University School of Advanced International Studies. It was founded to deal with trafficking in humans as a legal issue and human rights violation. It focuses on the promotion of human rights values and the protection of human security, especially the rights of women and children. It seeks to foster nongovernmental organization (NGO) development through coalition and capacity building, bringing citizens into the political and legal process, advancing education about human rights, as well as ending trafficking in persons. The Protection Project contributed to the drafting of the Victims of Trafficking and Violence Protection Act of 2000, assists in drafting model anti-trafficking legislation, identifies trafficking victims through field research and data collection, provides training and services to professionals working with victims of human trafficking, and maintains an online database on human trafficking.

Rand Corporation
http://www.rand.org/

The nonprofit Rand Corporation provides research and analysis for policy decision making. Its research areas include terrorism, homeland security, and national security. It contains the Center for Global Risk and Security, a Homeland Security Program, and a Center for Terrorism Risk Management. The Homeland Security Program assists local, state, and federal government to prevent and mitigate terrorist activity within U.S. borders. Projects in this program include national preparedness, critical infrastructure protection, cybersecurity, emergency management, terrorism risk management, security cost-benefit analyses, border security, enhanced capabilities for responders, domestic threat assessments, domestic intelligence, and manpower and training.

Terrorism Research Center (TRC)
http://www.terrorism.com/

TRC is an independent collaborative research and training institute. It studies terrorism, homeland security, and other low-intensity conflict issues.

Urban Institute.
http://www.urban.org

The Urban Institute gathers and analyzes research data on economic and social policy issues, including immigration. Its Center on Labor, Human Services, and Population has particularly focused on immigrant families and children.

Woodrow Wilson International Center for Scholars
http://www.wilsoncenter.org/index.cfm

The Woodrow Wilson Center was established by an act of Congress in 1968. It supports linkage of knowledge to the policy process. Scholars are brought to Washington, DC, to conduct research and interact with policymakers. The center has both Canada and Mexico Institutes and a Division of International Security Studies.

8

Print and Nonprint Resources

Books and Articles

Border Control Policy

Alden, Edward. 2008. *The Closing of the American Border: Terrorism, Immigration, and Security since 9/11.* New York: HarperCollins.

After 9/11 the George W. Bush administration sought to balance public security with maintaining openness at its borders. Edward Alden covers the impact of counterterrorism policy on visitors, business travelers, and the flow of professional or skilled workers and their ideas across the borders. As a case study in policy development and bureaucracy, it is based on interviews with federal officials, foreign government officials, university professionals, business executives, and individuals. The relationship of homeland security with economic openness, and its social and diplomatic impact on keeping a welcoming orientation are appraised.

Andreas, Peter. 2000. *Border Games: Policing the U.S.-Mexico Divide*. Ithaca, NY: Cornell University Press.

Andreas examines inconsistency in the rhetoric and application of border control policy. Border policing has been transformed from a relatively marginal activity to a costly, high-tech infrastructure seeking to curb migration and drug trafficking. This has occurred while the economies of Mexico and the United States—with the exception of labor forces—have become more integrated under the North American Free Trade Agreement. Andreas emphasizes that past immigration and drug-war policies have led to the escalation in border enforcement. Of importance, he stresses that the attempt to control the border is less about deterring migrants from coming and more to do with symbolically affirming U.S. sovereignty and appeasing the public. Andreas believes that globalization has not made borders superfluous but instead has increased their importance.

Campbell, Howard. 2009. *Drug War Zone: Frontline Dispatches from the Streets of El Paso and Juarez.* **Austin: University of Texas Press.**

In the first decade of the new century, drug trafficking–related violence reached unprecedented levels in Mexico and the Mexican border cities. This ethnographic study of community drug use in El Paso, Texas, and drug sales and smuggling in its sister city Ciudad Juarez, Mexico, provides an overview of the situation accompanied by oral history interviews with law enforcement from both sides of the border and drug traffickers. The narrative examines drug-trafficking organizations, their connection to government, and law-enforcement corruption, and strategy in the "drug war zone." Campbell maintains total commitment to control of drug trafficking produced a "security vacuum" connected to an overall increase in Mexican border crime. Overall, Campbell's research critiques the War on Drugs and suggests that policy alternatives must be considered.

Dunn, Timothy J. 1996. *The Militarization of the U.S.-Mexican Border, 1978–1992: Low-Intensity Conflict Doctrine Comes Home.* **Austin: CMAS Books, Center for Mexican American Studies, University of Texas.**

This social history is the classic study of the application of low-intensity conflict doctrine to the U.S.-Mexico border. Initially, border enforcement is situated within the years of pacification (1848–1919) and examined as a method of labor control (1918–1977). During the Carter and Reagan administrations (1978–1988) the Immigration and Naturalization Service (INS) began the use of military technology, integrated law enforcement and military personnel, and expanded the authority of the U.S. Border Patrol. From 1988 to 1992, a continued paramilitary buildup was associated with the War on Drugs. The militarization of the border is represented as a means of securing a region of strategic economic importance subject to political instability. Dunn views the outcome as serving to preserve asymmetry of power between the United States and Mexico and creating a precedent for further loss of civil and human rights.

Dunn, Timothy. 2009. *Blockading the Border and Human Rights: The El Paso Operation That Remade Immigration Enforcement.* **Austin: University of Texas Press.**

In 1993, in El Paso, Texas, Operation Blockade began a strategy of stationing U.S. Border Patrol officers at the border line in highly visible areas to deter unauthorized migrants from crossing in urban areas. Dunn examines how the prior policy of apprehending unauthorized entrants in urban El Paso led to violations of Mexican American citizens' civil rights, particularly students attending Bowie High School, right on the border line. In response, the line watch strategy of Operation Blockade led to the "prevention through deterrence" approach emphasized in the 1994 and 2004 National Border Patrol Strategies for the Southern Border. The consequences of this strategy for increased migrant deaths and human rights violations are considered and suggestions made for balancing issues of sovereignty with humanitarian concerns.

Guerette, Rob T. 2007. *Migrant Death: Border Safety and Situational Crime Prevention on the U.S.-Mexico Divide.* **New York: LFB Scholarly Publishing.**

Since the 1990s and the change in U.S. Border Patrol tactics, there has been an unprecedented increase in migrant deaths while attempting unauthorized entrance into the United States. Guerette presents research on the specific social and environmental causation of migrant death and evaluates the U.S. Border Patrol Border Safety Initiative. He found increasing spatial dispersion of migrants to remote and harsh terrain, disproportionate death rates for women migrants, and improved recordkeeping of migrant deaths. Using a situational crime-prevention framework, Guerette suggests methods for deterring migrants from hazardous crossing and considers safety practices before, during, and after life-threatening events to prevent deaths.

Maril, Robert. 2004. *Patrolling Chaos: The U.S. Border Patrol in Deep South Texas.* **Lubbock: Texas Tech University Press.**

Robert Lee Maril's ethnography focuses on a McAllen, Texas, U.S. Border Patrol station of 200 men and women over a two-year period. It closely follows 10 men and women on 10-hour patrols of the border as they perform surveillance and apprehensions of unauthorized migrants and drug smugglers. The book details the border police's insights into the effectiveness of placing vehicles on stationary "line watch" to deter people from crossing in dense brush country with low visibility. Maril criticizes the centralized USBP management hierarchy, its decision-making, and its androcentrism, which marginalizes women employees. He suggests that the issue of U.S. corruption should be confronted.

Massey, Douglas S., Jorge Durand, and Nolan J. Malone. 2002. *Beyond Smoke and Mirrors: Mexican Immigration in an Era of Economic Integration.* **New York: Russell Sage Foundation.**

Unauthorized Mexican immigration is presented as a part of the historical process of North American integration. Douglas Massey and coauthors indicate that the North American Free Trade Agreement of 1994 allowed for the passage of goods, services, information, and capital but not labor. The United States' policy of trying to deter the entrance of less-skilled Mexican workers has resulted in restriction of rights for immigrants and militarization of the border. This book views U.S. immigration policies enacted between 1986 and 1996 and its authorization of increased border enforcement as a waste of government investment. Unintended consequences include a change from circular, temporary migration to permanent migration, reinforcement of an underground economy for Mexican labor, and lowered wages for U.S. citizens. The authors suggest that the United States should recognize the demand for Mexican unskilled labor and regularize it while promoting economic development in Mexico as an employment alternative that will stabilize the situation.

Nevins, Joseph. 2002. *Operation Gatekeeper: The Rise of the "Illegal Alien" and the Making of the U.S.-Mexico Boundary.* **New York: Routledge.**

Operation Gatekeeper has utilized line watch and border walls to deter unauthorized immigration. Joseph Nevins historically situates this border-security practice in the context of a recession in California, ineffective government, and the social construction of unauthorized immigrants as "lawbreakers" and a threat to national security. Operation Gatekeeper is viewed as a result of the maintenance of boundaries despite the process of economic integration associated with the North American Free Trade Agreement and globalization. Instead globalization is viewed as a cause of a decreased sense of public security, which promotes border enforcement buildup with undesirable consequences for the integration of world regions and human rights, and increased migrant deaths.

Payson, Tony. 2006. *The Three U.S.-Mexico Border Wars: Drugs, Immigration, and Homeland Security.* **Westport, CT: Praeger Security International.**

Payson traces the history of the militarization of the border all the way through to the creation of the Department of Homeland Security and securitization. He views the "war over the enforcement of immigration laws," the War on Drugs, and the War on Terror as potentially reducing the autonomy of border regions and making a divide between border populations and Washington. The attempt to secure all points of entry and exit to the United States has become a barrier to economic, social, and cultural integration: a closing of the border. Border militarization is criticized and instead a multilateral "North American Solution" is proposed. Payson proposes a new vision of security based on multilateral cooperation.

Border Conditions, Crime, and Human Rights

Lee, Matthew T. 2003. *Crime on the Border: Immigration and Homicide in Urban Communities.* **New York: LFB Scholarly Publishing.**

Although immigrants are stereotyped as crime-prone, studies consistently indicate that the size of the immigrant population is associated with a decrease in violent crime. Matthew Lee's research uses multivariate analysis to compare the relationship between immigration and the homicide rate in Miami and the border cities of El Paso, Texas, and San Diego. The results show a negative relationship between Latino immigration and Latino homicide rates. Instead, the degree of Latino poverty and joblessness and residential instability, indicators of social disorganization, were positively associated with Latino homicide rates. The author suggests that economic deprivation, absence of labor market opportunity, and neighborhood instability, rather than immigration, must be addressed to lower homicide. Immigrant populations are a stabilizing influence on neighborhoods which can reduce levels of homicide.

Martinez, Oscar. 2006. *Troublesome Border.* **Revised edition. Tucson: University of Arizona Press.**

This volume details the conflictive history of the United States' relations with Mexico and the development of a transitional cultural zone at its border. Martinez covers contemporary issues such as the North American Free Trade Agreement (NAFTA) and economic integration, immigration, drugs, and violence. A chapter on Mexico's border population and the impact of its foreign independence provides a Mexican perspective on the U.S. impact. Finally, parallels to international situations at borders and suggestions about a bilateral approach are considered.

Martinez, Ramiro, Jr., and Abel Valenzuela, Jr. 2006. *Immigration and Crime: Race, Ethnicity and Violence.* **New York: New York University Press.**

Martinez and Valenzuela have gathered research essays that address the relationship between crime and immigration, race and ethnicity. National origin groups covered include Asian, Caribbean, and Latin American. Past theory and findings on immigration's relationship to crime are compared to the present. Topics include immigrant trends in victimization, juvenile delinquency, gangs, exposure to violence, drugs and homicide as well as border violence. Contributors indicate that fear of immigrant crime is not justified by the evidence. Instead, immigrants are subject to stereotyping, discrimination, and victimization.

Martinez, Samuel, ed. 2009. *International Migration and Human Rights: The Global Repercussions of U.S. Policy.* **Berkeley: University of California Press.**

The focus on increasing border control at the U.S.-Mexico border has overpowered consideration of the achievability and impact of securitization policy on other nations. Contributors examine how the United States and other industrialized countries' international trade, drug prohibition, immigration control, and national security policies have the unanticipated impact of increasing international migration. Essays include an examination of the impact of globalization on international migration, analysis of inspection at U.S. ports of entry, new discourse on unauthorized Mexican immigration and national security, profiling of Arab and Muslim immigrants, and human rights issues with detention. The contributors chart the many ways in which the criminalization and securitization of immigration have negative consequences for human rights.

Richardson, Chad, and Rosalva Resendez. 2006. *On the Edge: Culture, Labor, and Deviance on the South Texas Border.* **Austin: University of Texas Press**

This volume includes case studies of undocumented workers, immigration enforcement, drug smuggling, property crime, and the impact of Mexican criminal justice practices on U.S. citizens and Mexicans. It presents research on the motivations of Mexican undocumented migrants and the hardships faced in crossing the border while trying to avoid the U.S. Border Patrol and border bandits. It is one of the only studies of the cross-border issues of shoplifting and auto theft, especially among minors, and presents information on the problem of police corruption in Mexico and, to a lesser degree, in the United States.

Spener, David. 2009. *Clandestine Crossings: Migrants and Coyotes on the Texas-Mexico Border.* **Ithaca, NY: Cornell University Press.**

Academic debate has focused on the degree to which migrant smuggling is an organized effort connected to organized crime and human trafficking. Ethnographic research on unauthorized migration across the South Texas–Mexico border indicates that human smuggling is not a hierarchical, top-down, organized criminal activity. Extensive interviews with cross-border migrants and smugglers indicate it occurs within loosely structured horizontal networks that link migrants in sending and receiving communities with *coyotes* (human smugglers). The migrant-coyote linkage is explained as a result of the need to rely on costly additional help due to intensified border enforcement. Internationally, these efforts are viewed by liberal scholars as resistance to a closed-border policy enforcing global apartheid, the closure of access to the assets of wealthier groups and countries. The risks and suffering, even unto death during crossing attempts, is viewed as the imposition of structural violence due to the exercise of national sovereignty.

Staudt, Kathleen, Tony Payan, and Z. Anthony Kruszewski, eds. 2009. *Human Rights along the U.S.-Mexico Border: Gendered Violence and Insecurity.* **Tucson: University of Arizona Press.**

Public concern in the United States about the Mexican border control has led to unilateral efforts such as the militarization of border enforcement and the criminalization of immigration. This volume explores the violent consequences of U.S. policy for the developing country of Mexico. Part 1 contributors examine the social context in which migrant women experience sexual violence at Mexico's northern and southern borders; the risk of robbery or violence male and female migrants face from Mexican municipal police and railroad "security" workers and their human smugglers; the manner in which intensified border enforcement is making unauthorized crossing more difficult and causing deaths and abandonment of migrant women; and the impact of NAFTA's economic integration on the expansion of organized illicit markets from drugs to bootleg CDs. Part 2 presents research on femicide in Ciudad Juarez, Mexico, the border city in which over 400 women were murdered from 1993 to 2006. Femicide involves the rape, torture, and mutilation of one-third of the women victims, who were often *maquiladora* (Mexican factory) workers. Two-thirds of the women were killed as a result of domestic violence or routine opportunistic murders, issues that are overlooked on both sides of the border. Contributors examine how nongovernmental advocacy organizations and law enforcement responded and the implications for Mexico regarding adopting international human rights standards. In addition, problems with the United States' approach to protecting human trafficking victims are examined. The editor's conclusion discusses a "Border Security Industrial Complex" and its implications for violence against women, creation of human insecurity, and human rights issues. The authors suggest multilateral cooperation, legal immigration opportunities, and political, social, and economic reforms that include paying a living wage in Mexico as an alternative to present border policy.

Stowell, Jacob I. 2007. *Immigration and Crime: The Effects of Immigration on Criminal Behavior*. **New York: LFB Scholarly Publishing.**

Research indicates that the size of the immigration population in a community is negatively associated with the degree of violent crime. Overall, studies of the relationship between having immigrant status and crime have seldom examined variation by national origin. Previously, social disorganization theory predicted that the degree of structure, social disruption, and reduced educational attainment opportunities in immigrant communities would be correlated with crime. Findings based on multivariate analysis indicated that variation in level of neighborhood poverty and housing vacancies, which are associated with residential stability, differentially impacted national origin immigrant groups. Immigration was found to positively impact community social structure through its association with neighborhood poverty levels, and it had a negative effect on residential instability. Stowell concludes that although immigrants are less likely to engage in violent criminal activity, the national origin immigrant population has an indirect effect on crime through its positive impact on poverty and residential instability, key predictors of social disorganization theory.

Immigration and Interior Enforcement

Brotherton, David, and Philip Kretsedemas, eds. 2008. *Keeping Out the Other: A Critical Introduction to Immigration Enforcement Today*. **New York: Columbia University Press.**

This collection of essays examines the trend toward expansion of immigration enforcement before and after 9/11 and the development of a two-tier system of legal rights for citizens and noncitizens. The spiral of enforcement spending is shown to precede 9/11 during an era that provided initial rationales for the restriction of due process rights. Revocation of rights continued after securitization concerns about terrorism developed and Arab-Muslim men were subject to profiling and mass deportation without examination of the charges against them. This is connected to moral panic coalescing public attitudes favoring immigration restriction without evidence of extensive immigrant involvement in criminal activity or terrorism. Contributors address the impact of imprisoning noncitizens who are noncriminal detainees, prison conditions and abuse, the economics of expansion of immigration detention, and the mass deportation of unauthorized migrants and permanent resident aliens convicted of aggravated felony offenses. Essays conclude with a look at social causes and policy consequences of intense law-enforcement scrutiny merging federal, state, and local efforts and its impact on immigrant communities.

Dow, Mark. 2004. *American Gulag: Inside U.S. Immigration Prisons*. Berkeley: University of California Press.

Mark Dow covers the history of immigration law and the expanding use of detention both before and during the War on Terror. His field research covers the conditions faced by immigration detainees in Immigration and Naturalization Service (INS) detention centers and jails and prisons with contracts. Detainees, guards, and federal officials describe physical and psychological abuse, indefinite detention, racist attitudes, and other conditions in violation of human rights. Dow argues that many detentions are not a response to terrorism, but an aspect of INS unmonitored authority over unauthorized immigrants and asylum applicants within a prison system that holds many people who are not considered to have committed a traditional crime but are in violation of immigration law.

Orchowski, Margaret Sands. 2008. *Immigration and the American Dream: Battling the Political Hype and Hysteria*. New York: Rowan and Littlefield.

Margaret Sands Orchowski examines conservative, liberal, and independent viewpoints on the immigration issue. She considers that misinformation and political spin have complicated achieving an objective understanding of what is involved. This volume re-examines the history of immigration and offers an analysis of buzzwords and the framing of the issue. It presents the policy alternatives that are being politically debated and Orchowski's views on beneficial change.

The U.S.-Canada Border

Ackleson, Jason. 2009. "From Thin to Thick (and Back Again?): The Politics and Policies of the Contemporary US-Canada Border." *American Review of Canadian Studies* 39 (4): 336–351.

The policies and procedures of the 30-point Smart Border Action Plan have not been fully put into action. The new border-security procedures being implemented by the United States includes the Western Hemisphere Travel Initiative requirement that Canadians carry passports to cross the border. The Security and Prosperity Partnership are legging. Ackleson argues that the result is that when greater economic and security cooperation is needed it is not forthcoming, and he offers insight into obstacles to the process and ways to improve border-security efforts.

Adelman, Howard. 2002. "Canadian Borders and Immigration Post 9/11." *International Migration Review* 36: 15–28.

After 9/11, public discussion of terrorist routes into the United States focused on Canada as a "weak link." This essay examines the human rights implications for citizens and noncitizens of antiterrorism legislation passed in the Canadian Parliament to strengthen security. It discusses the transition of the previously unguarded border into a security barrier and the degree to which a common security perimeter might be developed. Regarding immigration policy, the Immigration and Refugee Act of 2000 and the post 9/11 Public Safety Act's new securitization procedures are highlighted. Finally, issues in the use of false documentation by refugees to gain entry and their disposition are discussed.

Hataley, Todd S. 2007. "Catastrophic Terrorism at the Border: The Case of the Canada-United States Border." *Homeland Security Affairs*, Supplement no. 1. http://www.hsaj.org/pages/supplement/issue1/pdfs/supplement.1.2.pdf.

The land crossings at the Canadian border are strategic for the economic viability of Canada due to its reliance on trade with the United States. A terrorist attack on border infrastructure, tunnels, and bridges would be catastrophic and jeopardize

Canadians' well-being. This essay examines the potential for disruption at the border and the use by terrorists of the Canadian border as a transit point into the United States.

Konrad, Victor, and Heather N. Nicol. 2008. *Beyond Walls: Re-Inventing the Canada–United States Borderlands.* **London: Ashgate.**

Since 9/11, there have been new policies for counterterrorism, trade regulation, emergency preparedness, and control of border crossing. The impact of "re-bordering" for Canadian and U.S. citizens is explored. Security-driven change is viewed as initiated by the United States and affecting the borderlands, its culture, and transnational communities. Chapters examine globalization and the development of borderlands theory, past practice at the Canada-U.S. border, cross-border trade with heightened security, passport compliance, the environment, and the Artic/Northern borderlands region.

Lennox, Patrick. 2007. "From Golden Straitjacket to Kevlar Vest: Canada's Transformation to a Security State." *Canadian Journal of Political Science* **40 (4): 1017–1038.**

Canada is rapidly becoming a security state that incorporates constitutional, bureaucratic, defense, and border initiatives to protect its citizens from terrorism. This change is explained as based in both asymmetry in Canadian-U.S. relations and the emergence of a transnational security paradigm—a common way of dealing with terrorism. Lennox argues that the power differential between the United States and Canada shaped the form of the changes but international concern with securitization led to rapid change.

Trafficking

Cook, Philip J., Wendy Cukier, and Keith Krause. 2009. "The Illicit Firearms Trade in North America." *Criminology and Criminal Justice* **9 (3): 265–286.**

Cook, Cukier, and Krause look at how the freedom to own weapons in the United States is associated with smuggling of weapons to criminal organizations in both Mexico and Canada. The U.S. federal gun control laws and state regulations allow for many situations in which "straw purchasers" can legally acquire firearms for illegal small-scale smuggling operations. Both Mexico and Canada have stronger legal controls on firearms than the United States. This article discusses how criminals, including narcotraffickers, evade the law to acquire weapons associated with increased inter-criminal organization violence.

Grayson, George W. 2010. *Mexico: Narco-Violence and a Failed State?* New Brunswick, NJ: Transaction Publishers.

There is speculation that drug trafficking and related violence in Mexico will undermine the ability to govern. Grayson examines Mexican history from Prohibition through the drug wars. He connects the crisis to the one-party rule of the Institutional Revolutionary Party (PRI) and its corruption and connections to organized crime. In 2000, the National Action Party (PAN) took the presidency and began a transition to a two-party democratic system. The historical and contemporary analysis examines the institutional structure of PRI rule and its decline, the Sinaloa and Gulf drug-trafficking organizations, President Felipe Calderon's strategy against narcoviolence, the implications for U.S. relations, and the impact of the Merida Initiative. In conclusion, Grayson considers whether Mexico might become a failed state due to eroded institutional capacity and the cost of the drug war and then discusses options.

Thachuk, Kimberly L., ed. 2007. *Transnational Threats: Smuggling and Trafficking in Arms, Drugs, and Human Life.* Westport, CT: Praeger Security International.

Thachuk's collection of essays covers nonstate criminal actors including terrorists, organized criminals, pirates, and entrepreneurs who engage in the smuggling and trafficking of people, goods, and services. Transnational threats occur across borders and are not subject to the control of any single sovereign state. Contributions on international criminal organization include writing on narcoterrorism, international human trafficking, and small arms trafficking. An essay on the threat of nuclear smuggling provides information on the likelihood of use of different types of radioactive materials. Regional studies cover various types of smuggling and trafficking in the Balkans, Central Eurasia, Africa, China, Japan, South Asia, the Andean region, the Caribbean, and the United States.

Velasco, Jose Luis. 2005. *Insurgency, Authoritarianism, and Drug Trafficking During Mexico's "Democratization."* **New York: Routledge.**

This statistically documented work focuses on the relationship between the democratic transition in Mexico and the unprecedented increase in narcoterrorism. The transition from the national one-party rule of the PRI to a two-party system including the PAN is represented as a weak institutional change in which drug-trafficking organizations have corrupted new government regimes and involved business in money laundering. Velasco promotes an antidrug strategy in which Mexico develops legitimate economic opportunity for its citizens and the United States addresses the demand for drugs among its own population. He concludes that weak states are especially vulnerable to the corruption of the international drug trade.

Terrorism

Eldridge, Thomas R., Susan Ginsberg, Walter T. Hempel II, Janice L. Kephart, and Kelly Moore. 2004. *9/11 and Terrorist Travel. Staff Report of the National Commission on Terrorist Attacks Upon the United States.* **http://govinfo.library.unt.edu/ 911/staff_statements/911_TerrTrav_Monograph.pdf.**

This examination of events and missteps in intelligence gathering and reaction prior to the 9/11 attacks is the seminal work on planning for counterterrorism. It explains the steps leading to the tragedy and issues a set of recommendations that remain relevant.

Winterdyck, John A., and Kelly W. Sundberg, eds. 2010. *Border Security in the Al-Qaeda Era.* **Boca Raton, FL: CRC Press.**

After 9/11, the manner in which nations protect their borders changed. The United States and Canada reorganized border services into new departments and other nations have passed laws to integrate border services to prevent terrorism. Contributors from Australia, Austria, Canada, England, Frances, Iran, Italy, and the United States address border-security issues. Each country's specific essay provides an overview of the following: (1) the history of terrorism and post-9/11 terror incidents; (2) the definition of terrorism used and its relation to border security; (3) how terrorism and suspected terror incident data is handled by border security; (4) organization and operation of border security and post-9/11 change; (5) how changes in border-security practices have impacted movement in people and goods and reporting on such in the mass media; (6) "preferred" explanations of terrorism used by governments or border security; (7) steps taken to strengthen national and border security and social, political, economic, and humanitarian impact of such change on citizens; (8) impact of border-security change on country's sense of sovereignty; and (9) examination of the impact of al-Qaeda on changes in border security and the results of such securitization for civil liberties and human rights. Emphasis is placed on how each country has dealt with terrorist attacks and whether political, legal, and military measures have been justified.

Periodicals and Publications

Immigration

Citizenship Studies
http://www.tandf.co.uk/journals/titles/13621025.asp

Citizenship Studies covers citizenship, human rights, and democratic processes from an interdisciplinary perspective including the fields of politics, sociology, history, and cultural studies. It seeks to lead an international debate on the academic analysis of citizenship, and also aims to cross the division between internal academic discussion and external public debate. It contains articles on debates that move beyond conventional notions of citizenship, and treats citizenship as a strategic concept that is central in the analysis of identity, participation, empowerment, human rights, and the public interest. Citizenship is analyzed in the context of contemporary processes involving globalization, theories of international relations, changes to the state and political communities, multiculturalism, gender, indigenous peoples and national reconciliation, equity, social and public policy, welfare, and the reorganization of public management. As a theoretically basic concept, citizenship provides new tools for formulating problems and providing practical analysis and advice in these fields.

Immigrants and Minorities
http://www.tandf.co.uk/journals/titles/02619288.asp

Founded in 1981, *Immigrants and Minorities* publishes research on the history of immigration and related studies. Its articles examine the social construction of "race" and ethnic and minority relations within a historical setting. International coverage includes research on the United States, Australia, the Middle East, and the United Kingdom.

International Migration
http://www.wiley.com/bw/journal.asp?ref=0020-7985

A policy-oriented journal, *International Migration* focuses on the migration research of sociologists, demographers, political scientists, economists, and other social scientists from all world regions. It covers policies relevant to international migration and publishes comparative research.

International Migration Review (IMR)

The peer-reviewed *International Migration Review* contains articles on sociodemographic, economic, historical, political, and legislative aspects of human migration and refugee movements. *IMR* offers original research, documentation notes, reports on key legislative developments—both national and international—an extensive bibliography and abstracting service, the International Sociological Association's International Newsletter on Migration, plus a scholarly review of new books in the field. It uses an interdisciplinary approach and provides international perspective for the analysis and review of international population movements.

Journal of Ethnic and Migration Studies
http://www.tandf.co.uk/journals/titles/1369183X.asp

The *Journal of Ethnic and Migration Studies (JEMS)* publishes the results of first-class research on all forms of migration and its consequences, together with articles on ethnic conflict, discrimination, racism, nationalism, citizenship, and policies of integration. It focuses on comparative research, for example, within Europe or between one or more European country and the countries of North America and Asia-Pacific, particularly advanced industrial countries. Certain articles are pertinent to informed policy debate and the implications of research for policy innovation or evaluate the results of previous initiatives. (Self-description)

Journal of International Migration and Integration
http://jimi.metropolis.net/

This quarterly multidisciplinary and interdisciplinary journal is published in English and Spanish. Its focus is current research, theory, and policy analysis on migration. Contributors include researchers, policy analysts, and service providers. Topics include the sending society impact of migration and diversity, demographic planning, public health, the effect of racism, discrimination and social exclusion of immigrant groups, securitization of immigration, and justice.

Migration
http://publications.iom.int/bookstore/index.php?main_page= contact_us

The International Organization for Migration publishes a description of its activities and policy essays several times a year. It is available in English, Spanish, and French.

Migration Letters
http://www.migrationletters.com/index.html

A quarterly interdisciplinary journal on international migration, *Migration Letters* publishes short accounts of research, articles focusing on debate, and comments. Topics include transnational mobility and voluntary or forced migration. Papers range from the theoretical to empirical and applied research or policy analysis.

Migration News
http://migration.ucdavis.edu/mn/

This quarterly online news source contains news and information on immigration and integration and has much useful information on current developments in U.S. immigration policy. Contributions are listed by region: North America, Europe, and Other. The email version is free.

Population Studies
http://www.tandf.co.uk/journals/titles/00324728.html

For over half a century, *Population Studies* has reported significant advances in methods of demographic analysis, conceptual and mathematical theories of demographic dynamics and behavior, and the use of these theories and methods to extend scientific knowledge and to inform policy and practice. The journal's coverage of this field is comprehensive: applications in developed and developing countries; historical and contemporary studies; quantitative and qualitative studies; analytical essays and reviews. Paper subjects range from classical concerns, such as the determinants and consequences of population change, to such topics as family demography and evolutionary and genetic influences on demographic behavior. (Self-description)

Immigration Law

Georgetown Immigration Law Journal
http://www.law.georgetown.edu/journals/gilj/

The *Georgetown Immigration Law Journal* is a scholarly publication dedicated to the advancement of legal knowledge in the field of immigration law. The journal is published quarterly and is dedicated to exploring and critically analyzing international and domestic events as they shape the field of immigration law. Each issue features articles by scholars and legal practitioners, as well as a significant number of student notes and a section reviewing current developments in immigration. Immigration law permeates a wide number of other substantive areas including constitutional, administrative, criminal, labor, and international law. Recent world events have increased awareness among the legal community of the importance of immigration law, with issues ranging from the meaning of citizenship to multinational corporate concerns about employing foreign persons. As a result, expertise in immigration law is required by both individuals seeking citizenship and big business attracting skilled workers. (Self-description)

Michigan Journal of Race and Law
http://students.law.umich.edu/mjrl/

The goal of the *Michigan Journal of Race and Law* is to serve as a forum for the exploration of issues relating to race and law, and to civil rights in general. The journal is recognized for publishing cutting-edge scholarship on a wide range of civil rights issues from diverse perspectives, most specifically those issues that are marginalized in mainstream legal discourse. Those perspectives include anything from critical race theory to law and economics, and everything in between. This flexibility has allowed the journal to cover a huge number of topics in-depth and with great effect. To that end, the journal publishes the views of scholars, students, practitioners, and social scientists. Since the inaugural issue, the journal has become nationally recognized as one of the leading civil rights journals in the country, and has also been consistently ranked among the top 25 specialty journals overall. (Self-description)

Human Rights

Social Justice: A Journal of Crime, Conflict, and World Order
http://www.socialjusticejournal.org/

Founded in 1974, *Social Justice* is a quarterly nonprofit educational journal that seeks to promote human dignity, equality, peace, and genuine security. Its early focus on issues of crime, police repression, social control, and the penal system has expanded to encompass globalization, human and civil rights, border, citizenship, and immigration issues, environmental victims and health and safety concerns, social policies affecting welfare and education, ethnic and gender relations, and persistent global inequalities. The journal has framed its vision of social justice with an understanding of the international dimensions of power, inequality, and injustice. In doing so, it has formed part of an international community of progressive intellectuals, activists, and movements. The connection to that community has helped *Social Justice* keep its bearings in times of stormy weather (such as the nasty squalls of the Reagan era or the hurricane winds at the end of the Cold War). *Social Justice* continues to promote social criticism as a distinctive form of knowledge and respects the theoretical implications of practice and the practical aspects of theory. We present divergent viewpoints in a readable fashion. (Self-description)

Recent issues include "Migrant Labor and Contested Social Space," "Beyond Transnational Crime," and "Immigrant Rights and National Insecurity."

Transnational Crime and Trafficking

Crime and Justice International
http://www.cjimagazine.com/

Crime and Justice International is published by the Office of International Criminal Justice at Sam Houston State University for a readership of academicians and law-enforcement professionals. Article topics include organized crime, border crime, trafficking, and terrorism.

Crime, Law, and Social Change
http://www.springerlink.com/content/0925-4994

Crime, Law, and Social Change is a peer-reviewed journal that publishes essays and reviews dealing with the political economy of organized crime, whether at the transnational, national, regional, or local level anywhere in the world. In addition, the journal publishes work on financial crime, political corruption, environmental crime, and the expropriation of resources from developing nations. The journal is also committed to publishing in the general area of human rights including historical and contemporary studies of genocide, essays on compensation and justice for survivors of mass murder and state-sponsored terrorism, analyses of international human rights organizations (both governmental and NGOs), and historical as well as contemporary essays focused on gender, racial, and ethnic equality. (Self-description)

Global Crime
http://www.tandf.co.uk/journals/titles/17440572.asp

Global Crime, formerly titled *Transnational Organized Crime*, is a social-science journal devoted to the study of crime broadly conceived. Its focus is deliberately broad and multidisciplinary and its first aim is to make the best scholarship on crime available to specialists and nonspecialists alike. It endorses no particular orthodoxy and draws on authors from a variety of disciplines, including history, sociology, criminology, economics, political science, anthropology, and area studies. Major topics include organized criminality, its history, activities, relations with the state, its penetration of the economy, and its perception in popular culture. Other topics include corruption, crime and women's studies, illegal migration, terrorism, illicit markets, violence, police studies, and the process of state building. The journal includes research articles, dispatches highlighting research in progress, and field reports from law-enforcement officials and book reviews. (Self-description)

Trends in Organized Crime
http://www.iasoc.net/trends.html#

Trends in Organized Crime is a peer-reviewed journal published four times a year. It presents a composite of analyses and syntheses of research on organized crime, drawn from a variety of sources. It publishes peer-reviewed, original research articles and excerpts from significant governmental reports. The contents also include reviews of important new books and presents analysis and commentary on current issues in organized crime. *Trends in Organized Crime* is an ideal resource for practitioners and policymakers, as well as the academic community. It is published in association with the International Association for the Study of Organized Crime (IASOC). (Self-description)

Terrorism

CTC Sentinel
http://ctc.usma.edu/sentinel/

The Combating Terrorism Center at West Point is an independent educational and research institution based in the Department of Social Sciences at the U.S. Military Academy, West Point. The CTC Center harnesses the Center's global network of scholars and practitioners to understand and confront contemporary threats posed by terrorism and other forms of political violence.

Perspectives on Terrorism
http://www.terrorismanalysts.com

An international initiative, this electronic journal permits traditional research and perspectives on terrorism and counterterrorism. Each posted essay is connected to a discussion board.

Studies in Conflict and Violence
http://www.tandf.co.uk/journals/tf/1057610X.html

Terrorism and insurgency are now the dominant forms of conflict in the world. Fueled by moribund peace processes, ethnic and religious strife, disputes over natural resources, and transnational organized crime, these longstanding security challenges have become even more violent and intractable, posing new threats to international peace and stability. *Studies in Conflict and Terrorism* aims to cast new light on the origins and implications of conflict in the twenty-first century and to illuminate new approaches and solutions to countering the growth and escalation of contemporary substate violence.

The journal thus seeks to publish the best theoretical and empirical studies that contribute to a better understanding of the causes of these conflicts and the measures required to achieve their resolution. In a world of diverse and changing threats, enigmatic adversaries, and continued uncertainty, the editor's goal is to provide fresh insight, thoughtful analysis, and authoritative prescriptions to the most pressing concerns that affecting global security in the twenty-first century. (Self-description)

Terrorism and Political Violence

http://www.tandf.co.uk/journals/titles/09546553.asp

Terrorism and Political Violence reflects the full range of current scholarly work from many disciplines and theoretical perspectives. It aims to give academic rigor to a field which hitherto has lacked it, and encourages comparative studies. In addition to focusing on the political meaning of terrorist activity, the journal publishes studies of various related forms of violence by rebels and by states, on the links between political violence and organized crime, protest, rebellion, revolution, and human rights. Symposia are a regular feature covering such subjects as terrorism and public policy; religion and violence; political parties and terrorism; technology and terrorism; and right-wing terrorism. (Self-description)

Terrorism and Security Monitor

http://jtsm.janes.com/public/jtsm/index.shtml

Jane's *Terrorism and Security Monitor* covers current issues in terrorism and counterterrorism worldwide. Contents include what's behind terrorist campaigns, tracking of trends in the strategy and operations of the world's terrorist and insurgent groups, and discussion of government policy responses to the terrorist threat. Key contents include regional coverage of terrorist activity, the root causes of terrorism and insurgency, terrorist use of weapons of mass destruction, biographies of terrorism leaders, and intelligence on the growing links between terrorism, insurgency, and organized crime. (Partial self-description)

Transnational Threats Update
http://csis.org/programs/transnational-threats-project/transnational-threats-update

The *Transnational Threats Update* is produced by the Transnational Threats Project and provides monthly reports and analysis on terrorism, drug trafficking, organized crime, money laundering, and arms trafficking. The newsletter draws on several U.S. and international media sources, including the Associated Press, Agence France Presse, Reuters, Xinhua News Agency, World Tribune, Afghan News, and others. (Self-description)

Government Reports

Beaver, Janice Cheryl. 2006. "CRS Report for Congress: U.S. International Borders: Brief Facts." http://fpc.state.gov/documents/organization/76897.pdf.

Beittel, June S. 2009. "Congressional Research Report for Congress: Mexico's Drug Related Violence." http://www.fas.org/sgp/crs/row/R40582.pdf.

Cook, Colleen W. 2007. "Congressional Research Service Report: Mexico's Drug Cartels." http://ftp.fas.org/sgp/crs/row/RL34215.pdf.

Government Accountability Office (GAO). 2005. "Information on Criminal Aliens Incarcerated in Federal and State Prisons and Local Jails." http://www.gao.gov/new.items/d05337r.pdf.

Government Accountability Office (GAO). 2006. "Border Security: Key Unresolved Issues Justify Reevaluation of Border Surveillance Technology Program." http://www.gao.gov/new.items/d06295.pdf.

Government Accountibility Office (GAO). 2008a. "Department of Homeland Security: Billions Invested in Major Programs Lack Appropriate Oversight." http://www.gao.gov/new.items/d0929.pdf.

Government Accountability Office (GAO). 2008b. "Secure Border Initiative: Observations on the Importance of Applying

Lessons Learned to Future Projects: Statement of Richard M. Stana: Director Homeland Security and Justice Issues." GAO Report 08-361. http://www.gao.gov/new.items/d081141t.pdf.

Government Accountability Office (GAO). 2009. "Briefing on U.S. Custom's and Border Protection Secure Border Initiative Fiscal Year 2009 Plan." http://www.gao.gov/new.items/d09274r.pdf.

Garcia, Michael John. 2006. "CRS Report for Congress: Immigration Consequences of Criminal Activity." http://fpc.state.gov/documents/organization/78335.pdf.

Government Accountability Office (GAO). 2004. *Over-Stay Tracking: A Key Component of Homeland Security and a Layered Defense: A Report to the Chairman, Committee on the Judiciary, House of Representatives.* Washington, DC: U.S. Government Printing Office. http://www.gao.gov/new.items/D0482.pdf.

Government Accountability Office (GAO). 2006. *Border Crossing Deaths Have Doubled Since 1995; Border Patrol's Efforts to Prevent Deaths Have Not Been Fully Evaluated.* Washington, DC: U.S. Government Printing Office.

National Drug Intelligence Center. "National Drug Threat Assessment 2009." http://www.usdoj.gov/ndic/pubs31/31379/index.htm.

Siskin, Alison, and Ruth Ellen Wasem. 2005. "Congressional Research Service Report for Congress: Immigration Policy on Expedited Removal of Aliens." Washington, DC: Government Printing Office. http://fpc.state.gov/documents/organization/54512.pdf.

United Nations Office on Drugs and Crime. 2006. *Trafficking in Persons: Global Patterns.* April. www.unodc.org/pdf/traffickinginpersons_report_2006ver2.pdf.

U.S. Department of State. 2008. *Trafficking in Persons Report 2008.* http://www.state.gov/g/tip/rls/tiprpt/2008/.

Bibliographies

The Internet provides many extensive bibliographies of value to the researcher; subjects include border security, unauthorized immigration, drug trafficking, and terrorism. Listed below are several bibliographies that address these issues.

Border Security

Homeland Security: A Selected Bibliography. May 2006. Compiled by Jeanette C. Moyer, U.S. Army War College Library. http://www.carlisle.army.mil/library/bibs/homesec06.pdf.

Human Security: An Extended and Annotated International Bibliography. November 1, 2001. Compiled by Sara Edson. Centre for History and Economics, King's College, University of Cambridge, United Kingdom for the Common Security Forum. http://www.humansecurity-chs.org/activities/meetings/first/bibliography.pdf.

Illegal Immigration and U.S. Border Security. May 2006. Compiled by Stephen B. T. Chun, Muir S. Fairchild Research Information Center, Maxwell Air Force Base, Alabama. http://www.au.af.mil/au/aul/bibs/illegalim.htm.

Unauthorized Immigration

Annotated Bibliography: Worksite and Interior Enforcement Issues. September 2007. Institute for the Study of International Migration. Walsh School of Foreign Service, Georgetown University. http://isim.georgetown.edu/Publications/SRFMaterials/ANNOTATED%20BIBLIOGRAPHY.pdf.

Undocumented Immigrants: An Annotated Bibliography. November 2005. Compiled by Alicia Burgarin, Steven DeBry, and Martha Jones, California Research Center. http://www.library.ca.gov/crb/05/06/05-006.pdf.

Human Trafficking

Data and Research on Human Trafficking: Bibliography of Research-Based Literature. October 2008. Compiled by Elsbieta M. Gozdziak and Michah N. Bump. http://www.ncjrs.gov/pdffiles1/nij/grants/224392.pdf.

Trafficking in Human Beings. 2009. United Nations Interregional Crime and Justice Research Institute (UNICRI). http://www.unicri.it/wwd/trafficking/bibliography/thb-bibl.php.

Drug Trafficking

Cork Bibliography: Drug Trade and Trafficking. January 2008. http://www.projectcork.org/bibliographies/data/Bibliography_Drug_Trade_and_Trafficking.html.

Narco-Terrorism. 2003. Compiled by Ron Fuller. Air University Library, Maxwell Air Force Base. http://www.au.af.mil/au/aul/bibs/narco/narco.htm.

Terrorism

Bibliography on Terrorism. 2008. Pinklet, The Peace Palace Library. http://andromeda.rutgers.edu/~wcjlen/WCJ/mainpages/bibliogs_body.html.

Terrorism and Counterterrorism: An Annotated Bibliography, Volume 2. September 11, 2006. Compiled by James J. F. Forest, Thomas A. Bengston Jr., Hilda Rosa Martinez, Nathan Gonzalez, and Bridget C. Nee, Combating Terrorism Center, U.S. Military Academy at West Point. http://www.teachingterror.com/bibliography/CTC_Bibliography_2006.pdf.

Weapons of Mass Destruction. 2006. Department of Justice, Federal Bureau of Investigation, FBI Academy Library. Quantico, VA. http://fbilibrary.fbiacademy.edu/bibliographies/weaponsofmassdestruction.htm.

Borders

U.S.-Mexico Border Issues: A Selected Bibliography from the Smithsonian Institution Libraries' Collections. Summer 2000. Compiled by Cecilia C. Perez, Smithsonian Institution Libraries Intern, University of South Florida, School of Library and Information Science.

DVDs

U.S.-Mexico Border Law Enforcement

Border Wars: Season 1. **2 discs; 250 mins. National Geographic, 2010. $29.97**

The efforts of U.S. Customs and Border Patrol to stop unauthorized immigration and drug trafficking are filmed by day and night in U.S.-Mexico Border locations including the Arizona desert. The programs detail the technology and methods used for apprehension at ports of entry, in urban areas and remote regions.

Border War. **52 mins. National Geographic, 2008. $19.95**

Unauthorized immigrants and smugglers try on foot and by car, even risking their lives to cross the U.S.-Mexico border. This DVD examines how migrants and drug smugglers attempt crossing the border and sometimes make it. Live action footage of U.S. Border Patrol officers using high-tech tracking is shown.

Now on PBS: Obama's Border Fence. **30 mins. PBS, 2009. $39.95 (public view) $19.95 (individual view)**

The Secure Fence Act of 2006 authorized the southwest border fence and the Secretary of Homeland Security was given waivers from lawsuits by environmentalists, property owners, and other concerned groups. As the fence is being finalized, this program discusses the "virtual fence" that the Obama administration inherited from the previous administration and Congress. Tests of the Secure Border Initiative in high technology for electronic surveillance have not indicated that it works.

Now on PBS: The Border Fence. **30 mins. PBS, 2001. $39.95 (public view) $19.95 (individual view)**

This program questions the degree to which the U.S.-Mexico border fence will be effective. It examines the impact of the fence on families who are concerned about their property and fear for their safety.

Enforcers: The Border Patrol. **100 mins. History Channel, 2008. $19.95**

In part 1, this Greystone documentary presents the history of the U.S Border Patrol and its enforcement of immigration law against smugglers and unauthorized migrants. Part 2 profiles the history of the Texas Rangers, who have also been active along the border.

Unauthorized Immigration and Crime

Frontline: World VII: Crimes at the Border. **24:41 mins. PBS, 2008. $54.95 (institutional viewing) $24.99 (individual view)**

Frontline and the *New York Times* partnered in this documentary about the business of human smuggling on the U.S.-Mexico border. Reporter Lowell Bergman interviews a Mexican smuggler who explains how smugglers are compensating for increased border enforcement and reports on a case of a corrupt border guard caught assisting human smugglers. Congressman Duncan Hunter (San Diego) and sociology professor Wayne Cornelius offer their perspective on the effectiveness and consequences of border controls. The report presents smuggling operations as increasingly expensive and organized—a high-paying business.

Border: The Divide Between the American Dream and the American Nightmare. **104 mins. Little Bonanza Productions, 2006. $19.95**

This documentary encourages debate about the problems and dangers of the border and critiques both Republican and Democratic views on immigration. It looks at both sides of the issue detailing the perspectives of the Minutemen, citizens volunteering to watch the border, ranchers, and immigrant rights groups including Derechos Humanos (a human rights organization), No More Deaths (human rights campaign) and the American Civil Liberties Union. Coverage includes recovery of the deceased and footage of a Mexican drug smuggling group. In addition, it details the impact of unauthorized immigrants on the California health care system. Director Chris Bogard's perspective emphasizes the problems associated with employers' encouragement of unauthorized migration and takes a position that opening the border would provide a source of eventual swing votes for the Democratic Party. Whether or not the viewer agrees with Bogard, the coverage of the politics of unauthorized migration and its impact will expand one's perspective. It has received awards as the best documentary at the California Independent Film Festival, Bronze Ram Award at the Houston Film Festival, and the Director's Choice Award at the Pensacola International Film Festival.

Rights on the Line: Vigilantes on the Border. **26 mins. American Friends Service Committee, 2009. $19.95**

The American Friends Service Committee, a human rights organization, presents a critique of the Minutemen citizen watch groups and border militarization.

Dying to Get In: Undocumented Immigration at the U.S.-Mexico Border. 40 mins. Brett Tolley, 2005. $19.95

Globalization is economically integrating developed and underdeveloped countries. Yet the United States deliberately did not include labor exchange across borders as a part of the North American Free Trade Agreement (NAFTA) and extensive unauthorized migration has occurred at the U.S.-Mexico border. This film examines how NAFTA displaced Mexican corn farmers through inexpensive U.S. corn imports and Mexicans must seek work. Trade and immigration policy has produced a situation in which Mexican migrants face high temperatures and dehydration, risking death to cross at remote areas of the border. This film covers the migrants' stories of the crossing and why they took this risk for economic survival. It asks the question of how U.S. citizens can achieve greater global responsibility.

The film received the following awards: Long Format News Digital Video Award (2007), Most Socially Relevant Student Documentary (2006), Hollywood Student Film Festival Finalist (2006), Best Student Film, Plymouth Film Festival (2006).

Letters from the Other Side. **New Day Films. $249; $4.99 (90-day flash streaming for individual use)**

In May 2003, 19 unauthorized migrants suffocated to death in a tractor trailer in Texas while attempting to enter the interior. This documentary interviews women and children in Mexico about how they feel about husbands and fathers who live in the United States. Two of the women lost their husbands in the 2003 tragedy, while others express their hopes and fears about husbands in the United States, who are also videotaped and share their thoughts with the families they left behind. The resultant videos are screened by an official at the Department of Homeland Security, who is unable to respond about how the United States will resolve this situation.

This film has received the following awards: Official Closing Night Film, SlamDance Film Festival (2006), Official Selection SXSW Film Festival, Official Selection, HotSprings Film Festival (2006).

Golden Venture. **70 mins. New Day Films, 2006. $295.00; $4.99 (90-day flash streaming for individual use)**

In 1993 the *Golden Venture*, a smuggling freighter, ran aground near New York City, carrying 286 migrants who had paid

$30,000 each to be smuggled from the Fugian province of China to the United States. Ten people drowned in the surf. Previously, they endured limited food, crowding, and disease below deck during the passage. In the United States, the Immigration and Naturalization Service detained them in county jails for up to four years, some gaining parole. Half were deported and 220 are living legally in the United States, vulnerable to deportation. Among the greater than 110 passengers deported, 60 have returned without authorization. In China, they allege, they were beaten, jailed, and forcibly sterilized but they are not eligible for political asylum. This film presents stories of the survivors and lawyers and paralegals who advocated for them. The immigration advocacy coalition included members of groups from the left and right and this film documents their work.

This film was an Official Selection, Tribeca Film Festival (2006).

Wetback: The Undocumented Documentary (Mojado: El Documetal Indocumentado). **92 mins. National Geographic, 2005. $19.95**

Despite the title, this documentary is a sympathetic presentation of the journeys of unauthorized entrants crossing borders to the United States and, ultimately, Canada. The southern journey begins in Nicaragua, crossing five borders in all. In Mexico, Nicaraguan migrants face gang members and, at the U.S. border, citizen watch groups. Seeking to enter Canada, which is perceived to have more jobs and less border control after 9/11, they must cross the United States. They come fleeing persecution or for employment. The film seeks to humanize the migrants' quest and win respect, not sympathy.

This film received the Best Documentary Award, Cinequest Film Festival (2005), Best Story, Pamplona Film Festival, Punto de Vista (2005), Spectrum Award (Full Frame) (2005, Audience Award), Chicago Latino Film Festival (2005), and was the Official Selection of Hot Docs (2005).

Invisible: Illegal in Europe. **88 mins. Documentary Channel, 2006. $24.99**

Europe faces extensive unauthorized immigration in search of economic opportunity. Without legal status, immigrants attempt to live in the shadows and participate in an underground economy. This documentary follows five unauthorized immigrants from different world regions who seek to realize a "European Dream."

Terrorism

Inside 9/11. 240 mins. National Geographic, 2005. $19.99

This documentary follows the evolution of Osama bin Laden from a freedom fighter in Soviet-occupied Afghanistan to al-Qaeda leader and Islamic terrorist jihadist. A timeline traces events through the 9/11 attacks on the World Trade Center. Focus is placed on 9/11 planner Khalil Shaikh Mohammed, hijackers Mohammed Atta and Ziad Jarrah, and sleeper cells. It looks at how 9/11 happened, including CIA and FBI failures in intelligence cooperation and flaws in airport security. It provides archival photos, news footage, and eyewitness interviews. An *Inside 9/11* interview archive is located at http://channel.nationalgeographic.com/channel/inside911/interactive.html.

Frontline: The Enemy Within. 60 mins. PBS Educational Media, 2006. $59.95

After 9/11, federal law enforcement was reorganized under the Department of Homeland Security. From the vantage point of five years later, policy response to terrorism and fear of terrorism are explained. It assesses the threat of international versus homegrown terrorism and presents the case of the purported JIS Conspiracy in Lodi, California. In addition, interviews with terrorism experts are presented.

Targeting Terror. 29 mins. Films for the Humanities and Sciences, 2010. $99.95

Terrorism's history, forms, and causation are examined in five nations: (1) the post-9/11 United States, which attempted to handle terrorism through civilian rather than military courts; (2) the United Kingdom, whose experience with the Irish Republican Army (IRA) is evaluated in terms of impact on handling Islamic terrorism; (3) Germany and Japan, former World War II aggressors whose counterterrorism efforts are subject to constitutional limitations; and Colombia, which used extradition as a tool against narcoterrorism. Some content may only be appropriate for adult audiences.

Our Own Private Bin Laden. **63 mins. (plus 102 mins. of bonus material). Films for the Humanities and Sciences, 2005. $179.95**

The United States is a former sponsor of Osama bin Laden, who was a revolutionary jihadist fighter against the Soviet Union when they occupied Afghanistan. This documentary examines the role of U.S. foreign policy in the genesis of 9/11. It looks at the actions taken during the Cold War by presidents Carter and Reagan such as the investigation and shutting down of the Bank of Credit and Commercial International. Then it looks at the CIA connection to bin Laden and the Afghani mujahideen as the Cold War ended prior to the War on Terror. Individuals interviewed include former National Security Advisor Zbigniew Brzezinski, who devised a plan to draw the Soviet Union into an expensive long-term conflict in Afghanistan, Benazir Bhutto, former prime minister of Pakistan, former CIA station chief in Pakistan Milton Bearden, and Noam Chomsky, scholar and activist.

The Balancing Act: Security and Liberty Post 9/11. **58 mins. Films for the Humanities and Sciences, 2004. $149.95**

The USA PATRIOT Act suspended certain constitutional rights for citizens and noncitizens as a part of the War on Terror. This CNN program examines the trade-off between personal freedom and security. The panel of experts discussing the issue include Viet Dinh, who wrote the act, Margaret Hamburg, a bioterrorism expert, and Professor Julieete Kayyem of the Harvard Kennedy School of Government. They talk about hypothetical attack scenarios for the United States, indefinite detention, Arab-American rights, the Freedom of Information Act, and the provisions of the USA PATRIOT Act.

Trafficking

Illicit: The Dark Trade. **54 mins. National Geographic, 2008. $24.95**

Moises Niam's *Illicit: How Smugglers, Traffickers and Copycats Are Hijacking the Global Economy* is the basis of this DVD. It explores how globalization has changed the nature of criminal opportunity, focusing on human smuggling, arms trafficking, money laundering, and music bootlegging. Smuggling activities are estimated to constitute 10% of the world's trade in goods. Smuggling has negative political consequences including corruption of officials and subversion of government. Because illicit goods and people cross borders, job loss, violence, and death can be a consequence.

Narco-State. **50 mins. National Geographic, 2009. $19.95**

The positioning of Mexico as the leading source of cocaine and other drugs has impacted Phoenix, Arizona. This program shows the operations of the Phoenix police department as they investigate a drug-related kidnapping, discover marijuana, and arrest suspects. The program also details the crime beat in the border city of Ciudad Juarez, Mexico, a leading transshipment point.

Lives for Sale: Human Trafficking. **60 mins. Films for the Humanities and Sciences, 2006. $169.95**

Slavery has re-emerged in the form of a black market in human beings for labor and the sex trade. Poverty leads migrants to seek employment abroad and, in the process, some become victims of exploitation at some point during their journey. This film features the Coalition to Abolish Slavery and Trafficking (CAST) and their work to free those trafficked. Interviews with U.S. Border Patrol agents and other law-enforcement officers add information on this human rights issue.

Dying to Leave: The Dark Business of Human Trafficking. **57 mins. Films for the Humanities and Sciences. 2003. $149.95**

Human traffickers are not choosey about how they transport people across borders, using sewage tunnels, shipping containers, ship holds, and even car chassis. Despite motivation to get ahead, many of those trafficked become sex workers and forced laborers. This Australian *Wide Angle* documentary looks at the social context of mass unauthorized migration, its connection to trafficking, and the situations endured by those who are enslaved.

Frontline: Sex Slaves. **60 mins. PBS Educational Media. 2006. $59.95**

This exploration of human trafficking uses hidden cameras to examine the activities of traffickers, pimps, and middle men who sell women. It uses the story of Katia, whose husband is searching for her, to illustrate the issue. It details the process of attracting women through offer of legitimate employment or smuggling services and how this can lead to entrapment involving rape, drugs, and confinement for prostitution.

Transnational Gangs

18 With a Bullet: El Salvador's American Style Gangs. **57 mins. Films for the Humanities and Sciences, 2006. $149.95**

During the era of revolutionary armed conflict in El Salvador in the 1990s, thousands fled to the United States. Since then, thousands have been deported to El Salvador, including youth socialized in Los Angeles gang culture. This *Wide Angle* documentary reports on the "18," a transnational street gang based on the L.A. 18th Street gang. The gang culture and organization replicated in San Salvador, capital of El Salvador, includes violent beating for initiation, helping peers, turf wars, and connections to members inside El Salvador's prisons. The result has greatly increased crime and violence in El Salvador. A film segment features Daljit Dhaliwal, a news anchor, discussing U.S. policy on deportation and its antigang initiatives with Assistant Secretary of State for Narcotics and Law Enforcement Affairs Anne W. Patterson.

National Geographic: World's Most Dangerous Gang. **53 mins. National Geographic Channel, 2007. $24.95**

MS-13 is a transnational gang with a violence-oriented culture and rituals now found in many different states and communities ranging from cities to small towns. This documentary traces their rise from a Los Angeles gang to an international organized crime organization. Interviews with law enforcement and gang members provide first-hand information. Some graphic content.

Femicide

Dual Injustice: Femicide and Torture in Ciudad Juarez. **17 mins. Wittness.org, 2009. $29.95 (institutional, K-12); $19.95 (home; may be available online)**

Witness.org, an international human rights organization, in partnership with Comisión Mexicana de Defensa y Promocion de los Derechos Humanos (CMDPDH), provides an overview of the violent deaths of women in Ciudad Juarez. Since 1993, more than 400 women have been tortured and murdered in this border city. This largely unprosecuted wave of femicide (violent deaths of women) is an international human rights issue.

Electronic Resources

Congressional Research Service. http://opencrs.com.
Executive Office for Immigration Review. http://www.usdoj.gov/eoir.
General Accountability Office. http://www.gao.gov.
GovTrack.us. http://wwwgovtrack.us.
U.S. Census Bureau. http://www.uscensus.gov.
Yearbook of Immigration Statistics. http://www.uscis.gov/graphics/shared/aboutus/.

Border

Morphing map of changes in the U.S.-Mexico border Source: PBS
http://www.pbs.org/kpbs/theborder/history/index.html
This map displays the changing contours? of the U.S.-Mexico border after the U.S.-Mexico War of 1848.

Ports of Entry

http://apps.cbp.gov/bwt/index.asp
A major issue about the impact of intensified border security is the impact that it has on travelers and commerce. The approximate wait times to pass through any Canadian or Mexican port of entry are posted.

Terrorism

Worldwide Incidents Tracking System
http://wits.nctc.gov/

This is an international terrorist incident tracking system maintained by the National Center on Counterterrorism. The NTC definition is ''terrorism occurs when groups or individuals acting on political motivation deliberately or recklessly attack civilians/non-combatants or their property and the attack does not fall into another special category of political violence, such as crime, rioting, or tribal violence."

Immigration

Children of Immigrants Data Tool
http://datatool.urban.org/charts/datatool/pages.cfm

This site provides online generation of charts on immigrant children for use in research and related reports.

U.S. Immigration Historical Trends Data Tool
http://www.migrationinformation.org/datahub/historicaltrends.cfm

Information on immigration patterns and the changing social characteristics of the immigrant population through time is provided. It allows tracing of the historic patterns of immigrant community formation and composition. Statistics include immigrant source countries since 1960, immigrants in the U.S. labor force, children in immigrant families, region of birth of the foreign-born, and immigrant age and sex distribution.

State Responses to Immigration: A Database of All State Legislation
http://www.migrationinformation.org/datahub/statelaws_home.cfm

This searchable data tool provides information on all immigration-related bills and resolutions introduced in state legislatures. They are classified by state, region, subject area, legislative type, and bill status. This time-sensitive site is periodically updated.

Glossary

admissible A noncitizen who may be granted entry to the United States because he or she is not excludable or has a waiver of exclusion.

aggravated felony Categories of crime or specific crimes resulting in a sentence of longer than one year which render an unauthorized or permanent resident alien deportable and excludable for a period of time or permanently.

alien A person who is not a citizen or authorized permanent resident of the United States.

amnesty A term that originally refers to a provision of the Immigration Reform and Control Act of 1986. A conditional amnesty allowed legalization of undocumented noncitizens who could offer proof that they had resided in the United States prior to January 1, 1982, and were able to support themselves.

apprehension The process of taking an unauthorized migrant or immigrant into custody.

arms trafficking The sale of weapons such as handguns or automatic rifles for cross-border movement in violation of national or international law.

Arrival/Departure Card The formal term for Form I-94. It is issued at all U.S. ports of entry by an officer of U.S. Customs and Border Patrol. The form states the legal period of stay, conditions, and status for the noncitizen. It is supposed to be returned upon departure.

asylees Individuals granted asylum in the United States because they are able to prove that they are unable to return to their home country because of past persecution or a "well-founded" fear of persecution if they are returned to the home country.

asylum Under U.S. law, a status that can be given to an alien physically present in the United States who satisfies the statutory criteria for classification as a refugee. After one year of continuous residence, the alien may petition for adjustment to permanent resident status.

asymmetrical political relations   A situation in which one country is more powerful than another country and dominates it, often engaging in unilateral or one-sided decision-making rather than bilateral decisions or, in the case of multiple countries, multilateral decisions.

asymmetrical warfare   The use of unconventional, subversive, and unexpected violent tactics and weapons by terrorists for disruption of governments. Indiscriminate attacks, technology-based terrorism, and weapons of mass destruction are examples of efforts to inflict mass casualties and disrupt societal operations and the security environment.

authorization   The process in which a visitor or immigrant proceeds from document acquisition and visa application through presentation and approval by an immigration inspector at a port of entry.

authorized stay   The period of time allocated to a foreign national for a stay in the United States. The return date is stamped on the I-94 form.

bilateralism   A method of decision-making in which two countries have equal influence.

biological weapon   A virus, bacteria, or other biological agent used to threaten or be intentionally released to harm human life. Examples: anthrax, smallpox, or other infectious disease.

biometric identification technology   Computer technology which allows the matching of facial features in digital photographs and fingerprints with suspected terrorists or persons attempting the use of a stolen or altered passport.

bioterrorism   The threatened or intentional release of viruses, bacteria, or other germs (agents) through the air, water, or food to harm of kill people, animals, or plants.

bipartisan effort   Political cooperation between the members of two or more competing parties.

black market   Financial sales of illicit goods in violation of national and/or international law. These may be sales which avoid paying a cross-border tariff or illegal sales of arms, drugs, and other contraband.

Board of Immigration Appeals (BIA)   Appeals of administrative decisions made by immigration judges in an immigration court are forwarded to the BIA. During an appeal, foreign nationals can be legally present in the United States.

Border Patrol   An organization within U.S. Customs and Border Protection. It monitors the border between ports of entry.

border security   Covers processes for maintaining orderly entrance and exit at a nation's borders, whether they have been crossed by land, at sea, or in the air. Inspection of people and goods is expected to realize an end-state of preventing unauthorized entrance and smuggling.

cell   A group of terrorists that operates autonomously but may be affiliated with a larger movement without being overly influenced by hierarchical control. This term is also applied to drug trafficking organization units.

cell-based terrorism environment   An environment in which semiautonomous groups of terrorists form cells which are only loosely connected to a hierarchical authority. The lack of central organization makes counterterrorism efforts more difficult.

chemical agents   Chemicals that can be used or converted into weapons of terrorism. Certain chemicals, such as pesticides, are readily found while others can be easily manufactured by terrorists with widely available instructional materials. Counterterrorism can involve tracking purchases of these chemicals.

civil law   The branch of law concerned with relations between individuals or organizations.

civil sanction   A fine issued under civil law impacting relations between individuals or organizations.

Consulate   An office of the U.S. government, typically located in a U.S. embassy, which handles visa applications and other consular duties.

contraband   Goods subject to a tariff or illegal items that are smuggled.

counterterrorism   Preventative policies for the identification and elimination of terrorist environments and groups. Counterterrorism laws that criminalize terrorist acts and intelligence operations to capture or assassinate terrorists are proactive counterterrorism activities.

crime   Actions or lack of action in violation of the criminal laws of a local jurisdiction, the state, or the federal government for which there is no legally acceptable excuse.

criminal law   The branch of law concerned with offenses against society, individual members, their property, and the social order.

criminal sanction   A fine or punishment issued under criminal law.

criminalization   The process by which a previously accepted or unclassified behavioral practice is made illegal through legislative action.

Customs   The division in U.S. Customs and Border Protection responsible for monitoring goods being sent across a border, confiscating contraband hidden in the goods, and collecting any applicable tariff.

cyberterrorism   A term referring to the use of technology to disrupt information systems.

debt bondage   A condition in which an individual is falsely induced or coerced to enter into a labor contract that does not pay enough to meet individual need or a past debt, such as for being trafficked across a border into a new country. The individual is forced to labor under harsh conditions without being able to clear his or her economic obligation. This situation, also referred to as peonage, is illegal in the United States.

deportation The former term describing the formal process of return of an alien who has been deemed removable due to violation of immigration laws. Deportation is ordered by an immigration judge and is not legally considered punishment. Now termed removal.

detention The process and condition in which foreign nationals are held in legally authorized confinement in ICE facilities and subcontracted jail or prison bedspace.

deterrence The use of criminal law and security procedures to increase the risk of an act, thereby preventing individuals from carrying it through. Examples are unauthorized immigration and antiterrorism law and security procedures.

dirty bomb A toxic explosive device using non-weapons-grade radioactive materials acquired from medical or other uses. The radioactive contamination could cause catastrophic damage by rendering areas uninhabitable. This is thought to be the type of weapon of mass destruction most accessible to terrorists.

domestic terrorist acts Terrorist acts committed by American citizens.

drug cartel Large sophisticated criminal organizations which contain more than one drug-trafficking organization (DTO) and cells with specific duties related to production, transport, distribution, security, and money laundering. The drug command structure is located outside of the United States but U.S. DTOs that are a part of the cartel or have an alliance with it assist in drug distribution.

drug trafficking The large-scale practice of transporting prohibited substances over the border for purpose of sale. It is differentiated from drug dealing, which involves street-level distribution and sales.

drug-trafficking organizations (DTOs) Complex organizations with developed command structures to produce, transport, and distribute mass quantities of one or more types of illegal drugs.

due process of law A right provided by the Fifth, Sixth, and Fourteenth Amendments the U.S. Constitution. It is generally understood to refer to the process in which legal proceedings are conducted so as to protect individual rights. For citizens involved in a criminal proceeding, these rights include being charged with a specified criminal offense; being heard before an impartial judge and court having jurisdiction over the case; accusations made in proper form with notice and opportunity to defend according to established procedure; and the right to obtain a lawyer and, under certain circumstances, to appeal.

emigrant A foreign national who leaves his or her country of origin for the purpose of immigration to a receiving country.

emigration   The process in which foreign nationals leave countries of origin for immigration to a receiving country. Historically and at present, the United States has been a major receiving country.

employer sanctions   Civil and criminal fines and penalties for any employer who hires, recruits, or refers for a fee aliens known to be unauthorized to work in the United States. These penalties were established by the Immigration Reform and Control Act of 1986.

enhanced security   Counterterrorism measures that "harden" targets to prevent or reduce terrorist attack severity.

equal protection under the law   The guarantee under the Fourteenth Amendment of the Constitution that all persons should be treated equally in legal proceedings. This right is currently interpreted as held by citizens and not foreign nationals in immigration court proceedings.

EWIs   The abbreviation for "entered without inspection." It refers to foreign nations who entered without inspection of documents by immigration officials. Most commonly this occurs by crossing the Canadian or Mexican land border away from a port of entry. A foreign national who is EWI cannot apply for legal entrance unless seeking asylum.

exclusion   A legal term for denial of entry of an alien to the United States. Before passage of the Illegal Immigration Reform and Immigrant Responsibility Act of 1996, the decision to exclude was made by an immigration judge in an exclusion hearing. After April 1, 1997, the adjudication of inadmissibility can take place in either an expedited removal process without an immigration judge and hearing or before an immigration judge at a hearing.

expedited removal   The process in which a foreign national or permanent resident alien considered to have no legal right to be in the country is deported (removed) without further judicial action.

expulsion   The process by which a foreign national is removed (deported).

felony   A criminal offense punishable by incarceration of at least a year, sometimes culminating in the death penalty.

globalization   Internationalization of trade, investments, services, information, and other human practices. Globalization has eroded the power of sovereign states and made certain individuals, organizations, and even criminal enterprises more powerful.

guest-worker program   A temporary migration program in which foreign nationals are admitted for specified time periods to do work in areas in which there as a documented shortage of workers.

human intelligence (HUMINT)   Intelligence gathered by human operatives on persons through tracking, interviews, and interrogations. In the United States, this activity is primarily carried out by the Central Intelligence Agency (CIA).

human rights   The basic rights and freedoms to which all persons are entitled. These rights are often considered to include the right to life and liberty, freedom of thought and expression, and equality before the law.

human trafficking   A process in which individuals seeking to migrate come under the control of criminal enterprise and through coercion, force, or fraud, lose their freedom and are forced to labor for no compensation, including in prostitution.

identity papers   Documents such as a visa and passport, which establish who a person is and what his or her country of residence is.

illegal alien or immigrant   A term often used in the media to refer to individuals present in the United States who entered without inspection of documents and approval by an immigration official or who entered legally and overstayed their visit.

immigrant   A person born in another country who has been granted permission to permanently reside in the United States, either as a legally resident alien or a naturalized citizen.

Immigration and Customs Enforcement (ICE)   The enforcement division of the U.S. Department of Homeland Security. This branch includes detention and deportation officers and immigration court trial attorneys.

immigration court   The administrative court for immigration matters. Immigration judges have the authority to administer removal (deportation) proceedings and to grant foreign nationals legal status to remain in the United States. Immigration court appeals are heard by the Board of Immigration Appeals.

inadmissibility   A person who seeks to come to the United States at a port of entry but does not meet the criteria in the Immigration and Nationality Act for admission and presence in the United States. The person may be placed in removal proceedings or, under certain conditions, allowed to withdraw an application for admission. Such a person is inadmissible.

intelligence   Data collected for an information database. The purpose can be to track entry and exit of individuals or to monitor terrorist activity, among other reasons.

interdiction   The process of intercepting unauthorized migrants, drugs, or contraband at the nation's borders. Interdiction is a strategy for controlling unauthorized immigration, terrorist entry, and drug trafficking.

international law   Laws agreed upon by governments that are enforced by international agreements.

jihad   Islamic term referring to a holy war against religious or political oppression.

law   Formally written rule of conduct for the operation of a society which proscribes or mandates certain behavior.

law enforcement   A term referring to all agencies responsible for enforcing the law and maintaining public order.

legal permanent resident   A status granting a foreign national permission to reside in the United States permanently and, if so desired, to apply for naturalization.

legalization   Elimination of laws and criminal penalties associated with having entered without documents or overstayed a visa. A process of changing the status of unauthorized immigrants to permanent resident aliens.

literacy test   A procedure initiated by the 1917 Immigration Law in which individuals must demonstrate that they are able to read and write before being allowed entrance as an immigrant.

migrant   An individual who has crossed a border without inspection of documents authorizing entrance.

militia   A citizens' group organized for provision of paramilitary activity such as patrolling a border.

misdemeanor   An offense punishable by incarceration, typically in a local jail, for a period whose upper limit is typically up to one year.

money laundering   The process in which money or assets acquired through criminal means is entered into the banking system disguised as legitimate business proceeds or income.

mujahedeen   Muslim fighters engaged in jihad, the fighting of a holy war.

multilateralism   A method of decision-making in which a group of countries have mutual influence in decision-making.

narcoterrorism   Drug trafficking–related violence involving terrorization, such as use of threats, torture, and beheading, which often occurs as a result of interdrug trafficking organization disputes or as an attempt to coerce government officials.

narcotraffickers   Latin American drug traffickers who use terroristic violence for intimidation.

naturalization   Process through which a noncitizen becomes a citizen which includes a residency and civics requirement.

new terrorism   An emergent type of terrorism with a loose cell-based form of organization that uses asymmetrical tactics including weapons of mass destruction with potential for high casualties.

nuclear weapons   Military weapons using weapons-grade plutonium and uranium with a high-explosive capacity inside a blast zone. Radioactive debris from these weapons can return to the ground as fallout. Fallout contaminates the region around the blast zone, irradiating it and making it uninhabitable.

overstay   A situation in which a noncitizen with a visa has stayed beyond the date of departure approved and recorded on an arrival/departure (I-94) form. Overstay is a grounds for penalizing the noncitizen through cancellation of a visa or denial of permission to visit based on overstay duration. Visa overstay is a major source of unauthorized immigration although only a small portion of all visa-related travel.

passport   A legal identification document issued by a country of origin which attests to citizenship for purpose of international travel.

permanent resident alien   An individual who is not a citizen of the United States but is legally and lawfully residing in the United States. All lawful permanent residents are required to have and carry a green card, which is a permit to work.

persecution   Harm committed by a government or people that a government is unable or unwilling to control.

port of entry   Designated locations at which international travelers and cargos can receive authorization to cross a border and enter a country. Individuals must present visas and passports and cargos must have accompanying paperwork and are subject to inspection to prevent smuggling. There are land, sea, and air ports of entry.

protocol   An international agreement regarding procedures that the parties to such a treaty agree upon, such as the Protocols on Human Trafficking and Immigrant Smuggling.

racial profiling   A type of criminal profiling solely based on the race or ethnicity of a person. Race or ethnicity is not acceptable as the principal descriptor for suspect apprehension but it can be a secondary aspect of a criminal profile. An example would be a traffic stop of a person solely on the basis of race.

radiological agents   Radioactive materials that can harm biological organisms when eaten or inhaled. Non-weapons-grade radiological agents used in medicine could theoretically be used to construct a "dirty bomb."

refugee   Under the Immigration and Nationality Act, a person outside of the country of nationality who is unable or unwilling to return because of persecution or a well-founded fear of persecution on the basis of race, religion, nationality, membership in a particular social group, or political opinion.

removal   The expulsion of a noncitizen from the United States on grounds of inadmissibility or deportability. A formal term used to refer to deportation.

rogue states   Nations that support terrorist activities and groups.

securitization   The process by which an activity not previously considered to endanger the public becomes subject to security precautions and procedure.

security checks   Background investigations carried out to determine if individuals should be allowed into the United States.

signal intelligence (SIGINT)   Systematic intelligence gathering through electronic intercepts of messages using high technology.

slavery   The process of holding a person under coercion for the purpose of forced labor.

sleeper cell   A group of terrorist operatives who establish themselves in residences in another country and await orders for a terrorist attack.

smuggling   Unlawful movement of goods and people across a national border.

sovereignty   The power of a government to rule and issue laws for a given territory. National sovereignty was first recognized in the Treaty of Westphalia (1648), which recognized principles of national territorial integrity, supremacy of a nation in law-making, and inviolability of national borders.

spillover violence   Drug-trafficking organization or terrorist-related violence which occurs inside of the borders of a country that is not the target of the violence or harbors groups that are targets of the violence.

terrorist incident   A threat or an attack carried out by terrorists.

trafficking   The organized movement of illicit goods or people across international borders.

trafficking victim   An individual who was recruited, provided, harbored, or obtained through force, fraud, or coercion and subjected to involuntary servitude, forced labor, or commercial sex.

transnational organized crime   Unlawful activity such as drug, arms, or human trafficking, practiced or supported by organized criminal groups across national boundaries.

transnational threat   A potential source of harm that originates outside the United States connected to criminal or terrorist activity.

unauthorized alien or immigrant   A person present in the United States who entered without authorization through the inspection of approved documents.

unauthorized immigration   The federal government term for the process through which an undocumented population comes to migrate and then reside in the United States.

undocumented alien or immigrant   A term used by immigrant rights advocates to describe a person present in the United States who entered without authorization through the inspection of approved documents.

unilateralism   A method of decision-making in which a powerful country dominates the decision-making of another country or group of countries.

visa A permit issued by a U.S. consulate which gives an individual permission to seek entry at a port of entry to the United States.

voluntary departure Relief given to a foreign national in removal proceedings when he or she agrees to leave the U.S. voluntarily by a certain date instead of being deported.

War on Terror A phrase adopted after the 9/11 attacks on the World Trade Center and Pentagon to refer to the concerted effort against terrorism led by the United States on a worldwide scale.

weapons of mass destruction High-yield weapons capable of inflicting mass casualties when used by terrorists. Examples include biological, chemical, radiological, and nuclear weapons.

World Trade Center a complex of two towers located in New York City which was damaged when bombed by Islamic terrorists in 1993 and destroyed by Islamic terrorists using two hijacked jet aircraft to crash into the buildings on September 11, 2001.

Index

About the Author

Judith A. Warner is a professor of sociology and criminal justice at Texas A & M International University (TAMIU). In 2008, she received TAMIU's Distance Educator of the Year Award and in 1991, TAMIU's Scholar of the Year Award. She is the editor of *Battleground Immigration* (2009), and co-editor of the *Journal of Social and Ecological Boundaries*. She has published in the areas of immigration, homeland security and domestic violence. Her research interests include border security, immigration and the intersection of race, class and gender.

For Reference

Not to be taken from this room

DATE DUE